THE COUCH AND THE TREE

THE COUCH AND THE TREE

Dialogues in Psychoanalysis and Buddhism

❑

Edited by

ANTHONY MOLINO

NORTH POINT PRESS

A division of Farrar, Straus and Giroux

New York

North Point Press
A division of Farrar, Straus and Giroux
19 Union Square West, New York 10003

Copyright © 1998 by Anthony Molino
Distributed in Canada by Douglas & McIntyre Ltd.
Printed in the United States of America
Designed by Jonathan D. Lippincott
First edition, 1998

Library of Congress Cataloging-in-Publication Data
The couch and the tree : dialogues in psychoanalysis and Buddhism /
edited by Anthony Molino.—1st ed.
        p.   cm.
    ISBN 0-86547-520-2 (hardcover : alk. paper)
    1. Psychoanalysis and religion.   2. Buddhism—Psychology.
I. Molino, Anthony.
BF175.4.R44C68   1998
150.19'5—dc21   98-27577

CONTENTS

Introduction ❏ vii

Part I: FOUNDATIONS

Joe Tom Sun, *Psychology in Primitive Buddhism* (1924) ❏ 3

Franz Alexander, from *Buddhistic Training as an Artificial Catatonia* (1931) ❏ 12

D. T. Suzuki, from *The Zen Doctrine of No-Mind* (1949) ❏ 26

Karen Horney, from *Free Associations and the Use of the Couch* (1952) ❏ 35

Shoji Muramoto (trans.), *The Jung-Hisamatsu Conversation* (1958) ❏ 37

W. Van Dusen, *Wu Wei, No-Mind and the Fertile Void in Psychotherapy* (1958) ❏ 52

Akihisa Kondo, *Zen in Psychotherapy: The Virtue of Sitting* (1958) ❏ 58

Erich Fromm, from *Psychoanalysis and Zen Buddhism* (1960) ❏ 65

Harold Kelman, *Psychoanalytic Thought and Eastern Wisdom* (1960) ❏ 72

Alan Watts, from *Psychotherapy and Liberation* (1961) ❏ 80

Takeo Doi, *Morita Therapy and Psychoanalysis* (1962) ❏ 86

Jack Kornfield, Ram Dass, and Mokusen Miyuki, *Psychological Adjustment Is Not Liberation* (1979) ❏ 96

Part II: CONTEMPORARY RESEARCHES
Meditation

Jack Engler, *Buddhist Psychology: Contributions to Western Psychological Theory* ❏ 111

Mark Epstein, *Beyond the Oceanic Feeling: Psychoanalytic Study of Buddhist Meditation* ❏ 119

V. Walter Odajnyk, *Zen Meditation as a Way of Individuation and Healing* ❏ 131

Biography

George R. Elder, *Psychological Observations on the Life of Gautama Buddha* ❑ 145

Mark Finn, *Tibetan Buddhism and Comparative Psychoanalysis* ❑ 161

Anthony Molino, *Slouching Towards Buddhism: A Conversation with Nina Coltart* ❑ 170

Critical Perspectives

Masao Abe, *The Self in Jung and Zen* ❑ 183

Adam Phillips, *Reflections on Buddhism and Psychoanalysis* ❑ 195

Jeffrey B. Rubin, *The Emperor of Enlightenment May Have No Clothes* ❑ 200

In Practice

Michael Eigen, *One Reality* ❑ 217

Paul C. Cooper, *The Disavowal of the Spirit: Integration and Wholeness in Buddhism and Psychoanalysis* ❑ 231

Stephen Kurtz, from *The Practice of Unknowing* ❑ 247

Theoretical Reflections

Joyce McDougall and His Holiness The Dalai Lama, *Is There an Unconscious in Buddhist Teaching?* ❑ 265

Gereon Kopf, *In the Face of the Other: Psychic Interwovenness in Dōgen and Jung* ❑ 276

Anthony Molino, *Zen, Lacan, and the Alien Ego* ❑ 290

The Couch and the Tree

Joseph Bobrow, *The Fertile Mind* ❑ 307

John R. Suler, *Paradox* ❑ 321

Polly Young-Eisendrath, *What Suffering Teaches* ❑ 344

The Contributors ❑ 355

INTRODUCTION

❑

Dialogue comes from the Greek *dialogos*. *Dia* is a preposition that means "through," "between," "across," "by," and "of." It is akin to *dyo* and *di*, meaning two. As a prefix in English *dia* suggests a "passing through" as in diathermy, "thoroughly" or "completely" as in diagnosis, a "going apart" as in dialysis, and "opposed in moment" as in diamagnetism. *Logos* comes from *legein*, "to speak." It may mean thought as well as speech—thought . . . that is conceived materially as breath, spirit, *pneuma*. Hence, etymologically a dialogue is a speech across, between, through two people. It is a passing through and going apart. Dialogue has a transformational as well as an oppositional dimension—an agonistic one. It is a relationship of considerable tension.   —VINCENT CRAPANZANO, "Dialogue"

❑

1

As of 1995, close to twenty-five hundred titles appeared indexed under the subject heading of "Buddhism" in the computer catalog of a major American university. Of these, only thirty-three (twenty-three in English) were listed under "Buddhism—Psychology." Against the backdrop of such a publishing record, the case can be made that, in the "dialogue" between Buddhism and psychoanalysis, no single work has superseded, in impact and importance, the 1960 classic *Zen Buddhism and Psychoanalysis*, with its groundbreaking essays by D. T. Suzuki, Erich Fromm, and Richard De Martino. And yet, more and more psychoanalytic texts are referencing and grappling with Buddhism, whether directly or indirectly. Mark Epstein's noteworthy *Thoughts Without a Thinker* is perhaps the best known of such recent explorations. But there are others as well, as the following examples attest:

> Psychoanalysis may indeed relieve suffering, but only in Zen-like fashion: not by trying to suffer less, but by submitting to what life is about. —Michael Guy Thompson, from *The Truth About Freud's Technique*

Winnicott may have found a niche in psychoanalysis for an experience valued in some Eastern religions, in which the "ego" cracks up, in which coherence or self narrative is regarded as a defense, and in which the path to knowing the self can be achieved only by forgetting this self . . . —Christopher Bollas, from *Cracking Up*

In fact, the aims and practice of bare attention are exactly the same whether taught by a Buddhist meditation master or by an experienced analyst such as Freud, Searles or Bion. —Nina Coltart, from *Slouching Towards Bethlehem*

What would an enlightened psychoanalyst look like? To return to the Buddhist model, the *sannyasin* is (thus) described by David Neel: freed from social and religious laws; freed from all bonds, he walks on the path which is known to him alone, and is responsible only to himself. He is par excellence an "outsider." In many ways this describes the life and character of Jacques Lacan . . . —Stephen Kurtz, from *The Art of Unknowing*

In Jung's words, a great deal of our suffering is neurotic, or unnecessary, suffering. Both Buddhism and depth psychology recognize that to let go of one's obsessions, and to break through them so that they no longer constitute the world, is a way to suffer less and be freer. —Polly Young-Eisendrath, from a conversation in *Elaborate Selves*

Erich Fromm was drawn to Zen Buddhism, I imagine, partly because of its lightness of touch, something not easily found in psychoanalytic theory . . . "One has to allow," Freud wrote to Ferenczi in 1914, "for a certain multiplicity of voices, even an alloy with such and such percent nonsense." Fromm's voice is a good one to have because he knew that the unalloyed voice is a contradiction in terms. —Adam Phillips, from *On Flirtation*

It is now nearly forty years since the publication of *Zen Buddhism and Psychoanalysis*. In line with Phillips' claim, my contention in compiling *The Couch and the Tree* has been that prevailing cultural and spiritual sensibilities are such as to encourage a new alloy of these two defining "voices" of contemporary culture. As a result, my aim in pursuing this alloy has been to produce a volume that might span and document the history of the interaction between the two disciplines, while also inspiring new contributions to the overarching dialogue between psychoanalysis and the multiple, manifold reality that is Buddhism today.

In some respects, I have approached the "dialogue" with an attitude similar to the one that inspires many literary translators to propose yet another version of a classic already translated time and again. In such instances, the argument is that every age is entitled to its own defining translation, say, of *The Divine Comedy*, or of Goethe's *Faust*. In similar fashion, I realized in the course of editing this book that no summary or defining statement—no alloy of retrospective and prospective soundings—existed for the particular sensibilities of our day and age. For all of the wondrous contributions, both past and present, that have sprinkled and fertilized the terrain of the dialogue, no single volume to date had attempted to combine a historical overview (and the critical assessment such an overview implies) with a survey of the "state of the art." In something of a paradox, over the course of nearly a century of engagement, the sound of one hand clapping was everywhere to be heard, but rarely were the two hands of Buddhism and psychoanalysis *thoroughly* coupled—in applause, prayer, handshake, or even in the embattled clasps of arms wrestling. Discreet but disparate virtuoso efforts—many, unfortunately, hardly known outside the inner circles of specialists—seemed to me to be constellated in celestial geometries where the dots of stars had yet to be connected. My intention, then, in imagining this book, was to connect the dots. To sound the terrain. To offer a reading—or a "translation"—of an ever-evolving text, of a genuinely compelling *discourse*, between two of the most powerful and defining *Weltanschauungen* that our history has generated.

2

The matter of translation is clearly central to any dialogue, to any understanding that is genuine and reciprocal. Within the specific context of this collection, perhaps no piece exemplifies this more than the translation of the famous Jung-Hisamatsu conversation of 1958, available here for the first time in English in a direct translation from the German protocol of Jung's secretary, Aniela Jaffé. (The only previous English translation—generally acknowledged as inadequate and pedantic—was from the Japanese translation of the German. See Shoji Muramoto's introduction for the history of the conversation and its translation.) While preparing my notes for this introduction, I was advised by a colleague and close reader of the manuscript to mention the role translation had played in the history of the dialogue between Buddhism and psychoanalysis. More specifically, he alerted me to the possibility that the relative paucity of translations of Buddhist texts into Western languages during the first half of this century had invariably limited the access of psychoanalysts to the wellsprings of

Eastern thought. Such a view explains, at least in part, the "lateness" with which psychoanalysis was sensitized to the Buddhist tradition. John Suler, in his substantive and thoroughly researched *Contemporary Psychoanalysis and Eastern Thought*, seems to suggest as much when he writes, in a chapter entitled "East Meets West": "What is so surprising is not that Buddha and Freud eventually shook hands, but that it didn't occur until some 100 years after the birth of psychoanalysis." In fact, with the early exceptions of Carl Gustav Jung, Franz Alexander, and Georg Groddeck, it wasn't until the 1950s that the dialogue was actually engaged—when, through the mediation of figures like Akihisa Kondo, D. T. Suzuki, and Richard De Martino, the generation of Karen Horney, Harold Kelman, and Erich Fromm made its way "east." In some respects, this emphasis on translation parallels the argument made by Kakuzo Okakura in his 1906 classic *The Book of Tea*, where he laments both the paucity, and the inadequacy, of the then-extant Western expositions of Zen and its historical antecedent, Taoism. Okakura's metaphor, borrowed from an unnamed author of ancient China's Ming dynasty, goes something like this: translation is like the reverse of a brocade. The threads are all there, but the refinement of design and color are altogether missing.

Undoubtedly, before psychoanalysis opened up to Buddhism, translations of the seminal Buddhist texts were few and far between, and their quality was questionable. Scrupulous, critical work like Muramoto's on the Jung-Hisamatsu conversation indirectly confirms this early shortcoming. Still, I hesitate to attribute a definite centrality to the argument that equates a flourishing of translations with the greater opening of Western minds to Buddhism. Suler himself, in fact, along with another prominent comparatist, Jeffrey Rubin, makes a more convincing point on the matter of the mistrust that has long characterized not only the relationship of psychoanalysis to Buddhism but of Buddhism to psychoanalysis as well. Freud's foreclosure on religion, his estrangement from the "heretical" Jung, as well as his reductionist reading of the "oceanic feeling" of mysticism are, by now, all proverbial. Lest we forget, Freud's writings almost exclusively constituted the psychoanalytic canon for the first generations of analysts, and to that extent helped define and structure the mind-sets of his disciples and followers up to and well through the years of World War II. In this light, is it reasonable to think that psychoanalysis *could* have opened up to Buddhism before the 1950s—especially considering the trauma and tragedy of the intervening war years, the fact that Japan (which proved, ultimately, to be the cultural and geographical pathway for the transmission of a Buddhist sensibility westward) and the Allies were enemies, and that the Master himself, Sigmund Freud, had only died in 1939? Or wasn't it precisely the post-atomic shocks that rattled the West, wasn't it precisely the horrors of the Holocaust that confronted the West with its own spiritual devastation and desolation that, in inaugurating the heyday of existentialism—by which psychoanalysis itself was soon to be engaged—acted as receptors for the ligand of Buddhism? It is no coincidence that the existential philosophies of religious thinkers such as Martin Buber and Paul Tillich, along with the mysticism of Thomas Merton, interlocked most readily with Buddhism. From a historical, or "foundational," angle, Harold Kelman's seminal article, "Psychoanalytic Thought and Eastern Wisdom," can be read in this light. In a way, within the context of the contemporary researches presented in this volume, readers will find Michael Eigen's essay, "One Reality"—with the author's portraits of Buber and Suzuki—to be a complementary study to, and retrospective commentary on, the work of early researchers like Kelman.

But back to the issue of mistrust. The foreclosure on Buddhism's part on the insights of psychoanalysis has, traditionally, been just as restrictive. Peter Matthiessen, for example, in his book *Nine-Headed Dragon River* tells of a Zen master who fiercely countered the suggestion that Zen and psychotherapy could both address the problem of human suffering. For the Zen master, in fact, the psychotherapist is often just another patient. "Can he cure this bowl? This table? Zen can do! Can psychotherapy cure birds?" According to Matthiessen, the master insisted that while psychotherapy could at best prune the twigs of a tree, the force and wisdom of Zen go "straight into the root."

This example of what Jeffrey Rubin calls an "Orientocentric" attitude (in contrast to the Eurocentrism that has marked the classical Freudian foreclosure of psychoanalysis and its implicit claim to a developmental, if not evolutionary, superiority with regards to Eastern thought) is also manifested—albeit more subtly—in the work of one of the foremost Buddhist philosophers of this century. In the preface to his fundamental treatise *Religion and Nothingness*, Keiji Nishitani, of the famous Kyoto School, sets out on his inquiry "by way of problems judged to lie hidden at the ground of the historical frontier we call 'the modern world,' with the aim of delving into the ground of human existence and, at the same time, searching anew for the wellsprings of reality itself." In the foreword to the book, however, Winston L. King of Vanderbilt University remarks somewhat surprisingly on what he sees as a striking shortcoming of Nishitani's work:

The relation of this volume to another important strand of American culture, with considerable inbuilt academic, religious, and personal interest, poses a problem. This is the psychological-psychiatric strand. Nishitani never mentions Freud, his successors, or opponents. Is it because Freudian-inspired techniques seem to be too much the mere manipulation of mental processes and emotional sets in order to better achieve traditional worldly goals, rather than the existential breakthrough Nishitani calls for? Yet this relationship, or lack of it, is of some consequence because part of the . . . interest in Zen has been attributable to the strength of the psychological-psychiatric "tradition" in America . . .

King's observation is both timely and telling. Critics like Rubin—whose essential work is represented here by an essay entitled "The Emperor of Enlightenment May Have No Clothes"—are correct to point out the dangers of a faddish Orientocentrism, in which "the valorizing and privileging of Asian thought" often involve "the neglect if not the dismissal of Western psychological perspectives." Against this background of reciprocal mistrust and misinformation, and of resultant prejudicial claims to monolithic understandings of our human condition, one of the aims of *The Couch and the Tree* is to situate itself precisely in a dimension of the dialogue which Rubin sees "not [as] a singular pattern of influence, but rather resembling a heterogeneous mosaic composed of elements that are . . . antithetical, complementary, and synergistic." Such a dimension, as I've suggested, must make room for celebration as well as criticism. For a recognition of the Other which eschews both facile exaltations and devaluations, as well as simplistic presumptions of sameness—what Rubin calls "pseudo-complementary/token egalitarian models." Ultimately, if I were to invoke a model for the kind of optimal relationship I envision for Buddhism and psychoanalysis, and which this volume hopefully represents, I'd call on the words of a mystic from another tradition, Kahlil Gibran, who in his book *The Prophet* reminds us that

> the pillars of the temple stand apart
> and the oak tree and the cypress stand not
> in each other's shadow.

3

It is not the primary concern of this introduction to revisit the public and published details of the sometimes discreet, sometimes momentous history of the "dialogue" between Buddhism and psychoanalysis. That has been done elsewhere, and better, than I could ever hope to manage. Among recent treatments of the subject, Rubin's own *Psychotherapy and Buddhism* and John Suler's *Contemporary Psychoanalysis and Eastern Thought* both provide exhaustive historical overviews of the meeting between the two disciplines, tracing its development through a series of defining influences, encounters, and publications. Working on the assumption, however, that at least some of the figures involved in the early history of the dialogue are no strangers to readers of this volume, I have included in the opening section entitled "Foundations" selections from the classic works of ground-breakers such as Franz Alexander, C. G. Jung, Erich Fromm, Karen Horney, Shin'ichi Hisamatsu, Harold Kelman, D. T. Suzuki, and Alan Watts. Where chronology is concerned, I have dated all contributions at their time of publication. (Several of the essays, such as Fromm's, Alexander's, and Kelman's, were lectures delivered earlier.) The lone exception is the excerpt from Karen Horney's *Final Lectures*, posthumously published in 1987, but situated here at the time the lecture was given, in 1952, shortly before the author's death.

This selection of essays by widely recognized figures—some of whom, such as Watts and Suzuki, were also instrumental in popularizing the dialogue through the "counterculture" of the 1960s—is complemented in the "Foundations" section by a collection of lesser-known but equally compelling essays and articles. Among these is perhaps the earliest published essay in the dialogue, the 1924 "Psychology in Primitive Buddhism" by Joe Tom Sun (pseudonym of the Chicago psychoanalyst Joseph Thompson). Aside from its own intrinsic historical and heuristic value, Tom Sun's piece is particularly instructive when viewed together with Alexander's contribution of 1931 ("Buddhistic Training as Artificial Catatonia"). Both point to a fact which is easily overlooked: namely, that the earliest, somewhat "renegade" psychoanalytic explorations of Buddhism were not principally informed by Zen. It is only later—with the advent of the generation of Horney and Fromm and, as I've suggested, the postwar opening toward Japan—that Zen becomes, for quite a time, the privileged vehicle and terrain for the dialogue. There are, of course, other reasons for this development: among these, the parallel lineage structures, in Zen and psychoanalysis, for the transmission of their respective forms of knowledge, as well as their common emphasis on the centrality of individual experience and perception. (See especially Okakura's *The Book of Tea* for an understanding of the premium placed on individualism in Zen Buddhism.)

The rest of Part I comprises a sampling of essays that highlight, again from a historical standpoint, both the work of key figures as well as the particular themes that characterized the dialogue's early years. These range from Akihisa Kondo's "Zen in Psychotherapy: The Virtue of Sitting" (1958)—which, while not a case history or clinical study, is one of the first papers to focus on prospects for cross-influences of technique—to Takeo Doi's 1962 "Morita Therapy and Psychoanalysis," a comparative study, by one of the major cross-cultural theorists of this time, which expands on the concepts implicit in Kondo's work. W. Van Dusen's brief but dazzling "Wu Wei, No-Mind and the Fertile Void in Psychotherapy" (1958) is an excursus, decades ahead of its time, into the challenging spaces and black holes of Taoism, the new physics, and schizophrenia. It is also one of the first interdisciplinary explorations to cite clinical material in support of its thesis. This aspect of comparative work, largely absent from the early efforts, becomes increasingly relevant in more recent studies. In the "Contemporary Researches" of Part II, in fact, psychoanalysts can be seen resorting increasingly and more freely to case material, to help illustrate both their synergistic intuitions and their antithetical intimations.

The "Foundations" section concludes with the transcript of a little-known symposium, on the theme "Psychological Adjustment Is Not Liberation," held in 1979 at the Mount Baldy Zen Center in California. Admittedly, both date and event reflect an arbitrary choice of sorts in the designation of an "end point" to a segment in time aiming to define a "classical" period in the dialogue between Buddhism and psychoanalysis. Similar choices, however, beleaguer all historians concerned with the identification and definition of epochs and cycles. In this instance, my decision was based in part on references made during the symposium that betray a certain historical context and sensibility, characteristic of the 1960s. For example, one of the participants in the symposium, Ram Dass—himself a noteworthy figure of the 1960s counterculture—refers at one point to "psychology as defined and practiced by people like Erikson, Maslow, and Rogers and the neo-Freudians, as well as the neo-Jungians and the gestalt therapy of Fritz Perls." This influential grouping, cited in the context of the symposium as representative of some of the foremost advances in psychological (and psychoanalytic) thinking at the time, is not one that would readily be mentioned today, or even in the 1980s. When compared with the thrust and tone, for example, of two of the earlier pieces presented among the contemporary researches—Jack Engler's 1985 "Buddhist Psychology: Contributions to Western Psychological Theory," and Masao

Abe's "The Self in Jung and Zen," also published in 1985—as readers we sense that somehow the terms have changed. From within psychoanalysis, the thinkers cited by Ram Dass only six years earlier no longer provide the primary context of investigation. Furthermore, the very emphasis on *liberation*—a theme also sounded by Alan Watts in the excerpt here presented from his 1961 "Psychotherapy and Liberation"—in a way also dates the piece. Not that liberation is any less of a concern today—politically, spiritually, or existentially. To the contrary. If anything, the word's loss in "currency," in a world caught in the throes of the vertigo of postmodernism, underscores its urgency—and warrants its reappraisal in a volume such as the present one. Nonetheless, it is partly the result of a philological exercise that I've chosen the symposium to close out Part I of this book. Additionally, however, it is also my belief that the piece serves nicely as a springboard from which to launch Part II of *The Couch and the Tree*. For in a way all of the contemporary researches here presented break off and emerge from Part I not merely because of chronology but because they all stand as imaginative answers to a question implied by Karen Horney's biographer, Susan Quinn, in her book *A Mind of Her Own: The Life of Karen Horney*, where she writes: "Had there been more time, there is no telling how Horney might have altered her views as the result of her new interest in Zen." Replace the word Zen with Buddhism, and you have, in Part II, some of the most compelling contemporary investigations pointing to just how psychoanalysis has altered *its* views—as well as to how Buddhism, for its part, has responded to and been engaged by such changes and challenges.

4

"Sometimes you remind me of a slobbering baby Buddha with a bib."

"There are times when I imagine you sitting under a tree, like a Buddha meditating, and I want to pick up a nearby stone bench and smash it over your head."
                                                    —Two patients, speaking from the couch

It was more than fifteen years ago when, in the course of a particularly difficult moment in my own psychoanalysis, I was led to a pocket-sized gem of a book by Eugen Herrigel, entitled *Zen in the Art of Archery*. As I now thumb through the yellowed pages of that little classic and discover, to my amazement, the feverish reverence I must have brought to my reading (uncharacteristically, my copy is entirely unmarked), I remember well its lesson, summed up for me today by what has come to be known as the fundamental koan of Zen Buddhism: "When it is impossible to do anything, what will you do?"

In the course of *doing* nothing—that is to say, if it is ever possible for the unenlightened among us to do no-thing—epiphanies sometimes chance upon us. Over the course of the next fifteen years, a series of epiphanous occasions opened the way for what is still an ongoing personal exploration of the relationship between Buddhism and psychoanalysis. There were, at first, the discoveries—almost invariably at times of personal developmental crises marking the passage into early adulthood—of popular books like Watts's *The Way of Zen*, Pirsig's *Zen and the Art of Motorcycle Maintenance*, and Sheldon Kopp's *If You Meet the Buddha on the Road, Kill Him!* Books read by millions of people, inspiring or deluding a generation or two of idealists, alienated teenage suburbanites, and genuinely damaged souls, for whom the fantasied "East" began to loom as an alternative geography, a saner sensibility, a realm of quietude, of refuge and escape . . . As I sit here writing, suddenly a surge of memory. Early 1970s. Still a teenager, I can remember picking up two books at a church-sponsored yard sale on a sweltering summer day in Philadelphia. Those two books, purchased together, are still part of my personal library: a clothbound edition of Hesse's *Siddhartha*, bought for a dime, and a volume entitled *Explorations in Psychoanalysis: A Tribute to the Work of Theodor Reik*, edited by Robert Lindner—himself an iconoclast, as I was later to learn. For sure, Lindner's was the first book I'd ever read on psychoanalysis, and I know I'd never before heard of Siddhartha Gautama. The Buddha, you see, wasn't much of a topic of conversation in our West Philly, Roman Catholic, Italian-American neighborhood.

If epiphanies can be retrospective, so be it. Where my experience is concerned, in the very life of my unconscious, the memory points to the possibility that the dialogue was instituted as such from the very start—*as dialogue*, in the way anthropologist Vincent Crapanzano conceives of the word in the epigraph to this introduction. For me, at some level, from very early on, there was no Buddha without Freud, and vice versa. Later in life I was fortunate to have studied for three college semesters with Richard De Martino, the third but often neglected contributor, alongside Erich Fromm and D. T. Suzuki, to the volume *Zen Buddhism and Psychoanalysis*. Student, colleague, translator, and interpreter of luminaries such as Suzuki himself as well as of Shin'ichi Hisamatsu, De Martino was a seminal figure in the postwar transplantation of Zen to American soil. It was thanks to De Martino that the dialogue for me became real, substantial, engaged. It was through him that I became familiar with the sutras and Karen Horney, with Dogen and Heidegger, Tillich and Hisamatsu, Abe and Lacan. It was also around that time, when I was enrolled in De Martino's classes, that I decided to train as a psychoanalyst, after I'd already been in analysis for several years. I now know for a fact that, already then, the embryo of *The Couch and the Tree* had begun to take form.

5

As I've already suggested, the section of this volume entitled "Contemporary Researches" has been compiled with the intent of bringing together the work of some of the most prominent modern-day commentators on the interrelationship between Buddhism and psychoanalysis. For obvious reasons, this section has been organized differently from the "foundations" of the dialogue presented in Part I. Whereas Part I was conceived as something of a historical record, the contemporary researches presented in Part II seek to expand the limits of that record in several directions. As mentioned, the greater use and relevance of clinical material will be reflected throughout Part II, and not only in the particular section entitled "In Practice," where such work will be highlighted. Moreover, what I earlier referred to as the "multiple, manifold reality that is Buddhism today" will similarly be reflected, as a direct consequence of the growing interpenetration of psychoanalysis with strands of Buddhist thought not previously privileged. Obviously, the necessarily limited scope of a project such as *The Couch and the Tree* precludes an in-depth presentation and/or exploration of the many "Buddhisms" other than Zen. Nor did it appear feasible, in conceptualizing this volume, to organize the papers presented in Part II under headings like "Psychoanalysis and Theravadin Buddhism," or "Psychoanalysis and Tibetan Buddhism." To have done so would have meant overlooking an exceedingly important point that Jeffrey Rubin makes in his book *Psychotherapy and Buddhism: Toward an Integration:*

> Psychoanalysis and Buddhism are not one thing. Since meaning, as Bakhtin knew, is the product of an interaction or dialogue between reader and text, rather than a monological essence waiting to be found in a neutral, fixed manuscript, there is no

singular, settled or definitive Buddhism or psychoanalysis. "Buddhism" and "psycho-analysis" are heterogeneous and evolving: a multitude of beliefs, perspectives, and theories, co-created and transformed by readers from different psychological, historical, sociocultural, and gendered perspectives.

In other words, to have proposed such an organization of Part II would have meant a neglect of the similarly complex and multiple reality that is contemporary "psychoanalysis," with its own schools and divisiveness, and with its own competing claims to truth. Consequently, my concern in Part II was to adequately represent the various schools of both disciplines, in the hope that any—perhaps inevitable—omissions or deficiencies would be more than compensated for by the breadth and substance of the con-tributions collected.

Along these lines, the first five groupings of Part II correspond to specific themes or dimensions of the dialogue that have either traditionally focused the attention of researchers (i.e., meditation studies, comparative theory) or have generated new and intriguing perspectives (biographical studies, *critical* reflections on the "nature" of self, and the aforementioned attention to clinical practice). There is no set boundary, however, to each grouping, nor can there be. Issues pertaining to the self, for example, are clearly discussed throughout the entirety of Part II; similarly, case material from clinical work is in no way restricted to the three essays collected under the heading "In Practice." The various headings, in fact, are intended to func-tion primarily as a mapping device to help orient and focus the reader through the pages of a work not necessarily intended for immediate, cover-to-cover reading. Such a mapping is also intratextual, however, to the extent that several of the essays appearing among the "Contemporary Re-searches" not only reference each other (i.e., Odajnyk on Epstein, Rubin and Bobrow on Engler) but extend the dialogue across generations and back to its "foundations." In this sense, it is particularly interesting to read the eminent Buddhist scholar Masao Abe's incisive critique of the Jung-Hisamatsu conversation presented in Part I (even as I must note that Abe's essay draws on the first translation, and not Muramoto's, of the conversa-tion); similarly, Mark Epstein, in his paper "Beyond the Oceanic Feeling," provides a bridge that spans the historical divide and connects directly with the early work of Joe Tom Sun and Franz Alexander; or, in what is one of the richest and most engaging contributions to the book, psycho-analyst Joyce McDougall and His Holiness The Dalai Lama discuss Bud-dhist understandings of the unconscious in a way which cannot help but invite fruitful and challenging comparisons with the essential Suzuki of Part I. (Within Part I, Suzuki's own essay and analysis of key Buddhist terms shed further light on the painstaking efforts of Muramoto, whose notes to the Jung-Hisamatsu conversation underscore some of the etymological and philosophical problems inherent to processes of cultural translation.)

Whereas the first five groupings of Part II thus organize some of the most cutting-edge thinking in the dialogue—centering, in some respects, on Adam Phillips' provocative "Reflections on Buddhism and Psychoanalysis"—the final group of essays is where, ideally, the present-day architecture of couch and tree can be most readily assessed. The three essays—by Joseph Bobrow, John Suler, and Polly Young-Eisendrath—comprise, at least in my estimation, at one and the same time some of the simplest and most profound writing presently being done. These three pieces—Bobrow's far-reaching "The Fertile Mind," Suler's swirling essay on paradox, and Young-Eisendrath's sobering and sensitive "What Suffering Teaches"—constitute the kind of space, if you will, where Freud's couch and the bodhi tree of the Buddha can both alternate *and* come together, to offer two of the saner resting places in today's dizzying and decentered world.

It is my contention—and one of the main ideas at the heart of this volume—that in a shrinking and increasingly homogenized global space, bereft nearly everywhere of organizing principles and value systems on which to ground a truly human ethos, Buddhism joins psychoanalysis as "one of the few remaining endeavors that will allow change and surprise —that is, that will allow life" (Julia Kristeva, *New Maladies of the Soul*). In this final group of essays, then, in looking to design a space where ethics and aesthetics might reflect not only their shared etymology but the ancestral, perhaps archetypal experience that first bound them in human thought and language, I hope to have collected some of the dialogue's foremost "parallel convergences"—lines of inquiry coursed by the kind of antithetical, complementary, and synergistic elements invoked by Jeffrey Rubin and, I would suggest, by almost every contributor to *The Couch and the Tree*.

6

This book owes its life to a great number of people, each and every one of whom was essential to its completion. First off, for their belief in and support of this project, I would like to acknowledge my editors at Farrar, Straus & Giroux/North Point Press: Jonathan Galassi and, principally, Ethan Nosowsky. I would like to thank as a group the editors and permission managers of the many publishing houses and journals whose dedicated efforts and timely assistance made this book possible. To this end, my cherished teacher and colleague, the late Marie Coleman Nelson, also offered precious assistance. Special thanks go to Wesley Shumar, Deidre Bair, Alan Roland, Francisco Varela, Samuel Laeuchli, Jan Middeldorf, and Professor Shigenori Nagatomo of Temple University for their personal intercessions on my behalf. My deepest gratitude, meanwhile, goes to Ms. Ruth Weibel, executor for the estate of Erich Fromm, and Gill Davies, formerly of Free Association Books. Their exceptional and most generous collaboration helped tie together, from a permissions standpoint, what were for some time the project's dangling loose ends.

Among the contributors to the volume, I would like to acknowledge Professor Masao Abe and Joyce McDougall for their especially gracious facilitations. I am grateful as well to Mark Epstein, who not only brought his "Beyond the Oceanic Feeling" to my attention but also led me to the early works of Joe Tom Sun and Franz Alexander. John Suler was similarly instrumental in helping me outline the contents of the volume, while also providing me very generously with copies of articles collected in the course of his extensive research. Polly Young-Eisendrath and Jeffrey Rubin were more than contributors: as friends, they both supported and helped expand the project, while also helping me surmount crucial obstacles in the course of its realization. I thank them both dearly. Last but not least of this very special group, my wife, Marina, patiently read and helped critique my introduction to the book as well as my own essay on the alien ego. While she may have been alien—as a biologist—to the discourses of both pieces, her love was alien neither to her careful reading nor to the two years' time it took me to complete *The Couch and the Tree*.

Finally, no single individual labored more on behalf of *The Couch and the Tree* than Shoji Muramoto. His tireless efforts—via phone, fax, and the relay of countless E-mail messages—to help me dialogue with and secure permissions from my Japanese interlocutors bordered continually on the miraculous. Very simply, Shoji's collaboration has been invaluable.

Without him, it is no overstatement to say, this book would not exist. I hope someday to have the pleasure of meeting him and thanking him in person.

In closing, perhaps no single psychoanalyst did more to bridge psycho-analysis and Buddhism than the late Nina Coltart. Nina died while I was preparing this volume, but not before having graced me with the gift of her friendship and the wisdom of her life story. Through her I also met Joe Bobrow, a distant colleague I now call a friend. It is with a sad smile, and a heart thankful for the times and tea we shared, that I dedicate this book to her memory.

Anthony Molino
Vasto, Italy, July 1998

Part I

FOUNDATIONS

❏

PSYCHOLOGY IN PRIMITIVE BUDDHISM

Joe Tom Sun

(1924)

❏

From time immemorial the Law of Cause and Effect has been accepted by the philosopher when considering matters relating to the physical world.

To the early Aryan thinkers cause and effect played so important a role that in speech there arose a single term to express the concept. This word was "Karma," and it was tersely and dynamically defined as: "That power by virtue of which cause is followed by effect."

The gift of gifts that was made by Buddha to mankind was his application of this Karmic Law, the law of cause and effect, to the moral world. In his discourses he contended this with inexorable consistency.

One of the most far-reaching contributions to philosophy made by Freud is his insistence upon psychic determinism; in the neuroses this is the relation existing between the symptom and its motivation. This is the application of the Law of Karma, not only to the physical and moral phases of life but also to the science of psychology.

This article first appeared in the journal *The Psychoanalytic Review*, vol. XI, pages 38–47, 1924. It is reprinted here, with minor editorial revisions, with the permission of the editors of *The Psychoanalytic Review*.

In perusing some of the primitive Buddhist texts the analyst cannot fail to be charmed at the sound psychological insight into human behavior that was achieved by Buddha and taught by him to his followers.

To the five senses of the old psychology the Buddhists added a sixth. This is called "mano," thought perception. Mano is regarded as the mental eye, it is on a par with other sense organs such as the eye or ear, and its function is to observe what takes place in the mind. Mano is at once recognized as being identical with the endopsychic organ postulated by Freud and termed consciousness. Consciousness Freud defines as a sensory organ for the reception of psychic qualities.

The Buddhist concept of mano and the Freudian thesis of consciousness may be regarded as one of the most concrete examples of the phenomenon of convergent evolution that is known to have transpired in the realm of philosophy.

The Buddhist writings do not contain any mention of the unconscious in the Freudian sense. They do contain, however, one of the most eternal of verities—namely, that desire (tanhā) is the outstanding obstacle to wisdom, and therefore the principal component of ignorance.

This, restated in the language of psychoanalysis, reads: The therapy of Freudian psychopathology is based upon the theory that uncontrolled desire (avijja, lack of wisdom, tanhā, desire), faultily attached libido, is the salient etiological factor in the neuroses.

Buddhist thought was preeminently devoted to reality. Many speculations were regarded not only as profitless but actually as pernicious. Among these were contemplations of first causes such as the origin of the universe and metaphysical matters such as the nature of the hereafter. These and kindred subjects were prohibited as well as dabbling in the affairs of one's neighbors. It was written: "Not about the perversities of others, not their sins of commission or omission, but regarding his own misdeeds and negligences alone should a sage be concerned." Dream interpreters were held in disregard, as were certain divinators who told fortunes from fragments of rags that were gnawed by mice.

Buddha taught the evil of illusion (maya) and the need for its substitution by wisdom. Freud teaches the pathogenesis of phantasy and contributed to therapeutics the technique of psychoanalysis to bring about the substitution of conscious thinking (wisdom, vijja) for unconscious thinking, phantasy (illusion, maya).

The teachings of Buddha and Freud are absolutely identical upon the subject of determinism as it applies to the individual personality. In the

Dhammapada it is written: "All that we are is the result of what we have thought; it is founded on our thoughts, it is made up of our thoughts. Freud, in speaking to Putnam, said: "We are what we are because we have been what we have been (the Law of Karma). And what is needed to solve the problem of human life is not moral estimates (maya, illusion) but more knowledge" (vijja, wisdom).

A deeper evaluation of the majesty of the oneness of these utterances will be felt when it is appreciated that they are separated by an interval of twenty-four centuries.

The philosophy of Buddha starts with the postulate of the existence of sorrow and ends with the goal of the elimination of sorrow. Again and again Buddha says: "Both then and now just this do I reveal, sorrow and the extinction of sorrow."

As to the existence of sorrow it was held to be inherent in living matter, quite on a par with motility, irritability and the other attributes of protoplasm. To Buddha birth, growth, old age and death appeared to be accompanied by such an unwarranted and unwelcome element of pain, disease and craving, collectively called sorrow (dukkha), that the escape from sorrow became the sole aim of his teachings.

Dukkha, sorrow in the Buddhist sense, not only refers to sorrow as consisting of the ills, trials and tribulations of everyday life, but refers almost entirely to the emotion that arises upon appreciating the impermanence and transiency of life, and all else in the universe. This is precisely one of the principal symptoms of many neurotics, the feeling of the futility of future efforts, the emptiness of life; it appears in many disguises.

With the object of eliminating sorrow, Buddha took under critical consideration the cause of sorrow. This cause he uncompromisingly stated to be desire (tanhā), which in turn is due to ignorance (avijja). This ignorance was by no means assumed to be lack of learning in material matters but referred almost entirely to faulty psychic functioning.

The elimination of desire is the most elemental of human activities. It is clearly formulated by Kempf in modern psychological terms under the neutralization theory.

With the elimination of sorrow it was assumed that there naturally would follow contentment—in other words the maximum happiness, which is tranquillity (nirvana). The profound psychic import of this tenet will at once be appreciated when one observes that it is identical with the pleasure-pain principle of unconscious thinking.

Buddha taught that psychic tranquillity (nirvana) can be obtained by the acquisition of wisdom. Wisdom again does not refer to academic accomplishments but signifies understanding of life in its broadest sense. Buddha outlined a definite path (maggā) along which it was necessary to travel in order to acquire the wisdom that would eliminate the sorrow arising from ignorance. This path of conduct was described as living one's life so that it should at all times be governed by right views, right aspirations, right speech, right acts, right means of earning a livelihood, right efforts, right thinking and right peaceful contemplation. In psychoanalytic language this is behavior motivated by the conscious mind of a reasoning personality instead of by the unconscious mind of the child, savage or neurotic.

The standard of morality that was held by Buddha may be inferred when one reads that evil may be done not only by acts and by speech but by evil thinking as well. The soundness of psychology's contention that somatic harm to the organism may result from faulty ideation has only recently been taken seriously by the Western scientific world. Jelliffe has just stated as a very important truth that emotional stimuli cause reactions as definite as psychical agents.

Buddha ranked desire, lust (rāga), as the foremost hindrance to leading a life of wisdom and tranquillity, with laziness and doubt (anxiety) following. To the student of Kempf, who upholds the ideals of virility, efficiency and happiness, these precepts of Buddha seem awe-inspiringly close to the best that modern philosophy has to offer.

In that the greatest hindrance to attaining nirvana was clearly recognized to be desire, the need to conquer desire became imperative. This was attained, not by the mechanism of repression, but by the most deliberate of conscious sublimation. This sublimation was not along the lines of extraversion in motor activity but by an introversion. This introversion took the form of a studious acquisition of knowledge of life, and above all an intensive contemplation (jhāna) upon what was learned. Meditation is one of the most important tenets in Buddhism. Memorizing without thought was regarded as without avail and meditation without study was held to be futile, it being but cloud divination.

Buddha enjoined a searching introspection of one's conduct and mind. Once a month the monks in a district would assemble for what was known as the disemburdening, a form of confession. The individual was required to arise in the meeting, at which several thousand might be present, and to publicly announce each transgression that he had committed against the regulations of the monastic order. This was a ceremony that could have been endured only by men of rare earnestness.

Profound insight into the psychology of the conscious mind was attained and later expounded in their philosophy. Emotion, for example, was frankly stated to be due to ignorance. A casual glance at the underlying motive for the majority of emotional outbreaks will make it clear that these are due to the mechanism of displacement, a by-product of ignorance, lack of psychic insight. Furthermore, a morbid emotion is not cured by merely teaching a patient its etiology. Its cure is, however, brought about by analysis (vijja, wisdom) which is characterized by instruction and the deepest of meditation—that is, free association and being led gently backwards from the present effect to the past cause.

It is recorded that when Buddha spoke before a gathering each listener thought that the doctrine was being expounded expressly for him. This is a direct reference to what is now understood as positive transference.

The manner in which Buddha helped a sufferer may be learned from this quotation: "I set up the individual mind of each one who seeks peace, bring it to quietude, unify it, gather it together." It would be difficult today to state the aim of an analysis more clearly, which above all is to unify a mind, to make conscious the unconscious—that is, to bring peace, an end to conflict and sorrow.

When the subject of the ego comes up one is touching upon the most difficult chapter in Buddhist philosophy. Not difficult to understand, but very frustrating to try to epitomize. On the one hand, it is extremely individualistic in that there is absolute responsibility for one's acts, the existence even of chance being denied: "By oneself one sins, by oneself one is purified." Buddhists do not pray; they have no projected anthropomorphic progenitor or mother-image intermediator who can relieve them of their sins. This is the theory of personal responsibility carried to its logical end. On the other hand, though individualistic it is at the same time extremely unselfish, as charity toward one's fellow beings, including kindness even to the lower animals, is held to be among the highest of virtues.

These two ideas, the intense individualism and consistent compassion, are so antipodal as almost to refuse to constellate.

Buddha taught that the ego was not a reality, that it was nonexistent, that it was an illusion, as it came from antecedent causes which in themselves were of an unstable nature, that what has a beginning must have an end, that what has an end is inherently impermanent, and that permanence was the sole criterion of reality.

The apparent ego is regarded as a mere integration of certain material and psychic factors. It is due entirely to the coming together, the occurring at the same time of the physical person consisting of the chemical elements of the body and the mental attributes such as sensation, perception, consciousness and character. None of these taken separately constitutes the ego; the ego, the personality, results from this ephemeral association of aggregates. To illustrate this there is the chariot simile. The chariot as such is regarded as nonexisting. What do exist, however, are the component parts of the vehicle—the pole, the frame and the wheels. None of these taken separately is a chariot, in fact when dissociated they are but a pile of spare parts, but when in certain ephemeral, unstable and transient relations to each other they constitute a carriage to which a name is given. This name is thereupon mistaken for an entity. Then there is the rainbow simile. The rainbow does not exist as such. What does exist, however, is an integration of raindrops and rays of light, producing the illusion, the rainbow.

To the Buddhist: "In the quest for the *I* the error already exists in the problem itself and transfers itself necessarily to all its conclusions" (Dahlke).

This attitude in no detail differs from the view expressed by White when writing: "What constitutes the individual? What constitutes the environment? These are pseudo-problems. They are the two elements of a dynamic relation, of a constant interplay of forces, in which their relative values are in a constant state of flux." One must keep in mind that flux, becoming, impermanence and illusion are phenomena, and that it is by phenomena alone that it is possible to assume the existence of reality, which as a matter of fact has as yet not been grasped (Spencer).

In psychoanalytical terms, a personality may be described as the integrating of the physical body with a set of psychic mechanisms. In fact this integration of mind and matter amounts to an indistinguishable interrelation in that both are but forms of energy. In a grave psychosis, when a dissociation takes the place of one of the systems such as perception, memory, foreconsciousness, motor or consciousness, there may follow a complete disappearance of the erstwhile rational ego, and there remains a wrangling mass of human spare parts, a deteriorated psychotic.

With an understanding of the Buddhist concept of the ego the question of the nature of the soul is disposed of, in that a soul is merely an ego after death. Any discussion of the difference between a live illusion and a dead illusion can only be entered upon by those skilled in metaphysics.

With the ego declared to be nonexistent, being but a transient association of mind and body aggregates, with the soul declared to be likewise illusion, yet with the most steadfast insistence upon personal responsibility for evil acts and an unshakable belief in the hereafter, the question arises: What is it that lives? What is it that carries on to the future existence? The answer to this rings clear to the Buddhist mind: "It is our acts." The proof of this is that it is to acts that Karma applies. It is to acts in that they are followed by reactions, which reactions again instantly function as causes for further effects. Therefore to acts alone is there permanence in that their effects never cease.

The personality of one today is the effect of antecedent acts, and is the cause of acts to come. If we are in distress, critical and unbiased inspection of the facts in the case will regularly show that our distress is due to lack of wisdom; little does it matter to the end product, wretchedness, by whom the unwise act is performed. The woman suffers severely from the acts she performed when a child, yet she is not the little girl who acted unwisely. However, she came from that child, and the grown woman profits or suffers in accordance with her childhood experiences and the manner in which she phantasied about them.

To the Buddhist, death is merely life looked at from another viewpoint; it is strictly a matter of energy transformation. One can imagine a live man, with a vast amount of energy latent in him, instantly killed by a falling beam. Biochemistry does not even hint at a solution of the problem of the difference between a live body and a body suddenly bereft of life. This difference is thinkable only in terms of energy. It is clear that people differ widely in energy values. In that wisdom conduces to health and strength and folly leads to disease and weakness it is evident that upon death each person liberates a different degree of energy. This difference in degree of energy released is the effect of antecedent behavior of the individual. It is our deeds that are immortal, it is to them that Karma and permanence, the test of reality, alone belongs. This body indeed dies when the life forsakes it, but the life does not die.

This energy liberated at death must be accounted for, just as the physicist accounts for the light wave that emanates from a snuffed candle. The Buddhist theory of rebirth (jāti) has been formulated to this end. Rebirth is assumed to be due to the energy that is liberated upon the dissolution of one personality energizing a new being. This, like all advances into the unknown, is theory and theory alone. But, mark well, its conditional acceptance explains much that is in urgent need of explanation. Embryology has taught us to locate in a fertilized ovum of one one-hundredth of an inch in diameter the capacity to recapitulate the phylogenetic history of a billion years of animal life in nine months. The Buddhist believes that the life energy that energizes this ovum is the effect of countless eons of antecedent causes such as being a monad, a multicellular organism and finally a mammal. The same fundamental concept is contained in the new psychology which views an organ as the somatic expression of psychic phenomena.

The Buddhist theory of rebirth alone answers the question of what it is that brings about the differences in mankind. Biology refers to it as variation. Variation, however, is strictly an effect of antecedent causes; the variation noted in the person under consideration is a cause only for that which is to follow.

The Buddhist knows that by living a life governed by conscious wisdom and not by unconscious craving there will result a personality but little afflicted by sorrow. Further, from the law of cause and effect, a sorrowless life in the present will condition a sorrowless life in the hereafter. This is a transference of character, yet a disavowal of personality and soul.

Skepticism as to a hereafter is a flight from reality, so also are the psychoses; both are due to the individual finding life so laden with sorrow as to make escape imperative.

A review of the neurotic cases passing before one will show that almost all of them are decidedly disoriented in their religious beliefs. They have lost the faith of their forefathers and are bewildered. One will further observe that mild neurotics are materially comforted by an intensive return to some manner of ceremony, usually in a new or bizarre cult. A high percentage of patients, upon their first being awakened to the somber seriousness of their having to gaze upon the image of their behavior as reflected by an opaque analyst, promptly abandon treatment, criticizing, compensating and regressing as they wend their way in a maze of religious activities.

The withdrawal of the ego from reality in the psychoses may be so complete as to place the patient beyond the pale of present psychoanalytic synthesis. In that skepticism is a severe fugue, there follows the most philosophical soundness for the statement of Reede that a penetrating analysis and permanent repair cannot be made of a patient who has completely lost his faith in the hereafter.

The Buddhist hereafter, Nirvana, is strictly a mental condition. It is not a place, it is not a negative state, it is not death. On the other hand, it is the living of a life with one's mind unhampered by the craving of unsated desire. It is a phase of mental life that is as much a reality to those who have attained to a glimpse of its emotion as is the concept of the unconscious mind to the Freudian scholar. It is equally difficult for the adept to demonstrate to the unprepared, there being no test-tube precipitate or jog in the sphygmograph line by which to point to the presence of either.

The fact is there are far more affinities between the Buddhist philosophy and Freudian psychoanalysis than exist between the latter and any other system for aiding humanity to attain the goal of increased energy intake, conversion and output (Jelliffe).

Philosophically the aim of both is identical, the elimination of sorrow and the attainment of happiness. In Buddhism the path is by enlightenment, in psychoanalysis by association-understanding of intrapsychic mechanisms, and both place the highest stress upon the need for sublimation.

In closing, it should be noted that not a trace of Freudian psychoanalysis as such exists in Buddhism. On the other hand, Buddha clearly discerned some of the most profound problems menacing mankind and through the mechanism of sublimation offered a rational scheme of libido control that was, prior to the teachings of Freud, absolutely unparalleled in the history of human endeavor.

from

BUDDHISTIC TRAINING AS AN ARTIFICIAL CATATONIA

THE BIOLOGICAL MEANING OF PSYCHIC OCCURRENCES

Franz Alexander

(1931)

❑

In what does the Nihilistic theory of Gautama Buddha consist, and what influence has it upon his disciples, who follow his teaching?

The common factor in the various Indian self-absorption methods is the goal-conscious, systematic withdrawal of all libidinal interest from the outer world, and the attempt to dispose narcissistically of all such freed quantities of libido. The important and interesting thing for us is that in self-absorption the intellectual functions are also drawn in. Even in Buddha's teaching the chief accent falls upon this inward perception. "Where there is no self-absorption there is no wisdom, and no wisdom where there is no self-absorption, and he who has both self-absorption and wisdom is near to Nirvana," says Buddha.[1]

The actual mental absorption is introduced by a general ascetic training, which consists in a systematic suppression of all emotional life. The chief

Translated by Margaret J. Powers. An earlier version of this essay was delivered as a lecture at the Seventh Congress of the International Psychoanalytical Association, Berlin, September 25, 1922. It later appeared in the journals *Imago* and *The Psychoanalytic Review* (vol. XVIII, no. 2, 1931). This excerpt comes from the latter (pages 132–45) and is reprinted here with the permission of the editors of *The Psychoanalytic Review*.

conditions are freedom from hatred, ceasing to desire property, denial of all fleshly pleasures, and sexual continence. Analytically regarded, this means that not only every genital but also every sadistic, oral-erotic, and anal-erotic outlet must be closed, in order to lead the libido to the ego, in its most primitive functions. The external means of accomplishing these demands consist in isolation, a peaceful composure of the body, and the observation and regulation of breathing. It is clear why breathing plays this especial role. It is the only constant periodical function which is accessible to the conscious will. After this ascetic preparation the first mental absorption sets in, which leads to Nirvana through the four steps of Jhana. The first Jhana step consists in a turning aside from the variety of external perceptions and inner imagination, and in the limitation of phantasy activity—concentration of thought upon a single theme. The objects of these meditations are different, yet are exclusively such as tend to depreciate the world and life in its entirety, meditations on the brevity and futility of human existence. Gradually these meditations pass over to increasingly gloomy observations of the hideousness and impurity of the human body, death, and the corruption of the flesh. These observations are bound with feelings of lively disgust with the body. The melancholic coloring is the chief feature of these sadistic, self-directed self-observations, the first stage of absorption, as emphasized by Heiler, in his research into religions. "In this phase of absorption the cosmic picture of the meditating monk is amazingly simplified, the entire world still only the inscrutable symbol of universal metaphysical evil . . . deep sorrow shakes the meditator, bitter contempt of the world fills him . . . all these transitory worldly desires and wishes die." It is thus that Heiler describes this phase of absorption, which, in the light of our clinical psychoanalytical knowledge, is exceedingly clear and especially interesting, inasmuch as it presents an experimentally induced melancholia. It is caused through the world, with all its multiplicity, ceasing to be a libido-object, after every worldly interest is artificially withdrawn, during the ascetic preparatory training, and now the entire withdrawn libido is directed to the individual's body. This assumes the role previously taken by the world and becomes the sole object. The libidinal interest of the ego is, at this stage, purely sadistic. The passionate frenzy against itself does not differ in any way from the well known clinical picture of melancholia. This condition is, however, far removed from the desired goal of absorption. The monk still feels disgust with his own body, and even this feeling must be conquered. If the conquest of disgust is successful, then the sadistic attitude toward the body will be replaced by a positive attitude. To put it clearly, the barrier erected during individual development, the feeling of disgust, the dam which is to protect the libido from narcissistic regression, is broken down and the entire libido, which until now found an outlet only in its sadistic component, streams back into the large reservoir of the ego. After the barrier of disgust is broken down no inhibiting factor is there to stop the transformation of object-libido into narcissistic libido—that is, to stop the regression of libido into primary form, self-love. This phase of positive attitude toward the ego is described in the Buddha text in the following words: "In this condition the monk is like a pool, fed from a source within himself, which has no outlet, neither to the east, nor to the west, north, nor south, and which also is not re-plenished by rain from time to time. This pool is fed from the cool stream of water within itself, with cool water streamed through, filled and flooded entirely, so that no single corner of the pool remains unsaturated: just so does the Bhikkhu drink from his physical body, fills and saturates himself completely from all sides with the joy and pleasurable feelings born out of the depths of absorption, so that not the smallest particle remains unsaturated." This is the second Jhana step. I think no analyst can more fittingly describe the condition of narcissism than is done in this text, if we substitute the word "libido" for "stream of water." For this reason this description seems to me especially interesting and important, because it is the description of a condition which we have only theoretically reconstructed and named "narcissism." The person's own body, indeed his entire body, becomes his sole object. This feeling of pleasure, a consummate voluptuousness of all organs, tissues, and cells, a pleasure completely freed from the genitals, an orgasm diffused through the whole body, is a condition which we ascribe to the schizophrenic in his catatonic ecstasy. We can consider the Buddhistic wording an introspective description of the mental situation during catatonia. This text justifies me methodologically in regarding Buddhistic absorption and Nirvana as psychological documents rather than as products of metaphysical speculation. Freud's conception of the development of object-libido from ego-libido is confirmed, point for point, in the artificial regression of absorption, and becomes an experimental truth. Furthermore, Freud's melancholia mechanism receives substantiation by the finding in the preceding melancholy stage of Jhana, which occurs when the world as object is lost, becomes sadistically depreciated, and when this sadism turns against the ego, which again recaptures its former developmental object-role from the outer world. The narcissistic step corresponds to the next further regression in that the barriers of disgust are broken down and the whole organism is flooded with positive libido. Perhaps the only new thing that we learn from this is in what sense a schizophrenic regression is deeper than one in melancholia. The deeper regression in schizophrenia comes about when the sadistic investment of the ego is replaced by a positive one. The protective role played by disgust, the disappearance of which is an old and well-known symptom of schizophrenia, comes clearly to expression: the conquest of disgust is the precondition for entering the second step of Jhana. Hate, disgust for the body, protects against love and is employed in the construction of the ego system in the form of feelings of disgust. If, then, schizophrenic regression corresponds to the narcissistic phase of individual development, melancholia must correspond to that postnarcissistic stage in which a critical agency is set up for the purpose of fighting the narcissism of the ego, which negatively invests the nucleus of the ego. In the self-accusations of the melancholic we hear the voice of the strict educator, whose criticisms and punishments are a pattern for a negative attitude of the ego against itself.

We have thus far seen that absorption systematically reverses the direction which development took in a constructive path, and then strives to demolish the entire physical and psychic personality. We may well be curious to learn where this repressive path can still lead, after the stage of narcissistic orgasm.

The third step of Jhana consists in a constant diminution of the feeling of pleasure of the second stage with a gradual transition into apathy. The narcissistic orgasm of the entire body is followed by a state of detumescence. The fourth stage is the condition of complete mental emptiness and uniformity. "Exalted above pleasure and pain, free from love and hate, indifferent to joy and sorrow, indifferent toward the whole world, toward Gods and Men, even toward himself, the monk lingers on the heights of *sancta-indifferentia*, on the threshold of Nirvana." Thus Heiler describes the last step of absorption. It is not difficult for us to recognize in this condition the last stage of schizophrenia, schizophrenic dementia, but it *is* difficult to evaluate and establish to which period of individual development it corresponds. According to Heiler, this condition is only quantitatively different from that of Nirvana; Nirvana means only its intensification.

We have several ways of approaching the analytical understanding of this state. First of all, physical behavior. Complete immobility with scarcely perceptible breathing; a limitation of metabolism, a kind of trance. In the final condition of the older autohypnotic Yoga absorption this physical effect is much more striking than in the Nirvana of the Buddhistic absorption. The unbelievable miracles of the fakirs, which seem to mock all physiology, take place in this autohypnotic state of Yoga practice. When we consider these miracles, we are struck by the remarkably stereotyped position of the body. Crouched together, the extremities folded up, with the head down, hanging from a tree, and similar things. Yet the greatest miracle is allowing oneself to be buried alive. It is not our province here to determine to what extent the stubbornly repeated rumors of forty-day burials rest upon truth. Sufficient other acts have been proven and the remarkable capacity of the fakir to influence his physiological function, even metabolism, has been established.

We are chiefly interested in the meaning of these customs, the meaning of which is involuntarily forced upon the analytical eye. Immobility, a remarkably uncomfortable position of the body, restriction, indeed almost cessation of breathing, burial. The sense is clear, a regression to the condition before birth, immobility, being folded together, without breathing, lying in the mother. The end-effects of Yoga practice which Buddha employed, only spiritualized, make it very probable that the end condition of his absorption, Nirvana, likewise means the deepest regression to the condition of intrauterine life, the more so since the physical characteristics are the same, immobility, being folded together, breathlessness—think of a Buddha statue. Nirvana is the condition in the mother's womb. "Without perception, without wishes, the peace in which there is no death nor being reborn, no Here, no Beyond, only an intermediate kingdom, that is even the end of sorrow," says Heiler.

But the intrauterine meaning of Nirvana will be much more obvious if we regard its psychic content and follow Buddha step by step through the four stages of Jhana into Nirvana. Here our analytical interest begins. The absorption was until now purely affective, yet Buddha promises his disciples knowledge, which is the true goal of absorption. Parallel with the physical and affective absorption runs the intellectual, the perception of the concealed connections of existence in the self to be attained by turning all intellectual power inwards. In the fourth stage of Jhana, Buddha recognized the eternal law of Karma, the cycles of eternal reincarnation. In birth, Buddha sees the cause of the threefold evils, age, sickness, and death. In the legend of the young prince who thrice sets forth upon a journey, Buddha explains to his followers the cause of his religious strivings, which leads him to turn away from the world, back into his innermost being. On first venturing forth, the young prince is induced to return by the sight of a helpless old man; at the second, the sight of sick people who are wallowing in their own excrements; and the third time by a funeral procession. The conquest of age, sickness, and death is the expressed goal of Buddhistic teaching and we may rightly call it a narcissistic religion in opposition to the transference religion, Christianity, which attempts to regulate the social life of humanity in its affective relation. We can even express it more forcibly. The aims of Buddhistic teaching are therapeutic, the conquest of age, sickness, and death. Their way is that of regression through introversion, and their cure Nirvana, the conquest, or nullification of birth. In his legend of the threefold exodus, Buddha three times curses birth: "Oh, shame, say I, of birth, that at birth age appears, sickness appears, death appears."[2] The cause of the threefold evil is birth, the cosmic law reincarnation, and Nirvana means its conquest. "In Nirvana the power which leads to existence is annihilated, no longer is there reincarnation—'says Buddha,' Man has regressed; sunk back into pure Being which is nothing but itself."[3]

I hope that I have succeeded in making it seem probable to you that the end goal of Buddhistic absorption is an attempt at psychological and physical regression to the condition of intrauterine life. We saw the introspective description of the different steps of the regressive absorption scale which correspond to the various steps of individual development, that the way to Nirvana can be likened to a cinema film which is turning in the reverse direction. Beginning by liberating the libido from the world, and leading through melancholy and then through the narcissistic catatonic phase, it finally attains the apparent alibidinous condition of Nirvana, the intrauterine state. We can understand this regression in the light of the libido theory until we reach the narcissistic phase. Analytical understanding is an equation which expresses the relation of the ego to the libido. The equation of the melancholy phase runs: sadistic investment of the ego as object; the equation of the narcissistic phase: positive investment of the ego as object. The question which remains open, according to the libido-ego equation of Nirvana, is that of the intrauterine condition, which, according to the description in the Buddhistic texts, appears to be alibidinous. The difference between object and subject vanishes, says Heiler in regard to this state. "The Complete has sunk back into pure Being, which is nothing but itself." Thus says Buddha. A distinction between subject and object is truly necessary to an understanding of the libido concept, and even the narcissistic libido takes the ego itself as object. This apparently alibidinous condition of Nirvana, pure existence, can be nothing other than the most complete restriction of the ego impulses and of the libido, one such as

Freud assumes for single-celled protozoa, or like the original narcissism of the sperm cells, which, according to his conception, were purely narcissistic.[4] According to this, the sensation of Nirvana would be identical with the complete coincidence of ego impulses and libido. This assertion, however, is a biological theory. What can that have to do with psychological sensation?

First of all, the intrauterine state is not a single moment in time, but comprises the developmental period from the fertilized cell up to the time of birth. In which phase of intrauterine life does Buddha discover the conquest of the cycle of reincarnations, the sinking back into pure existence? Indeed, where does Buddhistic regression really end?

We could easily form a picture of the melancholy phase of absorption. We found the description of the second stage of Jhana an excellent presentation of narcissism in the classical sense. In this state we could even recognize the catatonic ecstasy of schizophrenia. The psychological meaning of Nirvana, the sensation of the condition in the mother's womb, is difficult to imagine. That this condition is meant is entirely clear. Buddha himself calls it the conquest of birth, the conquest of eternal reincarnation. What does the expression "eternal rebirth" actually mean? For this we must seek some solution. One might easily get the impression that these statements about Nirvana are pure metaphysical conceptions, the fruit of some type of philosophical speculation. Yet we can at once discard this assumption. All other phases of absorption were psychological conditions and the path to them led through systematic, chronologically exact workings of the personality. The psychotechnique of Buddha made it possible voluntarily to trace this regressive path. The Yoga practice makes possible the physiological miracle, the voluntary restriction of metabolism; the absorption theory of Buddha produces a complete psychic regression. We are justified in assuming that the end state of this regression corresponds to a psychic experience as nearly related to the intrauterine condition as narcissistic absorption is to the actual narcissistic period of individual development. Yet I have a still more weighty proof that Nirvana really is a psychological regression to the intrauterine state, more precisely into a condition whose libido-ego equation is identical with that of the embryological period, a proof which I have withheld until now. I refer to the interpretation of Buddha's "salvation knowledge" in the fourth state of Jhana, which makes possible the entrance to Nirvana, the knowledge of the eternal repetition of rebirth. The meaning of these laws, the central core of Buddhism, can be understood in its deepest meaning only in the light of psychoanalytical interpretation. However, the philosopher Ziegler comes very near to this in his interpretations. Let us turn to his profound work *The Eternal Buddha*.

According to Ziegler, the whole way to self-absorption through the four steps of Jhana serves to free psychic processes from every tone of emotion, pleasurable as well as painful. All the painful feelings of the first stage and all the pleasurable ones of the second stage of Jhana which could induce the worshipper to persist at one of the stages must be overcome. Only in the fourth stage, when thought is cleansed of every pleasurable or painful undercurrent, can the liberating recollection of the reincarnations enter. We analysts are also acquainted with two kinds of resistance in our patients: those which depend upon unpleasurable affects and those tenacious defenders of the borders of narcissism which are based upon a tendency to persist in a pleasurable condition. The absorption scale corresponds to the chronological path of a well-conducted analysis. In conquering the melancholy phase the unpleasurable resistance is overcome and only then in the second stage ensues the conquest of narcissism.

Permit me to repeat the therapeutic meaning of the fourfold absorption in Ziegler's words: "In the same measure as the monk becomes more absorbed within himself, and the sources of each external experience are dammed up upon which we Occidentals are accustomed to base almost all our knowledge, and surely all our science—in just the same measure sources hitherto unknown to him begin to well up within him, the very distant whispering murmur of which his unusually sharpened ear ever more clearly perceives. He who has become strong in fourfold self-absorption has actually tempered and annealed for himself a new sense, which he can use as a drill is used by a geologist. Grown wise in himself and of himself— this monk is able above all things to recollect himself. This knowledge is recollection, and indeed in distinction and opposition to mere memory is to be understood throughout as *anamnesis* in distinction and opposition to mere *mneme*. . . . That the ascetic shall remember most accurately and vividly all the circumstances of his life down to the least detail is the most important outcome of the four Jhanani; that is the first relatively holy wisdom." I leave it to you to draw the parallel with psychoanalysis.

Shall we believe that the pious monk who followed Buddha's prescriptions was capable of such recollections? In the first three Jhana stages we saw that in case he did not recollect, he reenacted, formed transitory symptoms in Ferenczi's sense, a passing melancholia, a passing schizophrenia; he repeated the stages of his earlier development. It is theoretically conceivable that in the affectless, resistance-free fourth state, conscious memories arise. But how far this remembered knowledge, as Buddha calls it, goes is hard to establish. If we may believe Buddha, it goes very far. He halts not at all at the threshold of individual existence but passes over into a continuous state of regression. Let us hear what Buddha says of the condition of the fourth stage: "In such a zealous state of mind, refined, cleansed, purified, free of dross, supple, pliant, steadfast, invulnerable, I directed the heart toward recollected knowledge of previous forms of existence. I recollected many different forms of existence as if one life, then two lives, then three, then four, then five, then ten, then twenty—then a thousand, a hundred thousand, then times when many worlds were created, then times when many worlds declined, then times when many worlds arose—vanished."[5]

The meaning of those regressive recollections of all forms of existence, of all reincarnations until there is no more rebirth, until rebirth is finally dug out by the roots, until man is annihilated, can no longer remain in doubt. The regressive absorption, the turning of the film of life in a reverse direction, goes further, goes beyond birth and passes all stages of intrauterine life, and unrolls embryological development, which is nothing other than a short repetition of all forms of life in the geological rise and fall of many worlds of early times since the first birth. The question previously put—Where does the Buddhistic regression end?—can now be answered. Absorption goes back to the beginning of embryonic development.

I am perfectly aware of how improbable this sounds. Yet if you have followed me along the regressive path of absorption perhaps you will not deny that this path, which is a chronologically true demolition of ontogenetic development, finally leads to a primitive condition where ego impulses and libido completely merge, similar to the state which we can assume, according to Freud, to obtain for the germ cell. We know that neurotic symptoms make use of archaic forms of expression; it is really then only a quantitative question as to how old this form is. Whether it arises from the extra- or intrauterine condition is no fundamental matter. In the form of action, of repetition, every regression is thinkable, and I hope I have made it probable that the condition of Nirvana in Indian ascetics who have mastered the regression technique and whose entire libido through years of practice is withdrawn in this introverted narcissistic direction can be expressed as a libido-ego equation which is identical with that of the germ cell. But Nirvana means not only a complete regression to the beginning of development but at the same time a knowledge. The clairvoyant knowledge of eternal reincarnation, the recollection of all forms of life, all geological periods, which Buddha perceived after going through the fourth step of Jhana, is nothing more than our fundamental biogenetic law, except that Buddha discovered it by a completely different approach. He knew this law experientially by reliving, in his affective regression, his embryological existence. The difficulty we cannot resolve is how consciousness, or, as Buddha maintains, memory, can follow this deep regression so far. Here we meet our most difficult problem, whose solution is hardly possible, and which I shall in no way undertake. Nevertheless, permit me to point out that we meet the same problem daily in analytical practice and that just this commonplaceness explains why we have accustomed ourselves not to think about it.

This problem begins with Freud's thesis that the neurotic is always right. Our entire analytical striving rests upon this truth . . . that we listen to the neurotic and seek to trace a meaning in his symptoms. Freud's statement really means that the *unconscious* is always right. Now the above problem is brought somewhat nearer if we reformulate the sentence, "the unconscious is always right," more pretentiously: The unconscious knows everything—knows all that concerns the inner world. Ignorance of that which is within first begins with the Censorship. We find this thesis proven every day. The unconscious knows the "primal scene," knows of the amniotic fluid, and knows the fact of fertilization. Freud shows that it is unnecessary, in order to understand the knowledge of the unconscious, always to search for actual observations or even for early phantasies. He predicates the conception of inherent phantasies and with this predicates a phylogenetic knowledge. This knowledge is a sort of recollection. And as the memory of living matter is unlimited—in embryonic development are repeated even the occurrences of primeval times—so also the recollective knowledge of the unconscious is unlimited in time. The deepest layer of the unconscious cannot be other than the psychic reflection of those early biological events which we group together in the designation "embryological development." Upon this deepest layer, which we can designate as phylogenetic knowledge, Buddha strikes in his regressive absorption. For this embryological period a capacity for unlimited recollection is characteristic. Biologically regarded, it *is* nothing else but recollection. And yet it remains a riddle, this discovering of biogenic law by introspective means, the discovery, or rather the direct experiencing of it. This deepest layer of the unconscious, which is pure recollection, is furthest of all from consciousness, and with Buddha this is said to become conscious!

We can hardly picture that the recollected knowledge of Buddha retraces and psychologically reproduces embryological development. We know what a piece of work it is to make a neurotic symptom, and archaic regression, conscious, even aided by the entire stock of our analytical experience. It seems implied that Buddha, while in his schizophrenic regression, presents a symptom, interprets it at the same time, and in this way substitutes memory for repetition. Yet if we deny this there then remains only the other possibility, that Buddha found this law not by subjective means, but by the usual kind of objective knowledge, and then phantasied this into its theoretically correct place in the scale of absorption. The truth may be midway between these extremes. The dogma of rebirth is contained in the old Indian Atman. It is in the form of a theory of the transmigration of souls, a primitive intuitive presentiment of the theory of evolution, but in part perhaps chiefly based upon the objective observation of death, birth, and the similarities between men and beasts, and representing a deductive conclusion from such observation. We may also be dealing with a sort of *fausse reconnaissance*, as Heiler assumes, without recognizing the deeper meaning of that term. Heiler says: "We Occidentals can with difficulty picture to ourselves this anamnesis, this memory retrospect of previous existences. We can, however, psychologically understand how a person, all of whose desires and strivings focus on a flight from the painful recurrences of birth, in moments of the highest spiritual tension might, by a sort of *fausse reconnaissance* process, take the visual images which arise to be memories of previous reincarnation." But through Freud we know the deeper meaning of *fausse reconnaissance*. We recognize something which we know unconsciously, which we have repressed, or which is present in us as unconscious knowledge. The emerging phantasy pictures, in Heiler's explanation, arise from the unconscious. They enter during the repetition of embryological development, similar to a dream, or a free association, and are the last tributaries of the unconscious to surge into consciousness. However this may be, it is clear that Buddha has in some manner experienced the fundamental biogenetic law; his experience has not only biological but also geological validity. Yet this subjective experience is contained in every kind of knowledge, also in our seemingly purely objective type of knowledge of the outside world. Every intuitive comprehension of a truth, if it is accompanied by the subjective feeling of its being a discovery, or of having self-evidence, is a kind of *fausse reconnaissance*, a recognition of one's own self mirrored in the outside world. The connections within the self are just the same as in the external world—the self is only a special

part of reality. *"Ordo et connexio idearum idem est ac ordo et connexio rerum."*
And now I am again at my point of departure. I did not wish to prove the
reciprocal validity of biological and psychological occurrences, but to use
this concept to illuminate the phenomena of Buddha's self-absorption. The
oldest problem in philosophy reappears in this individual case. Yet all our
sense of wonder vanishes if we accept Spinoza's solution. There are two
roads to all knowledge. One can experience the world as an object, or
experience it directly, know it endopsychically. If the methods of both
forms of knowing are correct, then they must lead to the same result, and
this is the only true control. Indian culture has brought the subjective
method of self-submersion to completion, while our Occidental culture
fosters the method of objective knowledge. Only in psychoanalysis do the
two methods meet. Here I recall a statement of Groddeck that human
intelligence is nothing but the stupidity acquired through repression.[6] I
should like to amplify this sentence to the effect that in a certain sense
our entire consciousness is based upon such a relative stupidity, upon ignorance of that which is within. We leave the regulation of our instinctual
life to more primitive processes and agencies than our critical consciousness
such as conscience, the consciousness of guilt. The regulation of deeper
biological happenings is left to agencies which lie still further from consciousness and whose existence we are only beginning to appreciate.[7]
Through this stupidity in regard to our inner life we gain our knowledge
of the external world. This freedom comes from inner processes, which
take place automatically without the necessity of conscious interference
and permit us to direct all our attention toward the world.

When Buddha announced his absorption theory, a number of autohypnotic absorption methods, which one knows as Yoga practice, had already
been discovered. Seeking the truth, Buddha had at first chosen autohypnotic absorption and later discarded it as not leading to his goal. His main
methodological discovery was that absorption must take place under completely conscious circumstances in order to reach Nirvana. I will not again
point out the striking similarity between the analytical method and the
doctrine of Buddha. The overcoming of affective resistance and of narcissism, so that one is able to recollect instead of repeat the extension of
consciousness in a regressive direction toward the past, this is the doctrine
common to Freud and Buddha. Can we regard as accidental this remarkable
repetition in the history of both spiritual creations whose founders both at
first attempted to use hypnosis, which they found at hand as prescientific

practice? And was it also accidental that both then arrived at the conclusion that the chief and really difficult task is to establish the connection with consciousness?

Yet there remains an insurmountable difference between the two doctrines, deeply rooted in the difference between Indian and European culture. Buddhistic absorption goes much deeper in the direction of regression, yet it must pay dearly for this depth. Through this it allows the entire outside world to pass into oblivion, conquers the self, but loses the world thereby. The objective of psychoanalysis is more pretentious: it strives to conquer self without losing the outside world. The Buddhistic doctrine is more asocial; we find in the causes of absorption only biological factors such as age, sickness, and death, but no social factors such as the Oedipus complex. The world is given up, and the cure consists in regression to the condition where ego and libido, no longer driven by outer necessity, reach their ultimate boundaries. Buddha does not seek an adjustment to the world, as psychoanalysis seeks to achieve a new compromise, to establish a new boundary between ego and libido, adjusted to reality. This asocial feature of his doctrine also spelt its end, which came with a tragic crash. The neo-Buddhists overlook this failure if they expect from his doctrine a new salvation.[8]

Buddha denies himself the eternal life, which he has achieved through the conquest of death, by the entrance to Nirvana. Here is the first contradiction in the completely self-contained Nirvana philosophy. Buddha, voluntarily parting from life, directs the following words to his favorite pupil, Ananda: "If to thee though, Ananda, the Perfect One has given an important sign, an important suggestion, thou hast not been able to see it, hast not prayed for the Perfect One . . . may the Exalted persist throughout the ages, may the Welcome One exist throughout the ages, for the good of many, for the healing of many, out of pity for the world, for the use, welfare and succour of gods, and men. Hadst thou, Ananda, prayed for the Perfect One, so had thy words been twice unheeded, the third time answered. For this reason thou hast overlooked it, hast missed it."[9] Here we see, heavily shrouded, in the dark background, the Oedipus complex, the father conflict. Buddha departs, because his followers have not understood him, because he has remained alone, because even his favorite pupil, Ananda, does not seek to keep him from going. This incomprehensible "not asking to remain" means nothing other than an unresolved father conflict. According to Oldenburg, the silence of Ananda is explained by saying that the death god, Mara, had confused his reason.[10] Yet Buddha understands

Ananda's silence. He does not want to believe what he sees, and hints to Ananda that he expects from him a request to remain. But Ananda remains silent and Buddha departs. The attempt to eliminate reality completely has failed. He begins his analysis at a point which lies behind the Oedipus complex. He begins where we leave off, at the narcissistic boundary, at the borders of the organic.

And thus he instructs his disciples. He must go because his followers, under the pressure of the unconquered father complex, desire his departure. Buddha has not analyzed but repressed the object transference. Had he remained consistent, he would never have been able to announce his doctrine.[11] He completely withdrew from the world, yet one thread he left unsevered—his spiritual connection with his disciples. Here it is that he receives his mortal blow. He denied the world, and the denied world revenged itself upon him in the form of the unconscious parricidal wishes of his followers.

Notes

1. Heiler, *Die Buddhistische Versenkung* (Munich, 1922).
2. Leopold Ziegler, *Der ewige Buddho* (Darmstadt, 1922).
3. Heiler, 40.
4. Freud, *Jenseits des Lustprinzips* (2nd ed., 1922). (English edition, *Beyond the Pleasure Principle*, 1922.)
5. *Die Reden Gotamo Buddhos*, from the collection *Majjhimanikajo des Pali Kanons*, translated by Karl Eugen Neumann, vol. 1 (Munich, 1922).
6. Groddeck, "Über den Symbolisierungezwang," *Imago*, vol. 8 (1922), 72.
7. One thinks of the "ego-memory system" of Ferenczi ("Psycho-analytical Observations on Tic," *International Journal of Psycho-Analysis*, vol. 7, 1921).
8. I think first of Leopold Ziegler.
9. Ziegler, 159–60.
10. Oldenburg, *Buddha: Sein Leben, sein Lehre, seine Gemeinde* (Stuttgart-Berlin, 1921), 356.
11. Buddha actually wasn't sure whether he should keep his teachings to himself or announce them to mankind (Oldenburg, 159). Nowhere in the Buddhistic literature has sufficient account been taken of the deep contradiction between the absorption doctrine and Buddha's practical ethics, so far as I am able to follow. The goal of absorption, Nirvana, is a completely asocial condition and is difficult to combine with ethical precepts.

from

THE ZEN DOCTRINE OF NO-MIND

D. T. Suzuki

(1949)

❑

How is it possible for the human mind to move from discrimination to nondiscrimination, from affections to affectionlessness, from being to non-being, from relativity to emptiness, from the ten thousand things to the contentless mirror-nature or Self-nature, or, Buddhistically expressed, from *mayoi* (*mi* in Chinese) to *satori* (*wu*)?[1] How this movement is possible is the greatest mystery not only in Buddhism but in all religion and philosophy. So long as this world, as conceived by the human mind, is a realm of opposites, there is no way to escape from it and to enter into a world of emptiness where all opposites are supposed to merge. The wiping-off of the multitudes known as the ten thousand things in order to see into the mirror-nature itself is an absolute impossibility. Yet Buddhists all attempt to achieve it.

Philosophically stated, the question is not properly put. It is not the

This excerpt (pages 52–63) from the author's *The Zen Doctrine of No-Mind: The Significance of the Sūtra of Hui-Neng* (York Beach, ME: Samuel Weiser, 1972) is reprinted with permission of the publisher.

wiping-off of the multitudes, it is not moving from discrimination to non-discrimination, from relativity to emptiness, etc. Where the wiping-off process is accepted, the idea is that when the wiping-off is completed, the mirror shows its original brightness, and therefore the process is continuous on one line of movement. But the fact is that the wiping itself is the work of the original brightness. The "original" has no reference to time, in the sense that the mirror was once, in its remote past, pure and undefiled, and that as it is no more so, it must be polished up and its original brightness be restored. The brightness is there all the time, even when it is thought to be covered with dust and not reflecting objects as it should. The brightness is not something to be restored; it is not something appearing at the completion of the procedure; it has never departed from the mirror. This is what is meant when the *T'an-ching* and other Buddhist writings declare the Buddha-nature to be the same in all beings, including the ignorant as well as the wise.

As the attainment of the Tao does not involve a continuous movement from error to truth, from ignorance to enlightenment, from *mayoi* to *satori*, the Zen masters all proclaim that there is no enlightenment whatever which you can claim to have attained. If you say you have attained something, this is the surest proof that you have gone astray. Therefore, not to have is to have; silence is thunder; ignorance is enlightenment; the holy disciples of the Purity-path go to hell while the precept-violating Bhikshus attain Nirvana; the wiping-off means dirt-accumulating; all these paradoxical sayings—and Zen literature is filled with them—are no more than so many negations of the continuous movement from discrimination to non-discrimination, from affectibility to nonaffectibility, etc , etc

The idea of a continuous movement fails to account for the facts, first, that the moving process stops at the originally bright mirror, and makes no further attempt to go on indefinitely, and second, that the pure nature of the mirror suffers itself to be defiled, i.e. that from one object comes another object absolutely contradicting it. To put this another way: absolute negation is needed, but can it be possible when the process is continuous? Here is the reason why Hui-neng persistently opposes the view cherished by his opponents. He does not espouse the doctrine of continuity which is the Gradual School of Shen-hsiu. All those who hold the view of a continuous movement belong to the latter. Hui-neng, on the other hand, is the champion of the Abrupt School. According to this school the movement from *mayoi* to *satori* is abrupt and not gradual, discrete and not continuous.

That the process of enlightenment is abrupt means that there is a leap, logical and psychological, in the Buddhist experience. The logical leap is that the ordinary process of reasoning stops short, and what has been considered irrational is perceived to be perfectly natural, while the psychological leap is that the borders of consciousness are overstepped and one is plunged into the Unconscious which is not, after all, unconscious. This process is discrete, abrupt, and altogether beyond calculation; this is "Seeing into one's Self-nature." Hence the following statement by Hui-neng:

"O friends, while under Jen the Master I had a *satori* (*wu*) by just once listening to his words, and abruptly saw into the original nature of Suchness. This is the reason why I wish to see this teaching propagated, so that seekers of the truth may also abruptly have an insight into Bodhi, see each by himself what his mind (*hsin*) is, what his original nature is. . . . All the Buddhas of the past, present, and future and all the Sūtras belonging to the twelve divisions are in the self-nature of each individual, where they were from the first. . . . There is within oneself that which knows, and thereby one has a *satori*. If there rises an erroneous thought, falsehoods and perversions obtain; and no outsiders, however wise, are able to instruct such people, who are, indeed, beyond help. But if there takes place an illumination by means of genuine Prajñā, all falsehoods vanish in an instant. If one's self-nature is understood, one's *satori* is enough to make one rise to a state of Buddhahood. O friends, when there is a Prajñā illumination, the inside as well as the outside becomes thoroughly translucent, and a man knows by himself what his original mind is, which is no more than emancipation. When emancipation is obtained, it is the Prajñā-samādhi, and when this Prajñā-samādhi is understood, there is realized a state of *mu-nen* (*wu-nien*), 'thought-less-ness.' "

The teaching of abrupt *satori* is then fundamental in the Southern School of Hui-neng. And we must remember that this abruptness or leaping is not only psychological, but dialectical.

Prajñā is really a dialectical term denoting that this special process of knowing, known as "abruptly seeing," or "seeing at once," does not follow general laws of logic; for when Prajñā functions one finds oneself all of a sudden, as if by a miracle, facing Śūnyatā, the emptiness of all things. This does not take place as the result of reasoning, but when reasoning has been abandoned as futile, and psychologically when the willpower is brought to a finish.

The Use of Prajñā contradicts everything that we may conceive of things worldly; it is altogether of another order than our usual life. But this does not mean that Prajñā is something altogether disconnected with our life and thought, something that is to be given to us by a miracle from some unknown and unknowable source. If this were the case, Prajñā would be of no possible use to us, and there would be no emancipation for us. It is true that the functioning of Prajñā is discrete, and interrupting to the progress of logical reasoning, but all the time it underlies it, and without Prajñā we cannot have any reasoning whatever. Prajñā is at once above and in the process of reasoning. This is a contradiction, formally considered, but in truth this contradiction itself is made possible because of Prajñā.

That almost all religious literature is filled with contradictions, absurdities, paradoxes, and impossibilities, and demands to believe them, to accept them, as revealed truths, is due to the fact that religious knowledge is based on the working of Prajñā. Once this viewpoint of Prajñā is gained, all the essential irrationalities found in religion become intelligible. It is like appreciating a fine piece of brocade. On the surface there is an almost bewildering confusion of beauty, and the connoisseur fails to trace the intricacies of the threads. But as soon as it is turned over all the intricate beauty and skill is revealed. Prajñā consists in this turning-over. The eye has hitherto followed the surface of the cloth, which is indeed the only side ordinarily allowed us to survey. Now, the cloth is abruptly turned over; the course of the eyesight is suddenly interrupted; no continuous gazing is possible. Yet by this interruption, or rather disruption, the whole scheme of life is suddenly grasped; there is the "seeing into one's self-nature."

The point I wish to make here is that the reason side has been there all the time, and that it is because of this unseen side that the visible side has been able to display its multiple beauty. This is the meaning of discriminative reasoning being always based on nondiscriminating Prajñā; this is the meaning of the statement that the mirror-nature of emptiness (śūnyatā) retains its original brightness all the time and is never once beclouded by anything outside which is reflected on it; this is again the meaning of all things being such as they are in spite of their being arranged in time and space and subject to the so-called laws of nature.

This something conditioning all things and itself not being conditioned by anything assumes various names as it is viewed from different angles. Spatially, it is called "formless" against all that can be subsumed under form; temporarily, it is "nonabiding," as it moves on forever, not being cut up into pieces called thoughts and as such detained and retained as something abiding; psychologically it is "the unconscious" (wu-nien=mu-nen) in the sense that all our conscious thoughts and feelings grow out of the Unconscious, which is Mind (*hsin*), or Self-nature (*tzu-hsing*).

As Zen is more concerned with experience and hence with psychology, let us go further into the idea of the Unconscious. The original Chinese is *Wu-nien* (*mu-nen*) or *Wu-hsin* (*mu-shin*), and literally means "no-thought," or "no-mind." But *nien* or *hsin* means more than thought or mind. This I have elsewhere explained in detail. It is rather difficult to give here an exact English equivalent for *nien* or *hsin*. Hui-neng and Shen-hui use principally *nien* instead of *hsin*, but there are other Zen masters who prefer *hsin* to *nien*. In point of fact, the two designate the same experience: *wu-nien* and *wu-hsin* point to the same state of consciousness.

The character *hsin* originally symbolizes the heart as the organ of affection, but has later come to indicate also the seat of thinking and willing. *Hsin* has thus a broad connotation, and may be taken largely to correspond to consciousness. *Wu-nien* is "no-consciousness," thus the unconscious. The character *nien* has *chien* "now," over the heart, and might originally have meant anything present at the moment in consciousness. In Buddhist literature, it frequently stands for the Sanskrit *Kśana*, meaning "a thought," "a moment regarded as a unit of time," "an instant"; but as a psychological term it is generally used to denote "memory," "intense thinking," and "consciousness." *Wu-nien* thus also means "the unconscious."

What, then, do the Zen masters mean by "the unconscious"?

It is evident that in Zen Buddhism the unconscious is not a psychological term either in a narrower or in a broader sense. In modern psychology the scientists refer to the unconscious as underlying consciousness, where a large mass of psychological factors are kept buried under one name or another. They appear in the field of consciousness sometimes in response to a call, and therefore by a conscious effort, but quite frequently unexpectedly and in a disguised form. To define this unconsciousness baffles the psychologists just because it is the unconscious. The fact is, however, that it is a reservoir of mysteries and a source of superstitions. And for this reason the concept of the unconscious has been abused by unscrupulous religionists, and some people hold that Zen is also guilty of this crime. The accusation is justifiable if Zen philosophy is no more than a psychology of the unconscious in its ordinary definition.

According to Hui-neng, the concept of the unconscious is the foundation of Zen Buddhism. In fact he proposes three concepts as constituting Zen, and the unconscious is one of them; the other two are "formlessness" (*wu-hsing*) and "nonabiding" (*wu-chu*). Hui-neng continues: "By formlessness is meant to be in form and yet to be detached from it; by the uncon-scious is meant to have thoughts and yet not to have them; as to nonabiding it is the primary nature of man."

His further definition of the unconscious is: "O good friends, not to have the Mind tainted while in contact with all conditions of life²—this is to be Unconscious. It is to be always detached from objective conditions in one's own consciousness, not to let one's mind be roused by coming in contact with objective conditions. . . . O good friends, why is the Uncon-scious established as fundamental? There are some people with confused ideas who talk about seeing into their own nature, but whose consciousness is not liberated from objective conditions, and (my teaching) is only for the sake of such people. Not only are they conscious of objective condi-tions, but they contrive to cherish false views, from which all worldly worries and vagaries rise. But in self-nature there is from the first not a thing which is attainable. If anything attainable is here conceived, fortune and misfortune will be talked about; and this is no more than worrying and giving oneself up to vagaries. Therefore in my teaching, unconscious-ness is established as fundamental.

"O good friends, what is there for wu (of wu-nien, unconsciousness) to negate? And what is there for nien to be conscious of? Wu is to negate the notion of two forms (dualism), and to get rid of a mind which worries over things, while nien means to become conscious of the primary nature of Suchness (tathatā); for Suchness is the Body of Consciousness, and Con-sciousness is the Use of Suchness. It is the self-nature of Suchness to be-come conscious of itself; it is not the eye, ear, nose, and tongue that is conscious; as Suchness has (self) nature, consciousness rises in it; if there were no Suchness, then eye and ear, together with forms and sounds, would be destroyed. In the self-nature of Suchness there rises consciousness; while in the six senses there is seeing, hearing, remembering, and recognizing; the self-nature is not tainted by objective conditions of all kinds; the true nature moves with perfect freedom, discriminating all forms in the objec-tive world and inwardly unmoved in the first principle."

While it is difficult and often misleading to apply the modern way of thinking to those ancient masters, especially masters of Zen, we must to a certain extent hazard this application, for otherwise there will be no chance of even a glimpse into the secrets of Zen experience. For one thing, we have what Hui-neng calls self-nature, which is the Buddha-nature of the Nirvāṇa Sūtra and other Mahāyāna writings. This self-nature in terms of the Prajñāpāramitā is Suchness (tathatā), and Emptiness (śūnyatā). Suchness means the Absolute, something which is not subject to laws of relativity, and therefore which cannot be grasped by means of form. Suchness is thus formlessness. In Buddhism, form (*rūpa*) stands against no-form (*arūpa*), which is the unconditioned. This unconditioned, formless, and consequently unattainable is Emptiness (*śūnyatā*). Emptiness is not a negative idea, nor does it mean mere privation, but as it is not in the realm of names and forms it is called emptiness, or nothingness, or the Void.

Emptiness is thus unattainable. "Unattainable" means to be beyond perception, beyond grasping, for emptiness is on the other side of being and nonbeing. All our relative knowledge is concerned with dualities. But if emptiness is absolutely beyond all human attempts to take hold of in any sense whatever, it has no value for us; it does not come into the sphere of human interest; it is really nonexistent, and we have nothing to do with it. But the truth is otherwise. Emptiness constantly falls within our reach; it is always with us and in us, and conditions all our knowledge, all our deeds, and is our life itself. It is only when we attempt to pick it up and hold it forth as something before our eyes that it eludes us, frustrates all our efforts, and vanishes like vapour. We are ever lured toward it, but it proves a will-o'-the-wisp.

It is Prajñā which lays its hands on Emptiness, or Suchness, or self-nature. And this laying-hands-on is not what it seems. This is self-evident from what has already been said concerning things relative. Inasmuch as self-nature is beyond the realm of relativity, its being grasped by Prajñā cannot mean a grasping in its ordinary sense. The grasping must be no-grasping, a paradoxical statement which is inevitable. To use Buddhist terminology, this grasping is accomplished by nondiscrimination; that is, by nondiscriminating discrimination. The process is abrupt, discrete, an act of the conscious; not an unconscious act but an act rising from self-nature itself, which is the Unconscious.

Hui-neng's Unconscious is thus fundamentally different from the psychologists' Unconscious. It has a metaphysical connotation. When Hui-neng speaks of the Unconscious in Consciousness, he steps beyond psychology; he is not referring even to the Unconscious forming the basis of consciousness, which goes to the remotest part when the mind has not yet evolved, the mind being still in a state of mere sustenance. Nor is Hui-neng's Unconscious a kind of world-spirit which is found floating on the surface of chaos. It is timeless, and yet contains all time with its minutest periods as well as all its aeons.

Shen-hui's definition of the Unconscious which we have in his *Sayings* (par. 14) will shed further light on the subject. When preaching to others on the *Prajñāpāramitā* he says: "Be not attached to form. Not to be attached to form means Suchness. What is meant by Suchness? It means the Unconscious. What is the Unconscious? It is not to think of being and nonbeing; it is not to think of good and bad; it is not to think of having limits or not having limits; it is not to think of measurements (or of nonmeasurements); it is not to think of enlightenment, nor is it to think of being enlightened; it is not to think of Nirvāṇa, nor is it to think of attaining Nirvāṇa: this is the Unconscious. The Unconscious is no other than Prajñāpāramitā itself. Prajñāpāramitā is no other than the Samādhi of Oneness.

"O friends, if there are among you some who are still in the stage of learners, let them turn their illumination (upon the source of consciousness) whenever thoughts are awakened in their minds. When the awakened mind is dead, the conscious illumination vanishes by itself—this is the Unconscious. This Unconscious is absolutely free from all conditions, for if there are any conditions it cannot be known as the Unconscious.

"O friends, that which sees truly sounds the depths of the Dharmadhātu, and this is known as the Samādhi of Oneness. Therefore, it is said in the *Smaller Prajñāpāramitā*: 'O good men, this is Prajñāpāramitā, that is to say, not to have any (conscious) thoughts in regard to things. As we live in that which is unconscious, this golden-colored body, with the thirty-two marks of supreme manhood, emits rays of great effulgence, contains Prajñā altogether beyond thinking, is endowed with all the highest Samādhis attained by the Buddhas, and with incomparable knowledge. All the merits (accruing from the Unconscious) cannot be recounted by the Buddhas, much less by the Śrāvakas and the Pratyeka-Buddhas.' He who sees the Unconscious is not tainted by the six senses; he who sees the Unconscious is enabled to turn toward the Buddha-knowledge; he who sees the Unconscious is called Reality; he who sees the Unconscious is the Middle Way and the first truth; he who sees the Unconscious is furnished at once with merits of the Gangā; he who sees the Unconscious is able to produce all things; he who sees the Unconscious is able to take in all things."

This view of the Unconscious is thoroughly confirmed by Ta-chu Hui-hai, a chief disciple of Ma-tsu, in his *Essential Teaching of the Abrupt Awakening*: "The Unconscious means to have no-mind in all circumstances, that is to say, not to be determined by any conditions, not to have any affections or hankerings. To face all objective conditions, and yet to be eternally free from any form of stirring, this is the Unconscious. The Unconscious is thus known as to be truly conscious of itself. But to be conscious of consciousness is a false form of the Unconscious. Why? The Sūtra states that to make people become conscious of the six vijñānas is to have the wrong consciousness; to cherish the six vijñānas is false; where a man is free from the six vijñānas, he has the right consciousness."

"To see the Unconscious" does not mean any form of self-consciousness, nor is it to sink into a state of ecstasy or indifference or apathy, where all traces of ordinary consciousness are wiped out. "To see the Unconscious" is to be conscious and yet to be unconscious of self-nature. Because self-nature is not to be determined by the logical category of being and non-being, to be so determined means to bring self-nature into the realm of empirical psychology, in which it ceases to be what it is in itself. If the Unconscious, on the other hand, means the loss of consciousness, it then spells death, or at best a temporary suspension of life itself. But this is impossible inasmuch as self-nature is the Mind itself. This is the sense of the following passage which we come across everywhere in the *Prajñāpāra-mitā* and other Mahāyāna Sūtras: "To be unconscious in all circumstances is possible because the ultimate nature of all things is emptiness, and be-cause there is after all not a form which one can say one has laid hands on. This unattainability of all things is Reality itself, which is the most exquisite form of the Tathāgata." The Unconscious is thus the ultimate reality, the true form, the most exquisite body of Tathāgatahood. It is certainly not a hazy abstraction, not a mere conceptual postulate, but a living experience in its deepest sense.

Notes

1. *Mayoi* means "standing on a crossroad," and not knowing which way to go; that is, "going astray," "not being in the way of truth." It stands contrasted with *satori* (*wu*), which is the right understanding, realization of truth.
2. *Ching* in Chinese. It means "boundaries," "an area enclosed by them," "environment," "objective world." In its technical sense it stands contrasted with *hsin*, mind.

from

FREE ASSOCIATIONS AND
THE USE OF THE COUCH

Karen Horney

(1952)

❏

Ladies and gentlemen, last time we talked about the quality of the analyst's attention. I discussed three points: wholeheartedness, comprehensiveness, and productivity. I want to read a passage today from a book on Zen Buddhism in which is quoted a passage by Eckermann from his conversations with Goethe, a passage which describes the quality of wholeheartedness. I think it will summarize all or most of the important points we discussed last time. This is the passage:

> At dinner, at the table d'hôte, I saw many faces, but few were expressive enough to fix my attention. However, the headwaiter interested me highly so that my eyes constantly followed him in all his movements. And indeed he was a remarkable being.
>
> The guests who sat at the long table were about two hundred in number and it seems almost incredible when I say that nearly the whole of the attendance was performed by the headwaiter, since he put on and took off all the dishes while the

other waiters only handed them to him and received them from him. During all these proceedings nothing was spilled, no one was inconvenienced, but all went off lightly and nimbly as if by the operation of a spirit. Thus, thousands of plates and dishes flew from his hands upon the table and, again, from his hands to the attendants behind him. Quite absorbed in his vocation, the whole man was nothing but eyes and hands and he merely opened his closed lips for short answers and directions. Then, he not only attended to the table, but to the orders for wine and the like, and so well remembered everything that when the meal was over, he knew everybody's score and took the money.

Well, there you have a description of wholeheartedness and of a person who, in this particular performance, was entirely absorbed in what he was doing—operating with all his faculties while remaining at the same time quite oblivious to himself. This, I think, is a very difficult concept to grasp: at the same time having the highest presence and the highest absence. It is not only difficult to grasp as a concept, but it is difficult to be that way or to act that way. These descriptions are commonplaces of Zen because this is the very essence of Zen. This being with all one's faculties in something is, for them, the essence of living. You see this from the passage I cited by Eckermann. Here was a very ordinary situation and you see how the author's fancy and attention was captivated by the wholeheartedness of the headwaiter. But you know, of course, that such wholeheartedness is a rare attainment. Still, as a goal or an ideal it is good to keep wholeheartedness in mind so we can know how far away from, or how close we are, in approximating it. Sometimes we need to ask ourselves what factors might frustrate wholehearted attention.

I will add one thing. The headwaiter could not have performed in this way without training, skill, and experience. That's one thing on which we must fall back. Without training, such effectiveness is impossible. But then, with training and experience, this degree of absorption in what one is doing becomes possible, at least. There are many passages in Hemingway's *Old Man and the Sea* that describe a similar situation: being all there in the job one is doing.

THE JUNG-HISAMATSU CONVERSATION

A TRANSLATION FROM ANIELA JAFFÉ'S ORIGINAL

GERMAN PROTOCOL

translated by Shoji Muramoto

in collaboration with Polly Young-Eisendrath and Jan Middeldorf

(1958)

❏

TRANSLATOR'S INTRODUCTION

Shin'ichi Hisamatsu (1889–1980), a member of the Kyoto School and disciple of Kitaro Nishida, was a leading Zen philosopher of modern Japan. In 1958, as part of his comparative research into Eastern and Western religion and philosophy, he lectured extensively throughout the United States. On his way back to Japan, he visited with a number of prominent European thinkers for a series of conversations on Zen and Western thought. Among his interlocutors was C. G. Jung. Their conversation took place at Jung's home in Küsnacht, Switzerland, on May 16, 1958. Also present were interpreter Koichi Tsujimura, a student of Martin Heidegger's, and Aniela Jaffé, Jung's private secretary, who later compiled his autobiography.

How the dialogue unfolded is basically unknown; as of this writing, only Tsujimura is still alive. The only available documentation is Jaffé's transcribed protocol, derived from her shorthand notes of the meeting, and Tsujimura's Japanese translation of the German protocol. It is safe to as-

This new translation of the conversation, courtesy of Princeton University Press, is previously unpublished.

sume that Jung and Hisamatsu spoke their own languages, and that Tsujimura and Jaffé functioned as translator and transcriber, respectively.

Distortions resulting from mistranslation and misrecording were likely to
have occurred throughout the dialogue, of which no tape recording is
known to exist. We do not know, furthermore, whether and to what extent
both Jaffé, originally, and Tsujimura, later, edited the transcribed German
text. What we do know, however, is that a copy of the German transcription was sent to Hisamatsu and translated by Tsujimura. This Japanese
translation was first published in July 1959 by *FAS*, the journal for the
Zen-inspired FAS Society, founded by Hisamatsu in 1944. (According to
the Society's newsletter, "the acronym refers to the three inseparable dimensions of our existence: self, world and history.") Ten years later, in
1969, with the publication of *Eastern Nothingness*, Vol. I of *The Collected
Works of Shin'ichi Hisamatsu*, the same Japanese version appeared under the
title "The Unconscious and Wu-Hsin," together with an introduction by
Tsujimura and commentary by Hisamatsu.

Koji Sato, professor of educational psychology at Kyoto University, later
asked Jung's permission to publish a protocol of the text in *Psychologia*, an
English-language journal which he edited. But Jung refused. In a letter to
Sachi Toyomura, who had translated Tsujimura's Japanese version into
English, Jung explained the reasons for his refusal. The letter was later
published in Vol. III of *Psychologia* (1960), and is now available in a book
edited by Daniel J. Meckel and Robert L. Moore, *Self and Liberation: The
Jung/Buddhism Dialogue* (Paulist Press, 1992). Among his reasons for opposing this "most delicate and correspondingly dangerous procedure," Jung
mainly cites inevitable and profound gaps in his and Hisamatsu's understanding of each other's traditions.

In 1968, seven years after Jung's death and one year before the inclusion
of the Japanese version in *Eastern Nothingness*, Sachi Toyomura's English
translation was finally published in Vol. XI of *Psychologia*. The translation
was accompanied by a statement by Sato, who claimed that Jaffé's gift of
the German protocol to Hisamatsu could be interpreted as an expression
of permission for Hisamatsu to publish it. More than twenty years later,
Jaffé told me that Sato had misunderstood her intentions altogether, as she
had sent the protocol to Hisamatsu only as a "memento" (*Erinnerung*) of
his encounter with Jung.

As I have already suggested, the English translation published in *Psychologia* was not directly from the German text, but from Tsujimura's Japanese translation. Nor was it revised by any native speaker of English. Four

years later, in 1972, in reviewing the dialogue for *Psychologia*, Noma Haimes wrote: "Partly on account of a strange translation, the dialogue sounds like *Alice in Wonderland*." As Jung's letter to Toyomura suggests, he himself must have read the English translation—the quality of which may have played into his decision not to allow its publication. Now, however, even as Meckel and Moore, in republishing Toyomura's translation, have also clearly revised its English, the problem remains that the lone extant English version of the Jung-Hisamatsu dialogue is, at best, a retranslation of a Japanese translation of the original German protocol.

In the mid-1980s, I had the good fortune of meeting several times in Europe with Aniela Jaffé, to discuss the matter of the protocol and its translation. On January 3, 1985, following our first meeting and more than twenty-five years after the historic encounter between the two men, she wrote to me as follows:

> When I reflected on our very interesting dialogue, a problem occurred to me, and I want to talk about it. I suppose that Prof. Hisamatsu and Prof. Jung spoke with each other in English (though I don't exactly remember). But if that were the case, I could certainly not have taken such a detailed protocol. For I could only take shorthand in German. It is possible that I had taken notes in German in my notebook. But is it conceivable that Prof. Hisamatsu later elaborated on the text, especially his own comments?
>
> Even if both scholars had spoken German, it would hardly have been possible for me to complete such a detailed protocol, especially of the scholarly exchanges. Therefore, someone had to add to the text. This would be acceptable only if Hisamatsu were to have done so. If you should find the original of the "protocol" in the Jung archive [where I had been directed by Jaffé to find the original German text—SM] I would be delighted to be able to consult it.

It should be noted that Jaffé seemed to forget that Tsujimura had been present as a translator. The protocol, as a result, became all the more important. I later obtained permission from Lorenz Jung to make a copy of the document, use of which was allowed at the time only for reasons of "personal study and research." Upon securing the material, I immediately met with Jaffé again, and went over the document with her, comparing her transcription with the odd English text at our disposal. In further research I have since performed and published in Japan, I counted and commented on approximately fifty discrepancies between the two texts. (See my entry in *Annual Report from the Institute for Zen Studies*, Vol. XIX, 1993.) In the meantime, permission was finally obtained to publish a translation of the German protocol I had prepared in the course of my research. The following, therefore, is the first English translation to be published of Jaffé's original German transcription of the 1958 conversation between Shin'ichi Hisamatsu and Carl Gustav Jung.

May 16, 1958

SHIN'ICHI HISAMATSU: In the United States I witnessed the great spread of psychoanalysis and talked about it with many scholars. I am very glad to speak today with the founder of psychoanalysis.[1] I would like to hear your thoughts on the state of psychoanalysis today.

CARL G. JUNG: I would prefer to know your view first, so that I may understand the nature of the question. Eastern language is very different from Western conceptual language. In India, I had many conversations with philosophers and came to realize that I always need to clarify the question first, so as to know what my Eastern partner is thinking. If I assume that I know what he thinks, everything will be misconstrued.

SH: As I am no specialist in psychoanalysis, I would first like to understand its essential position, in order to then compare it with Zen.

CGJ: That is possible, but you must bear in mind that Zen is a philosophy and that I am a psychologist.

SH: In a sense, one might say that Zen is a philosophy, but it is very different from ordinary philosophy, which depends on human intellectual activity. One might also say that Zen is no philosophy. Zen is a philosophy and at the same time a religion, but no ordinary religion. It is "religion and philosophy."

CGJ: I must pose these questions in order to hear what you think, so that I can then direct my questions accordingly. You want to know what I think psychologically of the task that Zen poses for us. The task is in both cases—Zen and psychology—the same. Zen is concerned with how we deal with *wu-hsin*, no-mind.

SH: To date there have been many interpretations of *wu-hsin*. It is, therefore, absolutely necessary to find a true and strict definition for the term from the standpoint of Zen. This is extremely important. I would like to hear your thoughts on the matter.[2]

CGJ: It is the unknown which affects me psychologically, the unknown which disturbs or influences, whether positively or negatively. Thus I notice that it exists, but what it is, I don't know.

SH: Is this "unknown" something different from the unconscious? From the collective unconscious?

CGJ: The unknown disturbs or influences me in certain forms, otherwise I could not speak of it. Sometimes I sense that a personal memory is bothering me, or exerting an influence on me; other times I have dreams, ideas or fantasies that do not have a personal origin. Their source is not the subjective; rather they have a universal quality. For example, the image I have of my father is a personal image. But when this image possesses a religious quality, it is no longer solely connected to the personal realm.

SH: Is the nonpersonal unconscious a fundamental unconscious?[3] In other words, is the nonpersonal unconscious what you call the collective unconscious? Is this the most fundamental? Or perhaps just relatively more fundamental?

CGJ: The personal unconscious develops in the course of life, for example through experiences, the memory of which I repress. The other, the collective, is something instinctive, collectively developed and universally human. My collective unconscious is the same as yours, even though you were born in Japan and I here in Europe.

SH: Does the collective unconscious involve something common to all persons or something that is beyond the personal?

CGJ: One can only say that the collective unconscious is the commonality of all instinctive reactions found among all human beings. The possibility of our speaking with each other intellectually rests on our sharing a common foundation. Otherwise, we would be so different as to understand nothing.

SH: Fairy tales speak of various sufferings and joys. Do these all emerge from the collective unconscious?

CGJ: If, for example, you study a very primitive person with limited consciousness or, let's say, if you study a child—a child who cannot yet even say "I"—you find that the child is still in the general mental state of all children, or of all people before they achieve consciousness. Consciousness has developed through the course of history; it is a common experience. Ontogeny repeats phylogeny.[4] In the child, consciousness develops out of a collective unconscious state. Emotional life, worries, joys, sufferings, hate, love, these are already present before consciousness proper develops. You see this in animals as well. There are instinctive excitements observable in animals which are connected with the essence of the unconscious. Perhaps one could say that these are *klesas*—namely, properties or symptoms of the unconscious.

SH: From our viewpoint, *klesas* belong to the sphere of consciousness.

CGJ: Of course, consciousness is necessary, otherwise we could not establish that such things exist. But the question for us is: is it consciousness that creates the *klesas*? The answer is no, consciousness is their victim. Before consciousness, passions already exist. One cannot ask a raging animal whether it is raging. The animal is at the total mercy of its rage. The rage has seized it; the animal has not seized the rage.

SH: *Klesas* are usually thought to belong to consciousness, but how is this sphere of consciousness related to the unconscious?

CGJ: How is the unconscious related to consciousness? I really have no definite answer. But for us they are related: we see from experience that consciousness develops out of the unconscious. We can observe this in children, in primitive people and so on. And I see it as a physician. If I have to treat a person in the grip of the unconscious, the unconscious is like a landscape at night, when nothing of the mountains and lakes and woods is visible. Then, if a fire starts someplace, you can suddenly see all that's there—the lakes, the woods and so on. That is consciousness.

SH: Which then is our real self, our real, our putative "I": the unconscious or consciousness?[5]

CGJ: Consciousness refers to itself as "I." The self is no mere "I." The self is the whole personality—you as a totality—consisting of consciousness and the unconscious. This is the whole, or the self, but I know only consciousness; the unconscious remains unknown to me.

SH: In your view, the self is a totality. This prompts the following question: Is I-consciousness different from self-consciousness?

CGJ: In ordinary usage, one says self-consciousness, but that only means I-consciousness, psychologically speaking. The self is unknown because it indeed designates the whole of the person, both conscious and unconscious. The conscious person you are is known to you, but the unconscious person you are is unknown to you. The human self is beyond description, because it is only one-third, or perhaps two-thirds, in the realm of experience, and that part belongs to the "I." That which is known, however, does not encompass the self. The vernacular expression "self-consciousness" translates psychologically as I-consciousness. The self is much more than the "I."

SH: So the self is unknown?

CGJ: Perhaps only half of it is known, and that is the "I," the half of the self.

SH: Is the way the self is unknown the same as the way that the unconscious is unknown?

CGJ: It is practically the same. I do not know what is within the unconscious, I am not conscious of it.

SH: Is what we call "I" in ordinary life the same "I" that experiences so many different emotions? The ordinary "I" belongs to the sphere of consciousness. How is it related to the original unknown self? What place does the "I" have in the whole personality?

CGJ: The "I" is like a light in the darkness of night.

SH: In illness, a patient experiences many deep sufferings, and therapy perhaps consists of liberating the suffering patient from them. He is brought to a state of nonsuffering. If this liberation is the nature of psychotherapy, how is therapy related to the fundamental unconscious?

CGJ: If the illness is caused by things that are unconscious, then there is the possibility of healing by making these causes conscious. The causes do not always have to lie in the unconscious, however. There are cases in which the symptoms point to psychic causes. For example, there was a man who lost his consciousness, so to speak, and became only half conscious. It was as if he had lost his good judgment. The reason for this was that the child to whom his wife had given birth was not his own child. While he was not conscious of this fact, it had nonetheless darkened his consciousness. He then chased after an old love of his, but this was only because he was living in unawareness. He was unconscious of what was causing his suffering, and the therapy consisted in telling him that his wife had been unfaithful.

SH: What will become of this man when he has clearly recognized that the child is not his own? It could be that after learning the truth he becomes afflicted with another suffering. Does psychotherapy consist of making conscious the causes of suffering?

CGJ: In his case, yes, but not always. For example, there are other cases in which the causes are well known, in which a person already knows that a bad relationship with his father or mother is the cause of his suffering. Anybody can know as much. What everybody cannot know is the kind of consequences for the patient's character that result from the relationship. Nor do they know what kind of attitude he is now to have toward these consequences. Most patients say repeatedly, "Father and Mother are to blame for my illness," but the real question is: How can I treat the patient so that he becomes able to cope with his experience?

While the father's or the mother's responsibility may be a causal factor, when all is said and done, therapy hinges on the final question: What kind of meaning does my life have?

SH: Ordinary life has many kinds of suffering. Psychotherapy consists of liberation from suffering. What sort of changes in the sphere of the unconscious correspond to this liberation?

CGJ: This is the question of conscious attitude. In states of psychological suffering, it is important how I myself relate to a certain state, what kind of attitude I have. Let's say I am unhappy or sad because of something that's happened. If I think, "How horrible that something like this has happened," and cannot accept it, then I'll only suffer more. Each day has its own troubles, and the sun cannot always shine. Sometimes it rains or snows. If a person is able to adopt the attitude that both good and bad are part of life, that person will suffer less. With an objective attitude, he can find a way to release himself from his morbid neurotic suffering. If he can say "yes" to the suffering and accept it, the pain is suddenly diminished.

SH: A universal suffering is the fear of death. How can this suffering be treated by psychotherapy?

CGJ: There is no general rule or method, but only individual cases. People fear death for many different reasons. The course of therapy depends upon the *reasons* for this death anxiety. My anxiety of death is quite different from anxiety in a young, healthy man. Why does he fear death? There may be no apparent reason and yet he fears it. So the situations are quite different. Therefore, there is no general course of therapy. We must always consider the individual case. Why is an old man anxious about death? Why is a young man anxious about death? The two must be dealt with quite differently.

SH: I only mention the fear of death as an example, because death is unavoidable. But people suffer in many, many ways. We must almost always live in suffering. I want to ask you whether or not it is possible, within the framework of psychotherapy, for a person to disengage from all these various sufferings in one fell swoop?

CGJ: Are you asking whether there exists a method by which suffering is healed?

SH: Yes. Is there no generally valid remedy for it?

CGJ: Are you asking whether there is a method through which one could spare a person suffering?

SH: Yes. Can psychotherapy liberate us from suffering in one fell swoop?

CGJ: Liberate us from suffering? One tries to reduce suffering, yet some suffering is always present. There would be nothing beautiful if the beautiful were not in contrast with ugliness or suffering. The German philosopher Schopenhauer once said: "Happiness is the cessation of suffering." We need suffering. Otherwise, life would no longer be interesting. Psychotherapy must not disturb the problem of suffering too much in people. Otherwise, people would become dissatisfied.

SH: Suffering is, in a sense, necessary for life. You are right. Nevertheless, we have a genuine wish to be liberated from it.

CGJ: Of course, if there is too much of it. The physician strives to reduce suffering, not to put an end to it.

SH: In the case of physical illness, the physician tries to release the patient from it and to eliminate sickness from the human world. Is this not also true of mental illness?

CGJ: Of course!

SH: The great messengers of religious truth—Christ, for example[6]—have said that all humans suffer a common lot: the suffering of death, or of original sin. Their intention was to liberate humans from this fundamental suffering. Is it possible to think that such a great liberation could be realized in psychotherapy?

CGJ: This is not inconceivable, if you regard the problem not as a personal illness, but as an impersonal manifestation of evil. The concern of psychotherapy is in many cases to make patients conscious, through insight, of the *nidana* chain, of the unnecessary suffering fostered by lust, desire and passion. Passion ties us up, but through insight we are made free. The goal in psychotherapy is exactly the same as in Buddhism.

SH: The essential issue in this liberation is: how does one reach a fundamental self, one that is no longer captivated by the ten thousand things? How to get there, that is the problem. Is it necessary to liberate oneself from the collective unconscious as well, or from the conditions it imposes on us?

CGJ: If someone is caught in the ten thousand things, it is because that person is also caught in the collective unconscious. A person is liberated only when freed from both. One person may be driven more by the unconscious and another by things. One has to take the person to the point where he is free from the compulsion to either run after things or be driven by the unconscious. What is needed for both compulsions is basically the same: *nirdvanda*.[7]

SH: From what you have said about the collective unconscious, might I infer that one can be liberated from it?

CGJ: Yes![8]

SH: What we in Buddhism, and especially in Zen, usually call the "common self" corresponds exactly to what you call the "collective unconscious." Only through liberation from this self does the authentic self emerge.[9]

CGJ: This self of which you speak corresponds, for example, to the *klesas* in the Yoga Sutra. My concept of self corresponds, however, to the notions of *atman* or *pursha*. This personal *atman* corresponds to the self insofar as it is at the same time the suprapersonal *atman*. In other words, "my self" is at the same time "the" self. In my language, the self is the counterpart to the "I." What you call the self is what I would call the "I." What I call the self is the whole, the *atman*.

SH: The authentic self corresponds to the *atman*. In the common understanding *atman* still retains a faint trace of substance, but that is not yet what I call the true self. The true self has neither substance nor form.[10]

CGJ: So when I compare the self with *atman*, my comparison is an obviously incorrect one. They are incommensurable because the Eastern way of thinking is different from my way of thinking. I can say that the self both exists and does not exist, because I really can say nothing about it. It is greater than the "I." The "I" can only say: this is the way it seems to me. If one were to say that *atman* either has or does not have substance, I can only acknowledge what the person says—for I do not know what the true *atman* really is. I only know what people say about it. I can only say of it: "It is so" and, at the same time, "It is not so."

SH: Unlike the ordinary *atman*, the true self of Zen has neither form nor substance. It has no form, mental or physical.

CGJ: I cannot know what I don't know. I cannot be conscious of whether the self has attributes or not, because I am unconscious of the self. The whole human person is both conscious and unconscious. I only know that I may possess a certain set of attributes. What you say [concerning the ordinary *atman* and the true self of Zen—SM] is possible, but I can't know if that's really the case. I can, of course, make assertions. I can state metaphysical matters until I am blue in the face but, fundamentally, I don't know.[11]

SH: The true self is without form and substance, and is therefore never bound by the ten thousand things. That is the essence of religious liberation. This is also the religious character of Zen, with its insight into the value of transcending the passions and becoming the formless self.[12] That is why I said at the beginning of our conversation that Zen is both philosophy and religion.[13]

Professor Hisamatsu thanks Dr. Jung for having found, together with him, the connection between the unconscious and what we have called "the true self."[14] The connection has become very clear to him. He then proceeds to explain the true self further by using the metaphor of waves on water.[15]

Notes

1. Jaffé's note: C. G. Jung's psychology is called *analytical psychology*, to distinguish it from Freud's psychoanalysis.
2. Hisamatsu does not use the Chinese word *wu-hsin*, but rather its Japanese phonetic transcription, *mu-shin*. Like many other Buddhist terms, the word has settled into the Japanese language, albeit with some variation in meaning. Jaffé notes in the protocol that Jung takes *wu-hsin* to mean the unconscious.
3. The word "fundamental" (*ursprünglich* in Jaffé's protocol) is my translation of both *konpontenki* and *kongenteki* in the Japanese translation—terms which might be more exactly rendered "original." What Hisamatsu means to refer to is something metaphysical, and not genetically primal—though he would deny metaphysics in the Western sense. His meaning may be close to the German prefix *ur-*, as in Goethe's concepts of *Urpflanze*, *Urphänomen* and so on, because it is at once both metaphysical and accessible to experience. It is with some reservation, then, that I adopt the English term "fundamental" instead of "original."

   It is essential in this context to keep in mind Hisamatsu's lack of familiarity with depth psychology. He speaks of "the fundamental unconscious" in his own Zen sense of *wu-hsin*—and not in any psychological sense. Thus, even if the term "fundamental" were replaced by words like "original" or "primal," it is only the translator who grapples with such nuances of meaning and sophistication. Hisamatsu only uses the word "unconscious" in this dialogue with Jung; otherwise, he would never speak of it. In the Japanese text, in fact, the word "unconscious" is given in quotes, perhaps to suggest Hisamatsu's particular use and understanding of it.
4. Jung here refers to Ernst Heckel's famous biological thesis. The earlier English version of the conversation, based upon the Japanese translation, reveals that the Japanese translator was unaware of this. In that earlier version, "ontogeny" and "phylogeny" were respectively mistranslated as "the development of the individual" and "the development of psyche in history."
5. Since the days of Strachey's translation of Freud, the German term *das Ich* is usually

rendered "the ego" in the psychological literature. But throughout the conversation, both Hisamatsu and Jung seem to refer to an everyday—rather than a technical—understanding of the term, along the lines of what Bruno Bettelheim, in his book *Freud and Man's Soul*, takes to be Freud's own original intent. Therefore, I consistently use "I" instead of "the ego" as the translation of *das Ich*. I am grateful to Jan Middeldorf for his insistence on this point.

6. The Buddha is mentioned along with Christ in Tsujimura's translation.

7. Sanskrit word meaning "freedom from opposites," but different from *nirvana*. *Nirdvanda* refers to an idea in which dualism is presupposed and at the same time overcome. It is no wonder that Jung adopted this word, as it fits well with his mode of thinking which is expressed, for example, in his key concept of the "transcendent function"—namely, an attitude or a capacity to sustain the tension of opposites, from which a reconciling symbol can then emerge from the depths of the mind. The word *nirvana*, on the contrary, originally meaning "the extinction of fire," suggests an absolute transcendence or denial of dualism to nothingness—reflecting a mode of thinking which is foreign to Jung.

   Upon reading the German protocol for the first time, I asked Jaffé whether the word *nirdvanda* was not a typing error for *nirvana*. Firmly saying "No," she opened to page 377 of Vol. 11 of Jung's *Collected Works* (in the original German version of the *Gesammelte Werke*) and pointed to paragraph 435. The word *nirdvanda* was in fact there. However, in the editor's note to the expanded edition of Vol. 1 of Shin'ichi Hisamatsu's *Collected Works*, published in 1996, Gishin Tokiwa writes that translator Tsujimura clearly heard Jung speak of *nirvana*, and not *nirdvanda*. According to Tsujimura, he had translated the typewritten protocol he'd received from Jung himself, thus making unlikely, if not impossible, any translation errors of this sort. Tokiwa goes on to claim that there is no difference between *nirdvanda* and *nirvana*. Personally, I think the difference between the two Sanskrit words is not to be overlooked, especially where the dialogue between Zen and psychology is concerned.

8. Hisamatsu's immediately preceding question is, in my opinion, the gravitational center of the entire conversation, comparable with a critical confrontation between a Zen Master and his disciple in Zen *mondo* (question and answer). We are told, in fact, in Hisamatsu's commentary to the Japanese version of the translation appearing in Vol. 1 of his *Complete Works* that both he and Tsujimura found Jung's "Yes!" very unexpected. Unfortunately, however, we don't know what kind of "yes" it was. Was Jung's reply a heartfelt affirmation, an expression of exasperation, or a "yes" which was somehow forced from his mind, perhaps even against his will, by Hisamatsu's penetrating and somewhat intrusive questioning? Personally, I believe the latter was the case, and suspect that this was one of the reasons why Jung refused to have the conversation published in *Psychologia*.

9. Tsujimura's Japanese version includes this clarification of what is meant by the "authentic self": "That is the true self, or *doku datsu mu-e*: namely, the self which is alone, independent, and detached." The source of *doku datsu mu-e* is "The Record of Linchi," where not *doku datsu mu-e* but *doku datsu fu-e* is mentioned. Both *fu* and *mu* imply a negation, while *e* means "dependence."

   On the matter of "authentic self," the German *das eigentliche Selbst* cited in the protocol is perhaps Tsujimura's translation of Hisamatsu's term *honrai-no-jiko*. *Eigentliche* clearly suggests that Tsujimura—a student of Martin Heidegger—interprets *honrai-no-jiko* in the Heideggerian sense. Heidegger's concept of *Eigentlichkeit*, derived from his *Being and Time*, is usually translated *honrai-sei* into Japanese. The philosophers of the Kyoto School are generally sympathetic to Heidegger, whom Hisamatsu also met. (Their conversation, in fact, is recorded in Vol. 1 of Hisamatsu's *Collected Works*. It is altogether free of the many tensions evidenced in Hisamatsu's conversation with Jung.) Because *Eigentlichkeit* is translated as "authenticity" in English versions of *Being and Time*, I have opted to translate *das eigentliche Selbst* as "the authentic self."

10. To refer to something ultimate, or metaphysical, Hisamatsu uses in the Japanese version three different adjectival phrases: *honrai-no, shinjitsu-no* (or *shin-no*) and *kongenteki*, which I have rendered respectively as "authentic," "true" and "fundamental." Though originally Chinese terms, they have been used by modern Japanese philosophers to translate Western philosophical terms into Japanese. Hisamatsu seems to use the three adjectives without any clear differentiation among them in his terminology. Thus, while Hisamatsu elsewhere speaks of "the fundamental unconscious" in the Zen sense of *wu-hsin* (see note 3), we have reason to suspect that his use of terms like "authentic" or "true" refers to this same basic understanding.

Still, in this very passage Hisamatsu clearly states that "the authentic self that corresponds to the *atman* . . . is *not* yet what I call the true self"! I realize that such a statement seems in flagrant contradiction to the claim that "true," "authentic" and "fundamental" are all equivalent adjectives for Hisamatsu. In a sense, this passage reveals an inconsistency in the philosopher's use and understanding of the words "the true self." It may be due to a logical dilemma intrinsic to Buddhist philosophy—of which Hisamatsu was likely to be deeply aware, to the point of coining the concept of the "formless self."

Finally, it is interesting to note that, in the Japanese text, this same passage reads: "The authentic self, insofar as semantics are concerned, corresponds to the *atman*." Hisamatsu was aware of how difficult, if not impossible, it is to explain the meaning of the true self with the Indian concept of *atman*. He never identified the authentic self with *atman* in the Hindu sense. In my view, he borrowed the Hindu concept to explain his own concept to Jung, who did not share the same spiritual background but seemed to have some knowledge of Upanishad philosophy. Such confusion is common between people from different cultures trying to reach a common understanding.

11. Jung's final two comments evidence his harsh criticism of Hisamatsu's conviction, which, in its resistance to any psychological investigation, resembles those Jung observed throughout his life in clergy and believers. Basically, we can see Jung opposing his psychological viewpoint to Hisamatsu's ontology.

In this light, a freer translation of Jung's response might read: "Professor Hisamatsu, we must distinguish between your understanding of the true self of Zen—as one possible archetypal image of the self—and the archetype of the self as such. You may well know the self in your sense—be it fundamental, true or formless—but while I am sorry that I do not, neither of us can know the self as such."

Jung's opening statement here is also quite perplexing, and warrants close attention. Perhaps tautological in expressing his agnostic stance, the phrase "I cannot know what

I don't know" seems to turn Jung's own understanding of the unconscious upside down. It is not characteristically Jungian, or true, that one cannot know what one does not know. In the course of a lifetime, one can indeed come to know what one ignores at any given time. Conversely, it is Jung's unequivocal contention that only the unconscious is destined to remain forever unknown—despite one's efforts to know it. Thus, a phrase like "I don't know what I cannot know" somehow sounds more natural and consistent in a Jungian context than the cited "I cannot know what I don't know." We can perhaps assume that Jung's odd remark reflects an implicit refusal to further debate Hisamatsu's religious and philosophical convictions.

12. Hisamatsu's phrase "with its insight into the value of transcending the passions" is not present in the Japanese text. It was perhaps edited out by Hisamatsu himself or by Tsujimura. In addition, the next phrase, "and becoming the formless self," is somewhat different in the Japanese text, where it reads: "In short, becoming the formless self is the nature of Zen."

    On the matter of the formless self (*muso-no-jiko*, in Japanese): As a Buddhist, Hisamatsu does not regard the self as a metaphysical entity. This does not mean, however, that he advocates nihilism. He presents a concept of the self which is not metaphysical in the Western sense but, in a sense intrinsic to Buddhist philosophy, formless. It is the Mahayana understanding of the self as *bodhi* (awakening) that underscores, in fact, Hisamatsu's religion or philosophy of awakening. But while Hisamatsu's central idea is basic to the very origins of Buddhism, his idea of the formless self and other similar expressions (such as the fundamental, authentic or true self) mark—through his assimilation of Western philosophy—his unique contribution to the development of modern-day Buddhism.

13. Hisamatsu's remark "Zen is both philosophy and religion" actually reads "Zen is both philosophy and psychology" in the German protocol. While this likely reflects an error in typing, the substitution offers an interesting example of what Freud considered "the psychopathology of everyday life"!

14. I am not sure whom the "we" here refers to. Two answers are possible. One is, of course, both Hisamatsu and Jung. Another is Hisamatsu himself, together with those who share his position.

15. The metaphor of waves on water is originally found in the Lankavatara Sutra, a sutra supposedly preached by the Buddha on Adam's Peak in Ceylon. It later became the source for the text "The Mahayana Faith Awakening," whose original Sanskrit version by Asvagosha was lost but later recast through two Chinese versions by Paramartha and by Siksananda. To illustrate the metaphor, I offer the following excerpt, taken from Hisamatsu's own essay "The Characteristics of Oriental Nothingness":

    "Waves are produced by the water but are never separated from the water. When they cease to be waves, they return to the water—their original source. . . . While the water in the wave is one with the wave and not two, the water does not come into being and disappear, increase or decrease, according to the coming into being and disappearing of the wave. Although the water as wave comes into being and disappears, the water as water does not come into being and disappear. Thus even when changing into a thousand or ten thousand waves, the water as water is itself constant and unchanging. The Mind of 'all is created by Alone-Mind' is like this water. The assertions of the Sixth Patriarch, Hui-neng, 'Self-Nature, in its origin constant and without commotion, produces the ten thousand things,' and 'All things are never separated from Self-Nature,' express just this creative feature of Mind." (Translated by Richard De Martino, in collaboration with Jikai Fujiyoshi and Masao Abe.) See *Philosophical Studies of Japan*, Vol. 2, 1960.

WU WEI, NO-MIND AND THE FERTILE VOID

IN PSYCHOTHERAPY

W. Van Dusen

(1958)

❏

From the first not a thing is.
—HUI-NENG

Though clay may be molded into a vase, the utility of the vase lies in what is not there.
—LAO-TZU

❏

At the very center of psychotherapeutic experiences there is an awesome hole. With Western modes of thought the hole tends to be seen as a deficiency which the therapist plugs by an interpretation of what it means. My point is quite simple. The hole is the very center and heart of therapeutic change. To my knowledge the only place its dynamics are adequately described is in ancient Oriental writings. From them one can learn to make practical use of this fertile void around which psychotherapy turns.

The void is not unknown in the psychoanalysis of the Western world. Freud discovered it in orality, regression, the going back to an infantile state. At a deeper level he once characterized it as Thanatos, the death instinct. Otto Rank put it in the womb. Pathology began by the trauma of leaving the womb. In Jung the void is not as clear, but in general it is found in the archetypes of mother, earth and origin of things.

What will be treated here as the void is seen by Western psychoanalysis

This article first appeared in *Psychologia: An International Journal of Psychology in the Orient*, vol. 1, pages 253–56, 1958. It is reprinted here with the permission of the editors of *Psychologia*.

as a going back, returning to the origin, as a destruction and loss of ego development. The main implication is of a weakness, so that one has to start over instead of moving on from here. The going back can be totally destructive as in chronic schizophrenia or it can be productive as in the so-called therapeutic regression in the service of the ego. The void is seen primarily biologically as a mouth or a womb.

Using the phenomenological method, I discovered a world of tiny holes, most of which were smaller than the orality of the Freudians. In the phenomenological approach one simply attempts to discover the world of the patient as it is for him without reducing it to any pseudoscientific categories (obsessional, anal, etc.). In a careful examination of the worlds of others I ran across many blank spaces. For a moment the patient couldn't concentrate, couldn't hear me, couldn't remember what he intended to say, or he felt nothing. At first it appeared these holes or great blank spaces were characteristic of schizophrenics only. Certainly in schizophrenics the blank apathy can enlarge to fill their whole life space. But closer examination showed that these holes appear in all persons to a greater or lesser extent. More and more it came to appear that these blank holes lay at the center of psychopathology. The blank holes came to be the key both to pathology and to psychotherapeutic change. Though my knowledge of Taoism and Zen Buddhism is poor (grandmotherly, a Zen monk might say), it was these two that helped me understand the way in and out of the holes and their meaning.

First, what are the holes? They are any sort of defect—blankness, loss of memory, failure of concentration or loss of meaning. They can be of very brief duration so that the person is hardly aware of a lack of continuity to his thoughts or feelings. Or they can last for years, as in chronic schizophrenics, for whom decades can slip by without being noticed. In their lapses schizophrenics not only drop time but when it is dropped they can't recall what they intended to say or they forget they dropped time. A common mild example is to be unexpectedly caught by the gaze of another person and for a brief moment lose the sense of direction. Or, when in a group, you may lose the thread of conversation and several moments later realize your fantasies have wandered from the group. In the hole you feel you have momentarily lost your self. What you intended is forgotten. What would have been said is unremembered. When you try to trace your way back to where you were a moment ago you have lost the trail. You feel caught, drifting, out of control and weak.

These holes and blank spaces are important in every psychopathology.

In the obsessive-compulsive they represent the loss of order and control. In the depressive they are the black hole of time standing still. In the character disorders they represent an unbearable ambivalence. In schizophrenia they are the encroachment of meaninglessness or terror. In every case they represent the unknown, the unnamed threat, the source of anxiety and the fear of disintegration. They are nothingness, nonbeing, death.

It is extremely important to know what people do when faced with encroaching blankness. Many talk to fill up space. Many must act to fill the empty space with themselves. In all cases it must be filled up or sealed off. I have yet to see a case of psychopathology where the blankness was comfortably tolerated. Even in very chronic and apathetic schizophrenics there is a filling up of the space. One examined a door hinge for an hour because not to fill his world with something was to die. This void is familiar to the Taoist or Zen Buddhist. The pathology appears to be in the reaction to the void. Normal and often very creative individuals can allow themselves to become blank and think of nothing, with an expectation that they will come out of it with an idea for a painting or other work of art. Many have deliberately used the void to find creative solutions to problems. The neurotic and psychotic struggle against it.

In large part the culture of the Western world fosters this struggle. In the West the world is filled with objects. Empty space is wasted unless it is room to be filled with action. This contrasts markedly with Oriental painting, for instance, in which empty space is the creative center and lends weight to the rest of the painting. Subtly the culture of the West teaches one to fear and avoid blankness, emptiness, and to fill space as much as possible with our action with objects. Or we let the action of objects (cars, TV) fill our space. In the Orient emptiness may have a supreme value in and of itself. It can be trusted. It can be productive. In the *Tao Te Ching* it is commented that thirty spokes make up a wheel, but only in the emptiness of its hub is its usefulness. Walls and doors make up a house, but only in the emptiness between them is its livability.

Following the lead of the Orient, I explored the empty spaces. If the patient obsessively plotted every move and worried everything into existence, he was encouraged to drift. If he anxiously filled space with words, we looked for a while at wordlessness. The person who feared going down in depression permitted himself to go down and explore the going down. The findings are always the same. *The feared empty space is a fertile void. Exploring it is a turning point toward therapeutic change.* A case will illustrate some of these points.

The patient is a thirty-year-old schizophrenic who has been hospitalized nine years. He enters stiffly like a wooden puppet, sits awkwardly and avoids my gaze. I leave him alone. His eyes fix on my bookcase and he stares emptily. After several minutes I comment that he is at the bookcase and I ask him what it is like. In no way do I attempt to move him from the spot he has drifted to.

Slowly he says he is looking at the top books. They are decoration. That is, they have no meaning. They are part of the bookcase, they are decoration in the furniture. This he says with no affect, punctuated by a sudden touching of the top of his head and repetitive movements with his fingers. I try not to disturb his state. A slow exploration indicates that really the whole world is like the meaningless book-decoration he sees before him.

He accepts this as a black, hole-like world. In this black hole he can't think or remember and this threatens him. I'm a strange doctor not to fill up the space with questions to occupy him. In the nothingness he is nothing. When he touches the top of his head or his nose he exists for a moment, he feels himself there. Because I don't fill the void with questions he tries to remember what other doctors asked so he can ask himself these questions and answer them and thereby fill the void. A question should fill this empty space and move time on a bit. But he is dully threatened because he can't remember what he was trying to think of even though he repeats it over and over. It too goes out of existence. Again the dull concern: "I must concentrate, hold my mind from drifting and find questions to fill my space."

I ask him if he will let himself drift. Because my request fills the void he complies. We are silent. In a moment some feeling breaks forth. He reddens and laughs. He can't quite tell me what happened. Usually, in the past, these were feelings critical of me. I speak of drifting in the hole. When he drifts he seems to stumble on something new. Once before he found strong sexual desire (which is quite unusual for him). In one long session he drifted into a fantasy of a violent rape attack. Today he drifted and ran upon the fact that there was something in his left side. Explored further, it turned out to be a flat, oval black mass (the nigredo of Jung). In subsequent sessions it changed and became a feeling of life in him. As the hour ended, I asked whether he wanted to climb out of the hole. He said (with a trace more of affect) he would stay in it and see what else of interest might happen. I was pleased because he had discovered that of itself the void filled with new things. He didn't have to work so hard to fill it up.

The schizophrenic gives the purest example of the black void in human experience. Other disorders give examples of briefer and less empty voids. What I learned in these is quite simple. When we are threatened by the void and attempt to crawl out or fill it up by keeping our minds centered (the mind dusting of Zen), the void grows and encroaches upon our will. When a person sleeps in the void—i.e., allows himself to drift willy-nilly —he stumbles upon surprising new things in the void.

The complete dynamism is relatively simple. Let me use an analogy with night and day. The two alternate naturally and spontaneously. We do not make the night or the day. If we try to stay awake indefinitely and thereby deny the night, we are dragged into fatigue and eventually sleep. (The schizophrenic by his constant plugging of holes is dragged into timelessness.) On the other hand, we cannot sleep indefinitely. We will be thrust into wakefulness. (The alcoholic who tries to drink away his responsibilities is dragged into the wakefulness of a hangover.) The day wears on to night when all things rest. Out of the timeless black night a new day emerges. This is the cycle of the Chinese Yin and Yang. In psychotherapy all action is the day and all of the holes, the defects, are the fertile void of night. It seems simply that we are thrust forward into daylight imperfect. The fertile void of night comes into psychotherapy so that we might dissolve a little and come out a little changed into a new day. I no longer fear the fertile void for either my patient or myself. The way to day is through the night. The night or the void is the no-mind of Zen. It is not nothing nor is it something. It is a fertile emptiness. The only thing I can think of that is kin to it in Christianity is psychological openness to grace.

In Taoism and Zen there is a healthy understanding and respect for this night aspect of life. It is used in painting, in the tea ceremonies, in wrestling, in the building of houses; in flower arrangement it is the space around a graceful branch. It is known and respected in its permeation of Oriental life.

The patient comes to a therapist because he fears the void. If he didn't fear it, he would be a productive person and not need help. If the therapist also fears the void, he will be unable to help the patient. For each patient the void has different meanings. For the compulsive it may be disorder, for some it is age and death, for the young woman it may be the loss of self in sexual climax, for the early schizophrenic it is the force destroying the ego. The meaning of the void and how it appears in the transference relationship must be discovered anew in each case. A common way to try to fill the void is to find *the answers* as to what is wrong. Not only is there the major void in the presenting symptoms, there are also the many little ones that appear in the immediate relationship with the patient. The way out is through the voids. The fears that keep one from entering them can be explored. As these are studied, the voids become less fearsome. Finally the voids can be entered. In each case one comes out a little changed, as in the case of the schizophrenic above who came out with more affect than he had known in a long time. Often the therapist cannot predict the direction of change. It is spontaneous and natural. It is change from within the patient and not a change in any way planted by the therapist. When fully recovered the patient not only no longer fears the void but knows and can use its productivity.

"From the first not a thing is." If a thing still is (i.e., there is action or talk or the patient is toying with *the* answer), one has not yet reached the first which is the beginning. For literally at the first not a thing is. At this turning point one has no words, no actions, no answers. One may well not even remember.

In Wu Wei, the blankness, the state is characterized by total uncertainty. One doesn't know answers, one doesn't know solutions. Even the problems besetting one may be unclear. The uncertainty can be painful. "Somewhere in all this there should be a solution if I could only think clearly enough to find it," is the feeling. It is a void, no-mind, but it is certainly not empty. It is chaotic with possibilities. One feels helpless and waits. It is central that one's own will can no longer find the way out.

My apologies to the ancient teachers for a poor oversimplification of their work. But it must be done. Somewhere it is necessary to show not only that these teachings have practical value in psychotherapy but that their relevance is ever present.

ZEN IN PSYCHOTHERAPY

THE VIRTUE OF SITTING

Akihisa Kondo

(1958)

❑

Anxiety—and its attendant states of self-dissatisfaction, emptiness, meaninglessness—is not the discovery and exclusive possession of the twentieth century; it is as old as the human mind itself. For Dogen, founder of the Soto Sect of Zen Buddhism in Japan some 700 years ago, anxiety is a reflection of the uncertainty of human existence. When this anxiety is consciously and acutely felt, moreover, there commences the flow of the Bodhi spirit that leads to enlightenment. Anxiety, then, according to Dogen, is the driving force to enlightenment. Without it as a spur we are left to flounder in a shallow, insecure life, eternally caught in the vicious circle of ignorance. Anxiety when accepted, therefore, works as the striking of a match in the dark, giving us a revealing glimpse of our impasse and at the same time igniting our desire to break out of it.

For most people ordinary daily life is a streamlined facade of so-called happy living, a life filled with competitiveness, jealousy, possessiveness,

This article first appeared in the journal *The Chicago Review*, vol. 12, number 2, pages 57–64, 1958. It is reprinted here with the permission of the editors of *The Chicago Review*.

arrogance, humiliation, hate, love, aggressiveness, success, failure, and whatnot. At every turn our psychic energy is distracted and squandered in pursuit of this or that aim. We are trapped in the endless, blind, vicious circle of these drives. And because we are busily pursuing them, we do not have time to listen to our inner voice.

This voice comes from the depths of our real self. It may take the form of conscience, aesthetic feeling, creative thinking or activity, or just the warm, soft inner suggestion to return home. Whatever the form, it is the expression of something deep and basic, far beyond these forms. At the very moment when we hear and accept it we are actually affirming our real self. If we look deeper we find that listening to it is our unconscious act of faith—faith in our real self. Further, it is an unconscious act of our real self that leads us to have faith in it and to listen to its voice. However powerful and overwhelming our ignorant drives are, the Real Self is always working in and through us. But we do not have pure faith because our minds are too much preoccupied with other strong beliefs: in success, prestige, money, intellectual superiority. What we need is time and space so that, free from all interruptions and distractions, we can at least once a day collect our psychic energy and concentratedly bring it into direct contact with our inner, most powerful resources. In order to feel vividly this kind of pure faith we need to empty our mind, to liberate it from all false values, and to experience directly our real self in its wholeness.

Psychoanalysis in its recent development has clarified the nature of the blind drives which haunt us within the unconscious, and has exerted its efforts to helping people realize specifically by what drives they are driven. Horney called this kind of help a disillusioning process. She believed that when we become disillusioned of the idealized image of ourselves that handcuffs the development of our real self, our real self has a chance to grow. Her thinking in this regard is of course a great contribution to making clear how ignorant human beings are of themselves. She aimed at helping people realize and amply feel that the blind drives that are hindering them from listening to the voice of their real self ultimately come out of their idealized image that is illusory. From the Zen point of view, this is a fine step in discerning how grievously illusory are our ideas about ourselves and our life. Her approach, naturally, is analytical, and I am not in disagreement with her regarding its value—I myself find it very useful.

However, the analytical approach is not the only one. Especially as regards coming closer to one's self, the Zen way is specific and positive. Let me point out what Zen suggests.

In Zen practice, although the need to discern the illusory nature of our concepts, ideas, and emotions is considered important, concentration on sitting is stressed. It is sitting with a single mind. What does this mean? Those in the Zen temple will never give an answer to one who wishes to know before experiencing it. What they say, if anything, is simply, "Just sit!" This is meaningful, because they know from their experience that one can know the meaning of sitting only by actually practicing sitting. The answer must come out of oneself, by one's own experience. Single-mindedness is just single-mindedness and leaves no room for interrogation. It is a sheer act of faith in oneself. It implies, therefore, total respect for the real self. "What is real self?" is not to be intellectually understood, it is to be experienced. Zen regards sitting as the way in which to experience this Real Self. Enlightenment, the realization of the true self, comes out of the practice of sitting, out of the "sitting" state of mind, and this cannot be vicariously understood. This single-minded state, it must be pointed out, is not confined merely to static sitting, so called, but must carry over and be strengthened in all our dynamic activities.

Dogen's advice about sitting is substantially as follows: Avoid distracting contacts and activities. Don't eat too much or too little. Sit in a quiet place on a thick rug or mat, with a pillow under your seat and your legs crossed in half- or full-lotus position (or sit in a straight-back chair with your feet flat on the floor). Keeping the back straight, breathe naturally from the depths of the lower part of the abdomen. Don't think about good or bad, yes or no. Become concentrated but not in thoughts.

When we sit as he advises, all our psychic energy that has been scattered as a result of our pursuits and internal conflicts is collected into a unity again. Of course at first, since our mind has been accustomed to functioning distractedly, sitting is felt to be a constriction of our activities. We become impatient and irritable, build up conflicting ideas, and feel desperate. Zen practice has been called the strenuous way to enlightenment, and it re-quires considerable effort; therefore we shrink from it. But this point is the test of our determination. Will we follow our old easy futile way of life or enter upon the path to liberation? This is the crossroads. If we truly realize the futility, meaninglessness, and emptiness of our past way of life, our determination to seek emancipation will be stronger. In this connection I wish to point out the meaningfulness of Dogen's assertion that the consciousness of the Bodhi-Spirit as the propelling force for practicing Zen must be acutely experienced. If we continue to practice while fighting all kinds of temptations to escape, we come to experience a calmness that is charged with vitality. This comes about partly because our psychic energy is no more wasted in futile drives and partly because it has become unified. Nor is this all. Every part of our body and mind is filled with vitality. Actually we are not aware of mind apart from body or body apart from mind; only a total feeling of fullness exists. In this stage we are no longer separated from our sitting, so to speak. At this time, according to the school of Zen followed, some will concentrate on a koan, others will just practice sitting. Whatever the method, the result is the same: in place of the separatedness experienced before, more and more we enjoy oneness in ourselves. Our total being is strengthened as a consequence. We feel in ourselves tremendous stability, fullness, and harmony. We feel alive. So Dogen says, "Sitting is the gateway of truth to total liberation."

This is the virtue of sitting that is called the power of sitting. This power or virtue achieved through sitting is not restricted in its functioning to the time of sitting. Once it is achieved it mobilizes and expresses itself every moment, and is strengthened through its functioning at all times. This may be called the dynamic functioning of the state of mind developed in sitting. It is, of course, different from the state of so-called enlightenment. Nonetheless in the steady deepening and strengthening of the practice of sitting there is enlightenment ever fulfilling itself. Enlightenment, then, is the fruit of sitting practice and not its goal. Actually, from a strict Zen point of view, in the very single-mindedness of the sitting and in the very life in which it functions, the real self is expressing itself most strongly and naturally without any consciousness on the part of the individual himself necessarily. In this sense only can we say there is enlightenment. According to Dogen, "There is enlightenment in practice and practice in enlightenment." To be sure, there are different expressions of experiences corresponding to differences in personality. Yet when one lives in the fullness of this kind of sitting, seriously absorbed in the problem of his true self, it is not astonishing that he can suddenly become enlightened at any time, since his real self is always expressing itself and only his consciousness is unaware of it. Emyo sought instruction from the Sixth Patriarch, who answered, "All right, I will teach you. At the very moment when you do not think good or bad, right or wrong, what is your original face?" Emyo was suddenly enlightened.

As a student of Zen I have personally profited a great deal. But as a therapist of neurotic patients I am greatly indebted to Zen teaching for their recovery. Perhaps, therefore, the following brief observations relating to my therapeutic experience with patients will not be inappropriate.

In addition to interview sessions, I strongly recommend that patients practice sitting as Dogen suggests. Inevitably at first it is almost unbearable for them. Some complain of physical pains and strains. Some complain of irritability and the great difficulty of keeping a motionless posture. Others say they feel more depressed and lonesome. Still others complain that they are haunted by stabbing ideas and fantasies and frustrated by their inability to achieve a tranquil state of mind. And some see only meaninglessness in this kind of practice. These protests add up to one general complaint: the method is ineffective and only leads to an intensification of the symptoms. This is quite understandable. In the first place, since they are accustomed to resorting to measures that achieve a pseudo-solution to their problems, they have an established pattern of activity. Sitting alone prohibits them from following their accustomed way of life. They feel frustrated because they cannot follow their usual pattern of scattering their energy, which they take to be natural activity but which actually is an escape mechanism to avoid facing their problems. So they feel constriction. Second, when the dispersion of their energy in external activities is blocked, they have no other way to turn except inward. They now must see the inside of themselves. Again, in order to avoid facing their actual problems they start to juggle various ideas or fantasies. Nevertheless, especially for the shallow and aggressive patients, now comes the chance to experience themselves inwardly. Willy-nilly they see the problems they suffer from and hate to face. Because they hate to see the problem they hate the way they are brought to see it—that is why they think the method is ineffective. They feel their sufferings intensified because they have to see the problems causing their sufferings, the very problems from which they are trying to escape. In my interviews with the patient, of course I pay respectful attention to his complaints, as well as to the content of his ideas, fantasies, and emotional experiences, and I try to help him elucidate their meaning. But I suggest continuing to practice sitting, and advise him not to pay much attention to his ideas and fantasies, stressing only the importance of sitting itself. If the patient feels it difficult to sit more than fifteen minutes, I do not urge him to sit longer, but strongly advise him to sit regularly and devotedly every day. Usually patients concur in these instructions and begin to feel they can get along in their sitting. Not infrequently a patient reports that he does not know why, but he feels his irritability or anxiety considerably lessened. From the therapist's side it is very impressive that the patient, as he practices sitting steadily, begins to show, unconsciously, more intensive concentration in working on his problems in the therapeutic session. In other words, through the patient's practice of sitting his psychic energy has begun to become assembled, unified, and available for constructive work. I don't say that the patient after sitting for a period of time becomes enlightened. What I say is that he is helped considerably to become charged with more psychic energy and vitality. His dreams show a more constructive picture and his posture begins to show more stability. Often patients say, "When I sit I feel I am rooted and full of sap, where before I felt helplessly buffeted by every emotional wind or storm." Or "I feel as if there is a bubbling fountain within me. I don't feel tired or frustrated anymore." It is noteworthy that in these self-expressions images of water or trees abound.

I believe, from my experience, that any teaching is ineffective fundamentally, whether it be psychoanalysis or psychotherapy or Zen, unless it helps a person feel, experience, and become confident of his fundamental resourcefulness, his real self, his Buddha-nature, his inborn freedom and security, his uniqueness and universality, from the inside of himself and by himself. Neurotic or normal, we are all human beings. As human beings we share the same fate. The neurotic's case is merely an extreme one. But as Buddhism teaches, basically we are all alike in our ignorance of ourselves and in our capability of becoming emancipated from such ignorance through self-realization. Buddhism from the very beginning of its long history clearly recognized the nature of human existence and sought to emancipate human beings from their suffering. Zen, however it may be understood, has this aim.

I have tried to show how Zen intends to bring us to self-realization through sitting. This is a practice leading to single-mindedness, first, by assembling our psychic energy into a unity, and second, by strengthening it through constant practice in our daily living, leading to a stage where we are fully charged with strong vitality and power, where we sit and act with stability and security—in other words, the stage of no-mindedness. It is always a matter of chance when the Self will come to its own realization in our consciousness. The enlightenment experience comes about through the ripening of sitting, just as a fruit or a flower appears as the natural result of the growth of the tree. The roots of such enlightenment have been nourished for a long time in the rich soil of sitting.

It is almost routine to talk about enlightenment. It is the ultimate in the practice of Zen and surely it is important. But how important is it to talk about enlightenment all the time when for those who are enlightened it is pointless and for those who are not, incomprehensible, and frequently a hindrance in that it agitates their already too greedy preoccupation with enlightenment? It is my belief that, enlightenment or not, sitting is strengthening. How much so is something one has to experience for himself.

Sozan, a Zen Master, visited Tozan, a Zen Master. Tozan asked, "Who are you?" Sozan answered, "Honjaku is my name." Tozan said, "Say something more to the point!" Sozan said, "I shan't speak further." Tozan asked, "Why not?" "I don't call myself Honjaku," answered Sozan.

After a number of interviews I asked a patient of mine who was very much concerned that she was an illegitimate child (and who had been sitting according to my instructions), "Who were you before you were an illegitimate child?" She looked puzzled for an instant, then suddenly burst into tears, crying out, "I am I! Oh, I am I!"

Where is the Real Self in these contradicting statements?

from

PSYCHOANALYSIS AND ZEN BUDDHISM

Erich Fromm

(1960)

❏

Where does this whole discussion lead us with regard to the relationship between Zen Buddhism and psychoanalysis?

The aim of Zen is enlightenment: the immediate, unreflected grasp of reality, without affective contamination and intellectualization, the realization of the relation of myself to the Universe. This new experience is a repetition of the preintellectual, immediate grasp of the child, but on a new level, that of the full development of man's reason, objectivity, individuality. While the child's experience, that of immediacy and oneness, lies *before* the experience of alienation and the subject-object split, the enlightenment experience lies after it.

The aim of psychoanalysis, as formulated by Freud, is that of making the unconscious conscious, of replacing Id by Ego. To be sure, the content of

Excerpted from *Zen Buddhism and Psychoanalysis*, by Erich Fromm, D. T. Suzuki, and Richard De Martino (Harper and Row, 1960). An earlier version of this essay was delivered as a lecture in Cuernavaca, Mexico, in August 1957, at the Autonomous National University's conference on Zen Buddhism and Psychoanalysis. This excerpt (pages 135–41) is reprinted courtesy of the Fromm estate.

the unconscious to be discovered was limited to a small sector of the personality, to those instinctual drives which were alive in early childhood, but which were subject to amnesia. To lift these out of the state of repression was the aim of the analytic technique. Furthermore, the sector to be uncovered, quite aside from Freud's theoretical premises, was determined by the therapeutic need to cure a particular symptom. There was little interest in recovering unconsciousness outside of the sector related to the symptom formation. Slowly the introduction of the concept of the death instinct and eros and the development of the Ego aspects in recent years have brought about a certain broadening of the Freudian concepts of the contents of the unconscious. The non-Freudian schools greatly widened the sector of the unconscious to be uncovered. Most radically Jung, but also Adler, Rank, and the other more recent so-called neo-Freudian authors have contributed to this extension. But (with the exception of Jung), in spite of such a widening, the extent of the sector to be uncovered has remained determined by the therapeutic aim of curing this or that symptom; or this or that neurotic character trait. It has not encompassed the whole person.

However, if one follows the original aim of Freud, that of making the unconscious conscious, to its last consequences, one must free it from the limitations imposed on it by Freud's own instinctual orientation, and by the immediate task of curing symptoms. If one pursues the aim of the full recovery of the unconscious, then this task is not restricted to the instincts, nor to other limited sectors of experience, but to the total experience of the total man; then the aim becomes that of overcoming alienation, and of the subject-object split in perceiving the world; then the uncovering of the unconscious means the overcoming of affective contamination and cerebration; it means the de-repression, the abolition of the split within myself between the universal man and the social man; it means the disappearance of the polarity of conscious vs. unconscious; it means arriving at the state of the immediate grasp of reality, without distortion and without interference by intellectual reflection; it means overcoming of the craving to hold on to the ego, to worship it; it means giving up the illusion of an indestructible separate ego, which is to be enlarged, preserved as the Egyptian pharaohs hoped to preserve themselves as mummies for eternity. To be conscious of the unconscious means to be open, responding, to *have* nothing and to *be*.

This aim of the full recovery of unconsciousness by consciousness is quite obviously much more radical than the general psychoanalytic aim. The reasons for this are easy to see. To achieve this total aim requires an effort far beyond the effort most persons in the West are willing to make. But quite aside from this question of effort, even the visualization of this aim is possible only under certain conditions. First of all, this radical aim can be envisaged only from the point of view of a certain philosophical position. There is no need to describe this position in detail. Suffice it to say that it is one in which not the negative aim of the absence of sickness, but the positive one of the presence of well-being is aimed at, and that well-being is conceived in terms of full union, the immediate and uncontaminated grasp of the world. This aim could not be better described than has been done by Suzuki in terms of "the art of living." One must keep in mind that any such concept as the art of living grows from the soil of a spiritual humanistic orientation, as it underlies the teaching of Buddha, of the prophets, of Jesus, of Meister Eckhart, or of men such as Blake, Walt Whitman, or Bucke. Unless it is seen in this context, the concept of "the art of living" loses all that is specific, and deteriorates into a concept that goes today under the name of "happiness." It must also not be forgotten that this orientation includes an ethical aim. While Zen transcends ethics, it includes the basic ethical aims of Buddhism, which are essentially the same as those of all humanistic teaching. The achievement of the aim of Zen, as Suzuki has made very clear, implies the overcoming of greed in all forms, whether it is the greed for possession, for fame, or for affection; it implies overcoming narcissistic self-glorification and the illusion of omnipotence. It implies, furthermore, the overcoming of the desire to submit to an authority who solves one's own problem of existence. The person who only wants to use the discovery of the unconscious to be cured of sickness will, of course, not even attempt to achieve the radical aim which lies in the overcoming of repressedness.

But it would be a mistake to believe that the radical aim of the de-repression has no connection with a therapeutic aim. Just as one has recognized that the cure of a symptom and the prevention of future symptom formations is not possible without the analysis and change of the character, one must also recognize that the change of this or that neurotic character trait is not possible without pursuing the more radical aim of a complete transformation of the person. It may very well be that the relatively disappointing results of character analysis (which have never been expressed more honestly than by Freud in his "Analysis, Terminable or Interminable?") are due precisely to the fact that the aims for the cure of the neurotic character were not radical enough; that well-being, freedom from anxiety and insecurity, can be achieved only if the limited aim is transcended, that is, if one realizes that the limited, therapeutic aim cannot be achieved as long as it remains limited and does not become part of a wider, humanistic frame of reference. Perhaps the limited aim can be achieved with more limited and less time-consuming methods, while the time and energy consumed in the long analytic process are used fruitfully only for the radical aim of "transformation" rather than the narrow one of "reform." This proposition might be strengthened by referring to a statement made above. Man, as long as he has not reached the creative relatedness of which *satori* is the fullest achievement, at best compensates for inherent potential depression by routine, idolatry, destructiveness, greed for property or fame, etc. When any of these compensations break down, his sanity is threatened. The cure of the potential insanity lies only in the change in attitude from split and alienation to the creative, immediate grasp of and response to the world. If psychoanalysis can help in this way, it can help to achieve true mental health; if it cannot, it will only help to improve compensatory mechanisms. To put it still differently: somebody may be "cured" of a symptom, but he can not be "cured" of a character neurosis. Man is not a thing,[1] man is not a "case," and the analyst does not cure anybody by treating him as an object. Rather, the analyst can only help a man to wake up, in a process in which the analyst is engaged with the "patient" in the process of their understanding each other, which means experiencing their oneness.

In stating all this, however, we must be prepared to be confronted with an objection. If, as I said above, the achievement of the full consciousness of the unconscious is as radical and difficult an aim as enlightenment, does it make any sense to discuss this radical aim as something which has any general application? Is it not purely speculative to raise seriously the question that only this radical aim can justify the hopes of the psychoanalytic therapy?

If there were only the alternative between full enlightenment and nothing, then indeed this objection would be valid. But this is not so. In Zen there are many stages of enlightenment, of which *satori* is the ultimate and decisive step. But, as far as I understand, value is set on experiences which are steps in the direction of *satori*, although *satori* may never be reached. Dr. Suzuki once illustrated this point in the following way: If one candle is brought into an absolutely dark room, the darkness disappears, and there is light. But if ten or a hundred or a thousand candles are added, the room will become brighter and brighter. Yet the decisive change was brought about by the first candle which penetrated the darkness.[2]

What happens in the analytic process? A person senses for the first time that he is vain, that he is frightened, that he hates, while consciously he had believed himself to be modest, brave, and loving. The new insight may hurt him, but it opens a door; it permits him to stop projecting on others what he represses in himself. He proceeds; he experiences the infant, the child, the adolescent, the criminal, the insane, the saint, the artist, the male, *and* the female within himself; he gets more deeply in touch with humanity, with the universal man; he represses less, is freer, has less need to project, to cerebrate; then he may experience for the first time how he sees colors, how he sees a ball roll, how his ears are suddenly fully opened to music, when up to now he only listened *to* it; in sensing his oneness with others, he may have a first glimpse of the illusion that his separate individual ego is some*thing* to hold on to, to cultivate, to save; he will experience the futility of seeking the answer to life by *having* himself, rather than by being and becoming himself. All these are sudden, unexpected experiences with no intellectual content; yet afterwards the person feels freer, stronger, less anxious than he ever felt before.

So far we have spoken about *aims*, and I have proposed that if one carries Freud's principle of the transformation of unconsciousness into consciousness to its ultimate consequences, one approaches the concept of enlightenment. But as to *methods* of achieving this aim, psychoanalysis and Zen are, indeed, entirely different. The method of Zen is, one might say, that of a frontal attack on the alienated way of perception by means of the "sitting," the koan, and the authority of the master. Of course, all this is not a "technique" which can be isolated from the premise of Buddhist thinking, of the behavior and ethical values which are embodied in the master and in the atmosphere of the monastery. It must also be remembered that it is not a "five hour a week" concern, and that by the very fact of coming for instruction in Zen the student has made a most important decision, a decision which is an important part of what goes on afterwards.

The psychoanalytic method is entirely different from the Zen method. It trains consciousness to get hold of the unconscious in a different way. It directs attention to that perception which is distorted; it leads to a recognition of the fiction within oneself; it widens the range of human experience by lifting repressedness. The analytic method is psychological-empirical. It examines the psychic development of a person from childhood on and tries to recover earlier experiences in order to assist the person in experiencing of what is now repressed. It proceeds by uncovering illusions within oneself about the world, step by step, so that parataxic distortions and alienated intellectualizations diminish. By becoming less of a stranger to himself, the person who goes through this process becomes less estranged to the world; because he has opened up communication with the universe within himself, he has opened up communication with the universe outside. False consciousness disappears, and with it the polarity conscious-unconscious. A new realism dawns in which "the mountains are mountains again." The psychoanalytic method is of course only a method, a preparation; but so is the Zen method. By the very fact that it is a method it never guarantees the achievement of the goal. The factors which permit this achievement are deeply rooted in the individual personality, and for all practical purposes we know little of them.

I have suggested that the method of uncovering the unconscious, if carried to its ultimate consequences, may be a step toward enlightenment, provided it is taken within the philosophical context which is most radically and realistically expressed in Zen. But only a great deal of further experience in applying this method will show how far it can lead. The view expressed here implies only a possibility and thus has the character of a hypothesis which is to be tested.

But what can be said with more certainty is that the knowledge of Zen, and a concern with it, can have a most fertile and clarifying influence on the theory and technique of psychoanalysis. Zen, different as it is in its method from psychoanalysis, can sharpen the focus, throw new light on the nature of insight, and heighten the sense of what it is to see, what it is to be creative, what it is to overcome the affective contaminations and false intellectualizations which are the necessary results of experience based on the subject-object split.

In its very radicalism with respect to intellectualization, authority, and the delusion of the ego, in its emphasis on the aim of well-being, Zen thought will deepen and widen the horizon of the psychoanalyst and help him to arrive at a more radical concept of the grasp of reality as the ultimate aim of full, conscious awareness.

If further speculation on the relation between Zen and psychoanalysis is permissible, one might think of the possibility that psychoanalysis may be significant to the student of Zen. I can visualize it as a help in avoiding the danger of a false enlightenment (which is, of course, no enlightenment), one which is purely subjective, based on psychotic or hysterical phenomena, or on a self-induced state of trance. Analytic clarification might help the Zen student to avoid illusions, the absence of which is the very condition of enlightenment.

Whatever the use is that Zen may make of psychoanalysis, from the standpoint of a Western psychoanalyst I express my gratitude for this precious gift of the East, especially to Dr. Suzuki, who has succeeded in expressing it in such a way that none of its essence becomes lost in the attempt to translate Eastern into Western thinking, so that the Westerner, if he takes the trouble, can arrive at an understanding of Zen, as far as it can be arrived at before the goal is reached. How could such understanding be possible, were it not for the fact that "Buddha nature is in all of us," that man and existence are universal categories, and that the immediate grasp of reality, waking up, and enlightenment are universal experiences?

Notes

1. Cf. my paper "The Limitations and Dangers of Psychology," in *Religion and Culture*, ed. by W. Leibrecht (New York: Harper & Brothers, 1959), 31ff.
2. In a personal communication, as I remember.

PSYCHOANALYTIC THOUGHT AND EASTERN WISDOM

Harold Kelman

(1960)

❏

Eastern wisdom is not alien to the West. The West is becoming more aware of and congruent with it. Eastern and Western civilization are descendants of the magic world to which the East remained closer than the West. In evolving from the magic world East and West dealt differently with reference to the subject and object. "The Western mind fixes the object as the *ob-jectum*—that which is thrown against the subject—in a word, the opposite. The world surrounding the subject is an objective world. It is independent of the subject. What corresponds to the object in the West, in the East is better named—the other." The distinct cleavage, as in the subject-object dualism, does not occur. "A certain bond and affinity thus persists . . . embracing equally the grim and friendlier aspects of world and nature."[1] What characterizes the East is the subjectifying attitude, the West, the objectifying one. *"Eastern cognition is interested in consciousness itself. Western cognition is interested in the objects of consciousness."*

This paper was first presented at the Academy of Psychoanalysis, New York City, December 7, 1958. It later appeared in *Science and Psychoanalysis*, vol. 3, Jules Masserman, ed. (New York: Grune and Stratton, 1960). It is reprinted here with the permission of W. B. Saunders Company.

The guiding principle of the Eastern mind structure is juxtaposition and identity. In the West it is unity in variety. The East is essentially concerned with life in its intuitive and aesthetic immediacy and produced the world's religions. The West is primarily interested in the theoretically designated and inferred factors in nature and produced science. Wisdom, for the West, is what can be conceptualized. Reality is what can be explained by theories. "The East attempts to establish immediate contact with the Real. This communion and what derives from it is, to the man of the East—wisdom." The Western absolute is an abstraction or a deity so that even in *"unio mystica"*[1] a distinction between the human and divine remains, a dualism persists. The Eastern absolute is the Real. With its subjectifying attitude in the subject-other relation, by a process of dismantling consciousness of its contents, "the subject meets and experiences itself, freed from the interference of otherness altogether." Then all is pure subject, pure consciousness, pure being. The subject and all otherness are identical as is the absolute and the Real. Then there is "awareness without anything of which awareness is aware—hence a state of pure lucidity."

East and West differ in their attitudes toward time. "Time is the arch-enemy of all living." The West attempts to define it explicitly, to oppose and dominate it, only to become its victim. The East shows pronounced discretion toward time. The West postulates abstract and absolute time. In the East, time is ever filled, concrete time. It has no reality other than as time experienced. In the West emphasis is on the past and the future, i.e., away from here-now. In the East time is the absolute present. Past and future are absorbed into it. In China, time is experienced as succession. Past and future are absorbed in the eternal presence of the ancestral family. India's attitude toward time is almost ahistorical. "What reality there is in this world resides in the individual, not as a link and member of the historical process, but in him as such."

Some essential differences between East and West can be explicitly pointed at through an exercise in which the body is used and breathing is of central importance. Yogic exercises or Buddhist meditation in the lotus position are Eastern examples and for the West any form of sport. The disciple sits on the floor, cross-legged. He is actively at rest in the most solidly contained and earth-rooted position a human being can be. His attention is directed inward toward his breathing and its rhythmicity. His orientation is centripetal. Gradually he lets go of his attachments to time, place, person, causality, teleology, materiality, thinking, action, willing, the guiding notions of the West. In time he becomes less affected by thirst, hunger, fullness of bowel and bladder and other bodily sensations and feelings. By attending to his breathing he becomes his breathing, its rhythmicity, its spontaneity. These exercises guide him. They are a stream that carries him into his depths, to control of his heart rate, breathing and ultimately consciousness itself.

In the West exercise means being in the erect position, locomoting, centrifugally oriented and dominated by dualisms in will, thought, feeling and action, i.e., focusing on winning. Breathing is disregarded until the anguish prior to getting second wind obtrudes itself. The experience of breathing and playing being one (i.e., being the breathing or the piano playing without the experience of an I doing it) is not unknown to Western athletes and artists. Good teachers are good gurus. Roger Bannister experienced the being run rather than running and Leopold Auer helped his pupils become the "method of no method" and play brilliant violin with effortless effort.

To show how these differences between East and West came about we must begin with the magic world. The West not only severed its connection with it but kept increasing its distance from it. Egyptian hieroglyphics were phonetic syllabic, i.e., language already was becoming more abstract in its forms. One major function of Egyptian astronomy and mathematics was utilitarian. With the Greeks reason was enthroned and the body became an object to be worshipped. Administration from on top reached its peak with the Romans. The dichotomy between what is and what ought to be was codified in Roman law. Long before Christ, the idea of God as an object was evident. With the Renaissance, the ultimate of centrifugal living had been attained. Western man had become dissociated from his natural organic rhythms.

Centrifugal motion for acquisition was Western man's orientation, to acquire grace in heaven, power and things on earth, to move great distances by foot, on horse and ships, and to build empires. At his apogee, Western man regarded himself as Man. He felt he was the universe and master of all he surveyed.

Inherent in this centrifugal orientation were the seeds of its own dissolution. The scientific spirit guided Copernicus' (1473–1543) assault on the geocentric universe. Darwin (1859) derived God's creation from primitive forms. Freud (1856–1939) unseated man's exalted reason with his "unconscious forces." Einstein's "Special Theory of Relativity"—1905—undermined the absolute space and the absolute time Newton (1642–1727) postulated. Hiroshima—August 6, 1945—set in motion a crescendo of terror. The pride of technology spawned by the scientific method—Francis Bacon (1561–1626)—set free by Western man, catapulted him from his remaining heights. Against this awareness he struggles with mass conformity, mass rebellion, superficial entertainment and acquisition of more things. The awareness of his world's destruction remains acutely imminent.

This is the first time in human history that one individual, in control of mass destruction weapons, in a moment of mental aberration, could destroy the world. It has become a survival necessity that we have our finger on the pulse of each individual's inner experience. Abruptly each human being and his inner experiences have assumed world significance. Our present total context is an assault on our dualistic, mechanistic and materialistic Western thought. The inescapable fact is, there is no either/ or. No one can win a war and everyone loses it. There will neither be victors nor vanquished.

Western man, who has exercised his body, his reason and his willpower, has been forcefully thrown from his exalted heights to land precipitously on his haunches beside his Eastern brother who has been there through the centuries practicing his exercises in meditation. The great difference is that he remained there through choice while Western man was fleeing from that position. Although enforced, the Occident is now more receptive and open to Eastern wisdom in a way never before possible.

Only those who have become steeped in and explored what the West has and is contributing can be open to what the East can offer. They must be aware of the uniqueness of this time in human history. Also they must have experienced the limitations of dualistic thinking and sense impressions. And finally, their anxiety responses to Existentialism, the work of Martin Buber and Zen Buddhism must not be of such intensity that they are driven to be antagonistic, indifferent or to swallow one or all whole. That man has proselytized and prostituted love, religion and in recent times science cannot be held against them. That fads and frauds have been made out of the teachings of Existentialism, Buber, Zen and psychoanalysis does not discredit them. Man has always gone through phases of besmirching his dignity with indignities.

There are certain blocks to our being open and receptive for what the East has to offer. To the extent we are aware, they will stand less in our way. Our language is noun-oriented. We make propositions about things. Languages which are verb-oriented make propositions about events. They are more suitable for communicating immediacies. Our language, subject-predicate in form, creates a dualism and a hypostatization of processes.

Process languages facilitate experiencing. Our language is phonetic alphabetic, the ultimate in abstraction. Ideographic languages, like Chinese, which are painting, are closer to the intuitive and aesthetic, and better communicate feeling. The most expressive language I know is the sign language of mutes. It uses the whole body as a brush and for touching. Finally our Western mind-structure, with its emphasis on conceptualization and its built-in dualisms, blocks communicating experiencing and being, on which the East focuses.

Freud in forcing Western rational man to pay more attention to his feelings, symbolized by sex and "the unconscious," unwittingly moved him closer to the East. When patients came to Freud, as physician, he was relying on an ancient tradition. It started with the priest being also physician. After a period of separation of functions, it is the physician who is now becoming the priest. The patient came to Freud much as a disciple seeks out a master or guru. To this extent psychoanalysis is nonproselytizing, i.e., non-Western. At the deepest level, it is spiritual anguish which brings the sufferer to seek the helper, better named the more experienced one in self-investigation, in contemplation. In these regards, psychoanalysis is closer to Buddhism, Hinduism and Taoism than to Judaism, Christianity or Mohammedanism.

Once in the analyst's office the patient is required to become even more non-Western. He is told, "Say whatever goes through your mind."[2] To spell it out, he is required to be nonconventional, nonproselytizing, nonteleological, nonrational, nonlogical, nonconceptual, nontime-bound, nonspace-bound, nonmaterialistic, passively alert, choicelessly aware and threshold conscious. In short he is required to adopt a whole range of attitudes not only contrary to usual Western forms but quite consonant with many Eastern ones.

Freud asked the analyst to assume the same attitude in his "self-observation." He recommended that he model himself after "the surgeon who puts aside all his own feelings, including that of human sympathy, and concentrates his mind on one single purpose, that of performing the operation as skillfully as possible. . . . The justification for this coldness in feeling in the analyst is that it is the condition which brings the greatest advantage to both persons involved."[3]

Freud's model was the pure research viewpoint of nineteenth-century science. That he was caught in a dualism is evident in his opposites of sympathy and coldness. But if we take him literally when he suggests putting "aside all his own feelings," in a sense, he is defining the impersonal attitude of the guru or master which is the ultimate in being personal. Freud's limited interest in therapy and greater one in psychoanalysis as an investigative tool is almost Eastern. The basic premise of the East is that experiencing is understanding, is knowing, is enlightenment, is therapy carried to its ultimate.

Menninger[4] requires of the analyst, " 'The willpower of desirelessness': in other words, how to free himself from *the desire to cure*. . . . Elsewhere it was implied that the physician must sincerely want to get the patient well." The paradoxes and dualisms remain and also the nonteleologic attitude.

Psychoanalysis carried to its logical conclusion is Eastern in its techniques and Eastern in its ultimate aims and aspirations. It is not Eastern in its theories because the East does not theorize in a Western sense. Psychoanalysis and its theories are a product of the West and of the subject-object dualism. Between theory and technique there is a built-in dichotomy. Freud's theory fits the nineteenth-century scientific materialistic, rationalistic, dualistic man. With each contribution to psychoanalysis an additional facet to the image of man was added. Jung added a collective unconscious; Rank the creative will; Adler the masculine protest and social factors; and Reich, character. Recently, Sullivan, Fromm and Horney have emphasized in different ways cultural, social, interpersonal, intrapersonal and moral factors and the human situation.

Theories of man have shifted from the individualistic toward the interpersonal, holistic and the unitary. Instead of being posed as an object that must change and being opposed to a society that will not, man became a participant-observer and an aspect of the unitary process, individual-environment.

Concomitantly changes in the therapist's function occurred. Freud's pure research viewpoint, when applied to human beings, had to give way before countertransference. Ferenczi positively wanted the therapist to be symbol, surrogate and human being. As the therapist became participant-observer, the comprehensive concept of interpersonal transactions and the doctor-patient relationship became necessary. With the being of therapist and patient participating, the concept of *Begegnung* became essential for Existentialism.

The emergence of and interest in Existentialism, the work of Buber and Zen, to me are evidence that Western man is aware that his philosophic roots are inadequate. I feel these interests are a current phenomenon of the West and a phase on the way toward something different which will unify the contributions of East and West in ways heretofore not existent or envisaged. Existentialism is the formulated awareness of the emptiness, meaninglessness and nothingness of our previous ways of being on the basis of the subject-object dualism and the tragedy of it. It points at the experienced despair and hopelessness of hanging on to an outmoded way of being. It defines the fear of the responsibility of choosing to let go into freedom, a freedom with which the West has little experience. In terms of my notion[5] of the symbolizing process and the self system, Western man's present situation is experiencing the struggle involved in hanging on to and in letting go of the formed aspects of his self system in which are embedded the old and familiar individual, family, group, societal and Western forms of being. He is struggling against and hanging on to the underpinnings of Western civilization which Copernicus in an obvious way began to undermine. The difference between a Westerner and a disciple and master is that the Westerner, and maybe his analyst, still have their eyes on heaven and hell, and are centrifugally oriented and hanging on. The Occidental is being pushed off the precipice into the unknown, into formlessness, against his will, in terror, dread and despair. The Easterner makes this leap into formlessness through choice, in the natural course of his discipleship.

To the extent that the analyst can be the subject-other relation of the East, he can be the ultimate of the impersonal which is the ultimate in the personal. Then truly he will experience juxtaposition and identity and that pain is pain and pleasure is pleasure, neither to be exalted nor degraded. He will be aware that his patient is both identical with him in essentials and different from him in those aspects that enrich the essentials. He will feel him continuous with himself in identity and contiguous with him, as each experiences his own identity in his own right. To the extent this obtains, there will be more meditating, looking inward and being centripetally oriented, until centripetal and centrifugal become one, inward and onward become one and only different ways of looking at and naming the same process, being.

The analyst will have to be aware that the only place we can ever be and experience is here; that the only time we can ever be and experience is now; and that the only feelings we can ever be, not have, are present feelings. This means the only time and place we live is the moment. This being the moment, being it totally, is vastly different from the Western experience of urgency and emergency that demands relief and release and in which each moment is experienced as a matter of life and death but on quite a different plane. Total acceptance of the Western notion that we have to die to be reborn is more possible and widespread in the East. Each moment we die and are reborn. Each moment is new. This notion is not alien to us. Goldstein says, "If the organism is 'to be,' it always has to pass again from moments of catastrophe to states of ordered behavior."[6] And in quantum physics energy exchange is discontinuous.

With the feeling of the subject-object relation, the absolute now, reality indicated by the Chinese notion of *hsing*,[7] pointed at by Northrop's concept of pure fact[8] and Gabriel Marcel's Being[9] and being guided by the unifying hypothesis of the symbolizing process,[10] I feel vaster and deeper possibilities are now open to what is now called psychoanalysis which can and does move more in the direction of the Eastern master-disciple relation.[11]

References

1. W. S. Haas, *The Destiny of the Mind, East and West* (New York: Macmillan, 1956). [Quotations from Haas continue through to "What reality there is in this world . . ."]
2. Sigmund Freud, *Further Recommendations in the Technique of Psycho-Analysis*, vol. 2 (London: Hogarth Press, 1933), 355.
3. Sigmund Freud, *Recommendations for Physicians on the Psycho-Analytic Method of Treatment*, vol. 2 [n.p., n.d.], 327–88.
4. Karl Menninger, *Theory of Psychoanalytic Technique* (New York: Basic Books, 1958), 11, 27.
5. Harold Kelman, "Life History as Therapy, Part III: The Symbolizing Process," *American Journal of Psychoanalysis* 16 (1956), 145, 166.
6. K. Goldstein, *The Organism* (New York: American Book Company, 1939), 512.
7. W. Barrett, ed., *Selected Writings of D. T. Suzuki* (New York: Doubleday & Co., 1956), 112.
8. F. S. C. Northrop, *The Logic of the Sciences and the Humanities* (New York: Macmillan, 1948), 36–40.
9. Gabriel Marcel, in R. May, E. Angel, and H. F. Ellenberger, eds., *Existence* (New York: Basic Books, 1958), 40.
10. Kelman, "Life History as Therapy."
11. Harold Kelman, "Communing and Relating, Parts I–V," *American Journal of Psychoanalysis* 18, nos. 1, 2 (1958), 19, nos. 1, 2 (1959).

from

PSYCHOTHERAPY AND LIBERATION

Alan Watts

(1961)

❑

Psychotherapy and the ways of liberation have two interests in common: first, the transformation of consciousness, of the inner feeling of one's own existence; and second, the release of the individual from forms of conditioning imposed upon him by social institutions. What are the useful means of exploring these resemblances so as to help the therapist in his work? Should he take practical instruction in Yoga, or spend time in a Japanese Zen monastery—adding yet more years of training to medical school, psychiatric residency, or training analysis? I do not feel that this is the point at all. It is rather that even a theoretical knowledge of other cultures helps us to understand our own, because we can attain some clarity and objectivity about our own social institutions by comparing them with others. It helps us to distinguish between social fictions, on the one hand, and natural patterns and relationships, on the other. If, then, there are in other cultures disciplines having something in common with psychotherapy, a theoretical knowledge of their methods, objectives, and principles may enable the psychotherapist to get a better perspective upon what he is doing.

This he needs rather urgently. For we have seen that at the present time psychology and psychiatry are in a state of great theoretical confusion. It may sound strange to say that most of this confusion is due to unconscious factors, for is it not the particular business of these sciences to understand "the unconscious"? But the unconscious factors bearing upon psychotherapy go far beyond the traumas of infancy and the repressions of anger and sexuality. For example, the psychotherapist carries on his work with an almost wholly unexamined "philosophical unconscious." He tends to be ignorant, by reason of his highly specialized training, not only of the contemporary philosophy of science, but also of the hidden metaphysical premises which underlie all the main forms of psychological theory. Unconscious metaphysics tend to be bad metaphysics. What, then, if the metaphysical presuppositions of psychoanalysis are invalid, or if its theory depends on discredited anthropological ideas of the nineteenth century? Throughout his writings Jung insists again and again that he speaks as a scientist and physician and not as a metaphysician. "Our psychology," he writes, "is . . . a science of mere phenomena without any metaphysical implications." It "treats all metaphysical claims and assertions as mental phenomena, and regards them as statements about the mind and its structure that derive ultimately from certain unconscious dispositions."[1] But this is a whopping metaphysical assumption in itself. The difficulty is that man can hardly think or act at all without some kind of metaphysical premise, some basic axiom which he can neither verify nor fully define. Such axioms are like the rules of games: some give ground for interesting and fruitful plays and some do not, but it is always important to understand as clearly as possible what the rules are. Thus the rules of ticktacktoe are not so fruitful as those of chess, and what if the axioms of psychoanalysis resemble the former instead of the latter? Would this not put the science back to the level of mathematics when geometry was only Euclidean?

Unconscious factors in psychotherapy include also the social and ecological contexts of patient and therapist alike, and these tend to be ignored in a situation where two people are closeted together in private. As Norman O. Brown has put it:

> There is a certain loss of insight in the tendency of psychoanalysis to isolate the individual from culture. Once we recognize the limitations of talk from the couch, or rather, once we recognize that talk from the couch is still an activity in culture, it

becomes plain that there is nothing for the psychoanalyst to analyze except these cultural projections—the world of slums and telegrams and newspapers—and thus psychoanalysis fulfils itself only when it becomes historical and cultural analysis.[2]

Is not this a way of saying that what needs to be analyzed or clarified in an individual's behavior is the way in which it reflects the contradictions and confusions of the culture?

Now cultural patterns come to light and hidden metaphysical assumptions become clear only to the degree that we can step outside the cultural or metaphysical systems in which we are involved by comparing them with others. There are those who argue that this is simply impossible, that our impressions of other cultures are always hopelessly distorted by our own conditioning. But this is almost a cultural solipsism, and is equivalent to saying that we can never really be in communication with another person. If this be true, all study of foreign languages and institutions, and even all discourse with other individuals, is nothing but extending the pattern of one's own ignorance. As a metaphysical assumption there is no way of disproving it, but it offers nothing in the way of a fruitful development.

The positive aspect of liberation as it is understood in the Eastern ways is precisely freedom of play. Its negative aspect is criticism of premises and rules of the "social game" which restrict this freedom and do not allow what we have called fruitful development. The Buddhist *nirvana* is defined as release from *samsara*, literally the Round of Birth and Death, that is, from life lived in a vicious circle, as an endlessly repetitious attempt to solve a false problem. *Samsara* is therefore comparable to attempts to square the circle, trisect the angle, or construct a mechanism of perpetual motion. A puzzle which has no solution forces one to go over the same ground again and again until it appears that the question which it poses is nonsense. This is why the neurotic person keeps repeating his behavior patterns—always unsuccessfully because he is trying to solve a false problem, to make sense of a self-contradiction. If he cannot see that the problem itself is nonsense, he may simply retreat into psychosis, into the paralysis of being unable to act at all. Alternatively, the "psychotic break" may also be an illegitimate burst into free play out of sheer desperation, not realizing that the problem is impossible not because of overwhelming difficulty, but because it is meaningless.

If, then, there is to be fruitful development in the science of psychotherapy, as well as in the lives of those whom it intends to help, it must be released from the unconscious blocks, unexamined assumptions, and unrealized nonsense problems which lie in its social context. Again, one of the most powerful instruments for this purpose is intercultural comparison, especially with highly complex cultures like the Chinese and Indian which have grown up in relative isolation from our own, and especially with attempts that have been made within those cultures to find liberation from their own patterns. It is hard to imagine anything more constructive to the psychotherapist than the opportunity which this affords. But to make use of it he must overcome the habitual notion that he has nothing to learn from "prescientific" disciplines, for in the case of psychotherapy this may be a matter of the pot calling the kettle black. In any event, there is no question here of his adopting Buddhist or Taoist practices in the sense of becoming converted to a religion. If the Westerner is to understand and employ the Eastern ways of liberation at all, it is of the utmost importance that he keep his scientific wits about him; otherwise there is the morass of esoteric romanticism which awaits the unwary.

But today, past the middle of the twentieth century, there is no longer much of a problem in advocating a hearing for Eastern ideas. The existing interest in them is already considerable, and they are rapidly influencing our thinking by their own force, even though there remains a need for much interpretation, clarification, and assimilation. Nor can we commend their study to psychotherapists as if this were something altogether new. It is now thirty years since Jung wrote:

> When I began my life-work in the practice of psychiatry and psychotherapy, I was completely ignorant of Chinese philosophy, and it is only later that my professional experiences have shown me that in my technique I had been unconsciously led along that secret way which for centuries has been the preoccupation of the best minds of the East.[3]

An equivalence between Jung's analytical psychology and the ways of liberation must be accepted with some reservations, but it is important that he felt it to exist. Though the interest began with Jung and his school, suspect among other schools for its alleged "mysticism," it has gone far beyond, so much so that it would be a fair undertaking to document the discussions of Eastern ideas which have appeared in psychological books and journals during the past few years.[4]

. . .

The level at which Eastern thought and its insights may be of value to Western psychology has been admirably stated by Gardner Murphy, a psychologist who, incidentally, can hardly be suspected of the taint of Jung's "mysticism." He writes:

> If, moreover, we are serious about understanding all we can of personality, its integration and disintegration, we must understand the meaning of depersonalization, those experiences in which individual self-awareness is abrogated and the individual melts into an awareness which is no longer anchored upon selfhood. Such experiences are described by Hinduism in terms of the ultimate unification of the individual with the atman, the super-individual cosmic entity which transcends both selfhood and materiality. . . . Some men desire such experiences; others dread them. Our problem here is not their desirability, but the light which they throw on the relativity of our present-day psychology of personality. . . . Some other mode of personality configuration, in which self-awareness is less emphasized or even lacking, may prove to be the general (or the fundamental).[5]

It is of course a common misapprehension that the change of personal consciousness effected in the Eastern ways of liberation is "depersonalization" in the sense of regression to a primitive or infantile type of awareness. Indeed, Freud designated the longing for return to the oceanic consciousness of the womb as the *nirvana*-principle, and his followers have persistently confused all ideas of transcending the ego with mere loss of "ego strength." This attitude flows, perhaps, from the imperialism of Western Europe in the nineteenth century, when it became convenient to regard Indians and Chinese as backward and benighted heathens desperately in need of improvement by colonization.

It cannot be stressed too strongly that liberation does not involve the loss or destruction of such conventional concepts as the ego; it means seeing through them—in the same way that we can use the idea of the equator without confusing it with a physical mark upon the surface of the earth. Instead of falling below the ego, liberation surpasses it. Writing without apparent knowledge of Buddhism or Vedanta, A. F. Bentley put it thus:

> Let no quibble of skepticism be raised over this questioning of the existence of the individual. Should he find reason for holding that he does not exist in the sense indicated, there will in that fact be no derogation from the reality of what does exist. On the contrary, there will be increased recognition of reality. For the individual can be banished only by showing a plus of existence, not by alleging a minus. If the individual falls it will be because the real life of men, when it is widely enough investigated, proves too rich for him, not because it proves too poverty-stricken.[6]

One has only to look at the lively and varied features and the wide-awake eyes of Chinese and Japanese paintings of the great Zen masters to see that the ideal of personality here shown is anything but the collective nonentity or the weakling ego dissolving back into the womb.

Our mistake has been to suppose that the individual is honored and his uniqueness enhanced by emphasizing his separation from the surrounding world, or his eternal difference in essence from his Creator. As well honor the hand by lopping it from the arm! But when Spinoza said that "the more we know of particular things, the more we know of God," he was anticipating our discovery that the richer and more articulate our picture of man and of the world becomes, the more we are aware of its relativity and of the interconnection of all its patterns in an undivided whole. The psychotherapist is perfectly in accord with the ways of liberation in describing the goal of therapy as individuation (Jung), self-actualization (Maslow), functional autonomy (Allport), or creative selfhood (Adler), but every plant that is to come to its full fruition must be embedded in the soil, so that as its stem ascends the whole earth reaches up to the sun.

Notes

1. C. G. Jung, *Psychology and Religion: East and West*, vol. 2 of *Collected Works*, Bollingen Series 20 (New York: Pantheon, 1958), 476.

2. Norman O. Brown, *Life Against Death: The Psychoanalytical Meaning of History* (Middletown, Conn.: Wesleyan University, 1959), 170–71.

3. R. Wilhelm and C. G. Jung, *The Secret of the Golden Flower* (London: Routledge, 1931), 83.

4. Under the heading of "Contributions from Related Fields," the recent *American Handbook of Psychiatry* (New York: Basic Books, 1959) contains full articles by Eilhard von Domarus on Oriental "religions" and by Avrum Ben-Avi on Zen Buddhism.

5. Gardner Murphy, *Personality: A Biosocial Approach to Origins and Structure* (New York: Harper, 1947).

6. A. F. Bentley, *Inquiry into Inquiries* (Boston: Beacon, 1954), 4.

MORITA THERAPY AND PSYCHOANALYSIS

Takeo Doi

(1962)

❑

I am going to attempt here a comparison between Morita therapy and psychoanalysis. Before doing so, however, a brief exposition of Morita therapy would be required, because I presume this treatment method is not known to you, though in recent years there have been a number of publications, written in English, on this subject and you might have heard of its name. After describing what Morita therapy is like, I will try to interpret Morita therapy in terms of psychoanalytic language. I mean by this an interpretation of the psychodynamics of what takes place in Morita therapy. Then I will speculate on the philosophy behind Morita therapy or rather its cultural background. Lastly, in the light of what we learn about Morita therapy, I will venture to reexamine psychoanalysis and raise a few questions about it.

This paper was first presented on June 11, 1962, at the National Institute for Mental Health, Bethesda, Md. It appeared that same year in *Psychologia: An International Journal of Psychology in the Orient*, vol. 5, pages 117–23, and is reprinted here with the permission of the editors of *Psychologia*.

Morita therapy is so named because its founder is Dr. Shoma Morita,[1] who was professor of psychiatry at Jikei Medical College in Tokyo. It was in the early 1920s that he evolved a special treatment method for certain kinds of neurosis. The types of neurosis he selected for the treatment were neurasthenia, anxiety neurosis and obsessive neurosis, all of which he subsumed under the general category of *shinkeishitsu*, a Japanese word for the German *Nervosität*. The reason for his doing so was the following: that all three develop from the common constitution, which he named the "hypochondriacal constitution." By using the term "constitution" he meant the existence of a basic, possibly biologically determined, factor in these neuroses. But by attaching the adjective "hypochondriacal" to this term he tried to elucidate the psychological aspect of this basic constitution. It is extremely interesting that he took the hypochondriacal state of mind as a very ordinary one, in fact, a very natural human condition. Namely, he stated that this state of mind arises from the fear due to the self-preservative instinct; hence it is universal and exists to a greater or lesser degree in every man. Undoubtedly, the hypochondriacal constitution is the one in which there is a good deal of such an instinctive fear. Morita stops at this point and does not attempt a further analysis of this fear, inasmuch as he takes the hypochondriacal state of mind for granted in the first place. But starting from this seemingly naive theory of the hypochondriacal constitution, he constructed further a theory of symptom formation. The hypochondriacal constitution alone does not produce a disease of *shinkeishitsu*. But if one who has such a constitution develops an emotional or autonomous reaction to a certain stimulus and gets caught in such a reaction because of his "hypochondriacal mood," then it will turn into a permanent symptom, even though otherwise it was only to be a temporary thing. Because, Morita argues, such a reaction will get intensified by the undue attention that was aroused by the hypochondriacal fear, subsequently it will invite more attention to it, and thus set in motion the reciprocal effect of reaction and attention. He called the process of this reciprocal effect *toraware*, a Japanese word which means "to be caught." Incidentally, this is a very ordinary Japanese word, and we use it quite often in everyday conversation to express the feeling of being caught or involved or preoccupied. As against this morbid state of mind Morita set forth the ideal state of mind in which one's attention is not unduly arrested by anything and flows smoothly and continuously.

Morita's theory here expounded might look too unsophisticated to those who are immersed in psychoanalytic sophistication. Without attempting a critical examination of his theory, however, I will now proceed to describe his treatment method. This was developed from his philosophy of psychotherapy that what is most important in treating patients is how to prescribe and administer rest and training according to the need of each individual. For this purpose, he experimented first with keeping a patient or two in his own home. In other words, he practically lived with his patients. Gradually, as the number of patients increased, a part of his house was converted to a hospital ward, and the general scheme of his treatment method became more systematic. It is important to remember here that the Morita hospital was an extension of his home, physically as well as psychologically. Morita specifically called his method of hospital treatment "the home-like treatment." This tradition of carrying the home atmosphere into hospital life has been preserved to this day by his followers.

When Morita finally completed his treatment method, it consisted of four stages, each running for a week or more. In the first stage the patient is put to bed, and is told not to engage in any activity, such as seeing people, talking, reading or smoking, that might divert his attention from his sickness. The physician might come in to see him, but does not talk with him either. This isolation, of course, increases the patient's anxiety, but then the physician tells him not to fight it, just simply to bear it. Morita observed that the patient often experiences a sudden lifting of anxiety only if he stops fighting it. He also believed that this enforced isolation was useful for diagnosis of *shinkeishitsu*, because those of this type could go through this stage and eventually benefit from it, whereas others of different categories could not: for instance, hysterics would act out and schizophrenics would only become worse. After having struggled with his sickness and having become accustomed to his anxiety, the patient would begin to feel bored with staying in bed. When this sign of being bored is detected, the patient is ushered into the second stage of therapy.

In the second stage the patient is no longer allowed to stay in bed in the daytime, and is encouraged to engage in light manual tasks around the hospital, such as cleaning up the garden, washing the dishes, or working with some material. He is still prohibited from playing or reading or even talking beyond the bare minimum of necessity. Instead he is now asked to write a diary, on which the doctor makes short comments in writing each day. He is also invited to attend informal meetings, usually held in the evening, where he listens to what the physician or some other advanced patients talk about. The main purpose in this second stage is to make the patient aware of his desire for spontaneous activity and also to make him feel the simple joy of doing small things.

When the patient begins to feel like doing heavier work, he moves to the third stage. The emphasis is placed, as in the second stage, on doing things, not on getting some benefit from it. If the patient expresses a concern or worry about doing any specific task, it is pointed out to him, either directly or through comments on his diary, that he is "being caught" (*toraware*) by such a concern, and he is enjoined simply to engage in working. His complaints of symptoms, which he is still quite likely to note in his diary and also is allowed to make during informal meetings in the evening, only meet the laconic indifference or scorn of the physician.

Thus, if and after the patient gradually learns that he is able to work and to enjoy doing so, he enters the fourth stage of therapy, which prepares him to get back to the outside life. In this stage the patient is allowed to read only practical material like popular science, history, or biography. He still is not allowed to read novels or philosophy; also he is prohibited from concentrating on reading. His daily manual work must come first, and only in short intervals between the tasks is he allowed to read. He also gets the privilege of going out, but only on the pretext of doing errands. By this time he is comfortably enmeshed in interpersonal relations in the hospital, with the staff as well as with the patients. He has learned to be natural and comfortable with himself as he is and with others, a state of mind which often is described by the phrase *aru ga mama*, meaning "to take things as they are." This is also the state of mind which Morita described as the ideal, namely the one in which the mind is not unduly arrested by anything and runs smoothly. When he reaches this point the patient is discharged.

Now let us proceed to examine what takes place in Morita therapy in terms of the psychodynamics of the patient. I said earlier that Morita established the new diagnostic category of *shinkeishitsu* as an inclusive term for neurasthenia, anxiety neurosis and obsessive neurosis because all these three develop from the common hypochondriacal constitution. It is quite possible to question his reason for doing so, his theory of the hypochondriacal constitution, and also that of symptom-formation. But let us simply follow his intuition that there is something common in these three forms of neurosis in the way they present themselves to the physician. Here to our rescue comes *toraware*, the Japanese word which I explained earlier as meaning "to be caught," because these patients do seem to be caught in their symptoms, and the Japanese word *toraware* gives a perfect description of such a state of mind. So apart from Morita's theorizing on the state of *toraware* in terms of the so-called reciprocal effect of reaction and attention, we could simply start with the clinical phenomenon of *toraware*.

Here I should explain some of the results of treating those patients of the *shinkeishitsu* type with psychoanalytic treatment.[2] I have observed that almost invariably they come to develop in the course of treatment an enormous sensitivity over what the physician might feel or think about them, with the resulting diminution of their initial state of *toraware*. Then this sensitivity itself could easily be traced back to their hidden wish to be loved, to be taken care of. From repeated observations of such therapeutic processes, I have reached the following formulation over the dynamics of *toraware* in these patients. First, their primary wish to be loved has suffered a critical frustration, possibly in their early life. This leads either to the repression of the wish to be loved and also of the anger due to its frustration, or to their dissociation, which would result in distorted interpersonal relations. Then the feelings accompanying such distorted relations are displaced or introjected as hypochondriacal complaints, thus leading to the end stage of *toraware*. I have been helped in making this formulation by the presence of a unique word in the Japanese vocabulary, *amaeru*, which means "to depend and presume upon another's love" and "to indulge in another's kindness." I say it is a unique word, because there is no single word that corresponds to *amaeru*, so far as I know, in English or any other European language. *Amaeru* usually refers to what a child feels toward his parents, but can be applied to the similar feeling between two adults. I stated in my previous publications that the concept of *amaeru* is technically the same as what Michael Balint[3] called "passive object love." He incidentally pointed out that none of the European languages distinguish between the two kinds of object love, active and passive.

There are a good many things to be said about this interesting word *amaeru* and its concept. Assuming that the desire to be loved which it represents is more primitive and infantile than the desire to love, it is more vulnerable and subject to pathology. Further, assuming that the psychology of *amaeru* is what underlies that of *toraware* in *shinkeishitsu* patients, then this will throw some light on how Morita therapy works with these patients. In Morita therapy, as we saw above, the patient does not primarily aim to acquire an insight; he is only encouraged to reach a certain state of mind after being induced to experience the full effect of *toraware* which he cannot get rid of even if he wishes and tries to do so. His desire of *amaeru* or his dependency wishes may be noticed in passing by the physician, but they are never brought to bear on the patient. Rather, and this is an interesting feature, it seems that the way Morita therapy is conducted curiously circumvents the desire to be loved or to be taken care of on the part of the patient. He is left in isolation, with almost no support, in the first week. His complaints are paid no heed, and he is encouraged to engage only in manual work. True, he is in the hospital with many patients with similar ailments, some of whom may have improved even in his judgment. He also virtually lives with the physician and his assistants, who work along with him and even dine at the same table. These facts undoubtedly give considerable emotional support to the patient, but his hidden warped desire to *amaeru* remains untouched. But I wonder if this kind of technique somehow succeeds in making the patient transcend his pathology in *amaeru*, thus enabling him to recover his normal functioning. This obviously would not be the same as the result gained by psychoanalytic treatment, which laboriously tries to work out the pathology, but it may still be possible to attain the somewhat similar effect simply by its omission.

This is one account of how Morita therapy works in the light of my experiences of treating *shinkeishitsu* patients in psychoanalytic treatment. I do not say that it is the only correct account, nor that the possibilities contained in Morita therapy are exhausted by this account. In this context I would like to say a few words about the possible connection between Morita therapy and Zen Buddhism. It is a known fact that Morita himself not infrequently quoted from old Zen Masters for support of his thinking, and recently some of his followers have resorted mainly to the Zen literature for elucidation of the basic philosophy underlying Morita therapy. But what is really interesting about the possible connection between the two is the fact that, in spite of the obvious similarity between his thinking and Zen Buddhism, Morita disclaimed any special connection between the two. He admitted that he had earlier given Zen practice a try, but said that he had flunked. It is as though he were to say that having flunked he shed all influences of Zen from himself. In any event, it is known that he had a deep conviction that his theory was based upon rational scientific thinking, that he twice tried to communicate his thoughts to a German periodical of psychiatry, but each time was turned down on account of its being unintelligible. So it is quite likely that Zen-like thinking slipped against his will into the exposition of his theory, if not into its essence. And it is truly an irony of history that nowadays his theory is associated mostly with Zen Buddhism in the minds of Western scholars.

In my opinion, what definitely links Morita theory to Zen Buddhism is its conception of the ideal state of mind as the one in which the mind is not unduly arrested by anything and flows smoothly and continuously. In Morita therapy the patient is told not to shy away from his feelings, but rather accept them. Then this would not look different from what is set forth as the ideal in psychoanalytic treatment. But in the case of Morita therapy there seems to be a slight element of detachment in the way one accepts one's feelings. This is partly because in Morita therapy one does not go out to probe one's feelings as one does in psychoanalysis; rather one is encouraged to look at them summarily as things that simply happen; partly because one is practically made to stand aloof from the conflict-ridden self by engaging his whole person in manual work. As I mentioned earlier, Morita therapy does not aim at exploration of one's pathology, but I wonder if it also evades or perhaps transcends an issue of great importance by bypassing the pathology. In saying this I have in mind one interesting clinical phenomenon which one can observe in psychoanalytic treatment of *shinkeishitsu* patients. They would almost invariably experience a painful sense of "not having possessed their selves before" after they become aware of their hidden wish to *amaeru*. But this kind of experience will not occur to patients in Morita therapy, because here one is helped to attain a state of mind in which one is even forgetful of oneself. Truly this is related to the Zen ideal of no-self. Since the perception of one's individual separate self is most disturbing, it has to be dissolved in the feeling of unity with one's surroundings or with nature. Perhaps I should say "with Mother Nature," which is more meaningful psychoanalytically.

I would now like to look at this characteristic of Morita therapy again from a different angle. I think that the experience one is supposed to get in Morita therapy has something of an aesthetic quality. It certainly is not moralistic in spite of its confining patients to the home-like hospital life and its emphasis on manual work. The element of detachment from one's conflict-ridden life, which I spoke of, is undoubtedly congenial to aesthetic life. Even the emphasis on manual work is, as was explained before, not for any utilitarian purpose. Morita is said to have told patients, "Do lose yourself in whatever work you do." "Lose yourself" is a poor translation of his original words. They are literally "do become the act of doing anything you do." This, of course, does not exclude the genuine pleasure of work, rather it is meant to enhance it; hence it is tantamount to converting housework or any chore into artistic engagement. Thus this preponderance of aesthetic or artistic elements in Morita therapy fits in very well with the

Japanese culture in which it was born, since, as you probably know, or rather as I see it, the best quality of Japanese culture lies in its aesthetics and arts.

Now finally we come back to the task of examining psychoanalysis in the light of what we have learned about Morita therapy. Curiously enough, a very strange image of psychoanalysis emerges from the perspective of Morita therapy; that the former is a terribly moralistic treatment compared with the latter, in spite of the often-raised criticisms in Western societies that psychoanalysis is antimoral, or at least amoral. I here use the adjective "moralistic" not pejoratively, but then I have to qualify what I mean by this. For this purpose let me choose two problems of authority and dependency and see how they are dealt with in psychoanalysis. First, speaking of the problem of authority, one would almost automatically think that Morita therapy is authoritarian, while psychoanalysis is individualistic. I do not necessarily deny the validity of such a description, if one is to be satisfied by surface phenomena. But if one looks deeper, an entirely different picture comes to our view. Certainly in Morita therapy hospitals the patients would make deep bows to their physician and would not think of saying anything critical about him. So one may say that the authoritarian atmosphere prevails in Morita therapy hospitals. But what can one say about the fact that Morita therapists work alongside the patients and dine with them? They often even tell the patients that they have suffered from the same problem as the patients now do. So the prevailing atmosphere in Morita therapy hospitals is most congenial and warm in spite of the patients' due respect toward the physician. In contrast with Morita therapy, in psychoanalysis the patient faces his therapist as his equal. He certainly would not make deep bows to the therapist. He is even encouraged to say anything critical or negative about the therapist. He is free either to continue or discontinue therapy. But it is illusory to deduce from this apparent use of freedom that psychoanalysis is devoid of any function of authority. On the contrary, Freud himself stated that "Analysis . . . presupposes the consent of the analyzed; the situation of analysis involves a superior and a subordinate."[4] This is not to negate the freedom of patients, nor certainly to impose any moral demand on the patient, as Freud specifically stated to this effect elsewhere. But one has to be reminded that it takes perhaps even a greater authority to tell another human being, in this case a patient, that he is free to do whatever he chooses with his life. Furthermore, in psychoanalysis one is not even promised one's eventual cure, yet one should be prepared to remain in therapy for an indefinite length of time.

I wonder, then, what constitutes authority if this kind of commitment does not presuppose its existence, even though it may not be so named and recognized as such.

Speaking of the matter of length of treatment leads to another problem of dependency. The length of Morita therapy is comparatively short, and at most runs to only a few months, while the length of psychoanalytic treatment is by nature indefinite. It is true that in the case of Morita therapy the patients do often keep in contact with the physician even after their discharge, that at times they even form a group of ex-patients. But, as I said earlier, it is not in the nature of Morita therapy to deal with the patient's dependency wishes, rather it bypasses or possibly transcends them, whereas in psychoanalysis one has to labor with one's dependency wishes, has to probe every aspect of them; curiously enough, however, for that purpose one is allowed to depend upon one's analyst. But then one is required constantly to examine one's dependency on the analyst, eventually to save the golden core from the crude ore for future reference. I think this difference between Morita therapy and psychoanalysis on the matter of dependency is a reflection of different characteristics of Japanese society and Western societies. In Japanese society there are so many channels in which one can easily gratify one's dependency wishes. Only if one can transcend one's petty conflicts over dependency can one easily be integrated into the society. But in Western societies the requirement for an individual seems to be nominally high. Unless one becomes truly independent, one cannot satisfactorily function in those societies. Hence one would have to undergo a longer period of reeducation or longer apprenticeship, which is what psychoanalysis certainly looks like to the Japanese in comparison with Morita therapy.

I have been allowing myself to speculate on the cross-cultural differences between Japanese and Western societies. In comparing Morita therapy and psychoanalysis, one eventually has to confront the problem of a more basic difference between the two cultures in which these treatment methods were born. Not being trained in anthropology and cultural studies, I am not able to enlarge on this subject, but in order to further your thinking on the effect of culture on treatment method let me call your attention to the following fact. There is good evidence to believe that Morita himself suffered from the illness of *shinkeishitsu*, as did many of his followers. One may almost be justified to say that in the last analysis he evolved his treatment method out of his own struggles with his illness. Interestingly enough, one can't help feeling from reading Freud's biography that he himself suffered from *shinkeishitsu*. I refer here to his hypochondriacal symp-toms, anxiety attacks, and hidden mother attachment. But it seems that he approached this problem from an entirely different angle than Morita. As we all know, he tried to understand this in terms of sexual economy. To take the hypochondriacal state of mind as something ordinary, almost self-explanatory, did not occur to Freud as it did so naturally to Morita. Why this difference? If this question is meaningful, we are again thrown back on cultural differences between the two. I know Freud vigorously objected to the interpretation of his theory in terms of his personality and culture. But I don't think Morita would have objected as much to a similar attempt. Again, what accounts for this difference?

This, then, is my story comparing Morita therapy and psychoanalysis. I do not deny that I have oversimplified both for the sake of argument. But I shall be very happy indeed if my story has aroused a new curiosity about something you thought you were familiar with, and at least provoked you to some further thinking.

Notes

1. Shoma Morita, *Shinkeishitsu no hontai to ryoho* (Essence and Treatment of *Shinkeishitsu*) (1928), and new edition, with commentary by Hiroshi Kawai (Tokyo: Hakuyosha, 1960).

2. Takeo Doi, *Shinkeishitsu no seishinbyori* (Psychopathology of *Shinkeishitsu*), *Seishin-Shinkeigaku Zasshi (Psychiatria et Neurologia Japonica)* 60 [1958]), 733–44.

3. Michael Balint, *Primary Love and Psychoanalytic Technique* (London: Hogarth Press, 1956). See also "Amae: A Key Concept for Understanding Japanese Personality Struc-ture," *Psychologia*, 5 (1962), 1–7.

4. Sigmund Freud, "On the History of the Psychoanalytic Movement" (1914), in vol. 13 of *The Standard Edition of the Complete Psychological Works of Sigmund Freud*, ed. J. Strachey (London: Hogarth Press, 1953).

PSYCHOLOGICAL ADJUSTMENT IS NOT LIBERATION

A Symposium

Jack Kornfield, Ram Dass, and Mokusen Miyuki

(1979)

❑

MODERATOR: The question we would like to present to the panel this evening is whether psychological growth can be considered to be the same thing as spiritual growth?

KORNFIELD: I'd like to start from the perspective of the Abhidharma, the Buddhist tradition of analytic understanding, which describes the spiritual process as a transformation of certain mental factors, or qualities of mind. The Abhidharma model is rather simple in its major components. It describes our world or experience in three parts. First, there is consciousness or that quality of mind which knows different objects. Second, the sense perceptions of sight, sound, taste, smell, bodily feelings, and the perception of mind, which the Abhidharma also classifies as a sense organ. The third component is the whole category of qualities called mental factors, which determine how each moment of conscious-

This article first appeared in the journal Zero: Contemporary Buddhist Life and Thought, vol. 2, 1979. It is reprinted here courtesy of the former editor of Zero, Eric Lerner, and the current staff of the Mt. Baldy Zen Center (Mt. Baldy, California), which hosted the symposium in July 1978.

ness relates to the experiences of sights and sounds and so on. In Buddhist psychology, spiritual practice consists of the techniques for altering the predominance of these mental factors from attachment, aversion, and ignorance to the qualities of mindfulness or awareness, compassion, loving kindness, generosity, and equanimity. This alteration of mental factors begins to change the way we relate to experience from moment to moment. Seen from this point of view, there really is no difference between psychological and spiritual growth. Our different kinds of experiences are determined by the different qualities present in the mind, which arise in relation to our experience. From this perspective all the different traditions of religion and psychology can be judged by their ability to produce those factors of mind which are more wholesome or skillful and which allow for a clearer seeing and understanding of how things really are.

MIYUKI: If you talk about the Buddhist tradition in terms of psychological theory, you probably get some interesting pictures to play with. You can externalize those inner realities and mental factors and analyze their wholesome and unwholesome natures, and then consider how to transform these unwholesome ones into wholesome mental factors. But those are, by and large, games for the extroverted, and do not grapple with the question of the self or ego-consciousness. I feel it is more important to ask, where is the individual in this investigation and transformation? More specifically, where am I? From that angle, psychological growth in the Western sense may not be applicable to the Buddhist tradition, though spiritual growth may be. Spiritual growth may contain all the phases of life, the rational, irrational, the feeling sensations, and willpower. They are all included in a continuum of the various phases of life. In that sense spiritual growth is much more important and is much wider in scope than psychological growth.

RAM DASS: Thus far the answers reflect some confusion concerning what the word "psychological" refers to and what "spiritual" refers to. Jack clearly interpreted psychology in the most literal sense of the study of the mind, and is correct in saying that it is not antithetical to spiritual growth. In the contemporary Western culture framework, however, psychological growth is something very different. Psychology, as defined and practiced by people like Erikson, Maslow, and Rogers and the neo-Freudians, as well as the neo-Jungians and the gestalt therapy of Fritz Perls and so on, does not in the ultimate sense transcend the nature of ego structure. They really seem to be focused on developing a functional ego structure with which you can cope effectively and adequately with the existing culture. They have very little to say about how deeply identified you are with that ego structure.

Spiritual growth, however, concerns the identification with the ego structure and on that issue there is quite a gap between what is known as the psychological growth movement in America and the spiritual movement. The psychological world is primarily interested in worldly adjustment, happiness, and pleasure. Psychology treats unhappiness as a negative state and happiness as a positive state, while Buddha started out with the proposition that it's all suffering.

KORNFIELD: Part of the confusion between spiritual and Western psychological traditions may arise because of seeming similarity in teaching methods. The way that certain methods or tools are employed in Western psychology can help bring people to balance, but unfortunately they don't have the depth that is common in spiritual practice. In Western psychology, from what I can see, there is a predominant emphasis on the qualities known in the Abhidharma as analysis and investigation. This is true even in the best awareness traditions, like gestalt, where people pay very close attention in a mindful way to their inner process. Still there is a real neglect for the cutting power of *samadhi*, the stillness of the mind in meditation, through deep focus and inner contemplation. Thus a lot of psychological tools, which are similar to spiritual techniques, achieve different results because they do not penetrate the surface of mind. They lack these other important aspects: concentration and tranquility and equanimity, which empower the awareness to cut the neurotic speed. The Buddha's description of the phenomenon resembles movie frames that go by so fast that you need acutely developed attention in order to perceive that it's just one little blip after another on the screen. Western psychology hasn't developed this kind of depth and penetration in investigation. Instead, it's concerned with adjustment of personality. It is as if you climb the mountain a little way and you have a very small view of the fields and trees but don't have the power to see the whole landscape, that is, who you are in relation to everything else.

MODERATOR: On the other hand isn't it true that often this very quality of *samadhi* that separates psychological methods from spiritual practice becomes overdeveloped in relation to the analytic faculty among Western meditators who haven't experienced much quietness in their ordinary life. It becomes a great new toy and a way of circumventing the issue of personality. When *samadhi* is very strong there really is no personality. That experience is a wonderful escape from the struggle of personality in the world. Is there anything in the type of spiritual practice that is being taught in America that returns the meditator to his personality in order to undo the knots that were simply avoided?

KORNFIELD: That's exactly what a good teacher does. You develop *samadhi*, and when you come to him, anything that you're holding on to or avoiding is brought to light in the circumstances of the teacher-pupil relationship. Fundamentally your question points to the need for balance. Just as in the West there's been too much emphasis on the analytic process and not enough on depth of mind; in the East the greatest danger of Buddhist practice has been getting caught in tranquility or in states which are blissful or composed, but do not have a great deal of penetrating wisdom and investigation. We really need both.

MIYUKI: In Zen Buddhist practice you are encouraged to do all your daily activities, cooking, cleaning, working, etc., with the mind of *samadhi*. So how are we to interpret *samadhi*? *Samadhi* is never separate from the person, as you can see very clearly in the context of your own life here at this Zen Center.

Concerning the examination of the personality, I believe that you also need some special mind. Now is this special mind attained only by *samadhi* practice in meditation, or is it possible to attain it through some other method? I would like to maintain it is possible in other ways as well. This has been my experience with Jungian analysis, which works from the belief in the universality of human life and the human mind.

KORNFIELD: There are several avenues to approach this question from In terms of the absolute perspective of Buddhism all problems arise from a mistaken notion of the self, from not being able to penetrate through the illusion of self. But much of what I've heard tonight is from a much more relative level. On that level I feel we need to approach many of these problems more practically. I send quite a few of the people who come to my meditation retreats to therapists who I know are good and also have some spiritual understanding and perspective. At the same time I think there is a flip side of this question. There has been such an interchange between spiritual practice and psychological growth and human potential movements that there is a prevalent notion, at least in the psychological world, that Western psychology can actually get you to the same place as spiritual practice. I think this is really quite a dangerous assumption. From my observation of how psychological techniques work I see that although they can lead to some very useful growth and transformation, they do not develop the penetrating insight that helps one cut through the deeper layers of illusion and hallucinations about individual separateness. They also do not create the space for what we might call a mystical appreciation of the world. They are useful techniques but their limitations have to be explicitly stated or people can get caught in them as a dead end.

RAM DASS: I would like to reinforce what Jack said, concerning psychological systems taking over and preempting spiritual terminologies. By turning them toward worldly ends, they close the door conceptually to a lot of people who could go further spiritually, but would have to go into much deeper practices. Instead they are given labels like "enlightenment," and phrases like "I'm free" and "I've got it." I say "It's not it." It has nothing to do with it. I think we have to deal with these issues sooner or later, that we have to keep some perspective on the gap between these two different ends.

MODERATOR: Ram Dass, what about a character like your own teacher Maharajji. As you have so often described him, he is not particularly sane by any Western model of sanity. It seems the Western psychological notions of adjustment and sanity are very secular definitions. This goes to the heart of that equivalence that psychological movements make with spiritual movements. Perhaps their objectives are fundamentally different?

RAM DASS: Very much so. I don't think spiritual movements care that deeply about psychological health. They see it as a passing show. Most of the high spiritual beings are at least neurotic if not completely off their rockers. You go see the teacher Munindra in India and he is wearing funny-looking earflaps, and Maharajji's pants were always falling off. Their whole thing is absolutely weird from a psychological point of view. Read about the recent saint Ramana Maharshi, who sat around with ants walking all over him. Imagine a psychiatrist watching that. It seems to me that from the spiritual point of view "nuts" just means to be holding on to something. It is the clinging mind that is crazy. That's very different from the Western notion of sanity.

MIYUKI: Anthropologists these days are extremely aware that how we judge others really depends on one's cultural context. If you become a *sanyasin*, a wandering mendicant, in India, you are respected. Here you will have trouble with the authorities. In Japan too, the attitude toward people in mental hospitals is somewhat different from your attitude.

There mental illness is understood in terms of *ki*, the energy flow in a person. We say original *ki*, the *ki*, of *aikido*. *Ki* is both the macro and micro cosmic force, undifferentiated. It can be spiritual, can be mental, and can be physical. Mental illness is simply a coagulation of *ki*. So when I judge others I step back and say, "Ah, my *ki* and his *ki* do not come to be united in the place where I would like to be with him," that's all.

MODERATOR: Perhaps the participants are sidestepping the more difficult issue by pointing to the very easy black-and-white contrast of sanity and insanity. What about the gray area of neurosis where most of us spend our time? In other words, is it possible to do zazen if you're fixated on mother?

KORNFIELD: I don't really know what my mother would say about that. I see, as Ram Dass has stated so clearly, limitations in this spiritual practice. Many people are getting caught up in their own neurosis. However, in the course of spiritual practice, I have also observed what we would call psychological transformations, in which people become increasingly aware of different motivation patterns, different kinds of attachment, and different images of relationships in the most profound ways. Through practice, and through a sitting meditation discipline which is most central in Buddhism, I have observed many people going through the kind of growth that would also happen in psychotherapy. It's a by-product, but it's a usable by-product.

RAM DASS: Perhaps problems that would be psychologically maladaptive might eventually become irrelevant for a person who is on a spiritual path. A lot of the spiritual people I know have what might be diagnosed as maladapted neurotic patterns from a worldly point of view, but they don't seem to care much because that really isn't what their life is about.

I really think that there are even certain self-selecting, neurotic patterns which lead people to begin spiritual journeys. I don't think it's a random thing. I don't think this group here tonight is a healthy normal population. If we give them a standard psychological test the results are going to be off the edge. That's fine from my point of view, because normal patterns really aren't interesting anymore.

In the late 1960s a lot of what passed for the spiritual movement was really psychological in nature. As a result, when the psychological needs of the whole group of participants changed, a lot of these people fell away and are now good solid Middle Americans. They're nice people, and they have great scrapbooks and great memories. The percentage of people who are actually drawn by spiritual pulls is very small. I am quite sure those few serious practitioners have very neurotic patterns from a cultural point of view.

MIYUKI: This brings to my mind the Jungian distinction between the psychological problems of middle age and youth. In their youth most people are busy establishing their egos and attaching themselves to the external environment: getting through their education, developing a profession, marrying and having a family. The problems of this period of life differ from the middle-age crisis, which is a very different kind of neurosis. The middle-age crisis is more centered on the discovery of the unsatisfactory nature of human life, the discovery of human mortality. The Jungian expression of this is not so different from the Buddha's first Noble Truth, that all is suffering. The deep questions of the meaning of life are different from ordinary neurosis. In such a case a neurotic problem is really spiritual. Often Jung's patients expressed their gratitude for having such neuroses, because these neurotic symptoms were not necessarily symptoms of disease but rather manifestations of a functional person who now questions seriously the nature of life. It is clear that differing types of neurosis can produce very different effects. The mother complex should be differentiated from the neurosis that concerns the suffering over the meaning of life.

KORNFIELD: I appreciate your clarification of the modes of neurosis. I think it is important in the West to establish models which give people the faith and the inspiration to work with inner turmoil, beyond the point of becoming satisfied that they're comfortable. There really are two levels of practice. On one level of practice in any spiritual tradition people are working in order to become comfortable. That is, in a sense, the psychological level of practice, which aims, for example, at establishing a harmonious community where you can chant before meals, and keep enough precepts of conduct to allow people to live together without exploitation. That has become the goal, to a large degree, for the spiritual or counterculture or whatever-it's-labeled movement in this country. There is another level of practice, however, which is really inspired by the greatest teachers and saints. It comes from the most profound kind of archetypal possibility for human development. This level of practice requires a very deep transformation, a death of who you think you are. It requires working with all the things that bring comfort and then being willing to go far beyond that comfort through realms of different kinds of neurosis, through despair, through crisis. I think it is a very important thing that in the West that kind of possibility for transformation be kept alive and not become confused with other goals.

MODERATOR: Professor Miyuki, at one point in our discussion the other night you came out with the statement "It can be dangerous for Westerners to do meditation." As I interpreted that, you were saying that a Westerner, trying to sit down and do zazen, has something very different in his mind than someone from Japan. Could you perhaps elaborate on that?

MIYUKI: What I tried to say was that the individual ego structure is different in the East and West. I think the religious man in the West faces God at a distance all the time. You are ready to be judged by God. You take it quite personally. You are an individual, here. You can even sue your parents in America. In Japan, if you sue your parents you're really nuts. Before your parents will be judged, you'll be judged as crazy. In Japan your ego is very much tied to the family ego, and there is a strong identification with the collective ego. They are conscious of a greater social and spiritual totality. The Western ego, however, is very clearly separated and independent from the unconscious, as Jung would describe it. Whatever you do not see in the West doesn't exist. That is very clear for you. But for the Japanese it is not so clearly separated. The Japanese ego manifests in terms of operating harmoniously with the collective conscious and unconscious. Thus family structure is very important. So is the community structure.

RAM DASS: And how does this relate to the dangers of meditation?

MIYUKI: When you meditate, and this is also, in part, Jung's interpretation, you take all the ego energy and are drawn to some inner place which then stimulates the unconscious. In other words, states beyond the ego suddenly arise. If the individual ego is the only form of reality you have experienced prior to that, you could be psychologically disturbed. The ego has to continue to function, and if you suddenly absorb the energy that has been invested in the ego, and then activate the content within, you really could go crazy. But if the ego has always been close to a communal ego then there is less danger when these deeper states arise.

KORNFIELD: I'd like to put in a plug for my company in response to warnings by Dr. Miyuki about the dangers of meditation. I think what you say is true; that the ability to function in the world must be maintained in practice. Otherwise there has to be some institution, as there is in India, which can cover for people during the time they go through a transformation that does not allow them to be functional. But I do not think this dysfunction should be viewed as an automatic stage of practice. In all the Buddhist traditions, the mental training emphasizes first and foremost the factor of mindfulness that arises in relation to mental feelings, and experiences, without getting caught by them. As that mindfulness grows, it also has the function of deepening *samadhi*, which is not just the *samadhi* of withdrawal, but the *samadhi* of being very present in daily life moment to moment. If mindfulness or awareness is cultivated first, then the mind becomes prepared in a natural way for more difficult exposure to the unconscious, as well as the extremes in feelings and emotion that will inevitably come up in practice. In a sense, the balanced ego is strengthened to deal with those phenomena and still remain functional.

I'd like to comment on the importance we are giving to different ego structures that have developed in Japanese or American or Indian cultures. The real basic question in spiritual practice is not the particular structure of the individual or even collective ego, which is actually all in the realm of content of mind. Spiritual practice really focuses on the nature of the activity of mind. The work in practice is to come to a balance of two perspectives. One is a mystical or absolute perspective which transcends all kinds of ego structure, which sees through the self as any kind of solid entity and transcends any sense of duality. At the same time that must be balanced with an ongoing ability to function in the world. I see the spiritual practice of Buddhism transcending the cultural differences of Buddhism. I do agree, however, that it is essential to either remain functional within the world or find a protected environment, otherwise practice can be dangerous.

RAM DASS: I disagree with Jack. I think Professor Miyuki has raised an extremely profound point in differentiating between the types of ego structures. The narrow ego, identified with a very separate individual, immediately creates that kind of cliff-hanging quality that results when most Westerners start to do any kind of intensive meditation practice. I see a decrease in disciplined, intensive practice in the West these days because our ego structure cannot handle the more severe kinds of discipline or the deeper level of commitment needed. There are very few people prepared to delve deeply into this kind of practice. For one thing Westerners do not have the depth of resource that other cultures have provided their spiritual seekers. In India the practitioners are coming out of a culture steeped in the understanding of rebirth and karma. There is a social system to support their practice. All of this is so deep in their beings from the beginning that they have a greater understanding of what spiritual practice requires than we do.

The Western ego has thus far reasserted itself and said, "We will take from the spiritual movement the psychological systems which keep the ego very strong, systems that encourage us to say we're enlightened." In a way the West has done one of the worst things it could do to the Eastern traditions, though I do see people who are aware of this problem. They are struggling deeply and delving into their ego attachments. There are people who are willing to stay on that edge, and have gone way beyond their cultural wagon train. Ultimately the traditions imported from Asia will find only a few to carry them forward. If we are talking about mass phenomena of change, or larger numbers awakening, we are going to have to find new metaphors that are more suitable for our culture.

MODERATOR: Psychology has misappropriated a lot of spiritual terminology for its own sake. What about the other side of it? Do you think there are problems in translating and discussing Eastern spiritual practices using psychological jargon?

KORNFIELD: There can be an equivalent danger in that using the language and concepts from psychology to interpret or explain spiritual experience may cause their diminution by leaving out some vast areas of experience that are simply not covered by psychological terminology. However, I also see it as useful because it is a fact that psychology is a big part of our country's religion right now. Psychology and science both. I don't see that we have to abandon them, but just exercise a lot of care in our use of both psychological terms and the language of scientific technology, which is another part of our current religious worldview.

MIYUKI: In a way I am doing that kind of thing in my work. I think this is the period of transmission of Buddhism and you should appeal to some of the existing concepts in the culture. That was clearly done by the Chinese, who introduced Buddhism from India. They used the language of Taoism and then several hundred years later they cleaned it up.

KORNFIELD: I'd like to say one more thing. I like to think of the transmission of Buddhism in a very long-range perspective. It took a long time for Buddhism to go from India to China and I wonder if there were not similar problems in China when Buddhism arrived; whether it was co-opted or whether Buddhism was initially misinterpreted and lessened in its value by people who didn't take it to its fullest depth. I don't know the answer to that, but I have a certain faith that it will evolve in its own form in this country. There are a few people in each spiritual movement who will come to a deep enough understanding of Buddhist Dharma to keep it alive even after their teachers die. And that transmission, even among a very few at first, is enough, to create the possibility that the Dharma will eventually blossom in its own way in this culture.

Part II

CONTEMPORARY RESEARCHES

❏

MEDITATION

❏

BUDDHIST PSYCHOLOGY

CONTRIBUTIONS TO WESTERN PSYCHOLOGICAL THEORY

Jack Engler

❑

As a Western psychologist, I work primarily with patients suffering from psychotic and character disorders who repetitively oscillate between opposite and opposed ego states. I work very hard to help these individuals develop a sense of self: a sense of ongoingness in existence—a sense of stability, predictability, and personal continuity across time, place, and states of consciousness.

Yet these characteristics are precisely what Buddhist psychology diagnoses as the root of our deepest suffering: the attempt to hold on to something enduring in a universe of constant change. So when I switch hats

An earlier version of this essay was presented to the Conference on Inner Science with His Holiness The Dalai Lama at Amherst College in October 1984 in response to the question "What does Buddhist Inner Science of Mind have to contribute to Western psychological theory?". The conference was sponsored in part by a grant from the Institute of Noetic Sciences, and this talk was reprinted in their Spring 1985 *Newsletter*. The colloquium was the first between the Dalai Lama and Western scholars in the United States. A much fuller treatment of this topic can be found in Chapter 1 of *Transformations of Consciousness: Clinical and Contemplative Perspectives on Development*, which Jack Engler co-authored with Ken Wilbur and Dan Brown. Boston: New Science Library, Shambhala, 1986.

and go to the meditation center to teach *vipassana* or insight meditation, I do just the opposite from my clinical practice: I help students come to the realization that this enduring "self," which, from another point of view, I'm helping patients to develop, does not exist.

Buddhist psychology classifies and groups mental functions in the minute and detailed way it does precisely for the practical purpose of showing that there is nothing enduring and abiding, nothing we can call a "self" or soul or spirit in the sense of a self-existent, independent entity. Meditation is a practice which, by allowing one to observe somatic and mental experience, helps one move toward this realization.

So it might seem at first that Western and Buddhist psychologies are diametrically opposed, or at least start from very different assumptions.

Nevertheless, I think that's not the case. The two approaches can be integrated by recognizing that there are stages in the development of the self, or, more accurately, in the images or representations of self. It seems that our Western traditions have mapped out the early stages of that development and the Buddhist traditions have mapped out later or more advanced stages in which "decentering" from the egocentrism of early development culminates in selfless altruism. And neither tradition knows much about the other. They're talking about the same continuum of development, but about different segments of it.

THE SELF: ENDURING ENTITY OR MENTAL CONSTRUCT?

We can discern parallels between the two traditions by examining the theory of self-representation. Early in our lives, according to psychoanalytic theory, we begin developing certain schemas of who we are through our relations with others. Individual memory traces from these early experiences are gradually consolidated in more general, supraordinate schemas of who "I" am, who others are, and what my relations with them are like. The theory is somewhat detailed, but the point is that the self, as it has been understood from the perspective of newer developments in ego, object relations and self-psychology, is now seen to be exactly what Buddhist psychology and practice have always said it was: namely, a mental representation or construct, not an entity.

Moreover, it is constructed anew in each moment of experience. Each representation of myself, and each representation of an object in this world of self and objects, is actively constructed in our minds in an ongoing process, moment by moment. Psychodynamic theory understands this now, but it hasn't drawn the proper therapeutic implications.

Perhaps this is because the development of a sense of self is so important in early stages and is a central focus in much of therapy and clinical work. In fact, it would probably seem pointless to a Western psychologist to observe this moment-to-moment construction of self and object representations, even if he thought it were possible, which he would not. What good could come of it? Wouldn't it just produce psychic fragmentation? Mightn't it actually risk a kind of psychotic regression, back to those developmentally primitive states in which experiences remain disconnected and do not cohere?

But from the Buddhist point of view, experiencing the moment-to-moment construction and disappearance of self and object representations is exactly what meditation is all about. It takes an enormous amount of training to observe the process. But when you do observe it, the familiar universe of stable and enduring objects is effectively turned on its head. You are catapulted into a world of constant and total change, where nothing endures in either the inner or the outer universe for more than a few milliseconds. This is the universe that physicists and psychophysicists have now confirmed is the fundamental nature of "reality." Moreover, the capacity to observe and absorb this impartially does not lead to psychotic regression, but makes it possible to attain new levels of psychological integration and well-being.

The Pleasure Principle: An Innately Conditioned Response?

Classical psychoanalytic psychology tells us that the most primitive and enduring law of psychic life is the pleasure principle: the desire to maximize pleasure and minimize pain. In this view we are ineluctably driven by our reactions to pleasure and pain. There is an immediate and overriding action tendency to approach the pleasant and avoid the unpleasant. We in the West conceptualize this action sequence as being innate, automatic, spontaneous, and natural—an autonomic nervous system response beyond voluntary control.

Conversely, trained meditative observation reveals that this sequence is a volitional activity and in principle subject to self-regulation. A focal point in Buddhist training, in fact, is *unlinking* the experience of pleasure

and pain, satisfaction and discomfort, liking and not liking, from the tendency to react to these central-state affects through developing the capacity, moment by moment, to observe and experience all moments
impartially, with equanimity. One learns that the pleasant and the unpleasant can be experienced without preference or discrimination, and
without the impulsive need to cling to what one likes or push away what
one doesn't. In effect, meditation training returns what is discovered to be
a *conditioned* response to *voluntary* control. As a result, one can therefore
delay—and subsequently choose—one's response.

One of the major breakthroughs in Western psychodynamic psychology
in the last decade or two has been the emergence of an understanding of
affect that in many ways parallels the traditional Buddhist understanding.
Recent developments in psychoanalytic thinking, emotional theory, and
information-processing research have converged in identifying *two basic
components to affect*:

1. An initial moment of "hedonic appraisal" in which whatever is experienced is
   "appraised" according to its hedonic value as pleasurable, unpleasurable, or neutral;
   and
2. An immediately succeeding "felt action tendency" or "hedonic impulse" in which
   we react with approach or avoidance, depending on whether the experience is
   pleasurable or unpleasurable, or do not react if the feeling tone is neutral.

This primary sequence takes place in every moment of experience because *every* experience, no matter how fleeting, carries a hedonic or feeling
tone for us which we *always* register. Reactivity to it is the root of all
impulse and psychic drive states, enduring motivational dispositions, and
emotions such as joy, excitement, aesthetic pleasure, anger, disappointment, or surprise.

The problem that psychodynamic theory confronts at this point is fascinating. To psychodynamically oriented theorists, there does not seem to
be any way of disentangling or delinking that first moment in which we
experience something as pleasurable or unpleasurable from the impulse to
react with approach or avoidance that immediately follows. Even in this
new conceptualization of affect, both moments are seen as inseparable: the
experience of pleasure always leads to approach behaviors—wanting, de-
siring, grasping, clinging, prolonging; and the experience of not liking (or
pain) to avoidance—not wanting, rejecting, condemning, pushing away,

avoiding, denying, warding off. In other words, there is *always* reactivity in the mind.

That is actually an assumption, and an interesting one. Buddhist psychology makes just the opposite assumption. His Holiness The Dalai Lama identified those same two moments of affect as the separate mental functions of "feeling" and "desire."* This exactly accords with the Western view, except that Buddhist practice shows the link between these functions to be subject to self-regulation. But, in principle, there is no reason in psychodynamic theory why either pleasure or pain needs to lead innately and inevitably to reactive behavior.

There are other implications for psychodynamic thinking as well. There is also no reason any longer why, in principle, higher-order drive states such as libido or aggression need to be considered innate in personality, as Freud and psychoanalysts since him have assumed. Buddhist psychology maintains that the potential for these two drive states is extinguished at a certain stage of practice. Western clinicians have arrived at a similar theoretical position, but they have not yet seen the therapeutic implications of this new way of thinking about affect and higher-order emotional states.

REALITY TESTING AND PSYCHOLOGICAL DEVELOPMENT

What accounts for the operation of the pleasure principle fundamental to both psychologies?

According to Buddhist analysis, the cause is faulty reality testing. Ordinary reality testing is not only faulty, it is based on a particular type of misperception which inverts the actual order of things. We misperceive what is impermanent as permanent, what is incapable of affording lasting satisfaction as satisfying, and what is without enduring substance or selfhood as being substantial or an independently existing self. In other words, owing to faulty reality testing, we ordinarily perceive ourselves and objects to be just the opposite of the way they really are (*vipallasa* = "inverted view"). In this sense the critical diagnostic question in Buddhist meditation practice is the same as in Western clinical practice: is reality testing intact?

---

* "Feeling" (*vedana*) in Buddhist psychology designates the experience of hedonic appraisal, not the higher-order emotions which the term designates in Western psychology. "Desire" in Buddhist psychology, which is seen as the origin of suffering, designates precisely "hedonic impulse," the deeply conditioned tendency to react to pleasure/pain with approach/avoidance or clinging/condemning.

In our clinics this criterion differentiates normality and neurosis from psychosis. But in the meditative perspective, normal development itself is still deficient in reality testing. This is the reason Buddhist psychology can describe the normal state of ego functioning as "deranged" (*unmattaka*). What meditation does is reality-test inaccurate perceptions and show that things are just the opposite of the way we ordinarily experience them.

Buddhist diagnosis, in fact, distinguishes between three kinds of suffering, each springing from a different level of object relations experience. "Ordinary suffering" (*dukkha-dukkha*) corresponds to neurotic conflict between impulse and prohibition. In cases where ego development is less advanced, there is a kind of suffering (*dukkha-parinama*) which corresponds to the more severe character disorders and functional psychoses, in which core problems involve disturbances in the sense of self-continuity, fluctuating drives and affects, contradictory and dissociated ego states, lack of a stable self-structure, and lack of constancy in relations with the object world.

The third type of suffering, the suffering inherent in every conditioned state of mind (*dukkha-sankhara*), represents a category of psychopathology foreign to Western clinical theory. Such suffering is pervasive at all levels of personality organization, the normal as well as the abnormal: self- and object-seeking themselves are experienced as sources of suffering. Contradictory as that may sound in terms of current Western developmental theory, *the very attempt to constellate a self and objects that will have constancy and continuity across time, space, and psychological states emerges as the therapeutic problem* because of the inherently impermanent, mutable nature of reality and experience, and because of the nature of the self and its objects as mere momentary constructions. This means that, from a Western perspective, the two major goals of self and object relations development—the achievement of a self experienced as constant and continuous, an enduring recipient of experience and source of initiative; and the achievement of object constancy—from a Buddhist perspective, still represent fixation and arrest. Normal functioning and perception is a state of arrested development in this view.

It is this third level of psychopathology that Buddhist psychology and practice is designed to address. This has not been clearly understood either by Buddhists or by Western psychologists who tend to see the two traditions as either complementary or competing, but in either case without a clear awareness of the profound differences in their respective methods, aims and outcomes, and the problems they seek to remedy.

INTERVENTION

Buddhist insight meditation, like psychodynamic therapy, is an intervention designed to set ego and object relations development in motion from a point of relative arrest. As in psychodynamic therapy, the process of separation from limiting self-object ties is brought about by a controlled and partial return to more elemental ways of perceiving, conceptualizing, and feeling.

In psychoanalysis, this "regression" takes place in an interpersonal relationship and involves the transference of earlier behaviors to the psychotherapist so that they can be understood and worked through. The "return" that occurs in the classical stages of Buddhist insight meditation, however, does not take the form of regression. It is not a reliving or reexperiencing of earlier stages of development. Rather it is a controlled *"retracing" of the stages in the representational process by which self and objects are constructed* as it occurs in each moment. Insight meditation literally *reverses the way the world appears*, allowing the individual to gain control over each stage of his or her experience and construction of "reality."

TOWARD A FULL SPECTRUM OF HUMAN DEVELOPMENT

To sum up, what this amounts to in developmental terms is that you have to be somebody before you can be nobody. The farther reaches of meditation practice require a strong ego in the psychoanalytic sense of the capacity to assimilate, organize, and integrate experience, and a relatively well-integrated sense of self. With more compromised ego functions, or a self-structure that lacks sufficient inner coherence, continuity across time and states of consciousness, or a sense of its own fundamental goodness and worth, intensely practiced insight meditation based on moment-to-moment observation of mind/body experience can run certain risks: increasing anxiety at a minimum; producing fragmentation at worst.

So the issue in personal development, as I've come to understand it, is not self or no-self, but self *and* no-self. Both a sense of self and insight into the self's ultimate illusoriness are necessary to sanity and complete psychological well-being. But they must be attained in a phase-appropriate developmental sequence at different stages of self and object relations development.

What I think is needed is a conception of psychological development that in-

cludes the full developmental spectrum. From a clinical point of view, Buddhist psychology lacks this. It has little to say about the earlier stages of personality organization and the types of suffering that result from a failure to negotiate them. Western psychology in general and psychoanalytic theory in particular do not address the other end of the developmental spectrum. Their definitions of maturity and health reach no further than psychosocial identity, object constancy, mutuality in object relations, and more adaptive, less conflicted rearrangements of impulse and defense.

My hope is that as Buddhist, Western, and other ethnotherapeutic systems of practice begin to interact with each other, a more integrated, representative model of the spectrum of development, its vulnerabilities, and the therapeutic interventions necessary to repair them, may result. From Freud's psychosexual stage theory to Erikson's life cycle theory to Mahler's version of object relations theory, this has been the thrust and aspiration of psychodynamic thought. Part of this thrust has been implicit but not articulated in Buddhist thought. The one tradition has emphasized the importance of becoming somebody, in a psychosocial sense, so that we may love and work; the other, the importance of becoming nobody, in a spiritual sense, so that we may end the suffering of "clinging to self." As I have come to understand it as a psychologist and practitioner in both traditions, both a sense of self and a sense of no-self seem to be necessary to realize that state of optimal psychological well-being which Freud once described as an "ideal fiction" and the Buddha long before him had already described as "the end of suffering" (*Cula-Malunkya-sutta*, M. 63) and "the one thing" he taught.

BEYOND THE OCEANIC FEELING

PSYCHOANALYTIC STUDY OF

BUDDHIST MEDITATION

Mark Epstein

❑

Although Buddhism has consistently been identified as the most psychological of the world's religions (Schnier, 1957), psychoanalytic investigation of the meditative states that characterize the actual practice of
Buddhism has been extremely limited (Shafii, 1973). Freud's personal investigations into religious experiences did not include extensive experience
with those of the Orient (Jones, 1957, p. 351); to the extent that they
did, they were influenced almost exclusively by his thirteen-year correspondence with the French poet and author Romain Rolland, a student of
the Hindu teachers Vivekananda and Ramakrishna. This correspondence,

Versions of this essay were presented at the First Annual Conference on Buddhism and
Psychotherapy, New York, October 16–18, 1987 and the Fourth Annual Conference of the
Society for the Exploration of Psychotherapy Integration, Cambridge, Mass., April 21–24,
1988. It later appeared in *The International Review of Psychoanalysis*, vol. 17, Part 2, 1990,
and is reprinted here by permission of the author, in conjunction with the editors of *The
International Review of Psychoanalysis*.

which has been rather exhaustively reexamined in recent years (Hanly & Masson, 1976; Masson & Masson, 1978; Masson, 1980; Werman, 1977, 1986; Harrison, 1966, 1979), indicates that Rolland was interested in having Freud examine the meditative experience from a psychoanalytic perspective and that Freud was excited, but perhaps somewhat ambivalent, about such an undertaking (Harrison, 1979). "I shall now try with your guidance," Freud wrote in 1930, "to penetrate into the Indian jungle from which until now an uncertain blending of Hellenic love of proportion, Jewish sobriety, and philistine timidity have kept me away. I really ought to have tackled it earlier, for the plants of this soil shouldn't be alien to me; I have dug to certain depths for their roots. But it isn't easy to pass beyond the limits of one's nature" (E. L. Freud, 1960).

Rolland's descriptions of Hindu meditation inspired Freud to offer his well-known analysis of the "oceanic feeling" as a "limitless" and "un-bounded" ego-feeling of "oneness with the universe" that seeks the "restoration of limitless narcissism" and the "resurrection of infantile help-lessness" (Freud, 1930). This was Freud's only attempt at explaining med-itation practice, Hindu or Buddhist, and, while it does capture some truth about techniques that involve fusion with meditation objects, it takes no account of the investigative or analytical practices most distinctive of Bud-dhism. What is remarkable, however, is that throughout the history of psychoanalysis, both prior to and subsequent to Freud's formulation, med-itation has always been viewed in much the same manner as Freud de-scribed. The equation of meditation with preverbal, symbiotic union or regressive oneness with the mother (Fingarette, 1958; Shafii, 1973; Horton, 1974; Ross, 1975) has gone virtually unchallenged within the psychoana-lytic community. The most recent qualifications of this model have focused only on whether these experiences can be interpreted as adult adaptive ones, rather than purely regressive or defensive flights from reality (Horton, 1973, 1974, 1984; Meissner, 1984; Werman, 1986). This limited view stems not from an unwillingness to apply psychoanalytic investigation to the range of meditative states but from a basic unfamiliarity with what Buddhist meditation, at least, is actually about.

Buddhist meditation actually involves two distinct attentional strategies (Goleman, 1977), the first being concentration on a single object and the second, moment-to-moment awareness of changing objects of perception. The concentration practices stress the ability of the mind to remain steady on a single object, such as the breath or a sound, for extended periods. These practices, which involve restriction of attention, are preliminary, but may be developed to the point of trance or absorption. They are always associated with relaxation and pleasurable feeling states, are the basis for the hypometabolic psychophysiological state termed the "relaxation response" (Benson, 1975), and lead directly to what Freud described as the oceanic feeling. They are also related to hypnotic induction (Davidson & Goleman, 1977; Benson et al., 1981), and, as such, represent an attentional strategy with which Freud was actually quite familiar.

The *distinctive* attentional strategy of Buddhism, however, is that of mindfulness, of moment-to-moment attention to thoughts, feelings, images, or sensations as they arise and pass away within the field of awareness. Defined as "the clear and single-minded awareness of what actually happens *to* us and *in* us, at the successive moments of perception" (Nyanaponika, 1962), mindfulness encourages insight into the endlessly fluctuating nature of the mind-body process. The concentration practices are used to provide stability, but it is mindfulness that is unique to Buddhist meditation and it is mindfulness that precipitates psychological insights into the nature of the self that have not yet been explored from a psychodynamic perspective.

For, with only a handful of important exceptions, Buddhist sources were never distinguished from other mystical approaches by psychoanalysts attempting to understand such states. Focusing on the concentration practices only, analysts from Ferenczi, Jones, Alexander, and Freud to Lewin, Grunberger, and Chasseguet-Smirgel have repeatedly linked mystical states with prenatal or immediately postnatal harmony, union, merging, or symbiosis. Freud's description of the oceanic feeling is probably the most well-known of these formulations, but the insistence on such a direct clinical correlation was as strong before Freud's declaration as it has been ever since.

The theoretical groundwork for such comparisons was laid by Ferenczi (1913) in his "stages in the development of the sense of reality," in which he outlined the various grandiose, omnipotent, and merged subject-object feelings of the infant. In a paper entitled "The God complex," Jones (1913) equated "colossal narcissism" (p. 247) with what he termed an "unconscious fantasy" of complete identification with God. Jones (1923) was also the first to identify mystical ecstasy with the merger of ego and ego-ideal, describing a "regression to the most primitive and uncritical form of narcissism" (p. 283) in a variety of Christian, Hindu, and Buddhist mystical ecstasies. Schroeder (1922) clearly equated aspects of "prenatal union" (p. 447) with descriptions of both Eastern and Western mystical experiences, ascribing feelings of oneness, infinity, nothingness, omnipotence, and merging with the universe to predispositions of the prenatal psyche.

Alexander (1931), in a paper read in 1922 at the last Psychoanalytical Congress that Freud was to attend, read an analysis of a newly translated Buddhist description of advanced meditative states. But he chose a passage that emphasized concentration, and only concentration, practices. " 'In this condition the monk is like a pool . . .,' " he quoted, " 'filling and saturating himself completely from all sides with the joy and pleasurable feelings born out of the depths of absorption; so that not the smallest particle remains unsaturated . . . ' No analyst can more fittingly describe the condition of narcissism than is done in this text . . . It is the description of a condition which we have only theoretically reconstructed and named 'narcissism' " (pp. 133–34). Yet Alexander was also the first to recognize several essential parallels between Buddhist psychology and psychoanalysis that also intrigued Karen Horney and Erich Fromm (1960) a generation later. Alexander referred to the texts he studied as "psychological documents rather than . . . products of metaphysical speculation" (p. 134) and he called meditation a "psychotechnique" (p. 138) that enabled voluntary access to regressive states. He was clearly impressed with the sophistication of the texts that he uncovered, recognizing the essential psychological nature of their content. "I will not again point out the striking similarity between the analytical method and the doctrine of Buddha. The overcoming of affective resistance and of narcissism, so that one is able to recollect instead of repeat . . . this is the doctrine common to Freud and Buddha. Can we regard as accidental this remarkable repetition in the history of both spiritual creations whose founders both at first attempted to use hypnosis, which they found at hand as prescientific practice? And was it also accidental that both then arrived at the conclusion that the chief and really difficult task is to establish the connection with consciousness?" (p. 144).

The only analyst to acknowledge the importance of the mindfulness practices per se was a man named Joseph Thompson, who, in 1924, published an article entitled "Psychology in Primitive Buddhism" under the pseudonym Joe Tom Sun of Guam. He not only pointed out the similarities between meditation and free association but also noted the presence of transference phenomena in Buddhist theory and began to describe Buddhist notions of the structure of the self as seen in advanced stages of mindfulness and insight practice. There was no further development of this investigation, however. Ongoing interest in meditation focused once again exclusively on the concentration practices.

Federn (1928) amplified the notion of the primary narcissism of the infantile state, describing a primary ego-feeling, present from birth, that exists in an undifferentiated state and is experienced as encompassing the world, which he called the "ego-cosmic ego" (p. 307). He asserted that, in the adult state, this primary narcissism could be experienced "only in states of devotion and rapture, the highest degrees of which we call ecstasy and mystical union" (p. 293).

Thus, by the time of Freud's (1930) evocation of the oceanic feeling, the identification of mystical experience with concentration practices and with the narcissism of infancy was well established. Within the psychoanalytic literature, only Thompson's article hinted at any further possibilities. Subsequent literature has basically reinforced the premises so lucidly put forth in the early decades of this century. Marie Bonaparte (1940) described mystical ecstasy as re-creating the "paradise of our childhood or of our dreams" (p. 437) while Lewin (1950) analyzed the ecstatic experiences of manic patients as well as those of Christian mystics described by William James and concluded that "the ecstatic mood repeats or relives the nonverbal or never-verbalized experiences of union at the breast" (p. 149). Lewin also mistakenly equated the Buddhist goal of Nirvana with the Christian goal of heaven, betraying the same lack of familiarity with the mindfulness practices that had afflicted his predecessors. In clarifying Freud's notion of the ego ideal as the embodiment of primary narcissism with which an individual seeks in adult life to merge, Chasseguet-Smirgel (1975) also pays exclusive attention to mystical practices that promote a state of union, the equivalent of what she terms the "mother-prior-to-the-loss of fusion" (p. 217).

These traditional interpretations of meditation as satisfying the yearning to merge with an internalized image of a lost state of perfection are actually quite apt in regard to the concentration practices. Such techniques do involve limitation of attention to a single object and are always associated with feelings of delight that range from contentment or harmony to bliss, joy or rapture. In addition, they are used to provide a stabilizing force in the mind of the meditator and they are invariably associated with a sense of ontological security. The feeling state of these practices is indeed "oceanic" and the dynamic state is best expressed as a gratification of the desire to merge ego and ego ideal.

Yet the mindfulness practices are quite distinct from those of concentration and advanced stages of such practices lead to insights and states of consciousness that have nothing to do with the tranquillity of a mind that swells in absorption. Like free association and evenly suspended attention

(Epstein, 1988a), the mindfulness practices foster a therapeutic split in the ego, encouraging the ego to take itself as object, strengthening the observing ego's capacity to attend to moment-to-moment changes (Engler, 1983). Functionally (Stolorow, 1975; Rothstein, 1981), the development of mindfulness corresponds to a development of the synthetic capacity of the ego (Epstein, 1988b), that which maintains cohesion "on more and more complex levels of differentiation and objectivation of reality" (Loewald, 1951, p. 14). This synthetic function of mindfulness recalls Janet's concept of "pre-sentification," the capacity to attend to "the formation of the mind in the present moment" that allows reality to be grasped "to the maximum" (Ellenberger, 1970, p. 376). Such a capacity allows the ego to integrate and synthesize "what seems to move further and further away from it and fall into more and more unconnected parts" (Loewald, 1951, p. 14), precisely the kinds of experiences that are detailed in traditional Buddhist psychological texts on the progress of mindfulness.

Rather than promoting the merging of ego boundaries that characterizes the concentration practices, the mindfulness practices prompt development *within* the ego itself, encouraging a thorough and relentless scrutiny of each moment of consciousness that ultimately permits the impermanent nature of all experience to be discerned with finer and finer levels of perception.

Preliminary practices of mindfulness are uncovering, much as a beginning psychoanalysis is; unconscious material presents itself and the primary task of the meditator is an "adaptation to the flow of internal experience" (Brown & Engler, 1986, p. 195) that has been shown in Rorschach studies of somewhat more experienced meditators to produce records with "increased productivity and richness of elaborative associations" (p. 180). However, as meditation progresses, there is a fundamental shift from emphasis on intrapsychic content to an exclusive focus on intrapsychic process. Thus, when thoughts occur, only the generic process of thinking is attended to rather than the specific content of thought; emphasis is on the thought's insubstantiality, its transience, and the manner in which the meditator identifies with being the "thinker."

Thus, Buddhist meditation is not some Eastern variant of psychoanalysis; while its methods bear some profound similarities, there is an inexorable shift away from unconscious content once sufficient attentional skills are developed. Whereas pursuit of free association leads to identification of unconscious conflict and of intrapsychic constellations such as the Oedipus, pursuit of mindfulness uncovers unconscious material but "analyzes" it only insofar as "insight" into the transitory nature of thoughts, feelings, and the identifications which form the self-concept can be achieved. Because of the deliberate de-emphasis on content, insights in Buddhist meditation have little to do with drive derivatives or resistances and much more to do with illuminating the actual representational nature of the inner world.

The focus and ultimate target of this form of Buddhist meditation is exclusively the sense of "I" within the meditator. In advanced "insight" practices, attention is repeatedly brought to bear on the "sense of inherent existence" (Hopkins, 1984, p. 141), the belief in an "abiding" personality (Nyanaponika, 1962, p. 212), or the image of an independent, substantial, permanent, "self-sufficient entity" (Gyatso, 1984, p. 163) as it is experienced subjectively. The goal is not rejection or denial of ego, nor is it an undifferentiated merger or a state of union. In contrast, through the power of the synthetic capacity of the ego, developed through the cultivation of mindfulness, the goal is explicitly illumination of what, dynamically, has been termed the "self-representation as agent" (Rothstein, 1981). The goal is not to dispel the sense of I, which remains a necessary and useful concept, but to identify the self-representation as agent as a *representation*; as an image or simulacrum devoid of *inherent* existence.

Grasping the notion of inherent existence is crucial for a correct appreciation of Buddhist meditation. It is conveyed in the psychoanalytic understanding of the self-representation as agent conceiving itself "as existing actively to pursue and ensure its well-being and survival" (p. 440) and is perhaps best described as the "ideal ego," the narcissistic core of the representation as agent. This ideal ego is "the ego in so far as it believes itself to have been vouchsafed in a state of perfection—it refers to a positive state even if this state, in reality, is an illusion. In fact, the ideal ego is a self-image that is distorted by idealization but it may be experienced as more real than the ego itself" (Hanly, 1984, p. 253). It is this tendency to identify with an idealized image of the self, which Lacan (1966, p. 5) has termed the "specular I" (Morris, 1988, p. 199), that constitutes the belief in inherent existence targeted by the Buddhists. The point is to experience the self as it actually is phenomenologically, representationally, rather than as a fixed entity. No longer the "shackled captive" (p. 200) of the ideal ego, the meditator, consistent with modern object relations theory (Jacobson, 1964), realizes the manner in which the self-concept has been constructed out of internalized images of self and other.

"He sees the non-existence of a self of his own. He sees of his own self too that it is not the property of another's self. He sees the non-existence of another's self . . . He sees of another that that other is not the property of his own self . . . So this mere conglomeration of formations is seen . . . as voidness of self or property of a self" (Buddhaghosa, 1976, p. 763).

This is the essence of the Buddhist *anatta* (no-soul, no-self) doctrine, that the self as it usually appears is "falsely conceived" (Hopkins, 1987, p. 56) and lacking in inherent existence. The acknowledged goal of the investigative practices is termed "dispelling the illusion of compactness" (Buddhaghosa, 1976; Engler, 1983), revealing the self as it is convention-ally experienced to be essentially insubstantial. Again, this realization is not to be confused with a loss of self or a dissolution of ego boundaries. "Selflessness is not a case of something that existed in the past becoming non-existent; rather, this sort of 'self' is something that never did exist. What is needed is to identify as non-existent something that always was non-existent . . ." (Gyatso, 1984, p. 40). This realization is experienced as a relief, the Buddhist texts assure us, and it forms the cornerstone of Bud-dhist psychological and philosophical thought.

Thus, it is the ideal ego, rather than the ego ideal, that is the inheritor of primitive narcissism most targeted by the analytical meditations of Bud-dhism. Responsible for subjectively experienced feelings of solidity, per-manence, or immortality that constitute what the Buddhists term "inherent existence," it is the ideal ego that permeates the most deeply rooted images of self. Meditation practices that produce an experience of one-pointedness, of dissolution of ego boundaries and fusion with a primary object, do gratify the desire to unite ego with that which it yearns to become. While rec-ognizing the stabilizing impact of such experiences, traditional Buddhist psychology rejects the sole pursuance of such states. Opting instead for a very different attentional strategy, the practice of mindfulness leads ulti-mately to a confrontation with the most highly cherished images of the self, a confrontation that is much more likely to be terrifying (Epstein, 1986) than oceanic.

While the Buddhist practices lay great emphasis on illuminating the representational process, they make little direct effort to resolve intrapsy-chic conflict. Consistent with the view that the mindfulness practices re-inforce the synthetic function of the ego, Rorschach studies of subjects said to be experienced in Buddhist insight practices show no diminution of internal conflict, but only a marked "non-defensiveness in experiencing such conflicts" (Brown & Engler, 1986, p. 189). Indeed, there is no method of resolving intrapsychic conflict in these practices. What seems to change in experienced meditators is "not so much the amount or nature of conflict but awareness of and reactivity to it" (p. 210). There is ample opportunity, therefore, for such practices to be used defensively (Epstein & Lieff, 1981), for libidinal or aggressive urges to be dismissed as "just thoughts" or "just feelings." For clinicians engaged in psychodynamic work with those also pursuing a meditative practice, this is one vulnerability to remain alert to. There can often be a subtle aversion in this population to such derivatives, which, it can be pointed out, is not really consistent with a non-judgmental meditative outlook but is more likely to be a defensive co-optation of the meditative perspective.

When not used defensively, the insights of Buddhist meditation can complement dynamic work by informing the ongoing experience of the self. While not challenging the usefulness of the conventional notions of I or self, these insights attack the tendency to give such notions *ultimate* reality. In bringing the representational process into direct experience, the Buddhist practices confirm aspects of object relations theory and insist that such theory can be integrated on an experiential level, phenomenologically. Because of the insistence that the "I" that is illuminated was never intrinsically existent in the first place, the relevance of such insights is traditionally communicated through paradox or humor.

"Things are not what they seem," says a typical Zen sutra (Suzuki, 1978). "Nor are they otherwise . . . Deeds exist, but no doer can be found." This emphasis on the lack of a particular, substantial *agent* is the most distinctive aspect of traditional Buddhist psychological thought, but such a conception is not completely outside the realm of psychoanalysis. "Thoughts exist without a thinker," insists Bion (1967, p. 165). "The idea of infinitude is prior to any idea of the finite . . . the human personality is aware of infinity, the 'oceanic feeling.' It becomes aware of limitation, presumably through physical and mental experience of itself and the sense of frustration. A number that is infinite, a sense of infinity, is replaced, say, by a sense of threeness. The sense that an infinite number of objects exists is replaced by a sense that only three objects exist, infinite space becomes finite space. The thoughts which have no thinker acquire or are acquired by a thinker."

The traditional psychoanalytic formulation of the relationship between meditation and primary narcissism is correctly conceived but incomplete and undeveloped. Buddhist meditation seeks not a return to primary narcissism but liberation from the vestiges of that narcissism. Concentration practices do indeed evoke the ego ideal and the oceanic feeling in a manner well described by generations of analytic commentators, but the mindfulness practices, which define the Buddhist approach, seek to dispel the "illusory ontology of the self" (Hanly, 1984) encapsulated within the ideal ego. In so doing, such practices encourage an intuitive understanding of "thoughts which have no thinker," an understanding which must form the cornerstone of any comprehensive psychoanalytic study of Buddhist meditation.

References

Alexander, Franz (1931). "Buddhist Training as an Artificial Catatonia." *Psychoanalytic Review* 18: 129–45.

Benson, Herbert (1975). *The Relaxation Response*. New York: Morrow.

Bion, Wilfred (1967). *Second Thoughts*. New York: Jason Aronson.

Bonaparte, Marie (1940). "Time and the Unconscious." *International Journal of Psychoanalysis* 21: 427–63.

Brown, D., and Jack Engler (1986). "The Stages of Mindfulness Meditation: A Validation Study," In *Transformations of Consciousness*, ed. K. Wilber, Jack Engler, and D. Brown. Boston: New Science Library.

Buddhaghosa, Bhadantacariya (1976). *Visuddhimagga: The Path of Purification*, 2 vols., trans. B. Nyanamoli. Boulder, Colo.: Shambhala.

Chasseguet-Smirgel, Janine (1975). *The Ego Ideal*. New York: W. W. Norton.

Davidson, R. J., and Daniel Golman (1977). "The Role of Attention in Meditation and Hypnosis: A Psychobiological Perspective on Transformations of Consciousness." *Int. J. Clin. Exp. Hypn.* 25:291–308.

Ellenberger, H. F. (1970). *The Discovery of the Unconscious*. London: Allen Lane.

Engler, Jack H. (1983). "Vicissitudes of the Self According to Psychoanalysis and Buddhism: A Spectrum Model of Object Relations Development." *Psychoanalysis and Contemporary Thought* 6: 29–72.

Epstein, Mark (1986). Meditative Transformations of Narcissism." *Journal of Transpersonal Psychology* 18: 143–58.

——— (1988a). "Attention in Analysis." *Psychoanalysis and Contemporary Thought* 11: 171–89.

——— (1988b). "The Deconstruction of the Self: Ego and 'Egolessness' in Buddhist Insight Meditation. *Journal of Transpersonal Psychology* 20: 61–69.

——— and J. Lieff (1981). "Psychiatric Complications of Meditation Practice." *Journal of Transpersonal Psychology* 13: 137–47.

Federn, P. (1928). "The Ego as Subject and Object in Narcissism," 283–322, in *Ego Psychology and the Psychoses*. New York: Basic Books, 1952.

Ferenczi, Sándor (1913). "Stages in the Development of the Sense of Reality," 213–39, in *Contributions to Psychoanalysis*. New York: Basic Books, 1950.

Fingarette, Herbert (1958). "Ego and Mystic Selflessness. *Psychoanalytic Review* 45: 5–40.

Freud, E. L., ed. (1960). *Letters of Sigmund Freud*. New York: Basic Books.

Freud, Sigmund (1930). *Civilization and Its Discontents*. Standard Edition, 21.

Fromm, Erich (1960). "Psychoanalysis and Zen Buddhism," in *Zen Buddhism and Psychoanalysis*, ed. D. T. Suzuki, Erich Fromm, and R. De Martino. New York: Harper and Brothers.

Goleman, Daniel (1977). *The Varieties of Meditative Experience*. New York: E. P. Dutton.

Gyatso, Tenzin (1984). *Kindness, Clarity and Insight*. Ithaca: Snow Lion.

Hanly, Charles (1984). "Ego Ideal and Ideal Ego." *International Journal of Psychoanalysis* 65: 253–61.

——— and Jeffrey Masson (1976). "A Critical Examination of the New Narcissism." *International Journal of Psychoanalysis* 57: 49–66.

Harrison, I. B. (1966). "A Reconsideration of Freud's 'A Disturbance of Memory on the Acropolis' in Relation to Identity Disturbance. *Journal of the American Psychoanalytic Association* 14: 518–29.

——— (1979). "On Freud's View of the Infant-Mother Relationship and of the Oceanic Feeling—Some Subjective Influences." *Journal of the American Psychoanalytic Association* 27: 399–422.

Hopkins, Jeffrey (1984). *The Tantric Distinction*. London: Wisdom Publications.

——— (1987). *Emptiness Yoga: The Middle Way Consequence School*. Ithaca: Snow Lion.

Horton, Paul C. (1973). "The Mystical Experience as a Suicide Preventive." *American Journal of Psychiatry* 130: (3)294–96.

——— (1974). "The Mystical Experience: Substance of an Illusion." *Journal of the American Psychoanalytic Association* 22: 364–80.

——— (1984). "Language, Solace, and Transitional Relatedness." *Psychoanal. Study Child*, 39: 167–94.

Jacobson, E. (1964). *The Self and the Object World*. New York: International Universities Press.

Jones, Ernest (1913). "The God Complex," in *Essays in Applied Psychoanalysis II*. London: Hogarth Press, 1951.

——— (1923). "The Nature of Auto-Suggestion," in *Papers on Psychoanalysis*. Boston: Beacon Press, 1948.

——— (1957). *Sigmund Freud: Life and Work, Vol. III, The Last Phase, 1919–1939*. London: Hogarth Press.

Lacan, Jacques (1966). *Écrits: A Selection*. New York: W. W. Norton, 1977.

Lewin, Bertram D. (1950). *The Psychoanalysis of Elation*. New York: W. W. Norton.

Loewald, Hans W. (1951). "Ego and Reality." *International Journal of Psychoanalysis* 32: 10–18.

Masson, Jeffrey (1980). *The Oceanic Feeling: The Origins of Religious Sentiment in Ancient India*. Dordrecht, Holland: D. Reidel.

——— and T. C. Masson (1978). "Buried Memories on the Acropolis: Freud's Relation to Mysticism and Anti-Semitism. *International Journal of Psychoanalysis* 59: 199–208.

Meissner, William W. (1984). *Psychoanalysis and Religious Experience*. New Haven and London: Yale University Press.

Morris, H. (1988) "Reflections on Lacan: His Origins in Descartes and Freud." *Psychoanalytic Quarterly* 57: 186–207.

Nyanaponika, Thera (1962). *The Heart of Buddhist Meditation*. New York: S. Weiser.

Ross, N. (1975). "Affect as Cognition: With Observations on the Meaning of Mystical States." *International Review of Psychoanalysis* 2: 79–93.

Rothstein, A. (1981). "The Ego: An Evolving Construct." *International Journal of Psychoanalysis* 62: 435–45.

Schnier, J. (1957). "The Tibetan Lamaist Ritual: Chod." *International Journal of Psychoanalysis* 38: 402–07.

Schroeder, T. (1922). "Prenatal Psychisms and Mystical Pantheism." *International Journal of Psychoanalysis* 3: 445–66.

Shafii, Mustafa (1973). "Silence in Service of the Ego: Psychoanalytic Study of Meditation." *International Journal of Psychoanalysis* 54: 431–43.

Stolorow, Robert C. (1975). "Toward a Functional Definition of Narcissism." *International Journal of Psychoanalysis* 56: 179–85.

Sun, Joe Tom (1924). "Psychology in Primitive Buddhism." *Psychoanalytic Review* 11: 38–47.

Suzuki, Daisetz T. (1978). *The Lankavatara Sutra*. Boulder, Colo.: Prajna Press.

Werman, David S. (1977). "Sigmund Freud and Romain Rolland." *International Review of Psychoanalysis* 4: 225–42.

——— (1986). "On the Nature of the Oceanic Experience. *Journal of the American Psychoanalytic Association* 34: 123–39.

ZEN MEDITATION AS A WAY
OF INDIVIDUATION AND HEALING

V. Walter Odajnyk

❏

In his groundbreaking essay "Psychoanalysis and Zen Buddhism," Erich Fromm argues that the goals of his humanistic version of Freudian psychoanalysis and Zen are identical. Practitioners of both disciplines seek "insight into one's true nature, the achievement of freedom, happiness and love, liberation of energy" (Suzuki, Fromm, and De Martino, p. 122), and the transcendence of egocentric preoccupations through the attainment of an experience of a "new harmony and a new oneness with the world" (p. 87). In summarizing the psychoanalytic method of achieving these goals, Fromm says that they consist of "de-repression" or "overcoming repressedness" and of "becoming conscious of the unconscious." He noted that the psychoanalytic method requires special training of consciousness, just as special training is required in Zen meditation. But having little or no experience with the actual practice of meditation, Fromm could not actually compare the two. Nor could Fromm comment upon the specific psychological dynamics of the Zen method of training consciousness to overcome repression and unconsciousness.

This essay is previously unpublished.

In his attempt to build a bridge between Western psychology and the Eastern conception of Self-realization, Fromm broadens Freud's theory in a manner that would certainly make the founder of psychoanalysis cringe:

> If one follows the original aim of Freud, that of making the unconscious conscious, to its last consequences, one must free it from the limitations imposed on it by Freud's own instinctual orientation, and by the immediate task of curing symptoms. If one pursues the aim of the full recovery of the unconscious, then this task is not restricted to the instincts, nor to other limited sections of experience, but to the total experience of the total man; then the aim becomes that of overcoming alienation, and of the subject-object split in perceiving the world; then the uncovering of the unconscious means the overcoming of affective contamination and cerebration; it means de-repression, the abolition of the split within myself between the universal man and the social man; it means the disappearance of the polarity of conscious vs. unconscious; it means aiming at the state of the immediate grasp of reality, without distortion and without interference by intellectual reflection; it means giving up the illusion of an indestructible separate ego, which is to be enlarged, preserved as the Egyptian pharaohs hoped to preserve themselves as mummies for eternity. To be conscious of the unconscious means to be open, responding, to *have* nothing and to *be*. (1960, pp. 135–36. [See also Fromm excerpt in this volume.])

The influence of utopian Marxism in Fromm's vision is readily apparent. Like all utopian schemes and movements, Marx's vision manifests a projection of the archetype of Self or wholeness. The projection of the archetype of Self by Marx and Fromm, and by anyone else for that matter, onto nature, society, class, family, ethnic or religious groups, or even onto psychoanalysis and Zen, is an expression of unconsciousness.

Fromm does acknowledge that the "full recovery of consciousness" is a much more radical aim than the general psychoanalytical one of curing neurotic traits and symptoms. He admits that among depth psychologists, the full scope of this aim is approximated only in Jung's concept of individuation or wholeness.

For the archetype of wholeness to become a true source of liberation and expanded consciousness, it has to be withdrawn from its naive projection onto external reality so that it may be realized within the individual. In the "shrinking" and withdrawal of unconscious projections onto external objects, both Zen and psychoanalysis do have a common goal, although again, only the Jungian school states that the reason for withdrawing the projection is so that wholeness may be realized within the individual. (An attempt to compare the methods and aims of Eastern meditation and those of Jungian psychology may be found in my book *Gathering the Light: A Psychology of Meditation*.)

A recent, Freudian-based attempt to unite psychoanalysis with Eastern meditation is found in Mark Epstein's *Thoughts Without a Thinker: Psychotherapy from a Buddhist Perspective*. Epstein has meditative experience, which stems from the Vipassana tradition. Unlike Zen, which emphasizes one-pointed concentration, Vipassana meditation consists of the careful observation and analysis of, or insight into, the ongoing processes of mind formation. In this regard, because Vipassana is much more conceptually oriented than Zen, it is not surprising that it appeals more to intellectuals or thinking types of personality than to feeling or intuitive types. Consequently, there is much more writing and intellectual output by Vipassana practitioners than by Zen practitioners. I have heard some meditation teachers joke that Vipassana meditators tend to become psychotherapists, while Zen meditators become plumbers and carpenters.

To my thinking, Mark Epstein succeeds in building a bridge between Freudian theory and practice and the Vipassana form of meditation. Yet I marvel at how Epstein (at least in this book) can simply ignore Freud's pronouncement that religion is an illusion, and thereby dismiss or avoid Freud's related observation that mystical feelings of oneness or cosmic consciousness represent escapist regression to infantile narcissism or to the fetal experience in the womb. Nevertheless, Epstein demonstrates how various states of mind encountered during the practice of insight meditation can work in tandem with psychotherapeutic methods and perspectives to cure the effects of childhood trauma and neglect.

Epstein admits, however, that while mediation often brings to the surface psychological problems that require attention, it does not directly address them. Psychotherapy, on the other hand, does; however, psychotherapy is limited if it offers only partial ego development and the attainment of what Freud called a state of "common unhappiness." Buddhist meditation, Epstein argues, "offers a complementary method of ego development" beyond that which, from a therapeutic point of view, is considered adequate for "normal" functioning (p. 155), and can move the patient "beyond recognition and reconciliation to the far shore of relief" (p. 180).

ZEN MEDITATION AND HEALING

Generally, I agree that a combination of psychotherapy and meditation is the best way to approach psychological and spiritual growth and development. In this essay, however, I want to reverse my usual therapeutic stance and suggest that Zen meditation alone may accomplish the task of alleviating neurotic traits and symptoms, and provide, in addition, an experience of individuation or wholeness.

Let me first note some anecdotal evidence. After experience with Zen meditation many people report that even though they can't explain why, they feel better, emotionally and physically. Mentally, they feel more alert and less confused and conflicted. They feel that they have a better perspective on their emotional problems and have become more accepting of difficult relationships and of life's vicissitudes. One meditator, for example, stated that for most of his adult life he had felt burdened and pressured by the demands of the external world—pressures of work, time, and obligations. He felt he had expended a tremendous amount of psychic energy in pushing back against these pressures, just to have what he called "some breathing space for himself." After several years practicing meditation, even though these stresses had not vanished, he no longer felt that the world was closing in on him as much: he didn't have to push back as hard. Another meditator, who began sitting in a disciplined, almost rigid fashion which reflected his personality, began to observe that as his armor loosened, he became more tender and less harsh with himself and others. Another meditator noticed that as her psychological energy became somehow "purer," "cleaner," and "brighter," she felt more alive and vital. If she stopped meditating for a time, she felt that she sank back into a more lethargic, slower, and heavier way of feeling and being.

How can we explain these changes and experiences? Certainly they are not the result of suggestions or even visualizations, since in Zen the instruction is simply to observe the breath and concentrate the mind. Nothing else is suggested. Meditators are warned not to have expectations and are told to try to ignore or at least not put any stock in feelings of well-being, tranquillity, and so on. Therefore, something in the very nature of the practice is responsible for these and similar changes.

The common factor in every form of meditation is *concentration*. However, many people concentrate for long periods of time on various activities and mental occupations in their everyday life, and yet do not experience the beneficial effects associated with meditation. We must, therefore, conclude that there is something different about *how* one concentrates during meditation. The major difference seems to be that during meditation one is conscious of the act of concentration. But there is more to it than that. One also becomes conscious of distractions that interfere with the observed state of concentration and deliberately ignores them, tries not to get caught up in them. In other words, consciousness is used to protect the act of conscious concentration.

Furthermore, during meditation, the objects of concentration differ from those upon which people concentrate during their daily activities. In Vipassana meditation, for example, the focus is on one's breath and on the careful observation of the external and internal stimuli that constantly enter and leave the field of awareness. In Zen meditation, the focus may be on one's breath or on a syllable or phrase that comprises a koan, but in addition all external and internal distractions are ignored, so that the entire focus can be on the object of concentration. In advanced stages of Zen meditation, significant changes take place in the quality of concentration and in the nature of one's awareness or consciousness. Most people experience the beneficial effects of meditation long before they reach these advanced stages, however. Therefore, for an explanation of these effects we have to look at the basic nature of meditation practice.

My thesis is that during meditation, psychic energy is withdrawn from its habitual flow among our instincts, drives, fantasies, thoughts, feelings, complexes, ego defenses, persona, etc., and transferred to the effort of concentration or to the object of concentration. The same is true of the practice of "mindfulness": being aware of what one is doing every moment even when not meditating. To begin with, most of us have to overcome tremendous resistance on the part of the body and the psyche to maintain this artificially induced and suspended way of being. It goes against our natural tendencies not to lose ourselves in fantasy and activity but to maintain constant awareness. Instincts and complexes may put up a desperate fight, for they experience this withdrawal of habitually allotted energy as a threat to their well-being and survival. Several studies indicate that particularly in Westerners, meditation can make things worse: tension, anxiety, and depression may arise as powerful instinctive drives (fear, anger, sex, aggression, etc.) reassert themselves with a vengeance. In the past, this struggle was conceived as a fight with the devil and legions of evil.

Normally, with the help of constant distractions and through the mechanisms of suppression and repression, we keep these disturbing forces in the psyche at bay. During meditation, when distraction is forsworn and the attention is focused, the contents of the unconscious come to the surface and disturb consciousness. These are called *shadow* issues, in Jungian terms, and the initial stages of meditation, like those of therapy, usually bring about an experience of the *nigredo*. (*Nigredo* or blackness is an alchemical term descriptive of the first stage of the *opus*, characterized by passion, violence, depression, disorientation, death, dismemberment, decomposition, and dissolution. Since the alchemists projected their unconscious contents and processes onto the unknown qualities of matter, they also emotionally participated in and identified with the transformation of material substances, from which they tried to fashion or extract the "philosophers' stone." One of Jung's major accomplishments in the history of Western thought was to decipher the heretofore incomprehensible symbolism of alchemy and demonstrate that alchemical symbolism refers us to the fundamental contents and dynamics of the collective or transpersonal psyche.)

When they come face to face with these powerful and previously repressed or unconscious elemental forces of the psyche, many people give up the practice of meditation. For in its initial stages, meditation may be counterproductive of its announced goals: equanimity, serenity, clarity, and wholeness. For those for whom the threat of psychosis is real, retreat is the better part of valor and the wiser course. When this is the case, psychotherapy should step in and deal with the problems that surface.

But others feel that they are able to withstand this onslaught. They patiently persist through the Dark Night of the Soul, and eventually, *Deo concedente*, or God willing, as the alchemists used to say, things begin to quiet down. Analogous to the behavior of the wild ox pictured in the Zen Ox-herding series, the instincts and emotions become tame. And at this point, feelings of bliss, serenity, and inner peace may begin to suffuse the personality.

How do we explain this transformation? I believe that by consciously focusing the mind on the object of meditation and thereby altering the natural, habitual flow of psychic energy, we gradually "starve" and "shrink" the drives and complexes. In other words, Zen meditation, under certain conditions, achieves the same goals as psychoanalysis and psychotherapy —not through analysis, catharsis, interpretation, and reasonable ego adaptation, but simply by way of the continuous withdrawal of psychic energy from the problem areas of the psyche. By sitting still and withdrawing energy from the instincts and the complexes—which includes the ego complex, for one has to forget oneself as well—psyche and body are able to create conditions of health, well-being, and wholeness. This is why many meditation teachers, having experienced these therapeutic effects themselves, often counsel their students to simply continue or even intensify their meditation practice, believing that in time psychological problems will disappear.

Where the meditator's basic ego structure is fairly solid and the problems are neurotic in nature, this may be valid advice. But where pre-Oedipal fault lines exist in the personality structure, intensifying one's meditative efforts may be counterindicated. The practice of meditation simply uncovers the fault lines, aggravates them, and provides no treatment.

But meditation *does* succeed in alleviating or even eradicating neurotic symptoms and maladjustments. That such an outcome is possible means that the body and psyche themselves have a notion of health, balance, and equanimity. These goals are not consciously created. What we need to do, it seems, is get out of the way: we need to stop our conditioned, ego-defensive, and ego-driven way of functioning. For Westerners, who usually feel that they have to *do* something to make health or happiness possible, this is a momentous discovery. It is hard to imagine that good can come of non-doing, of trusting our deepest nature, of letting it take its course, and giving up control. Perhaps we haven't been around long enough. Jung conjectured that some of our ceaseless activity, inquisitiveness, and desire to manipulate and control the world indicates the relative youthfulness of the Western psyche, in comparison with that of the East.

MEDITATION AND INDIVIDUATION

In the same manner that it may cure neurotic traits and symptoms, meditation can also lead us to the attainment of individuation. In coining the term "individuation" for what is commonly called the process of maturation, Jung emphasized his belief that the essential feature of maturation is the development of an individual standpoint.

Individuation consists of two phases. In its initial phase, *separation* of the individual from the initially given matrix is required: on the one hand, from the domination of the instinctive drives and the unconscious psyche, and on the other, from the psychological and behavioral imperatives of family and social milieu. Usually, the bread-and-butter issues of psychotherapy are concerned with this task, necessary for establishing a conscious and autonomous ego-personality. Issues of narcissism, identity, self-esteem, competence, relationship, power, and sex characterize this phase of the process.

The second phase of individuation is the movement toward *integration* and wholeness. In other words, full maturation requires the development of a conscious relationship to the psychic and social matrix from which one previously worked so hard to separate. Indeed, past a certain point in one's life, excessive preoccupation with the issues that constitute the first stage of development—ego autonomy, identity, power, sex, etc.—indicates the persistence of regressive traits in a personality not yet fully mature. Under ideal conditions, the second phase of individuation becomes characterized by active involvement in spiritual, cultural, social, political, and humanitarian endeavors. Attainment of this phase is described by Abraham Maslow as self-actualization, by Alfred Adler as social awareness, by Erik Erikson as generativity, and by Jung as wholeness or completed individuation.

Now, how exactly does Zen meditation foster the process of individuation? First of all, in its monastic form, Zen separates the individual from family and society. An initiatory ritual requires that Zen monastics renounce their attachments to family and forgo the usual blandishments of secular life. Second, monastic rules and style of life are designed to overcome the dominance of instinctive and unconscious impulses. By insisting on constant mindfulness and periodic self-examination, the monastic ethos aims to forge a personality that is free of the unconscious acts and impulses that usually rule our lives in such basic matters as food, sleep, and sex, as well as in the more complex areas of ego, control, and recognition. Even though lay practitioners of Zen meditation do not undergo such intense training, they, too, are usually exposed to these principles. During weeklong retreats even lay practitioners follow a monastic routine.

All of the above separation takes place psychologically even before one begins to meditate. The act of meditation intensifies these factors, for during meditation one is totally alone. More than that, in Zen one works hard to let go of all thoughts, feelings, images, and sensations. One could hardly ask for a greater separation of the individual from both the inner and the outer world. In this manner, the regular practice of meditation is an alternative method for achieving the first phase of individuation that is the usual task of psychotherapy.

What about the second phase—integration and wholeness? Just as an individual's almost exclusive preoccupation with one's personal goals and ambitions, with one's family, ethnic, religious, or national group eventually turns to wider cultural and humanistic concerns, a similar turn occurs in meditation. As we remain detached from all distractions/objects that impinge upon our personal awareness from within and without, gradually an opening or widening of consciousness and being takes place. As writer Tony Schwartz noted about his experiences during an extended period of meditation: "Some lifelong barriers were coming down. I felt my heart opening. It was thrilling." (1995, p. C1.) Those who persist in the practice of meditation eventually obtain a glimpse of the absolute *beingness and at-one-ment* that encompass the individual as part and parcel of the cosmic whole. Here the separation of the individual comes to an end, and a compassionate, loving concern with all of life, with all existence, takes over.

EGO CONSCIOUSNESS AND SELF-REALIZATION

Even though Zen meditation may lead to an experience of the transpersonal core of the psyche, that experience alone is not necessarily an indication of a fully developed or mature personality. Jung's notion of individuation or wholeness encompasses a maturation and an integration of both ego and Self. The danger with spiritually inclined people is that they pursue Self-realization at the expense of personal development. For it is possible to pursue spiritual development in a split-off way. In extreme cases, something like an idiot savant results: a person with a highly evolved spiritual perspective but essentially infantile, socially unadapted, with instinctive impulses and egoistic concerns. The entire package is presented in a spiritual wrapping, and uncritical devotees feed into the pathology of immature masters and gurus with disastrous consequences for all concerned.

It is also important to note that there is a significant difference between Jung's notion and the Zen Buddhist's notion of Self. In a discussion between Jung and Shin'ichi Hisamatsu, a Zen scholar and professor of Buddhism, Hisamatsu said: "There is neither form nor substance in the True Self of Zen." Jung replied: "Even if you say so, I cannot in fact know what I do not know. I cannot know if the Self has various states or not, because I am quite unconscious in these regards. The whole of the human being consists of consciousness and the unconscious." (Meckel and Moore, 1992, p. 112.) The latter is Jung's definition of the Self. Therefore, for Jung, there are limits to how much a person can know about the characteristics of the Self.

Jung might agree that the Zen scholar's description may be a manifestation of the Self that appears under certain conditions, e.g., those promoted by Zen Buddhist concepts and meditation methods. Jung might also agree that the *a priori archetype of the Self* has neither form nor substance—but he would also insist that that is a purely hypothetical notion. One can't say anything for certain about the a priori nature of the archetype since our knowledge of it is always filtered through the conscious psyche. We can describe the phenomenology of the Self, but never its a priori form. For Jung, therefore, various religious conceptions and experience of God or of the ultimate nature of reality or Being may all be valid manifestations of the Self. Personal and cultural considerations determine which of these manifestations resonated with our mental, imaginal, and emotional makeup and, therefore, which of the archetypal manifestations of the archetype of the Self represents our God. Similarly, the major characteristics of mystical experiences are universally identical, but their meaning and significance are defined by the specific personal temperament and cultural context in which they take place.

In the end, however, both Zen Buddhism and Jungian psychology share the same overriding goal—the alleviation and transcendence of human suffering. Even the methods for the attainment of the goal are similar. Both, in Jung's words, affirm "the *self-liberating power of the introverted mind*" (1969, par. 737) and pursue that introversion through careful self-observation, meditation, and active imagination. Other similarities in methods include: conscious pursuit of personal and moral development, and a creative and fruitful integration of personal consciousness with the perspectives and aims of the transpersonal Self.

It is an axiom of Jungian psychology that the ego must maintain its individual standpoint when confronted with the often overwhelming, charismatic powers of the Self. Jung puts it this way:

> God wants to be born in the flame of man's consciousness, leaping ever higher. And what if this has no roots in the earth? If it is not a house of stone where the fire of God can dwell, but a wretched straw hut that flares up and vanishes? Could God then be born? One must be able to suffer God. That is the supreme task for the carrier of ideas. He must be the advocate of the earth. God will take care of himself. My inner principle is: Deus *et* homo. God needs man in order to become conscious, just as he needs limitations in time and space. Let us therefore be for him limitation in time and space. An earthly tabernacle. (1973, pp. 65–66)

Under favorable circumstances Zen meditation is a technique that can help cure various neurotic traits and symptoms. In addition, it can lead to a conscious encounter with the archetype of the Self. Such an encounter tends to relativize the otherwise often overwhelming experiences of human suffering. Nevertheless, during these encounters, and afterward, it is essential that we retain our sense of reality, our awareness of human limitation, and our commitment to ethical conduct.

References

Epstein, Mark (1995). *Thoughts Without a Thinker: Psychotherapy from a Buddhist Perspective.* New York: Basic Books.

Jung, C. G. (1969). *Psychology and Religion: West and East.* Collected Works, vol. 11. Princeton: Princeton University Press.

———— (1973). *Letters.* Vol 1: 1906–1950.

Meckel, Daniel J., and Robert L. Moore (1992). *Self and Liberation: The Jung-Buddhism Dialogue.* New York: Paulist Press.

Odajnyk, V. Walter (1993). *Gathering the Light: A Psychology of Meditation.* Boston: Shambhala.

Schwartz, Toby (1995). "A Father's Adventures in Enlightenment." *The New York Times,* March 23, 1995.

Suzuki, Daisetz T., Erich Fromm, and Richard De Martino (1960). *Zen Buddhism and Psychoanalysis.* New York: Harper & Row.

BIOGRAPHY

❑

PSYCHOLOGICAL OBSERVATIONS ON THE

LIFE OF GAUTAMA BUDDHA

George R. Elder

❑

INTRODUCTION

Toward the beginning of his long *Histoire du Bouddhisme Indien*, the great Indologist Etienne Lamotte remarks: "Buddhism would be inexplicable if we did not place at its foundation a personality sufficiently powerful to have given it its impetus and to have stamped it with those essential traits which have persisted through history."[1] He is referring, of course, to the powerful "personality" of Siddhārtha Gautama; and his statement signifies the premier place that the study of this personality—properly speaking, psychology—should have within the field of Buddhist studies. It is a fact, nevertheless, that there has been virtually no psychological analysis of Gautama; and studies of the traditional Life from any other perspective are generally less common than treatments of what the Buddha taught. Lamotte frankly admits that it is "discouraging" to take up the study of the

An earlier version of this essay appeared in the book *Buddhist and Western Psychology* (Prajna Press, 1983; Nathan Katz, editor). This new version, also published in the journal *Psychological Perspectives* (issue 35, Spring–Summer 1997), is reprinted here with the permission of Professor Katz.

Life. E. J. Thomas—who has written a classic, *The Life of Buddha: As Legend and History*—tells us also that in the "Triple Jewel the great problem has always been the person of Buddha."[2] For both of these scholars, and for others as well, the problem is named in the full title of Thomas' work: it is the problem of "legend and history."

A reading of the first century C.E. Mahāvastu makes apparent the implications of this dilemma. Its "history" informs us that Gautama returned to Kapilavastu to visit his family sometime after the Enlightenment; but the plausibility of this event is embedded in a story much less likely. The "legend" tells us that Gautama was accompanied by roughly 20,000 disciples, one of whom flew on ahead to reassure the family. Gautama himself, upon arriving, is said to have taken a walk in the air about head height, then to have risen to the height of a tree in order to cause fire to issue from the top half of his body and water to flow from his lower half—followed by fire from the right side of his body and water from his left, through twenty-two combinations![3] What is a scholar to make of such materials? In the nineteenth century, H. H. Wilson concluded that it is "not impossible, after all, that Śākya Muni is an unreal being, and that all that is related of him is as much a fiction as is that of his preceding migrations."[4] This conclusion is interestingly akin to the docetic theology of the Mahāsaṅghikas at the Second Council. But it is standard among scholars today to conclude that there really is a historical personality reflected in the sources even though the facts of that history are largely inaccessible, obscured by legend and myth. As a result, scholarship in this area is usually confined to a curious amalgam: the history of the legend, the likely development of unlikely events.

Here, I think, we can begin to see the usefulness of a psychological approach to the Life of the Indian man named Siddhārtha Gautama who became Buddha. It is not that this approach has special access to historical facts which are no doubt gone. Rather, psychology states that what remains in the sources—what all scholars refer to as "imaginary"—is itself a *fact* of the imagination which, with the proper attitude of reverence and openness, can reveal the nature of the psyche. If we notice that Buddhist legends or myths were in the past popularly taken as miraculous external events while we today see them more clearly as mental, then we reach the understanding that the less likely stories of religion reflect a less conscious level of psychological development—i.e., they refer to contents of the unconscious. Further, if we accept the hypothesis, advanced by the Swiss psychologist

C. G. Jung, that what has gone before us psychologically is somehow pre-served within the deeper structure of our own psyches, then we come to the most significant conclusion of all: that the imaginary material of the Life of Gautama Buddha does not so much discourage as challenge us to explore its symbolism for insight into the nature of our own unconscious selves.

The texts on the Life are so rich and of such a variety that we had best focus upon a single one: I suggest the *Nidānakathā* or *Statement of Intro-duction* (to a commentary on the *Jātaka*), a Singhalese compilation from the fifth century C.E. I will be looking at only the second section of this text, the *avidurenidāna* or "Introduction to Less Distant Events," which covers the life of Siddhārtha from the time that he was said to have been in Tuṣita heaven up to the time of his Enlightenment. And I will quote freely from H. C. Warren's translation of this work while regularizing the Pāli terms to Sanskrit.[5]

THE COMING INTO EXISTENCE

According to the *Ratnagotravibhāga*, a rather late Mahāyāna scripture writ-ten in the fourth or fifth century C.E., there are twelve "acts" (*karma*) which must be performed by every Buddha in his last—and human—life-time. As Alex Wayman translates, they are: (1) The descent from Tuṣita; (2) Entrance into the womb; (3) Rebirth; (4) Skill in worldly arts; (5) Enjoyment of the harem women; (6) Departure from home; (7) Arduous discipline; (8) Passage to the terrace of Enlightenment; (9) Defeat of the Māra host; (10) Attaining Complete Enlightenment; (11) Turning the Wheel of the Law; (12) Departure into Nirvāṇa.[6] These acts amount to a necessary pattern for becoming a Buddha. Since *buddha* in Sanskrit means "awake"—a term recognized by Buddhism itself as a symbol for the psy-chological event of becoming "conscious"—we can say that this "last life of a Buddha" is a model for becoming a more conscious human being, a paradigm of what Jung calls the process of individuation.

Our section of the *Nidānakathā*, however, opens onto a very strange world—in a heaven called Tuṣita where "Gautama" is not yet Gautama but a god, among innumerable other gods. Much is being assumed: not only that the *durenidāna* has already been told—those distant events from the time that the future Gautama was named "Sumeda," more than a hundred thousand aeons earlier—but also that the ancient Indian cosmology was in place. That cosmos was a three-storied universe (of heavens, earth, and hells) filled with five different kinds of sentient beings whose destinies were determined by the twin laws of karmic retribution and transmigration. While each of these features deserves some psychological comment, suffice it to say that these cosmological details differ so much from what we know of our external universe that they necessarily reveal—by a sort of wonderful default—the *mind* itself as a "universe" filled with "living beings" of various kinds and determined by "laws."

Within that strange psychological universe, the hero of our story is not yet conscious, not yet "born" as a human being here on earth. We are being told, I believe, that beyond our conscious ego existence ("earth") there exists within the region of the unconscious ("heaven") a numinously charged potential for consciousness. This is what Jung called the archetype of the Self and what Buddhists refer to as the "embryo of the Tathāgata" (*tathāgata* is an epithet of the recurring Buddhas, meaning "thus come and gone"). There is an embryo or precious seed of Enlightenment within us all.

The "heavens" are activated! A "Buddha Uproar" has gone up to announce the future birth of one who will become "awake"; and the "gods of all ten thousand worlds come together into one place" to ascertain who it is that will become a Buddha and to "beseech him to become one." This is an extraordinary view of ourselves. It implies that we are "called" to our vocation for psychological development by the archetypes or "gods" and that this call comes first of all from beyond our awareness within the depths of the unconscious psyche. Further, an impending emergence of consciousness is obviously no small event for the psyche: it has the support of all the forces of libido which "come together" or are constellated. And something of what it actually means to be conscious is anticipated by "Gautama's" performing in Tuṣita the "Five Great Observations"—i.e., he discriminates.

With each discrimination, there is imagery of the "middle" or of "union" or of the "fourth." It is this sort of imagery, as Jung has demonstrated, which points to psychological wholeness—the conscious integration of previously unconscious contents. For example, the country chosen for Gautama's birth is the "Middle Country," which probably is located historically in the foothills of the Himālayas in northeastern India but where—says our text—are "born" all Buddhas, all Pratyekabuddhas, all Arhats, Cakravartins, and higher classes—i.e., all those in Indian Buddhism who are perceived to possess a superior development of awareness. Clearly, this is a symbolic claim.

The most significant discriminations have to do with the Buddha's future family. He chooses the high *kṣatriya* class and a father named Śuddhodana who is said to be a "king." While historically it is likely that Siddhārtha Gautama was of this warrior class and that his father was Śuddhodana (a common enough name which may mean "he whose rice is pure"), it is nevertheless not very likely that the father was actually a king. Here, then, a psychological element intrudes perhaps to show the extraordinary power and value of one who is to become "awake." There is a striking contrast here with the story of Jesus Christ, who is also associated with consciousness as "Light of the World"—but whose value is initially obscured in a lowly manger. It should be said, however, that the image of Gautama's "royal father" introduces the profound ambiguity of Cakravartin psychology—i.e., "Universal Monarch" psychology—yet to emerge in the story.

The choice of mother is also colored by the psyche. Her name is Māyā, a name Buddhists themselves make nothing of and which, therefore, is quite likely a historical fact. But Māyā can mean not only "maker" (from *mā*, "to measure") but also "maker of illusion" or simply "illusion"—a range of possibilities that has caused only a bit of a stir among scholars. From a psychological point of view, however, she could not be better named: as the symbolic "Mother" of the ego, she would represent the nonrational realities of the unconscious which project themselves into the external world as our illusions. At the same time it is within the womb of this maternal unconscious that we find the embryo of our awareness. She will be present, I suggest, throughout the Life of Buddha in other symbolic forms—as "tree," as "full moon," as "earth."

The story tells us that Siddhārtha's mother died seven days after his birth and that the boy had to be raised by Māyā's sister, Prajāpatī, who was also a member of the father's harem. This may be biographical. The Jungian analyst Edward F. Edinger has written about the psychology of the "lost parent" in the context of the questionable paternity of Jesus Christ:

> When the personal father is missing and, more particularly, when he is completely unknown, as may happen with an illegitimate child, there is no layer of personal experience to mediate between the ego and the numinous image of the archetypal father. A kind of hole is left in the psyche through which emerge the powerful archetypal contents of the collective unconscious. . . . If, however, the ego can survive this danger, the "hole in the psyche" becomes a window providing insights into the depths of being.[7]

For Jesus, this will mean not only an inability to adapt in his youth to the masculine principle of the psyche but also that he will be driven to find a "heavenly father" visible through that "hole" in his life. Something similar can be said about Siddhārtha Gautama. The death of his personal mother, if it is true, helps us to understand the inordinate influence of Gautama's father over the boy. At the same time, it explains the drive in Siddhārtha to seek a vital connection to the feminine principle—which the personal mother is supposed to provide—but which he will have to discover instead beneath the "tree" of Enlightenment, at "full moon," by way of an "earth-shaking" religious experience.

It should be said, however, that Jung noticed this feature of death in the infancy of Gautama and offered a transpersonal interpretation. He said it refers symbolically to the archetype of the "dual mother"—i.e., the psychological pattern that an unconscious connection to the outer personal mother must "die," at the appropriate age, if one is to discover that "other mother" within.[8] From this angle, the stepmother Prajāpatī ("mistress of creatures") is a symbol of the creative unconscious.

THE YOUTH

Let us explore some of the events surrounding Gautama's youth. In the twelvefold scheme of the *Ratnagotravibhāga*, they are expressed in the acts called "Skill in worldly arts" and "Enjoyment of the harem women." In the first of these, Gautama is sixteen years of age and is called upon by his people to demonstrate his proficiency in the "manly art" of war. The prince responds without the need of training by exhibiting what the *Nidānakathā* refers to as a "twelvefold skill" in the art of archery; other versions inform us that Gautama's skill included such things as being able to string a bow that would otherwise take the strength of a thousand men.[9] The story seeks to reveal to us the strength and readiness of the Self actualized as ego. But we are also being taught what is necessary for the development of consciousness: one must develop the skills that belong to one's station in life. There is no premature "religious" attitude here, no monastic introversion in youth which would sap the development of the ego. The divine "vocation" of the psyche includes the establishment of a confident ego capable of engaging in an extroverted way the worldly reality which challenges it.

Since we are observing an archetypal portrait of what is required for psychological development, these principles must apply to "Enjoyment of the women." The scene in the *Nidānakathā* is one of sybaritic luxury:

> And the king built three palaces for the Future Buddha, suited to the three seasons —one of nine stories, another of seven stories, and another of five stories. And he provided him with forty thousand dancing girls.

Other versions have Gautama claim:

> I used no sandalwood that was not of Benares, my dress was of Benares cloth, my tunic, my under-robe, and cloak. Night and day a white parasol was held over me so that I should not be touched by cold or heat, by dust or weeds or dew.[10]

Put simply, these materials announce that unless one develops the capacity to enjoy the sensual life—the "wine, women, and song" most appropriately enjoyed in one's youth—there will be no Buddhahood.

What remarkable stories these must be for a Westerner to hear! One imagines a Christian youth looking to the Life of Christ for insight into how to lead the proper kind of adolescence and young adulthood only to find that the guiding hero is already thirty years old and, seemingly, without a youth at all. Should this young Christian search the scriptures and find that single story of a twelve-year-old Jesus who rebelled against his parents to teach all day in the temple, he will find here no adequate image—of meaningful work and healthy sexuality—around which to express burgeoning young life. But it has to be admitted that what we have just analyzed from Buddhist scriptures is not what one hears from Buddhists themselves who tend to be adult monastics teaching indiscriminately the adult psychology of monasticism. It may be, however, that what orthodox Buddhism tends to understate in the paradigm of the Life of Buddha is compensated within the religion itself by the unorthodox "sensual" traditions of Buddhist Tantra.

There is a profound ambiguity in all of this. Gautama's youth is full of pleasure—actually, it is too full. His skills come too easily, without the need to train; three palaces are more than enough and forty thousand dancing girls are too many. After all, the people had demanded that the prince demonstrate his skill in archery because they were worried that "Siddhārtha is wholly given over to pleasure" and would not be able to respond realistically in time of war. In the *Aṅguttaranikāya*, the Buddha tells his congregation: "I was refined (Pāli, *sukumālo*) . . . most refined (*parasukumālo*), extremely refined (*accantasukumālo*)."[11] It is clear that the young Gautama has been caught in an "extreme of pleasure." Edinger helps us understand that what we are observing is the psychology of inflation. He writes:

> I use the term inflation to describe the attitude and the state which accompanies the identification of the ego with the Self. It is a state in which something small (the ego) has arrogated to itself the qualities of something larger (the Self) and hence is blown up beyond the limits of its proper size.[12]

Yet Edinger goes on to explain—in a manner consistent with the meaning of a Buddhist "model" of individuation—that the act of inflation is a kind of "necessary crime" that prompts the ego to develop fully to prepare it for the drama of what has yet to unfold.

The driving force of the father exacerbates Siddhārtha's inflation. Śuddhodana has heard from prophecy that his son has the potential to become one of two kinds of exceptional men: a Buddha or a Cakravartin. This latter term means literally "Wheel Turner" but is usually translated loosely as "Universal Monarch." Stories say that the Cakravartin possesses a "divine wheel"—alluding to the chariot wheels of a warrior—rolling in each of the four directions conquering all in its path. Hearing the prophecy, the father knows exactly what he himself wants:

> It will never do for my son to become a Buddha. What I would wish to see is my son exercising sovereign rule and authority over the four great continents and the two thousand attendant isles, and walking through the heavens surrounded by a retinue thirty-six leagues in circumference.

It is obvious that this parent is also inflated; he is caught in what Buddhist doctrine calls the problem of "I and mine" or craving and clinging. While this sort of father may have been experienced personally by Siddhārtha—especially if the loss of his mother is historical—he is surely also the archetypal image of obstructing authority. Without reflection, Śuddhodana simply knows what is "best" for his son: if Siddhārtha has the opportunity to perpetuate to a higher degree what the father has accomplished in part, then that is the proper course. But what an extraordinary expectation in this particular case! For the father, in only wanting what is "best" for his son, is also willing to sacrifice his son's potential for Buddhahood—i.e., he is willing to sacrifice his son's higher consciousness. Hearing further that

Siddhārtha's Buddhahood is inevitable should he see "four sights"—an old man, a sick man, a dead man, and a monk—Śuddhodana sets a guard and proclaims: "From this time forth . . . let no such persons be allowed to come near my son." And so it is that we find ourselves in the presence of an Indian prince with his palaces, his fine clothes, the women—the very image of an overprotected son shielded from reality.

There is a secret connection, however, between the opposites, "Buddha or Cakravartin." Both are surrounded by the imagery of psychological wholeness: the Buddha, as we have seen, by the imagery of the "fourth" and the "middle"; the Cakravartin by the imagery of the "four directions" and the "mandala" wheel. Further, ancient Indian tradition claimed that the body of every Great Being (*mahāsattva*) possesses invisibly "thirty-two characteristics and eighty minor marks"—made visible in painted and sculpted images of the Buddha. But the Universal Monarch is also a Great Being with these same Buddhist features except for the crucial underlying fact that he is not "awake" but "asleep." Thus, we are shown in most striking fashion that the inflated state does arrogate to itself and imitate the wholeness of the Self; that is the secret of its attraction and power. But the inflated one is also unconscious and does not really know what he is doing.

There may be a larger cultural issue here. In the "wheel" of the Wheel Turner there are echoes of the patriarchal Āryan chariots that conquered matriarchal India a thousand years before the birth of Gautama. The Āryans no doubt crushed the feminine principle of the Indian psyche as they literally drove over those broad-hipped clay fertility goddesses which have survived among the archaeological finds of the Indus Valley. But by the dawn of Buddhism, this battle was long over. Where, then, would the libido or psychological energy—freed from its previous historical task— flow next? Would it continue to be channeled through the symbol of the "Cakravartin" and conquer even to the "ends of the earth"? Or would this energy be influenced by the image of a "Buddha" and turn back, introvert, and conquer instead an inner world of ignorance? The Buddhist story, of course, turns (as did the immediately preceding Upaniṣadic period of Hinduism) toward the task of developing consciousness. It also seeks to recover aspects of the once-conquered feminine. In this way, we can say that Gautama's personal problem is a particular manifestation of the collective problem of his people. His solution to that problem will be a guide for the larger cultural dilemma; and the people of India will revere him.

THE BREAKTHROUGH

A state of inflation is like a balloon and must sooner or later burst against the demands of reality. For Siddhārtha, this reality is expressed by the imagery of the forbidden "four sights"—the old man, the sick man, the dead man, and the monk—which the future Buddha did see despite his father's efforts. Objectively these sights are not extraordinary; but they have an extraordinary effect upon an "extremely refined" prince. Our text says that Gautama was "agitated in heart"; the Aṅguttaranikāya has him say, "As I reflected on it, all the elation in youth (Pāli, yobbanamado, literally, "intoxication of youth") utterly disappeared."[13] Inflation turns to deflation; or, as Jung would put it—borrowing a term from Heraclitus— Siddhārtha Gautama experiences an enantiodromia. Jung explains:

> I use the term enantiodromia for the emergence of the unconscious opposite in the course of time. This characteristic phenomenon practically always occurs when an extreme, one-sided tendency dominates conscious life; in time an equally powerful counter-position is built up, which first inhibits the conscious performance and subsequently breaks through the conscious control.[14]

Here, Gautama's "extremity of pleasure" gives way to an "extremity of pain." It is an event in the biography that appears in Buddhist doctrine as the first of the Four Delusions (all is "pleasure," sukha) which must give way to the first of the Four Noble Truths (all is "pain," duḥkha). Indeed, it is only in the light of the psychology of Guatama's Life that the extremity of the first Noble Truth makes any sense—since, objectively, life is not always painful. The pain here is part of the paradigm: without it, Siddhārtha Gautama would not have discovered the two sides of life, both of which are real, and thus deserve this title of being "awake" concerning the opposites which shape our experience. Nor, without duḥkha, would this overprotected prince have felt the sting that drove him away from the overbearing authority of his father—to seek his "lost Mother" in the midst of all this Cakravartin psychology.

At the age of twenty-nine, Gautama leaves his family (his doting father, his favorite wife, and newborn baby boy) with a touch of cowardice in the middle of the night without announcing his plans. After six long and difficult years, he becomes "awake" at the "dawning of the sun." His Enlightenment arrives, says scripture, in the lush spring season, the same season as Gautama's birth; it comes at the time of full moon, as it was at the birth but also at the conception. In other words, timing is critical in the development of consciousness. But this "time" seems especially to be the time of the fertile Mother archetype who creates in her natural way, not as we have planned but . . . when it is time. The time is also "evening" when, symbolically but also literally, the sharpness of consciousness is dulled and the unconscious begins to act without obstruction.

Gautama rises up like a "lion"—for ancient India, an animal of strength and courage; for modern psychology an image of the ego's strength enhanced by the forces of the individuating Self behind it. And he proceeds to the "tree" of his Enlightenment. This sacred tree recalls the cosmological symbolism of "Mount Meru," which traditionally is said to stand at the center of a flat, round earth; for around the tree lies the "broad earth" like a "huge cart-wheel lying on its hub." What an extraordinary way to inform us that Siddhārtha's breakthrough will require his wholeness (symbolized by the mandala "wheel") by having to face specifically the psychology of a "Wheel Turner." Yet it is also precisely here that the youthful development of a strong ego will begin to pay off; the work ahead will not be easy. When Gautama stood on the southern side of that earth: "Instantly the southern half of the world sank, until it seemed to touch the Avīci hell, while the northern half rose to the highest of the heavens." He walked around to each of the four directions only to find that the same disorienting event took place. Where is that "immovable spot" on which all the Buddhas find security? And the answer comes: it is at the *center*, sitting down cross-legged on the *earth* with one's back to the *tree*, facing the *East*—all rich universal symbols. Understood psychologically, we must make every effort—in the midst of an individuation crisis—to find the central place of the Self which values both conscious and unconscious processes, stay in touch with the feminine or feeling dimension of the psyche which grounds us in reality, and anticipate the natural unfolding of our destiny as we keep our "eyes on the prize"—the light of a greater awareness.

Gautama, the "lion," is perhaps too confident about all this. He exclaims:

Let my skin, and sinews, and bones become dry, and welcome! and let all the flesh and blood in my body dry up! but never from this seat will I stir, until I have attained the supreme and absolute wisdom!

And at precisely that moment, Māra appeared. "Māra" (literally, "killing") is the name of an Indian deity sometimes referred to as "Lord of this world."

The epithet is derived from the fact that this male god's heaven is said to be located at the very top of the cosmic Realm of Desire which includes the earth. Gods in that heaven are generally referred to as *paranirmitava-śavartin* because they enjoy "having power over what has been created by others."[15] And so we arrive at a portrait of Māra as a greedy, powerful god willing to kill for what he wants. What he wants now is that Gautama not become Enlightened:

> "Prince Siddhārtha is desirous of passing beyond my control, but I will never allow it!" [He] went and announced the news to his army, and sounding the Māra war-cry, drew out for battle . . . the host swept on like a flood to overwhelm the Great Being.

That Gautama is called a "Great Being" reminds us that this epithet is common to Buddha and Cakravartin. And that is significant because Māra himself is a perfect portrait of a "divine" Cakravartin—the archetypal war-rior who conquers all in his path.

In this way, just as we have seen a secret connection between Gautama and the Wheel Turner, we begin to see a secret connection between Gau-tama and his divine adversary. But this relationship is hinted at by the text if one considers the data psychologically. Māra first appeared in the *Nidānakathā* when Gautama departed from home. The text reads: " 'I shall catch you,' thought Māra, 'the very first time you have a lustful, malicious, or unkind thought.' And, like an ever-present shadow, he followed after, ever on the watch for some slip." This god represents the unconscious "shadow" side of the prince, even the negative side of the Self—that lust or greed (*kāma*), the malice (*vyāpāda*), the unkindness or cruelty (*vihiṃsa*) which are aspects of the power complex behind Gautama's inflation and behind his downfall. The same psychological point is made when Māra advises his army not to try to conquer Gautama from "in front": "We will attack him from behind"—i.e., from the negative side of this man's psyche that is not sufficiently conscious and which is his vulnerability.

At this point in the story, of course, Gautama does not know what is happening to him; that is his problem. He is not yet "enlightened" about the reality of the destructive shadow—nor does he know the creative Mother—and cannot possibly grasp the meaning of his pain. Thus, he must go on fighting (we have competing Cakravartins here!) with an adversary he thinks is outside and has nothing to do with himself. Were he to grasp the disturbing fact that Māra is also Gautama, there would follow the chastening of a too sanguine view of himself but no longer a conflict; a dangerous deity would become an integrated content of consciousness—and an aspect of the Self would be realized. At the same time, this ancient Indian would discover something about the nature of "deity" as an external manifestation of one's own unconscious; as the tantric Buddhists put it a thousand years after the death of the Buddha, the "gods do not exist" apart from the Mind of Enlightenment.[16] Finally, he would learn that a collective unconscious force lay behind the personal obstructions of his father and behind his people's self-destructive attitude toward life.

It remains to be seen if the imagery of our story supports this analysis along the lines of a psychology of integration as opposed to a psychology of repression. We are told that when Māra's nine storms failed to drive Gautama away from his "immovable spot," the deity "drew near"—as the religious experience deepened in its intensity and opened up into a curious dialogue. The dialogue, announcing relationship and the beginning of the dialectic process required to integrate unconscious contents, is reminiscent of Job's with the Hebrew god, insofar as a sort of legal debate takes place. Here, the god claims Siddhārtha's spot: "Siddhārtha, arise from this seat! It does not belong to you, but to me." Gautama answers in kind: "This seat does not belong to you, but to me." Gautama then goes on to ask if Māra has any "witness" (sākṣī) to his having done good deeds in the past to support his claim—whereupon Māra's army eagerly perjures itself: "I am his witness! I am his witness!" There is in this episode, and in the story of Job as well, a sober message about ourselves: we naively assume that archetypal forces of the psyche will respond to our ego's logic and that these forces are subject to the reasonable constraints of conventional law.

But Gautama's naiveté—as the paradigm requires—is necessary, for it creates a dilemma that leads to unexpected consequences. Very cleverly, the god Māra turns the question back upon his opponent: "Siddhārtha, who is witness to your having given donations?" The future Buddha is alone: he has left his family, and a small group of followers called the "Band of Five" has left him. All that remains is his rather dubious resolve. It must be obvious that Gautama's vigorous "will" to Enlightenment is precisely what evoked—almost like a prayer—the "Will" of Māra to oppose him. It had happened before as the prince left home: faced with a heavy palace gate, he had claimed "I will" leap over the wall, his courtier claimed "I will," his horse claimed "I will"—and, despite their success, there stood Māra.

From all of this, we might venture some conclusions about the mysterious operations of the power complex, especially when there is the psychological demand from the Self that it be made conscious. As long as the ego is simply identified with the complex, there is no apparent problem, even if one ends up without power. But as soon as this content moves toward consciousness, the complex appears to break away from identification with the ego to confront it in projection. Paradoxically, one begins to see "outside" one's self the unconscious content with which one is unconsciously identified. A "battle of wills" ensues and—locked in contention with one's own larger Self—one falls into a psychological paralysis or the kind of standoff depicted by our story.

And then, at this point in the imaginative history, the unexpected occurs. Gautama is forced to do something that no self-respecting Cakravartin would ever think to do:

> And drawing forth his right hand from beneath his priestly robe, he stretched it out towards the mighty earth, and said, "Are you witness, or are you not, to my having given a great seven-hundred-fold donation in my Vessantara existence?"

This is the scene which became the favorite source for Buddhist art: the Great Being with his "thirty-two marks"—including a golden skin and bump on the head, a tuft of hair in the middle of his forehead, elephantine shoulders—sitting cross-legged and reaching out with his right hand over his right knee for help. Gautama reached out beyond his terrible conflict for the grace that comes from the divine feminine principle when one's masculinity is defeated; and some versions say he "touched" Her.

> And the mighty earth thundered, "I bear you witness!" with a hundred, a thousand, a hundred thousand roars, as if to overwhelm the army of Māra. . . . And the followers of Māra fled away in all directions.

The "earth," Pṛthivī, is a goddess in her own right within Indian religion; but here she symbolizes one man's surrender of will and disidentification from a compulsive urge to power—"and Māra and his army flee." The withdrawal of the army "outside" Gautama would symbolize the withdrawal of projection. But, as our story suggests, projections are withdrawn only when the conscious ego position is humbled or relativized and gets in "touch" with the "earth"—which I suggest is one of the symbolic forms of the unconscious Mother of illusions (māyā). That she should be a supporting "witness" alludes to one of the images that cluster around the process of gaining insight. In the Gospel of John there is the forensic figure of the Paraclete (Greek, *parakletos*, "called to one's aid" in a court of law)—the saving "witness," the holy "spirit of truth"—rooted in the feminine figure of Wisdom in the Hebrew Bible. Getting in touch with her transforms an ordinary man named Siddhārtha Gautama into the extraordinary figure we all know as Buddha.

While this essay must come to a close here, the Life story of Siddhārtha Gautama does continue. He is said to discover the "Three Knowledges" in the three watches of the night of his Enlightenment and then to unravel near dawn the twelve members of "Dependent Origination." But I take these statements as doctrinal or conscious elaborations of the essential events that already have been told imaginatively by legend or myth. And, yes, there are more than four decades of teaching and a moving death at the age of eighty, important historical and symbolic materials. Yet their significance lies in one man's mid-life discovery of what I would call the "Soul" of Buddhism—a notion that superficially conflicts with the Buddhist doctrine of *anātman* ("no soul" or "nonself") but which is profoundly compatible with the Hīnayāna perception of a "Mother of all Buddhas," with the Mahāyāna perception of a divine feminine reality called the "Perfection of Insight" (*prajñāparamitā*), and in agreement with the late Tantrics who say it is with Her we must unite. Gautama, ultimately, found the Mother he never had.

Notes

1. Etienne Lamotte, *Histoire du Bouddhisme Indien* (Louvain: Institut Orientaliste, 1958), 16.
2. Edward J. Thomas, *The Life of Buddha*, 3rd ed. (London: Routledge and Kegan Paul, 1949), 211.
3. *The Mahāvastu*, trans. J. J. Jones (London: Luzac and Co., Ltd., 1956), vol. 3, 93ff.
4. Thomas, *The Life*, xvi.
5. Henry Clarke Warren, trans., *Buddhism in Translations* (1896; reprint, New York: Atheneum, 1970), 38–83.
6. Alex Wayman, "Buddhism," in *Historia Religionum*, ed. C. J. Bleeker and G. Widengren (Leiden: E. J. Brill, 1971), vol. 2, 393.
7. Edward F. Edinger, *Ego and Archetype* (Baltimore: Penguin Books, 1972), 132.
8. C. G. Jung, *The Collected Works*, ed. Herbert Read et al., Vol. 5: *Symbols of Transformation* (Princeton: Princeton University Press, 1956), par. 494ff.
9. Thomas, *The Life*, 48.
10. Ibid.

11. *Aṅguttara-nikāya*, ed. R. Morris (London: Pāli Text Society, 1885), part 1, 145.

12. Edinger, *Ego and Archetype*, 7.

13. *Aṅguttara-nikāya*, 1.145.

14. Jung, *Collected Works*, Vol. 6: *Psychological Types* (1971), par. 709.

15. Lamotte, *Histoire*, 761.

16. Alex Wayman, *Yoga of the Guhyasamājatantra* (Delhi: Motilal Banarsidass, 1977), 11.

TIBETAN BUDDHISM AND

COMPARATIVE PSYCHOANALYSIS

Mark Finn

❏

Buddhism has been a minor but recurrent interest of psychoanalysis. Freud, critical of religion in general, confessed that he had no personal knowledge of contemplative experience. However, Horney (1987) and Fromm (1950) as well as a number of more recent analytic writers, have found in Buddhist practice a psychology and a profound psychotherapeutics which both mir‑ rors and challenges psychoanalysis. Buddhism, while a religion on the one hand, has always essentially been a "therapy" with clinical approaches to the universal problems, recognized by psychoanalysis, of desire and self‑ deception. Deliverance or cure comes through psychological means, not divine intervention. Because the practice of Buddhist meditation is solitary, the importance of the teacher-student relationship has been underappre‑ ciated. It is in the examination of this relationship that the parallels be‑ tween Buddhism and psychoanalysis go beyond metapsychology to actual clinical discovery. This paper will argue that the biography of a Tibetan Buddhist figure is in part an account of psychodynamic transformation in‑

This essay is previously unpublished.

volving transference, resistance, and the resolution of the psychological difficulties arising in childhood and described by psychoanalysis.

To the limited extent that Buddhism has been considered by psychoanalysts, three general attitudes have emerged. The first, or classical, view equates meditative experience and regression, with the only question being whether the experience is adaptive or not (see Horton, 1974). The second view, represented by Transpersonal psychology, has argued that meditation represents an advanced state of psychological experience not contained by psychoanalytic categories and requiring new models of human possibility (see Engler, 1983). A third view has been more impressed by the parallels between Buddhist and psychoanalytic therapeutics (see Finn, 1992; Epstein, 1995; Rubin, 1996). This later sympathetic view appreciates the therapeutic value of meditation and the contemplative ground for psychoanalysis suggested in authors like Winnicott, Bion, and Loewald. Both meditation and psychoanalysis are techniques for the deployment of attention in a form at once disciplined and spontaneous. The paradoxical Buddhist teaching of the two truths helps clarify this relationship. (See Finn, 1992, for a more extended discussion.) The first truth is the relative truth of cause and effect, categorized distinctions, and historical sequence. The second truth is the absolute truth of no distinctions, no conditions, and no time. They are seen as inseparable and yet distinct. Like body and mind, not one and yet not two; both one and two. Thus, the psychological and the spiritual are both indivisible and yet separate. Eternity and personal history are similarly intertwined. (See Loewald, 1978, for a psychoanalytic consideration of this issue.)

Most discussions of psychoanalysis and meditation, whether critical, idealizing, or sympathetic, have focused on the experience of the individual meditator. In focusing on the individual, however, it is possible to forget that, generally, the practice of meditation takes place within the context of a structured relationship with a spiritual teacher. The teacher is an expert at the techniques the individual meditator is pursuing. The teacher is also an expert in creating a certain type of relationship, encouraging on the one hand, frustrating on the other.

The parallels between the Buddhist teaching relationship and psychoanalysis have not gone unnoticed. Stunkard (1951) wrote, in reference to Zen Buddhism: "The interpersonal situation it encourages bears striking similarity to transference manifestations in psychotherapy."

Before turning to the case itself, let us recall Shafer's (1983) attempt to establish clinically meaningful criteria for psychoanalysis that might cut across the tangle of various "analytic persuasions." The four components of the analytic attitude, according to Shafer, are as follows: First, the analyst maintains an attitude of neutrality so as "to allow all of the conflictual material to be fully represented, interpreted and worked through." Second, the analyst avoids either/or thinking, so that "much time in analysis is spent interpreting the analysand's need to see things as either black or white." Third, the analyst analyzes, by which Shafer means "the analyst's focus is on the interpretation of psychical reality." Fourth, the analyst aims to be helpful by "the maintenance of a respectful affirmative attitude" so that "the analyst is always ready to review the difficulties presented by the analysand, not in a negative light, but rather as meaningful, even if still obscure, expression of the very problems that call for analysis (pp. 5–12).

The case comes from a Tibetan spiritual biography. Tibetan spiritual biographies serve an array of narrative purposes: they record the legends of a particular spiritual lineage; they provide inspiration to practice meditation and they are used liturgically for chanting and devotion. I would argue that it is also possible to regard the biographies as narrative models of psychological transformation. This is the reverse of the situation encountered in psychoanalysis, where the "theory" implies certain ideas about what is important in the story of a human life. To use Shafer's terms, the various analytic persuasions are, in effect, narrative representations of psychic life. If that is a reasonable view, then it is interesting to consider that within a specific school of Tibetan Buddhism several different biographies are honored, each describing very different personalities, different teaching relationships, and different "outcomes." In some stories celibates take wives or mistresses; in others, monasticism is embraced. Some of the protagonists become the founders of institutions while others renounce organizations to practice in the wilderness. I emphasize this narrative variability because the narrative to follow demonstrates that the Tibetans understood the relevance of infantile sexuality more usually associated with a traditional Freudian position. Elsewhere, I have discussed another Tibetan biography in terms derived from object relations theory and notions of early attachments. The coexistence of these various psychological narratives within a single school may represent, in story form, the type of integrated, multi-theoretical approach to psychoanalysis suggested by Shafer (1983) among others.

What follows is a summary of the biography of the Indian Buddhist

Naropa and his teacher Tilopa (Guenther, 1980). Naropa went on to become the teacher of the Tibetan translator Marpa and is, therefore, considered a founding figure of Tibetan Buddhism.

Naropa was born to a royal family and as a child showed an early aptitude for spiritual scholarship. He pursued the study of Buddhism, but his parents despaired that he would not continue the family line. Not wishing to upset them, Naropa married, although he never would produce an heir. After eight years of marriage, he left home to join the faculty of Nalanda University, the leading Buddhist university of his era. He became a great scholar and defeated all opponents in debates. For eight years more he taught, until one day, while studying grammar, he had a very unusual experience. A terrifying shadow fell over him. When he looked up he saw an old woman with thirty-seven ugly features described variously as red, deep, hollowed eyes, a forehead large and protruding, a face with many wrinkles, ears that were long and lumpy, etc. She asked, "What are you looking into?" He replied, "I study the books on grammar, epistemology, spiritual precepts, and logic." "Do you understand them?" the lady asked. "Yes," replied Naropa. "Do you understand the words or the sense?" she asked. "The words," replied Naropa. The old woman rocked with laughter and began to dance, waving her stick in the air. Thinking she might feel still happier, Naropa added, "I also understand the sense." But then the woman began to weep and tremble. Naropa asked, "How is it that you were happy when I said I understood the words, but became miserable when I added that I also understood the sense?" She replied, "Happy because you, a great scholar, did not lie and frankly admitted that you only understood the words; sad, because you told a lie by stating that you understood the sense, which you do not." "Who then understands the sense?" asked Naropa. "My brother," replied the old woman. "Introduce me to him wherever he may be," implored Naropa. "Go yourself," said the woman, "pay your respects to him and beg that you may come to grasp the sense." And with these words she disappeared like a rainbow in the sky.

Naropa then resolved to find his true spiritual teacher. First he had a vision instructing him to seek the guru Tilopa. He went east for many months until he came to a narrow footpath blocked by a leper woman without hands or feet. He told her to step aside, but she replied that she could not move. Naropa closed his nose in disgust and leapt over her, but the leper woman rose in the air to a rainbow halo and said, "How can you find the guru with your habit-forming thoughts and limitations?" Naropa then realized that the leper woman was, in fact, the very guru that he sought, so he resolved to learn from the experience and try again.

Next, he encountered a stinking bitch crawling with vermin. Again, he closed his nose and tried to jump over her. Again the revolting figure appeared in the sky with a rainbow, this time saying, "All living beings are one's parents. How will you find the guru without developing compassion?" Again, he resolved not to allow revulsion to turn him away from the teaching, but again it happened. Next, he met a scoundrel who was playing tricks on his parents, whom Naropa resolved not to associate with, and who, of course, again became a rainbow. And so forth. Time and again Tilopa appeared, disguised as people committing all sorts of heinous crimes; and every time Naropa resolved not to be turned away. Eventually, he despaired of ever finding his teacher. He became suicidal and prepared to cut his veins with a razor. But, at this point, Tilopa appeared to him in human form and accepted him as a student. Tilopa then oriented him to his training by offering him various symbols of what he could expect. For example, Tilopa burned a cloth to show Naropa that his emotional instability would burn in the process of illumination. The offering of fruit symbolized the emergence of his true self.

After this orientation, the teachings themselves followed in twelve episodes. For each, Tilopa would sit motionless and mute for a year. Naropa would circumambulate him with folded hands, requesting instruction. At the end of the year, Tilopa would make a bizarre, dangerous request, such as asking Naropa to jump into a fire. After Naropa barely survives the experience, Tilopa asked indifferently, "What's wrong with you?" Naropa would complain of his suffering and Tilopa would explain that he was giving up some form of neurotic accumulation and that he should continue to look into the mirror of his mind. The mirror of mind is described as the home of the *dakini*. The *dakini* in Tibetan Buddhism is a personal deity, regarded as fundamentally psychological in nature, who represents the innate enlightenment of the individual in a female form. Specifically, the *dakini* unites sexual passion and anger as an expression of awakened mind. The *dakini* can be regarded as an example of a transitional object in spiritual practice (see Finn, 1992). The *dakini* is neither real nor unreal, external or internal, profane or sacred. She is psychologically approached as something outside so something inside can be attended to.

It is not necessary for our purposes to go into all the teachings in detail, but a later episode is instructive. After the usual motionless sitting, Tilopa and Naropa encountered a king and queen with their retinue. Tilopa requested that Naropa throw the queen down and drag her about; Naropa did so and was badly beaten by the king and his retinue. Again, Tilopa healed him from the injuries and offered him the following instruction:

> When (the meditator) has come to a stage where the possibilities of taking birth in various forms dawn upon him and when he sees his prospective parents engaging in coitus and feels hatred towards his father and love for his mother (provided he should be a male, while in the case of a female it would be the other way about) he transforms his mother's womb into (what is called) "Samayasattva" and himself enters there as Jñānassattva from his father's mouth, nose, or other part of the body. Conceiving the human body as a particularly well-suited foundation for the mantra-behaviour, he attains authentic existence after having been reborn. (Guenther, p. 74)

Tilopa concluded that it would be a mistake to assume either that evil has been abandoned or that good has been obtained through such an experience. In fact, at this point, notions of good and evil have nothing to do with what is taking place and would confuse real understanding. Shortly after his experience Tilopa instructs Naropa in what is called the practice of the lower gate. These are the famous tantric instructions for sexual intercourse as a means of spiritual practice. In these practices sexual bliss and mystery are seen as continuous with the mystery and bliss of genuine religious attainment.

The final teaching involves Naropa dismembering his own body to make a circular mandala offering to Tilopa, at which point Tilopa says to him, "This body of yours, Naropa, with its sullied pleasure, has no reality, yet it should be the source of your delight eternal." He goes on to offer Naropa a skull filled to the brim with a stinking, impure mess which turns out to be delicious. Tilopa says that without meditation the mess is vile. Similarly, if there is no meditation, the emotions may seem to be the cause of *samsara* (suffering), but in meditation they become the bliss of *nirvana* (liberation.)

It is said that, at the culmination of his teaching, Naropa's mind and the mind of his teacher became one. Naropa then went on to impress a king and win his daughter as a consort. He also became an unpredictable spiritual teacher.

While the fantastic aspects of this story are impressive, I am also struck by the psychodynamic coherence of the material. The relationship between Tilopa and Naropa seems to be understandable within the context of what Shafer is calling the analytic attitude, and the specific content of the teachings seems to be consistent with analytic theories of personal unfolding. Like many modern analysands, Naropa has accomplished a good deal in the external world. Nevertheless, he suffered from an apprehension of inner incompleteness. He also, like modern analysands, knew a great deal intellectually about the mind, the teachings, and perhaps even about his own difficulties, but he knew the words and not the sense.

Naropa's early experiences with Tilopa have a compelling parallel to analytic experiences as well. He devalues Tilopa at the beginning and is only able to see his teacher as diseased or evil or threatening, which is characteristic of modern narcissistic analysands. The teachings that he receives in glimpses from the many miraculous beings include the directive that he realize that all beings are his parents and that he is in relationship with all phenomena through the experience of early objects. The Buddhist teaching that all beings are one's parents is meant to awaken compassion and relationship to all of creation while again establishing the inseparability of absolute spiritual truth and relative psychological truth. In his despair Naropa is able to surrender his intellectual judgments and truly enter a dependent relationship with Tilopa. What follows in the twelve episodes of the teaching is all too familiar to analysands: the experience of a repetitive cycle of crisis and involvement on the part of the teacher Tilopa, eventually culminating in an engagement with Oedipal material, a reclaiming by Naropa of his sexuality and his own body, and a new freedom to go out into the world in a way defined by himself and not by either internal or external tyrannies.

In spite of the superficially magical qualities in the story, it appears that Tilopa meets Shafer's criteria for an analytic attitude. Certainly, he is radically neutral in Shafer's sense of creating a space where all of Naropa's conflicts can emerge. Second, Tilopa is a master of going beyond either/or thinking. His entire rhetoric and method are based on the radical deconstruction of the dualistic perception of reality. He does not preach theology but interprets events for their psychological meaning, and he always directs Naropa's attention to the inner source of eros and aggression. Lastly, Tilopa is consistently helpful to Naropa as he struggles to gain a genuine relationship to his mind and body. It is striking that this story should parallel so closely what Freud found in himself and the Greek tragedy of Oedipus. Where are we left as we ponder these parallels? Freud (1933) wrote:

> It is easy to imagine, too, that certain mystical practices may succeed in upsetting the
> normal relations between the different regions of the mind, so that, for instance,

perception may be able to grasp happenings in the depths of the ego and in the id which were otherwise inaccessible to it (p. 71).

Julia Kristeva (1987), in comparing psychoanalysis with the Chinese traditions of Confucianism and Taoism, reflects that "Freud's discovery, inspired by and for the benefit of the suffering individual, may well effect that ludic metamorphosis that leads us, at the termination of treatment, to regard language as body and body as language." She concludes: "Is psychoanalysis perhaps also our China within?" (p. 35). Naropa knew the words but not the sense. Looking for the sense, he found his body. Kristeva asks whether psychoanalysis is our China within. I am suggesting here that it may also be our Tibet.

Loewald (1978) argues no less when he asserts that it was only a hesitation in Freud's character that prevented him from seeing that the timelessness of the unconscious was identical to the experience of eternity in religious literature. As he concludes: "Certain forms of religious experience to which I have alluded are aspects of unconscious mentation, aspects that in much of modern civilization are more deeply repressed than 'sexuality' is today" (p. 74). Perhaps this very repression, which contributes to a certain tension between the categories of spirit and psyche, can itself be subjected to analysis: so that analytic insight can be appreciated in spiritual terms and the spiritual experience at the heart of analysis can be embraced without embarrassment. This isn't a new point of course, but, perhaps by its very nature, easily forgotten.

References

Engler, Jack H. (1983). "Vicissitudes of the Self According to Psychoanalysis and Buddhism: A Spectrum Model of Object Relations Development." *Psychoanalysis and Contemporary Thought* 6: 29–72.

Epstein, Mark (1995). *Thoughts Without a Thinker: Psychotherapy from a Buddhist Perspective.* New York: Basic Books.

Finn, Mark (1992). "Transitional Space and Tibetan Buddhism: The Object Relations of Meditation." 109–18, in *Object Relations Theory and Religion,* ed. Mark Finn and J. Gartner. Westport, Conn.: Praeger.

Freud, Sigmund (1933). *New Introductory Lectures on Psychoanalysis.* New York: W. W. Norton.

Fromm, Erich (1950). *Psychoanalysis and Religion.* New Haven: Yale University Press.

Guenther, H. V., trans. (1980). *The Life and Teaching of Naropa.* Boston: Shambhala.

Horney, Karen (1987). *Final Lectures.* New York: W. W. Norton.

Horton, Paul C. (1974). "The Mystical Experience: Substance of an Illusion." *Journal of the American Psychoanalytic Association* 22, 364–80.

Kristeva, Julia (1987). *In the Beginning Was Love*. New York: Columbia University Press.

Loewald, Hans (1978). *Psychoanalysis and the History of the Individual*. New Haven: Yale University Press.

Rubin, J. (1996). *Psychotherapy and Buddhism*. New York: Plenum Press.

Shafer, R. (1983). *The Analytic Attitude*. New York: Basic Books.

SLOUCHING TOWARDS BUDDHISM

A CONVERSATION WITH NINA COLTART

Anthony Molino

❑

AM: How did you chance upon Buddhism, and what has been the history of your attraction to and involvement in it?

NC: I talk a bit about that in *Slouching Towards Bethlehem*, insofar as I see myself as having a religious temperament. I do believe such a thing exists. I mean, there are people who go through their lives absolutely cold to religion. It doesn't mean anything to them at all. There are also people who, quite the opposite, have religious temperaments and look for worship, belief . . . dependence, if you like . . . elements that are usually associated with religion. Early on, from my late teens until I was

---

This interview with Dr. Nina Coltart is excerpted from a much longer conversation of ours, published in its entirety in my *Freely Associated: Encounters in Psychoanalysis with Christopher Bollas, Joyce McDougall, Michael Eigen, Adam Phillips and Nina Coltart* (London: Free Association Books, 1997). The final version of the conversation, which took place over the course of two days, September 12 and December 7, 1996, in Dr. Coltart's home outside of London, was reviewed and approved by Dr. Coltart only a few weeks before her sad and untimely death on June 24, 1997. I consider it a fateful privilege to have been entrusted with this final testament of sorts, which is reprinted here with the kind permission of Free Association Books.

about thirty, I was quite a devout practicing Christian, and it did a great deal for me. During that time I knew some good, decent Christians, and that was certainly a help. And, of course, I believed in God, and took Communion regularly.

And yet, as soon as I developed an active sex life—which was rather late for me, not surprisingly, in my late twenties—almost overnight I stopped believing in God. I think this happens to a lot of people, except it doesn't really get talked about very much. It's a phenomenon I've encountered in other people as well. And when I say stopped, I really mean stopped. Suddenly, and unequivocally. I haven't ever quite worked out why active sexuality should stop making a person believe in God. I mean, I've got some ideas about it, but not very many. In a way, I don't really care any longer. It all seems so long ago. But of course I still had a religious temperament. I was also a depressed young woman, and I wanted to be an analyst. So then I had an analysis; and though I never indulged a fanatical credulity in psychoanalysis the way some people do, it did occupy my attention for several years. But almost as soon as I'd finished I started looking around for something to sponge up my religious proclivities. It's not that I leapt out of one and into the other, however. There was a gap of four or five years before I became actively involved with Buddhism. . . .

I remember having an instinctive feeling that I wanted to learn to meditate. This was because my analysis, although it helped with my depression, didn't do much for my anxiety. I felt that if I could learn to meditate properly, I would be helped to manage my anxieties. I remember learning of a weekend retreat, run by a Buddhist monk as part of an ongoing adult education program. I applied to attend it, and did. The monk running the program subsequently turned out to be one of the greatest Buddhist teachers in the West. He virtually brought Theravadin Buddhism to this country, and set up the first Theravadin monastery, of which there are now six. Many people think this sounds rather ironic, but I regard my life as a series of strokes of luck. I had one or two strokes of bad luck, sure, but I've had some real strokes of good luck in my life. One of them was that weekend—at which I not only learned the rudiments of meditation but came to be taught by someone who subsequently became recognized as a great Theravadin teacher. Sheer luck! I remember thinking, "I want this man to be my teacher." And I've never looked back. That must have been twenty-five years ago. . . .

AM: Have your practice and commitment been as unwavering as your early

Christianity? What about the evolution of your Buddhist practice over
the years?

NC: By the time I started in Buddhism, I was older. I'd been analyzed, I
was established in my career, I was moving toward being successful in
my career. In many ways I was grown up and more mature, and I brought
far less depression to it. I did bring with me need and a capacity for
anxiety, but I think the evolution of my Buddhist practice has been
altogether peaceful, much more so than my earlier years as a Christian.
It's not true to say I didn't go into it with the kind of devotion I'd
brought to Christianity, because I did. But then that's part of having a
religious temperament. But my Buddhist development and practice have
been quieter. Slower, and gentler. . . .

You can listen to countless Buddhist teachings or sermons and many,
if not all of them, say the same thing. They all evidence how the Buddha
was a great teacher, precisely because he knew that, for the few things
in this life that really matter to sink in and be properly taught, they've
got to be repeated over and over again in different ways. Moreover, if
you've got a good teacher, as I've had, a lot of the teaching is very
amusing to listen to. There's lots of jokes. Teachers all hammer home
at the same themes, always from slightly different angles, until you really
begin to simplify your heart. By purifying your heart and simplifying
your mind, you come to realize that you don't have to keep scrambling
about like a monkey thinking your important thoughts. You learn to get
deeper into meditation, where the whole aim is to empty your mind of
thought. Meditation in the Buddhist tradition is not thinking, contrary
to the Christian tradition, in which you're literally given a theme to
think about. The two traditions couldn't be more radically different
in this way. Buddhist meditation is a sustained effort: watching the
breath to clear the mind, getting behind the scrambling monkey of
thought in order to stop it. Being able to do so, ever more and more
profoundly, and experiencing its effects, has been for me a slow but
steady process.

AM: In your most recent book, *The Baby and the Bathwater*, you mention
a defining period of twelve years in which Buddhism became absolutely
central to your life. Can you discuss the importance of that period?

NC: I referred to twelve years of Buddhist practice insofar as it took me
that long before I realized the third sign of being. There are three signs
of being in Buddhism: *dukkha*, which is suffering; *anicca*, which refers to
the transience or impermanence of all things; and *anatta*, which means

no self. In an essay from my first book, *Slouching Towards Bethlehem*, I comment that *anatta* is the one sign that Westerners find hard to swallow. We're all so ego-bound. The whole of psychoanalysis is bound up with the concept of the ego. The whole idea of being a no self takes the Western mind ages to penetrate, to be realized. And yet, as I think I said in *Slouching Towards Bethlehem*, I initially didn't bother about this very much. I thought, "Well, if I practice Buddhism faithfully and listen to the teachings, I will probably come to that point of realization. And if I don't, I don't." And in twelve years, really, of very regular practice and listening to teaching, I did come to it. I'd realized that I had realized it. *Anatta* had become real for me. . . .

Now this, of course, has considerable impact on what was, let's say, already an "interest" of mine—namely, the idea of one's own death. If one is not a self, if the ego is a construct, the result of a conditioning we come to accept, well then, what is there to fear? In any case, it's always been my impression that people fear dying much more than death . . . but that too hasn't been much sorted out in the West. I mean, it does require a lot more contemplation and attention. I myself continue to practice. It's not that I got to the point of realizing *anatta* only to think, "All right, that's it, now what should we do next?" To this day I continue my Buddhist practice; insofar as it centers on meditation, it is interminable.

AM: I'm intrigued when I hear someone like you say that she's realized the no self, only to acknowledge—as you've done earlier in our conversation—her own ego's historical need for defenses, as well as her own psychotic anxieties. How can a person who's realized the no self speak of an ego that is still so vulnerable?

NC: And so well functioning, a lot of the time! It's a question of levels of attitude, of levels of experience. The Buddha himself, if you read some of the scriptures or *sutras*, as they are called, was very good on this score. He was a very astute psychologist. He realized the difficulty of the question you've just asked. Here we are, we're cast into the world, we all have our cultures and languages and personal histories to contend with. We have to talk to each other. We have to be. We have to function. Increasingly in the world we're asked to cope with cultural inputs. We can't turn our backs on the world and say, "Well, sorry, folks, I'm a no self. I don't take part in that sort of thing." We have to observe the conventions of the culture that we live in, or else we'd have no life. I guess we would crouch in a corner meditating for twenty-three hours a day, possibly managing to totter to the shops and get a bit of food to sustain ourselves. . . .

For the longest time, we've had tools for thinking about the self, and the way the mind operates. Freud himself, of course, gave us a way to understand the structure of the mind—one which, while thoroughly flawed and subject to countless revisions, I quite accept. Conventionally, of course, we all are selves to ourselves. Other individuals are selves to us and, as individuals, are different from the next individual. Such a view, indeed such an experience, is all part of the convention that life and living demand of us. It doesn't alter in the least the fact that the three signs of being—suffering, impermanence, and no self—are still fundamental truths, with a capital "T." Everything else involves the conditions of going from day to day, of putting one foot in front of the other—from communicating with our friends at a micro-level, to trying to make sense of all sorts of global phenomena on a macro-level of existence.

AM: Is it this recognition of social and cultural realities that keeps Buddhism, in your view, on this side of nihilism?

NC: Buddhism is not, as is often thought, nihilistic. Not at all. It is the recognition of precisely what we've been talking about that keeps it from being so. Nor is it lugubrious. I mean, it's very serious and, at heart, actually pretty austere. There's a great deal of laughter in Buddhist monasteries—real, genuine heartfelt laughter. A lot of life is seen to be very ironic and very funny. Personally, I've never laughed so much as when listening to some of the abbots' sermons or talks, at the monastery just up the road. And yet, Buddhism is basically an austere religion. Contrary to Christianity, it doesn't have much, for example, in the way of consolations or comforts—except, that is, for what I regard as the three bare truths, which prove themselves through one's own efforts, as one tries to live out the fundamental precepts of the Middle Way. Such efforts make you happier, as the Buddha always said they would. In fact, the Buddha's message, in short, was: "Be good and you'll be happy." It's what all the Victorian and Edwardian nannies have been saying for years!

AM: On the matter of Buddhism and the self, I was flipping through a copy of Anthony Burgess' autobiography recently, a book called *Little Wilson and Big God*, when I found the following quote:

What do we mean by the ego? It is an existential concept, I believe, and the ego I examine is multiple and somewhat different from the ego that is doing the examining.

Even the ego that began this book in September of 1985 is not the one that has completed it in 1986. In other words, the book is about somebody else, connected by the ligature of a common track in time and space to the writer of this last segment of it which cheats and looks like the first.

As a Buddhist, what do you make of Burgess' remarks?

NC: That sounds remarkably like the sort of sermons I've heard from advanced monks! Certainly, if you've gotten as far as thinking that there is no self—or, I would prefer to say, as *realizing* that there is no self, because you don't get that far by thinking—you're going to accept fairly readily that the self who got up this morning is not, by any means, the self that you experience yourself as now. Of course, we go on experiencing ourselves as selves because, as I've already suggested, you can't not do so. But between then and now conditions have changed, hundreds of thoughts have been thought, hundreds of moments have been lived through. Burgess is quite right. There is a kind of ligature, possibly called memory, which connects the first part of his book to the last, or the beginning of our conversation to where we are now. But nothing much less tenuous than that.

AM: Increasingly, many parallels are drawn between psychoanalysis and Buddhism. What are the principal ones you've found? And what application, if any, has Buddhism found in your clinical practice?

NC: At the risk of sounding like my own salesman, I'd have to send you to buy my first book, *Slouching Towards Bethlehem*, where there's a chapter on Buddhism and psychoanalysis in which I talk in some detail about the ways in which they've never clashed for me. I've always seen them as potentiating and strengthening each other. That was always my experience. In the early stages of both, you might say, the paths have much in common. Many people who go into either, or both, are in more or less anguished states of mind for which they want help. Along both paths you begin to look into yourself: reflecting on your past, in analysis; and on your conditioning—which after all is your past—in Buddhism. Through both you learn how very influential those early effects were, and you learn to begin to examine them by free association. There's no clash here, none whatsoever. The paths tend to diverge further on because Freud always said he was not setting out to develop a religious system. He was not trying to provide a philosophy of life, nor was he trying to teach morality. Far from it. In many ways, he was trying to undermine morality as he and his times knew it. And this is where

Buddhism and psychoanalysis begin to diverge, but in a way that never seemed to me to matter all that much. . . .

Whatever analysts say about being nonjudgmental, or about being neutral on matters of morality is, of course, absolute bunkum. Analysts are making judgments all the time. The entirety of one's moral fiber, one's whole moral outlook, is involved in every single session, and in the tiniest of clinical judgments one makes. It can't not be this way. Therefore, the fact that Buddhism aims, on one level, to help establish and strengthen a moral base doesn't seem to me to be in conflict with psychoanalysis. Not at all. At least not as long as analysts don't start imposing their own strong moral judgments on patients. Again, I don't see how there's any conflict, because analysts can't help expressing indirectly their own morality to patients. Patients aren't fools. They're going to hear the echoes of that morality. They're going to pick it up. They're going to know if an analyst is trying to impose that morality on them, or not. . . .

With regard to any clinical applications, I think they are indirect at best. If you go into Buddhism and stick with it, you can't help having your way of thought influenced. But you have to be careful about not becoming a moral teacher or a pedagogue. A lot of my patients would probably be surprised on finding the chapters I've written on Buddhism, in both my first and last book. That is to say, it's only indirectly that they'd come to know that Buddhism was something I practiced. I would not extol Buddhism or teach Buddhism to a patient. Only very, very occasionally, toward the end of a long therapy or analysis, might I mention it, almost en passant, and perhaps provide the address of a Buddhist Association. But I'd do so only if I felt this person to be on a search of his own, looking for information about a path to pursue, and only if I knew him well enough to know that Buddhism might prove suitable. But I wouldn't do more than that. I wouldn't start teaching Buddhist precepts, or anything like that at all.

As regards my own practice, and how Buddhism has affected my clinical work with patients, one of the earliest things I noticed was the deepening of attention. I'd written a paper on attention in my first book, where I refer to "bare attention," which is a very Buddhist phrase. Bare attention has a sort of purity about it. It's not a cluttered concept. It's that you simply become better, as any good analyst knows, at concentrating more and more directly, more purely, on what's going on in a session. You come to concentrate more and more fully on this person who is with you, here and now, and on what it is they experience with you: to the point that many sessions become similar to meditations. When this happens, I usually don't say very much, but am very, very closely attending to the patient, with my thought processes in suspension, moving toward what Bion called "O": a state which I see as being "unthought-out," involving a quality of intuitive apperception of another person's evolving truth. All this undoubtedly became easier to do as a result of my Buddhist practice. Sessions became more frequently like meditations. That is about the most powerful effect Buddhism had on my clinical practice.

AM: I can't help but wonder about the effects a Buddhist training might have on the countertransference sphere. What has your experience been along these lines?

NC: It's an interesting way of looking at the relationship between the two paths. My immediate response, without having given your observation any prior thought, is that a Buddhist training might facilitate certain aspects of being oneself in a clinical situation. One of the things an analyst has constantly to learn to do—although with any luck we all do get better at it over time—is to sort out our own countertransferences. Learning to sort out our own personal reactions to the patient, and to what's going on between us, from the insidiousness of projective identifications. Such an exercise, of course, is vital. I would say that Buddhism makes this process easier because it not only gives a person, by clearing one's mind of too many scrambling thoughts, the capacity to fade out of the picture temporarily; it also opens up the space for something which the patient is busily trying to lodge into you. To this end, I would have to think that an analyst with this kind of sensitivity would be less defended, and all the quicker to recognize the nature of such a dynamic. . . .

Although I've never reflected on this question before, I think what I'm saying is true. It feels right. . . . There are two main forms of meditation in Theravadin Buddhism. One is *samatha*, where you simply watch the breath until you imagine you'd be bored to death with it. And yet it's not actually boring; it's a very good way of quieting the mind. The other is called *vipassana*, which involves getting to a stage of quieting the breath whereby a sort of internal detachment occurs from one's own powers of observation. It's a sort of self-splitting really. You can observe your thoughts running past you. You're not trying to control them or squash them or anything like that, but let them run on, as they are, of their own accord. *Vipassana* is the art of studying the thought stream. Now, if you've done a lot of this kind of meditation, it can't but help in studying the countertransference, because you do get to know all sorts of layers of your own thoughts by doing *vipassana*. I've not thought of this before, but it's fascinating to try to work it out here on the spot with you. If you've done a lot of *vipassana* and have managed to foster this split attitude of observation detached from thinking and reacting, yes, it's got to help the countertransference as well, hasn't it?

AM: I'd like to end our discussion on Buddhism with one general question regarding what you've called the "religious temperament." Alongside Freud's many accomplishments, he also helped close the doors of psychoanalysis to such temperaments or sensibilities. Recently, however, people as different as the Jewish mystic Michael Eigen and the Marxist Joel Kovel have been advocating and encouraging a return of the spiritual within psychoanalysis. Even beyond the reaches of Buddhism, how do you view the relationship of psychoanalysis to spirituality?

NC: I simply couldn't begin to address such a question! I don't know if even you have a sense of how simply colossal a question it is. I would have to sit and think about the question quite a bit more. It's not one I'd want to answer off the cuff. But I have read quite a lot of Michael Eigen. I'm a great admirer of his. . . .

AM: What if I were to reframe the question, or refocus it for you?

NC: Yes, please do.

AM: From both your own practice and what you know of the British scene, is there a greater opening toward and acceptance of the religious and spiritual temperaments, or is there still a foreclosure operating against them?

NC: There's still a foreclosure. Definitely. I have no doubt at all that the whole notion of spirituality, anything tainted with the very word "religion" creeping in under the cracks of the doors of psychoanalysis is still very much a taboo subject. I would certainly say that in the British Society, you do get islands of interest . . . odd people here and there who obviously have religious temperaments, or an interest in some form of spirituality. Joe Berke, for instance, has become a practicing Orthodox Jew. One or two other friends of mine have also gone deeply into Judaism and its practice. I certainly know of at least one practicing Christian psychoanalyst. . . .

AM: Neville Symington also seems to have opened up . . .

NC: Neville Symington has opened up a lot with his recent book, *Emotion and Spirit*, and he's done so very, very well. I mean, it's an immensely readable and thought-provoking book. Nevertheless, I think there's still a lot of foreclosure in the field at large. Of course, the Kleinians are a religion in and of themselves, and operate as if they were a high church with the truth to proclaim. But we won't go any further into that. . . .

Works Cited

Burgess, Anthony (1986). *Little Wilson and Big God* New York: Weidenfeld & Nicolson.
Symington, Neville (1994). *Emotion and Spirit* London: Cassell.

Nina Coltart: Selected Bibliography

The Baby and the Bathwater (1996). London: Karnac Books; Madison, Conn.: International Universities Press.
How to Survive as a Psychotherapist (1993). London: Sheldon Press; Northvale, N.J.: Jason Aronson, Inc.
Slouching Towards Bethlehem (1992). London: Free Association Books; New York: Guilford Press.

CRITICAL PERSPECTIVES

❑

THE SELF IN JUNG AND ZEN

Masao Abe

❑

I

The most conspicuous difference between Buddhism and Western psychology is perhaps found in their respective treatments of the concept of "self." In Western psychology, the existence of a "self" is generally affirmed; Buddhism denies the existence of an enduring "self" and substitutes instead the concept of *anātman*, "no-self."

In Western spiritual traditions one of the classical examples of the affirmation of an enduring self is Plato's notion of the immortal soul. The basis of the modern Western conception of the self was established by Descartes' *cogito ergo sum*, which led to a dualistic interpretation of mind as thinking substance and matter as extended substance. Christianity, which is not based on human reason but divine revelation, emphasizes self-denial or self-sacrifice in devotion to one's God and fellow human beings. Even so, as a responsible agent in an I-Thou relationship, the human self is affirmed

This essay first appeared in *The Eastern Buddhist*, vol. XVIII, no. 1, Spring 1985 (pages 57–70). It is reprinted here with the permission of the author, in conjunction with the editors of *The Eastern Buddhist*.

as something essential. Although it is a relatively new scientific discipline, modern Western psychology shares with older Western spiritual traditions the affirmation of the existence of a self.

In ancient India, the Brahmanical tradition propounded the idea of at-man or the eternal, unchanging self which is fundamentally identical with Brahman, the ultimate Reality of the universe. The Buddha did not accept this age-old notion of *atman* and discoursed instead about *anātman*, no-self. As Walpola Rahula states:

> Buddhism stands unique in the history of human thought in denying the existence of such a Soul, Self, or Atman. According to the teaching of the Buddha, the idea of self is an imaginary, false belief which has no corresponding reality, and it produces harmful thoughts of "me" and "mine," selfish desire, craving, attachment, hatred, ill-will, conceit, pride, egoism, and other defilements, impurities and problems. It is the source of all the troubles in the world from personal conflicts to wars between nations. In short, to this false view can be traced all the evil in the world.[1]

Throughout his life, the Buddha taught the means to remove and destroy such a false view and thereby enlighten human beings.

To those who desire self-preservation after death, the Buddhist notion of no-self may sound not only strange but frightening. This was true even for the ancient Indians who lived in the time of the Buddha. A bhikkhu once asked the Buddha: "Sir, is there a case where one is tormented when something permanent within oneself is not found?" Not unaware of such fear, the Buddha answered, "Yes, bhikkhu, there is." Elsewhere the Buddha says: "O bhikkhus, this idea that I may not be, I may not have, is frightening to the uninstructed worldling."[2] Nevertheless, the Buddha preached the notion of no-self tirelessly until his death, simply because the doctrine is so essential to his teaching: to emancipate human beings from suffering and to awaken them to the fundamental reality of human existence.

To properly understand the Buddhist notion of no-self, it would be helpful to consider the following five points:

First, the doctrine of no-self is the natural result of, or the corollary to, the analysis of the five *skandhas* or five aggregates—that is, matter, sensation, perception, mental formations, and consciousness. According to Buddhism, human beings are composed of these five aggregates and nothing more.[3]

Second, the notion of no-self—that is, the notion of no substantial unchanging own-being—is applied not only to human beings but also to all beings. This is why one of the three essentials peculiar to Buddhism is that "all *dharmas* [i.e., all entities] are without self." Thus, not only conditioned, relative things, but also unconditioned, absolute things are understood to be without self, without their own-being. Accordingly, not only *samsara*, but also *nirvana*, not only delusion, but also enlightenment, are without own-being. Neither relative nor absolute things are self-existing and independent.

Third, the notion of no-self entails, therefore, the denial of one absolute God who is self-existing, and instead puts forward the doctrine of dependent origination. That is, in Buddhism, nothing whatever is independent or self-existing; everything is dependent on everything else. Thus, all unconditioned, absolute, and eternal entities such as Buddha or the state of *nirvana* co-arise and co-cease with all conditioned, relative, and temporal entities, such as living beings or the state of *samsara*.

Fourth, in accordance with these teachings, the ultimate in Buddhism is neither conditioned nor unconditioned, neither relative nor absolute, neither temporal nor eternal. Therefore, the Buddhist ultimate is called *śūnyatā*—that is, "Emptiness." It is also called the "Middle Way," because it is neither an eternalist view which insists on the existence of an unchanging eternal entity as the ultimate, nor an annihilationist view which maintains that everything is null and void.

Fifth, if one clearly understands that the Buddhist notion of no-self is essentially connected with its doctrine of dependent origination and *śūnyatā* or Emptiness, one may also naturally understand that the Buddhist notion of no-self does not signify that mere lack or absence of self, as an annihilationist may suggest, but rather constitutes a position which is beyond both the eternalist view of self and the nihilistic view of no-self. This is forcefully illustrated by the Buddha himself when he answered with silence both the questions "Is there a self?" and "Is there no-self?" Keeping silence to both the affirmative and negative forms of the question concerning the "self," the Buddha profoundly expressed the ultimate Reality of humanity. His silence itself does not indicate an agnostic position, but is a striking presence of the true nature of human being which is beyond affirmation and negation.

In the light of these five points, I hope it is now clear that the Buddhist notion of no-self does not signify a mere negation of the existence of the self, but rather signifies a realization of human existence which is neither self nor no-self. Since the original human nature cannot be characterized as self or no-self, it is called No-self. Therefore, No-self represents nothing but the true nature or true Self of humanity which cannot be conceptualized at all and is beyond self and no-self.

In the Buddhist tradition, Zen most clearly and vividly emphasizes that the Buddhist notion of No-self is nothing but true Self. Rinzai's phrase "true person of no rank" serves as an example. "No rank" implies freedom from any conceptualized definition of human being. Thus the "true person of no rank" signifies the "true person" who cannot be characterized either by self or by no-self. "True person of no rank" is identical with the true nature of human being presenting itself in the silence of the Buddha. Unlike the Buddha who emphasizes meditation, however, Rinzai is an active and dynamic Zen master, directly displaying his own "true Self" while demanding his disciples to actively demonstrate this "true Self" in themselves. The following exchange vividly illustrates this dynamic character:

> One day Rinzai gave his sermon: "There is the true person of no rank in the mass of naked flesh, who goes in and out from your facial gates [i.e., sense organs]. Those who have not testified [to the fact], look! look!"
> A monk came forward and asked, "Who is this true person of no rank?"
> Rinzai came down from his chair and, taking hold of the monk by the throat, said, "Speak! Speak!"
> The monk hesitated.
> Rinzai let go his hold and said, "What a worthless dirt-stick this is!"[4]

In this exchange, "true person of no rank" represents a living reality functioning through our physical body. Furthermore, Rinzai is asking his audience to notice the living reality functioning in himself by saying "Look! Look!" and demanding from the monk a demonstration of his own true nature, taking him by the throat and saying "Speak! Speak!" Zen does not intend to provide an explanation or interpretation of the nature of true Self, but rather to precipitate a direct and immediate testimony or demonstration of it through a dynamic encounter between master and disciple.

II

In seeking to point out the similarities and dissimilarities between modern Western psychology and Buddhism, especially Zen, with regard to their understanding of the concept of the "self," let us examine a dialogue between Shin'ichi Hisamatsu (1889–1980) and Carl Gustav Jung (1875–1961).

Shin'ichi Hisamatsu was a professor of Buddhism at Kyoto University. He is regarded as one of the outstanding Zen thinkers of contemporary Japan. But Hisamatsu was also a Zen layman who had attained a very profound, clear-cut Zen awakening, and his subsequent thinking and way of life were deeply rooted in this awakening. He was an excellent calligrapher, tea master, and poet as well. In all, he was a real embodiment of the Zen spirit, outstanding even among contemporary Zen masters in Japan.[5] This dialogue with Carl Jung took place at Jung's home in Küsnacht, on the outskirts of Zurich, on May 16, 1958. While there were many stimulating exchanges and many interesting points raised in the course of the dialogue, I would like to focus here on the issue of self as understood by Jung and Hisamatsu.

After a discussion about the relation between consciousness and the unconscious, Hisamatsu asked, "Which is our true Self, the 'unconscious' or 'conscious'?" Jung replied:

> Consciousness calls itself "I," while the "Self" is not "I" at all. The Self is the whole, because personality—you as the whole—consists of consciousness and the unconscious. It is the whole, or in other words, the "Self." But "I" know only the consciousness. The "unconscious" remains unknown to me.[6]

This is Jung's well-known distinction between I, or ego, and self. To Jung, "ego" is the center of the field of consciousness and the complex entity to which all conscious contents are related, whereas "self" is the total personality, which, though always present, cannot fully be known.[7]

Later in the dialogue, the following exchange occurs:

> *Hisamatsu:* Is "I-consciousness" (ego-consciousness) different from "Self-consciousness" or not?
>
> *Jung:* In ordinary usage, people say "self-consciousness," but psychologically this is only "I-consciousness." The Self is unknown, for it indicates the whole, that is, consciousness and the unconscious . . .
>
> *Hisamatsu:* What? The self cannot be known?
>
> *Jung:* Perhaps only one half of it is known, and it is the *ego*. The *ego* is the half of the "self."

Hisamatsu's surprise is understandable, because in Zen practice the self is to be clearly known. *Satori* is "self-awakening"—that is, the self awakening to itself. The awakened self is characterized as *ryōryōjōchi*—that is, "always clearly aware."

Here we can see an essential difference between Jung and Zen. In Jung, self as the total personality consists of the consciousness as "I" or "ego," which is known to itself, and the unconscious, which remains unknown. Furthermore, the unconscious includes the personal unconscious, which owes its existence to personal experience, and the collective unconscious, the content of which has never been conscious and which owes its existence exclusively to heredity. Whereas the personal unconscious can sooner or later present itself to consciousness, the collective unconscious, being universal and impersonal, consists of preexistent forms, or archetypes, which give definite form to certain psychic contents, but which can only become conscious secondarily.[8] It would therefore be appropriate to say that in Jung, the collective unconscious, as the depth of the self, is seen from the side of the conscious ego as something beyond, or as something "over there," though not externally but inwardly. It is in this sense that the unconscious is unknown. In contrast to this, according to Zen, the self is not the unknown, but rather the clearly known. More strictly speaking, the knower and the known are one, not two. The knower itself is the known, and vice versa. Self is not regarded as something existing "over there," somewhere beyond, but rather is fully realized right here and now.

We must therefore recognize clearly that although both Jung and Zen discuss the concept of the self, the entity of the self is understood by them in fundamentally different ways. According to Zen, in order to awaken to the true Self, it is necessary to realize No-self. Only through the clear realization of No-self can one awaken to true Self. And the realization of No-self in Zen would reflect the realization of the nonsubstantiality of the unconscious self as well as of the conscious ego, to use Jungian terminology. In Jung, self is the total personality, which cannot be fully known. It consists of the conscious and the unconscious. But in Zen the true Self is awakened to only through overcoming or breaking through the self in the Jungian sense. I will try to clarify later how this process can occur, but at this point I would merely like to observe that there is no suggestion of the realization of the No-self in Jung. Since the No-self—that is, the nonsubstantiality of self—is not clearly realized in Jung, it therefore remains as something unknown to the ego.

III

The dialogue now turns to the case of a patient's mental suffering and the method of curing the infirmity. Hisamatsu asked, "How is therapy related to the fundamental unconscious?" Jung replied, "When a sickness is caused by things of which we are not conscious, there exists the possibility of cure through making the causes conscious. The cause, however, does not always exist within the unconscious. Rather there are also a fair number of cases in which the various symptoms indicate the existence of conscious causes." Emphasizing the existence of the worries and difficulties in our daily life, Hisamatsu then raises several other questions. "[If] the essence of cure is liberation from worries . . . what sort of changes in the sphere of the unconscious correspond to this liberation?" "Is it possible or not for a human being to discard all of his suffering at a stroke, and can this be achieved by psychotherapy?"

> Jung: How can such a method be possible? A method which enables us to free ourselves from suffering itself?
> Hisamatsu: Doesn't psychotherapy emancipate us from suffering all at once?
> Jung: Liberate man from suffering itself? What we are trying to do is to reduce human suffering. Still some suffering remains.

At this point in the conversation, Jung's reaction to the possibility of sudden emancipations from suffering itself was quite negative. Referring to Jesus Christ and Gautama Buddha, Hisamatsu says, "The intention of these religious founders was to liberate human beings from fundamental suffering. Is it really possible that such great freedom can be achieved by psycho therapy?" Jung's response to this question is not simply negative.

> Jung: It is not inconceivable, if you treat suffering not as an individual sickness, but as an impersonal occurrence, such as a disaster or an evil . . . [The patient] is entangled in the klesa, and can be liberated from them through inner wisdom. The aim of psychotherapy is exactly the same as that of Buddhism.

This leads to a crucial point in the dialogue:

> Hisamatsu: The essential point of this liberation is how we can be awakened to our Original Self. The Original Self is the self which is no longer bound by a myriad of things. To attain this self is the essential point of freedom. It is necessary, therefore, to release oneself even from the collective unconscious and the bondage which derives from it.

Jung: If someone is caught in a myriad of things and thus bound within it, this is because he is caught within the collective unconscious at the same time. He can be freed only when he is liberated from both of them. One person may be dragged along more by the unconscious, another by things. In short, through liberation, man must be brought to a point where he is free from the compulsion to chase after a myriad of things or from being controlled by the collective unconscious. Both are fundamentally the same:

Nirvāṇa.

Hisamatsu: In what you have just said about the unconscious, Professor Jung, do you mean that the collective unconscious is something from which, in its nature, we can free ourselves?

Jung: Yes it is.

Hisamatsu: What we generally call "self" is the same as the self [*Selbst*] characterized by you, Professor Jung. But it is only after the emancipation of this self that the "Original Self" of Zen emerges. It is the True Self described in Zen as the Self which is realized in absolute emancipation and is without dependence on anything [*dokudatsu mue*].

At this point, Jung answered affirmatively Hisamatsu's question as to whether the collective unconscious is something from which one must be emancipated for real freedom. Earlier in the dialogue, he answered negatively a question concerning the possibility of gaining freedom from suffering all at once. Toward the end of the conversation, however, Jung clearly agreed with Hisamatsu on the need of overcoming even the collective unconscious for a complete cure of the patient. According to Koichi Tsujimura, who acted as interpreter for the dialogue, Jung's affirmative response surprised people in the room, for if the collective unconscious can be overcome, then Jung's analytical psychology must be fundamentally reexamined.

IV

Looking back over the dialogue, I would like to make three remarks:

First, the psychotherapeutic method of relieving a patient's suffering and the Zen method of dissolving a student's suffering are different. In Jungian psychotherapy, to cure a patient's suffering, the analyst tries to help the patient become aware of the causes of his suffering, which previously had been unconscious, or he tries to help the patient realize the aim or meaning of his life, or he tries to help change the patient's attitude toward psychic worry and make him more accepting and positive. But as Jung says in the conversation, there is no universal rule or method for the cure. There are only individual cases, and in psychotherapy the analyst must cure the patient's worries as fully as possible in each individual case. As Hisamatsu points out in his additional note, however: "If each disease is treated individually, then when one disease is gone, another disease will come along. Hence, we shall never be delivered from sickness forever. This in itself may be said to be a disease in a very profound sense."

Hisamatsu calls this "the vicious circle" of psychoanalytic therapy. Unless the root of all possible diseases is dug out and cut away, the vicious circle of psychoanalytic therapy will not be overcome. What, then, is the root of all possible psychic diseases? According to Jung it is the collective unconscious or the unknown self which is responsible for hindering us psychically. Instead of analyzing psychic diseases one by one, Zen tries to dig out and cut away the very root of the human consciousness beyond consciousness, including the Jungian or any other hypothesized realm of an unconscious. Zen insists that only then can complete emancipation from human suffering be achieved and the true Self be awakened. The realization of No-self, which is indispensable for the awakening to true Self, is simply another way of describing "cutting away" the root of human consciousness.

Second, in Jung, the collective unconscious is something unknown which must be intensively analyzed to discover the cause of a patient's suffering, but it is at the same time a realm that can never be completely known. By definition, the collective unconscious remains an unknown "x" for both analyst and analysand. In Zen, through zazen and koan practice with a Zen master, the Zen student not only digs out the root of the unknown "x" but also becomes one with it. For the Zen student the unknown "x" is not something "over there." It comes to be realized as "here and now." In other words, it is totally, completely, and experientially realized by the student *as the unknown* "x." In this total, experiential realization, it ceases to be an *object* to the student, and instead the two become one with each other. Now the student *is* the unknown "x" and the unknown "x" *is* the student. Only in this way can the student overcome the unknown "x," "cut off" its root, and awaken to his true Self.

This event can be illustrated by a *mondō* (a question-and-answer exchange) between Bodhidharma, the first patriarch in the Zen tradition, and Hui-ko, who later became the second patriarch. In deep anguish and mental perplexity after many years of inner struggle, Hui-ko approached Bodhidharma and asked him:

"My mind is not yet pacified. Pray, Master, pacify it."
"Bring your mind here and I will pacify it." said Bodhidharma.

"I have sought it for many years," Hui-ko replied. "I am still unable to take hold of it. My mind is really unattainable."

"There! Your mind is pacified once and for all," Bodhidharma confirmed.[9]

Instead of analyzing the causes of Hui-ko's suffering, Bodhidharma asked Hui-ko to bring forth his mind. Confronted with this straightaway command, Hui-ko, who had sought after his mind for many years, clearly realized that the mind is unattainable. Suddenly, he totally and experientially realized the mind to be the unattainable and the unattainable to be the mind; there was no longer even the slightest gap between himself and the unattainable. His internal perplexity was resolved in this existentially complete realization of the mind as the unattainable. Recognizing this, Bodhidharma immediately said, "There! Your mind is pacified once and for all."

In Jung, the depth of mind is *objectively* regarded from the side of the conscious "I" as the unknown collective unconscious. In contrast, by overcoming such an objective approach, Zen straightforwardly enters into the depth of mind and breaks through it by becoming completely identical with it. In Zen, this breaking through is called the Great Death—because it signifies the complete denial of human consciousness, including any such Jungian notion of the collective unconscious. And yet the Great Death in Zen is at one and the same time a resurrection in the Great Life—because in this breaking through of mind, not only is the realization that mind is unattainable or unknowable included, but also the realization that the unattainable or the unknowable is precisely the true Mind or true Self. This is why "No mind" in Zen is not a negative but a positive entity. That is to say, unlike the Jungian unconscious, No-mind in Zen is not an extra-conscious psyche, but rather is the true Mind or Original Mind which is realized beyond Jung's framework of the mind.

A significant aspect of Zen in this connection is perhaps the emphasis in koan practice on the Great Doubt. Most koans, such as Joshu's *Mu* and Hakuin's "Listen to the sound of the single hand," are designed to drive a Zen student into a mental corner, to break through the wall of the human psyche, and to open up an entirely new spiritual dimension beyond analytic or dualistic thinking. For example, the koan "Show your Original Face before your parents were born," does not refer to one's preexistence in a temporal sense, but rather asks of a student to demonstrate his or her original nature which can be *immediately* realized at the depth of existence. Only when the student demonstrates it can he or she break through the framework of a self-centered psyche. The phrase "Original Face *before your parents were born"* can be understood to refer to that which lies beyond even the hypothesized collective unconscious and which is impersonal, universal, and yet is the root-source of your own being and which is unknown to the "I" which is limited by time and space.

Zen emphasizes the importance for a Zen student to become a "Great Doubting Mass": "At the base of Great Doubt lies Great Awakening." This emphasis on Great Doubt implies that a Zen student must dig up and grapple with the unknown "x" so thoroughly that he turns into the unknown "x" itself. To become a Great Doubting Mass is to turn into the unknown "x." To turn into the unknown "x" is to come to know existentially that the unknown "x" is nothing but the true Self. And that knowing is the Great Awakening to the true Self, characterized as *ryōryōjōchi*, "always clearly aware." Koan practice has proved an effective way to lead a student to the Great Awakening through Great Doubt.

Third, despite the essential differences between Zen and Jungian psychology in their understandings of self and their respective methods of curing human suffering, I believe there are also points at which these two disciplines can profitably learn from each other, although the scope and depth of their mutual learning may perhaps not be equal. Since Zen is so overwhelmingly concerned with cutting off the root of the human consciousness in order to attain No-self as true Self, or to attain No-mind as true Mind, it tends on the whole to neglect psychological problems that occur sometimes in the process of Zen practice, in particular the delusory apparitions known as *makyō*.[10] But if Zen learns from Jungian psychology about the theory of the archetype as an unconscious organizer of human ideas, and the process of individuation, it might help the Zen practicer to better understand such mental fabrication.

Modern Western psychology, and particularly Freudian and Jungian psychology, have claimed to discover the existence of a psyche outside consciousness. With this discovery the position of the ego, until then absolute as the center of human consciousness and the active source of man's spiritual act, was relativized.[11] In Jung, the ego is no longer identical with the whole of the individual but is a limited substance serving as the center of non-unconscious phenomena. If this relativization of the ego is strengthened—that is, the substance of the ego is understood to be even more limited—it could help open the way to the realization of No-self. But in Jung, instead of a relativization of the position of ego, the position of the self as the total personality based on the collective unconscious is strongly maintained. If the collective unconscious is something ultimate in which human suffering is rooted, then, as Hisamatsu suggests in his dialogue with Jung, Jungian psychotherapy may not be free from an inevitable "vicious circle," because even though it can relieve a particular disease separately and individually, other forms of psychic disease may recur endlessly. Only when the true source is reached beyond such possible psychological realms as the collective unconscious can human beings go beyond the root of suffering itself and be released from the "vicious circle" of particular manifestations of suffering. Zen offers a way to break through even the collective unconscious and similar theories about the structure of the mind.

In this respect, it is extremely significant that in his dialogue with Hisamatsu, Jung seemed eventually to agree with the possibility and necessity of freedom from the collective unconscious. Ultimately, Jung and Zen seem to agree that there is hope for human beings to be emancipated from suffering itself, rather than their being destined to remain in a samsaric cycle, finding relief from one suffering only to be faced with another.

Notes

1. Walpola Rahula, *What the Buddha Taught* (New York: Grove Press, 1959), 51.
2. Rahula, 56.
3. Rahula, 52 and 57.
4. D. T. Suzuki, Erich Fromm, and Richard De Martino, *Zen Buddhism and Psychoanalysis* (London: George Allen & Unwin, 1960), 32 (with a slight adaptation).
5. On Hisamatsu's life and thought, see my articles "A Buddhism of Self-Awakening, Not a Buddhism of Faith" in *Añjali: A Felicitation Volume Presented to Oliver Hector de Alwis Wijesekera on His Sixtieth Birthday* (Peradeniya, Ceylon, 1970), 33–39; and "Hisamatsu's Philosophy of Awakening" in *The Eastern Buddhist*, vol. 14, no. 1 (Spring 1981), 26–42; for his obituary, see 142–47 of the latter.
6. All quotes from the conversation between Jung and Hisamatsu are taken from the Meckel and Moore translation in *Self and Liberation: The Jung/Buddhism Dialogue*, edited by D. J. Meckel and R. L. Moore (Mahwah, N.J.: Paulist Press, 1992).
7. C. G. Jung, *Aion: Contributions to the Symbolism of the Self*, in *Collected Works*, vol. 9.2 (New York: Pantheon Books, 1959), 3, 5.
8. C. G. Jung, *Archetypes and the Collective Unconscious*, in *Collected Works*, vol. 9.1 (New York: Pantheon Books, 1959), 43.
9. Daisetz T. Suzuki, *Essays in Zen Buddhism*, First Series (London: Rider, 1949; reprinted 1973), 190; adapted.
10. The eighteenth-century Zen master Hakuin was an exception; his disciple Tōrei discusses some of the psychological problems that may occur in the process of Zen practice in his *Shūmon mujintō ron* (The Inexhaustible Lamp of Zen), Taishō 81: 581a–605b.
11. Jung, *Aion*, 6.

REFLECTIONS ON BUDDHISM

AND PSYCHOANALYSIS

Adam Phillips

❑

If we ask where can we find ourselves, where are the various versions of the self we've invented, one answer is in language. Both Buddhism and psychoanalysis are eloquent testimony to how we go about describing selves, as they introduce us to a cast of characters, a repertoire of familiar and unfamiliar figures: the Asian self, the familial self, the no self, the self-contained, self-reliant, and self-directed Western individual, the Great Self, and selflessness. And of course once you've got a group of characters, there's a drama. What are they going to do with each other? What do they believe consciously and unconsciously they're capable of doing together?

One belief they seem to share is that there is something to be done, that there are projects: fulfilling one's role in the social hierarchy, seeking enlightenment or cure, making oneself enviable, going to conferences. Something, in other words, is wanted—even if wanting itself is considered to be part of the problem. Talking about it in this way might make it

This essay, published here for the first time, is derived from comments made by the author at *The Suffering Self*, a two-day dialogue between psychoanalysts and Buddhists held in New York City on April 9–10, 1994.

sound as though we're in a kind of supermarket of cultural forms, where we can simply choose whatever sounds best. But the word "we," of course, is part of the problem here. Who is "we" supposed to refer to? Its varied usage presents us with a paradox.

On the one hand, selves are embedded in—that is, made possible by—specific forms of life. To describe a self is to describe a world, a culture that makes a place for such a self. And yet selves, or other versions of selves, might also resemble, or we may wish that they resemble, commodities: transportable, available if we can afford them, something we can try out for a while. In a way, like people, such descriptions of selves can increasingly be seen as socially mobile, or under severe economic constraints. Some might say there are as many selves as we can imagine. And others might say that there is something radically wrong with a culture that produces a self that can believe such a thing.

The history of psychoanalysis has, to some extent, reflected this dilemma of whether the solution is the problem or the problem the solution. But psychoanalysis has only been alive in its muddles; its clarities have been stultifying. Is the aim of analysis, as some of Freud's work suggests, to strengthen character, making the ego a kind of psychic imperialist? Where id was there ego shall be, etc.? Or, as the early Freud and Lacan suggest, is it precisely a strong ego, or rather the illusion of a strong ego, that people are suffering from? Is knowing who you are, turning yourself into a quasi-fictional character with so-called insight, the project? Or is the project discovering and learning to tolerate and enjoy the fact that you don't know who you are, and that in fact you have no way of knowing? Is this so-called self a kind of continual process of surprise or an idol to be revered and endlessly fashioned?

It was, of course, only analysts after Freud who seemed to need the concept of self. Freud himself leaves us with two instructive possibilities: either implicitly the word "self" can be used to refer to the sum of the parts he's described, a kind of superordinate term for id, ego, and superego; or, because of these parts he described, by their very nature and relationship, there can be no unitary "self" that such a word could refer to. A word like "self," Winnicott wrote, naturally knows more than we do. It uses us and can command us. Freud may have distrusted what the word supposedly knew . . . what some Buddhist critics refer to as the reification and absolutization of the self.

It is, I think, reassuring that psychoanalytic means tend to turn to psychoanalytic ends. The patient is not cured by free association, Ferenczi writes, he is cured when he can free-associate. The patient is not cured because he remembers, Lacan writes, he remembers because he is cured. Both of these statements reveal a commitment to process: to the idea that psychoanalysis makes possible something open-ended. The patient is deemed to be suffering from the fact that he has come to certain conclusions about himself. The self by definition is that which is forever unfinished.

The risk is that psychoanalysis can become subtly and not so subtly conformist; that in its theoretical repertoire of possible and acceptable selves, psychoanalysis offers more of the problem that Buddhism addresses—that is to say, the unconscious compulsion to reify "self," to secure it by making it somehow seem real, substantial, and present. Perhaps an inappropriately pragmatic question in this context might be: What do we want the idea of a self to do for us? How would our lives be better, as William James might have asked, if we had "selves"? It's my impression that any given self, any sense of representations we've collected into a self-image or self-story, is invented for a project. It intends, as it were, a certain kind of performance, which in turn intends a wishful transition: toward a state of no-self, perhaps, or self-integration or wealth or domination of other people, or whatever. At least in the first instance, the culture provides the individual with the repertoire of possible projects. Thus it is misleading, for example, for Winnicott to distinguish between true and false selves, since the individuals inherit their criteria of authenticity from their culture. It may be more useful to think of a person, at least in psychoanalytic language, as the conscious and unconscious performer of a *preferred* self. Both psychoanalysis and Buddhism offer descriptions of such preferred selves and how they might be fashioned. Ultimately, when we try to define the nature of the self, we are not, I think, talking about who we are, but about who we want to be.

Their approaches to the causes of suffering involve both psychoanalysis and Buddhism in stories about origins and stories about agency: stories about when the pain begins, and what or who has made it happen. And to understand one's life, or the stories about it, is to understand what's wrong with one's life: for living a life entails imagining what one lacks. What we call suffering is the acknowledgment of this insufficiency. Our relationship to suffering, what we make of it, the role we assign it in our psychic economy, is integral to the perplexing logic of life. Psychoanalysis, one could say, is the art of turning pain into meaning: a project that it shares, despite its own disclaimers, with many religions.

When people turn pain into sexual excitement, psychoanalysts call them perverse. When they turn pain into meaning, they call them corrective or insightful or good patients. Psychoanalysts, like Buddhists perhaps, assume that suffering is something we're compelled to work on and with. Our survival, not to mention the very beginnings of our lives, has depended on how we have done this. But where do we get our descriptions from—both of what suffering is and from what it is we are suffering? How do we know, at any given moment, that suffering is what we are doing?

Great religious leaders, and secular leaders like Marx and Freud, are people who tell us what we are suffering from. Their conceptions of cure or enlightenment or liberation show us what we lack. They reveal the cause and nature of our suffering. They become, or we make them, the masters of the causes of suffering. What's appealing about figures like Buddha and Freud is not that they attract worshippers, but that both of them have given us good, convincing accounts of the causes of suffering and, of course, of the causes of idolatry. Both of them suggest, from quite different perspectives, that our suffering is the consequence of false belief. The question becomes, then: To what extent are they inviting us, explicitly or implicitly, to believe in them? Are we cured or enlightened by learning to speak their languages? by attending to those things—grief, desire, delusion—they consider to be important? Their own life stories and work are, perhaps inevitably, and at least in part, a critique of the belief systems they inherited; and both of them, I think, can be described as doing something quite paradoxical: not necessarily, or only, replacing one belief system with another, but making us wonder about belief itself. But if belief is somehow integral to suffering, what can we replace belief—or, for that matter, attachment—with?

Both Freud and Buddha suggest that suffering is a consequence of fixed belief. Idolatry is a form of torture, often socially legitimated. A kind of addiction. The risk, then, is that concepts like causality and suffering become scientific or quasi-religious idols, assumptions we come to worship. Embedded in specific cultural contexts, both imply unquestioned worldviews and ways of life. And though a concern like "the *causes* of suffering" might seem to provide a link between psychoanalysis and Buddhism, it also stands, in point of fact, as a question. In what sense is the phrase "the causes of suffering" meaningful to both groups? The cause of suffering, one would think, is a universal preoccupation, but on this subject or indeed any other, how will we know if Buddhism and psychoanalysis are similar and/or different? Or to put it another way, who's to say? Especially if we consider that there is not one thing, one social practice, called psychoanalysis, any more than there is one Buddhism. Who, then, is in the position to make the useful or the credible link, and what do we want the links to do for us?

For some people, like Mark Epstein, it's both plausible and necessary to translate the Buddhist explanations of suffering into the language of psychoanalysis. Here Freud's "oceanic feeling" fits neatly into the Buddhist cosmology, as do any number of references from the writings of Guntrip, Eigen, Shaffer, and even Winnicott, who all make Buddhism and psychoanalysis seem both complementary and mutually illuminating. As Michael Robbins explains: "Both conceive of suffering as the product of disharmony or division within the mind." But he also qualifies this by suggesting that "it's certainly worthy of consideration that suffering may actually be experienced differently in each culture." Ultimately, it's the differences, the *obstacles* to translation, that preoccupy such thinkers. In this view, each model may finally be inadequate to describe the other; maybe psychoanalysis and Buddhism cannot be transferred or translated into the culture of the other.

For how can we tell, and who's to say, if one person or culture has understood another person or culture? Our wish to respect difference can be used to avoid contact; our denial of difference can make contact impossible. It will have escaped no one's attention just how interestingly symmetrical the positions of Epstein and Robbins are on the causes of suffering. For Epstein, translation is more than possible; for Michael Robbins, it may be misleading. We all know the political consequences that suffering entails in fantasies of purity. And we now live in patchwork cultures in which such fantasies are both harder to sustain, requiring more and more violence, and always something of a temptation. Personally, I would prefer to live in a world in which people can find and use what moves them, mostly for reasons they don't understand, to take them in directions of which they are unaware. Not a quest for purity, but for enlivening combinations. Perhaps each of us should take whatever appeals to us out of psychoanalysis and Buddhism, and from whatever else, to make something of our own. And if someone were then to object, "But this is really not psychoanalysis you're practicing," or "This is not really Buddhism," we should take it as a compliment. On the causes of suffering we need as many good stories as we can get hold of.

THE EMPEROR OF ENLIGHTENMENT

MAY HAVE NO CLOTHES

Jeffrey B. Rubin

❏

A Zen master's life is one continuous mistake.
—DOGEN

❏

Psychoanalysis and Buddhism are both deeply concerned with the problem of human suffering. One key purpose of psychoanalysis, according to Freud, was to eliminate neurotic misery. A central task of Buddhism is to achieve Enlightenment, which is said to eradicate suffering. Each tradition presents a highly sophisticated theory and methodology for attempting to alleviate human misery. There are strengths and limitations in each conception.

Here I shall challenge certain foundational assumptions of the Theravadin Buddhist conception of Enlightenment in light of psychoanalytic conceptions of self and cure, and I shall utilize Buddhist perspectives on selfhood in order to pinpoint certain limitations in psychoanalytic conceptions of health.

Since Buddhism, like psychoanalysis, is heterogeneous, composed of various schools of thought adopting different philosophies and types of practices, there is thus no monolithic definition of Enlightenment. It has been described in various ways in different Buddhist traditions and even within

This essay is taken, in its entirety, from the author's *Psychotherapy and Buddhism: Towards an Integration* (Plenum Press, 1996). It is reprinted here with the permission of the author, in conjunction with the publisher.

the "same" tradition. To Zen master Dogen, the founder of Soto Zen, Enlightenment meant "intimacy with all things," while an esteemed Tibetan Buddhist monk-psychiatrist has described it as "no unconsciousness" (Lobsang Rapgay, personal communication). In the Theravadin Buddhist model presented here, Enlightenment is described as completely purifying the mind of "defilements," e.g., greed, hatred, and delusion, which is said to result in the total cessation of suffering.

I shall raise two sets of questions about this conception: its possibility and its desirability. My remarks are meant in the spirit of encouraging further dialogue about important, complex, and neglected issues.

In an oft-quoted remark, Freud maintained that one purpose of analysis was to replace "neurotic misery" with "common human unhappiness." From the psychoanalytic perspective, some suffering—the neurotic kind—can and should be ameliorated. But *some* suffering is basic to human existence. Buddhism differs from psychoanalysis in its belief that suffering itself can be eliminated when one attains Enlightenment.

Enlightenment is often presented as the summum bonum or highest good of human existence. Buddhists, as well as representatives of other Eastern traditions, caution that descriptions of Enlightenment are inadequate. Nozick's (1989) description is worth quoting. Enlightenment is said to be

> blissful, infinite, without boundaries or limit, ecstatic, full of energy, pure, shining, and extremely powerful . . . it feels like an experience of something, an experience revelatory of the nature of a deeper reality . . . This experience seems to reveal reality to be very different from the way it ordinarily appears. (pp. 243–244)

The self, as well as reality, is then experienced very differently with its boundaries either "extended or dissolved" (p. 246):

> Not only does the person feel during the enlightenment experience that his deepest self is very different, often he is transformed as a result of the experience. The enlightenment experience of a very different mode of self-organization enables him also to encounter the everyday world differently, now less clouded or distorted by the interests of the limited self. (p. 247) . . . The enlightenment experience not only ends your identifying with the self as a particular delimited entity, it might be an experience of being no entity at all . . . If you don't have to possess or choose any essence at all, then to think you have one is a mistake. (p. 248)

Enlightened is defined, in the most comprehensive study of enlightened meditators that has ever been done, as the permanent transformation of consciousness leading to freedom from suffering and life without discontent: a state of "perfect wisdom and compassion and freedom from any kind of suffering" (Brown & Engler, 1986b, p. 207).

In Theravadin Buddhist psychology, the Arahant, one worthy of praise for slaying the demons of greed, hatred, and delusion, is the exemplar of ideal mental health and Enlightenment. The Arahant is described as a being in whom "no unhealthy mental factors whatsoever arise in the mind" (Goleman, 1980, pp. 133–134). The Arahant evidences

1. an absence of greed for sense desires, anxiety, resentments, or fears of any sort; dogmatisms such as the belief that this or that is "the Truth"; aversions to conditions such as loss, disgrace, pain, or blame; feelings of lust or anger; experience of suffering; need for approval, pleasure, or praise; desire for anything for oneself beyond essential and necessary items

2. a prevalence of impartiality toward others and equanimity in all circumstances; ongoing alertness and calm delight in experience, no matter how ordinary or even boring; strong feelings of compassion and loving kindness; quick and accurate perception; composure and skill in taking action. (Goleman, 1980, p. 134)

Enlightenment, that condition of panoramic awareness, nonreactivity, selflessness, wisdom, compassion, and love that has been deified for thousands of years in various religious traditions, appears to be an ideal that is completely innocent of self-deception, corruption, and suffering. It promises to eliminate the egoism, desire, and fear that most people feel mired in (Kramer & Alstad, 1993).

Enlightenment is a compelling vision of what we might become. A world beyond suffering is not to be denied out of hand or sloughed off easily. In assuming that human suffering is inevitable, analysis adopts a depressogenic stance toward the universe, which itself contributes to human suffering. The analyst in me who is keenly aware of the limitations of this vision of the world longs for a viable alternative, and the contemplative in me believes that the Buddhist vision may be the most interesting candidate we have.

An American once asked the Dalai Lama how one could identify true Buddhist teachers. The Dalai Lama replied, "Watch them. See how they behave" (Tworkov, 1994, p. 157). The rash of grossly self-centered and conspicuously unenlightened behavior exhibited by Buddhist teachers in recent years—documented by Sandy Boucher (1988) in *Turning the Wheel: American Women Creating the New Buddhism*—challenges the pervasive idealization of the ideal of Enlightenment and suggests that it would be prudent both to not uncritically accept this notion and to inquire further into the psychological dynamics that might be unconsciously operating.[1] In order to do this it will be helpful to briefly explicate the meditative process as it relates to Enlightenment.

In his "deconstructivist" model of the normative Theravadin meditative process Engler (n.d.) has likened the basic task of meditation to a deconstruction of the nonveridical perceptual process and the "constructions which bias perception and thought" (p. 725) and create a "world" of internal representations of self and others. Meditation practice, in this model, "traces the cognitive and affective pathways by which self and objects literally come into being . . . [and one] learns to correct the faulty reality testing which leads to non-veridical percepts of self and objects" (p. 724).

As the meditator's distractedness lessens and his concentration and attentiveness deepen, mental phenomena are recognized immediately after their arising. "Dispelling the illusion of compactness" (Nyanamoli, 1976) occurs when the meditator's concentration and attentiveness is sufficiently refined and his capacity to remain steadily aware for extended periods of times increases. Engler (1984) provides a cogent summary of the series of transformations that occur:

> The normal sense that I am a fixed, continuous point of observation from which I regard now this object, now that, is dispelled . . . my sense of being a separate observer or experiencer behind observation or experience is revealed to be the result of a perceptual illusion, of my not being normally able to perceive a more microscopic level of events. When my attention is sufficiently refined through training . . . all that is actually apparent to me from moment to moment is a mental or physical event and an awareness of that event. . . . No enduring or substantial entity or observer or experiencer or agent—no self—can be found behind or apart from these moment-to-moment events to which they could be attributed (an-atta = no-self). (p. 41)

When the meditator's attentiveness remains stabilized at this level of perception, deeper insights about the nature of self and object representations emerge: The meditator experiences

> how a self-representation is contructed in each moment as a result of an interaction with an object . . . and conversely, how an object appears not in itself . . . but always relative to my state of observation . . . I discover that there are actually no enduring entities or schemas at all; only momentary constructions are taking place. (Engler, 1984, p. 42)

As nonselective and reactive attentiveness continues to deepen, the meditator experiences that

> the stream of consciousness literally break[s] up into a series of discrete events which are discontinuous in space and time. . . . Representation and reality construction are therefore discovered to be discontinuous processes. . . . When this total moment-to-moment "coming to be and passing away" (udayabbaya) is experienced, there is a profound understanding of the radical impermanence (anicca) of all events. . . . I become aware of the selflessness (anatta) of mind, body, external objects and internal representations . . . any attempt to constellate enduring self and object representations, or to preferentially identify with some self-representations as "me" and expel . . . or repress . . . others as "not me," is experienced as an equally futile attempt to interrupt, undo or alter self and object representations as a flow of moment-to-moment constructions. (Engler, 1984, pp. 42–44)

As the meditator sees through and lets go of her illusory internal world of representations, she experiences a profound loss: the ontological foundations of her world are undermined. This initiates a "mourning" process involving pain and despair over the impossibility of recovering the lost object (world). This leads to what Engler (n.d.) terms a "reorganization" of one's inner world involving

> decathecting both (a) the need for the lost external object and (b) its internalized image. (p. 728) . . . Unlike normal mourning . . . the meditator is not simply confronted with the loss of a single object but with the loss of all his objects, of the object world as such, internal as well as external. (p. 730) . . . In meditation, there is thoroughgoing object loss. (p. 731) . . . [I]n meditation there is a renunciation of self-object ties altogether. . . . There is no new identification and no more object seeking. . . . In meditation all object ties are finally "outgrown." (p. 733)

This mourning of self and object loss and the renunciation of all object ties may be viewed, according to Engler (n.d.), "as the final step in separation-individuation: the end of suffering and ultimate individuation" (p. 734).

The concept of Enlightenment, as I understand it, is underwritten by at least two assumptions about human life and development. It presupposes that the mind can be permanently transformed and completely purified and that there is a stage of development, beyond egocentricity and the vicissitudes of conflict, that is irreversible and everlasting.

Spiritual teachers are often presented as being beyond self-blindness. There seems to be little evidence that many spiritual teachers discourage such idealized images. This is not surprising, since admitting that one had pockets of self-blindness or proclaiming one's psychological fallibility would not exactly attract a steady following of students.

In 1983, five of the six most esteemed Zen Buddhist masters in the United States, who presumably were selected by an enlightened teacher abroad to teach, were involved in grossly self-centered and conspicuously unenlightened behavior, such as sexually exploiting nonconsenting students and illegally expropriating funds from the community.[2] Leaving aside the fact that this is a complex phenomenon that is based on multiple historical, cultural, and psychological factors . . . an urgent question confronts us: If enlightenment is an irreversible transformation and purification of the mind, then why have these troubling incidents occurred?

Explanations of these incidents have been unconvincing. The problem tends to be (1) rationalized as, in the words of one Buddhist teacher, "crazy wisdom" that the unenlightened cannot understand; (2) minimized as an isolated aberration of an unevolved individual; or (3) connected to sociocultural differences between Asian and Western cultures.

Lest one defensively claim that these problems are incidental or accidental, it is worth reflecting on one of the conclusions of the previously cited study of enlightened Buddhist meditators that these individuals evidenced residues of psychopathology as well as extraordinary development, remarkable clarity, and profound compassion (Brown & Engler, 1986b). These meditators were, in the words of Drs. Brown and Engler, "not without conflict, in a clinical sense. They show evidence for the experience of drive states and conflictual themes such as fears [and] dependency struggles" (pp. 210–211). Brown and Engler's (1986a) Rorschach studies of enlightened meditators indicate that "these allegedly enlightened advanced practitioners are not without intrapsychic conflict . . . each of these Rorschach's evidenced idiosyncratic conflictual themes such as fear of rejection; struggles with dependency and needs for nurturance; fear and doubt regarding heterosexual relationships; fear of destructiveness" (pp. 188–189).

The observations of Jack Kornfield (1988), an esteemed American teacher of Theravadin Buddhism who studied with indigenous Buddhist masters in Asian monasteries for many years and has taught Buddhist meditation throughout the world for almost two decades, concur. He points to two of the "limitations" and insufficiencies of meditation practice: (1) unresolved personal, relational, and occupational issues that meditation practice does not alter in meditation students and teachers, and (2) "major upheavals and problems around power, sex, honesty, intoxicants etcetera

. . . in a majority of the twenty or more largest centers of Zen, Tibetan, and Vipassana practice in America . . . centering on the teachers (both Asian and American) themselves" (p. 10).

Brown and Engler's findings were explained in terms of the failure of the subjects of their study to attain the highest "stages" of Enlightenment. It was proposed that these subjects had only attained lower levels of Enlightenment and that conflict might be eradicated on higher stages. This claim was neither tested nor proven, so it remains essentially speculative in the absence of further evidence.

The psychological reductionism and oversimplicity of linear stage models of mind obscure the complexity and asymmetry of human development and mental life; for most people there probably is no uniformity to their identity and stage of development. One's empathy for others, for example, may be significantly less developed than one's own self-knowledge. The vast knowledge gained by psychoanalysts about the ubiquity of self-unconsciousness casts grave doubt on Buddhist claims about permanent and irreversible self-transformation and wisdom.

The practice of psychoanalysis teaches one that mental life is fluid rather than static, involving the continual, dialectical interplay of various states of consciousness, subject-positions, or self-states and modes of being that are sometimes at cross-purposes and in conflict. Living a human life is thus more like sailing, confronting exigencies that are both ever-changing and unpredictable, than attaining any sort of permanent and irreversible state. Conflict can no more be eliminated from mental life in the psychoanalytic model than the vagaries of the wind can be permanently eliminated from sailing.

Buddhist models of the mind also acknowledge that the mind, like the universe, is always in flux. But, with its recognition that everything changes—except Enlightenment, which is posited as an unchanging achievement—Buddhism attempts to eat its cake of flux and have it too.

Understanding the mind, like achieving physical health, is not a static attainment. Mental health, as psychoanalyst Melanie Klein (1960) suggested, is an ongoing job requiring continual attentiveness and persistence. Freedom, as John Maynard Keynes aptly noted, requires eternal vigilance (Joel Kramer, personal communication).

The acting out in spiritual communities on the part of Buddhist teachers, as well as the previously cited empirical research on Enlightenment, suggests that psychological conditioning from the past that inevitably warps personality cannot be completely eradicated and that there is no conflict-free stage of human life in which the mind is permanently purified of conflict. This is consistent with psychoanalytic insights about the essential nontransparency of the human mind; that is, the inevitability of unconsciousness and self-deception.

For an individual to be enlightened, they would have to be certain that they were completely awake without any trace of unconsciousness or delusion. Even if that existed in the present, it is not clear to me how one could know for certain that would never change in the future (cf. Kramer & Alstad, 1993). From the psychoanalytic perspective, a static, conflict-free sphere—a psychological "safe house"—beyond the vicissitudes of conflict and conditioning where mind is immune to various aspects of affective life such as self-interest, egocentricity, fear, lust, greed, and suffering is quixotic. Since conflict and suffering seem to be inevitable aspects of human life, the ideal of Enlightenment may be asymptotic, that is, an unreachable ideal.

In questioning the ideal of Enlightenment and claiming that the Emperor of Enlightenment, if you will, may have no clothes, I do not mean to neglect or devalue those moments of extraordinary clarity, self-acceptance, inner spaciousness, peace, and abiding love that meditators for millennia have experienced. Nor do I wish to deny that Buddhist teachers may have deep insights about self and life that might be illuminating for others as long as the context of teaching is based on an egalitarian, mutually respectful and empowering relationship rather than an authoritarian, hierarchical connection characterized by deification and submission.

What I do wish to question is the notion of a mind that is somehow permanently without any ripple of unconsciousness, self-deception, and selfishness. In doing this I hope that it is still clear that I recognize and have deep respect for the profound transformative possibilities of meditative *practice*, which teaches psychoanalysis that humans are capable of much greater self-awareness, compassion, and inner peace than psychoanalysts usually recognize.

While Buddhist practice may be profoundly self-enhancing, Buddhist ideals of Enlightenment are not without certain problematic consequences, which become more apparent when juxtaposed with a particular psychoanalytic conception of health, namely, self-integration or self-enrichment (cf. Atwood & Stolorow, 1984; Rizzuto, 1994). By self-integration I refer to the experience that analysands in successful treatment have of being more able to know, tolerate, embrace, integrate, and communicate formerly disavowed facets of their inner, personal reality. This fosters greater self-knowledge and self-acceptance and leads to an enriched engagement with oneself and the world. One's perspective of self and the world becomes less rigid and more inclusive as new internal and external experiences are accommodated to more readily. One becomes more tolerant of difference, in oneself and others, and develops a less egocentric and more inclusive and compassionate perspective on self and others. This perspective on health suggests that the Buddhist view is not only incomplete, it is, in at least three ways, also limiting.

First, eradicating suffering is central to the Buddhist view of health. The one thing I teach, asserted Buddha, is the cessation of suffering. A deeply unconscious assumption in Buddhism is that suffering is bad. *Is all suffering bad?* Certainly suffering is painful. It is natural to wish to avoid it, but if we reflect on times of self-transformation and growth in our own lives, they were probably often accompanied by suffering. Suffering that is worked through can deepen and enrich a human life, by generating greater knowledge, openness, sensitivity, compassion, and passion.

Because suffering can be edifying, one wonders why Buddhism is so preoccupied with the goal of removing it. Does the Buddhist goal of eradicating suffering bespeak an unconscious aversion to life that could actually be self-limiting because it removes one from engagement with life's existential and emotional vicissitudes and the self-knowledge that it can foster? In a world in which the suffering of women or Afro-Americans was prematurely removed, the discontent that sowed the seeds of the feminist and civil rights movements may have been uprooted and the moral outrage that fueled constructive social change and transformation may have been compromised.

The ideal of Enlightenment can foster self-impoverishment by encouraging meditators to unconsciously renounce and become detached from the complexity and passion of an embodied human existence. Might it not be an enriched Buddhism that simultaneously worked on eradicating human misery while it investigated the possible unconscious meanings and benefit of its own unconscious attachment to the project of disengaging from this facet of life?

Second, in emphasizing the deconstruction of self, the decathexis of both internal representations of other people and ourselves, the emptying of our inner psychological world and the mourning that it fosters, the Theravadin Buddhist model delineated earlier pinpoints one important facet of the healing process. Nonattachment, in the Buddhist sense, to outmoded ties to self and others certainly contributes to the process of lessening human suffering and expanding the possibilities for human liberation. As attachment and the grasping and aversion it fosters lessens, we are then freer to respond with greater openness and concern to ourselves and others.

Is the emptied inner world of Enlightenment that Engler depicts spacious and free or self-alienating and impoverished? Are all ties with others negative? Are all relationships enervating? Do relationships ever promote empathy and the mitigation of suffering? Was the novelist Toni Morrison (1993) way off the mark when she said in a recent interview that love is a space where freedom can be negotiated (p. 113)?

Intimacy can be promoted or obstructed by Buddhism as well as psychoanalysis. Buddhist theory can simultaneously encourage and inhibit greater human relatedness. Its commitment to a non-self-absorbed relationship with self, others, and the world can contribute to less exploitative conduct, while its self-nullifying view of subjectivity may interfere with genuine intimacy that is based, at least in part, on mutuality between two individuated individuals. Individuation does not flourish on the soil of self-negation.

The Theravadin Buddhist stance toward the world as embodied in the ideal of Enlightenment neglects the radical insight in psychoanalyst Heinz Kohut's (1977) claim about the lifelong necessity of vital ties with other human beings. It seems to minimize our inevitable embeddedness in relationships and their potential value. Participation in relationships can contribute to both greater self-awareness and increased self-validation. An enhanced sense of ourselves and capacity for agency and moral action can result.

Like the philosopher Immanuel Kant's (1968) dove, which regarded the resistance of the air as an obstacle and imagined that it could fly better in the vacuum of "empty space" (p. 47), Buddhism seems to view affective life as an obstacle to living instead of an irreplaceable aspect of life. In the model of self-integration or enrichment that I am advocating, past experiences and affective life, including relations with self and others, are not so much weeds to be eliminated as they are manure to fertilize.

In such a conception, the self can be likened to a symphony composed of a variety of instruments—consciousness and unconsciousness, self-centeredness and selflessness, rationality and imagination, and so forth— each with its own idiosyncratic sound and application. The self is impoverished if certain instruments are not played. The best music occurs when no instrument dominates or is excluded and when there is communication and cross-fertilization between them.

Third, the self-deconstruction that meditative practice promotes can lead to irresponsible self-disengagement[3] as well as self-impoverishment. Assuming that self and object representations are merely, in Engler's words, "constructs" (artifacts of the constructivist activity of perception) fosters a denial or minimization of self-existence that creates greater self-unconsciousness. For we are then predisposed to not notice facets of ourselves, such as greed or self-centeredness, that clash with our cherished self-conceptions. The privileging of self-negation and the consequent devaluing and repression of self-centeredness ultimately engenders the egotistical behavior sometimes acted out in Buddhist communities. The destructive self-centeredness that has plagued certain spiritual teachers and communities and caused suffering for all concerned is the natural result of such a self-nullifying stance toward human subjectivity. The perceptual disavowal of self is not the experiential working through of its historical legacy. The troubling interactions and incidents of exploitation that I have described above are sown from the seeds of such self-disavowal.

Self-disavowal can be particularly disastrous for people who have traditionally been marginalized in Western society, such as women and racial or religious minorities. Such people have often been crushed or invalidated on a sociocultural as well as a personal level. In theoretically calling into question the very category of persons, deconstructivist theories about the self interfere with a viable view of human agency, and thus inhibit political engagement. For if there is no subject, then there is no one who is alienated or oppressed, and thus no evil to challenge and no one to contest it. Such a stance toward the self denies and minimizes one's oppressed position within the asymmetrical social status quo. This can be crippling or disabling by implicitly or explicitly perpetuating the self-alienation and marginalized status of the oppressed even as it may theoretically undermine authoritarian doctrines that present reified visions of persons and are oppressive.

The emptied inner world of the Enlightenment experience sounds more barren and impoverished than expansive and liberating. Renouncing self and others leads not to freedom but to self-alienation. Freedom derives not from renunciation of ties to self and others but from freedom within the context of relatedness. In a world like ours in which profound self-alienation and emotional disconnection predominate, the psychoanalytically derived view of self-enrichment I have presented as an alternative to the Buddhist model of self-renunciation, a view of humans that values self-expansion and enrichment and connectedness to others, might foster less suffering than a model of self-renunciation and self-purification.[4]

The model of self-enrichment is a valuable way of thinking about the analytic process and health. A great deal of human suffering might be alleviated if more people, non-Buddhist and Buddhist alike, engaged in such a process.

But Buddhism teaches psychoanalysis that the notion of self-integration can also be a limiting and imprisoning type of self-experience, a suboptimal state of being that may foster self-restriction and self-alienation and thereby contributes to human suffering. Since selfhood is not a singularly definable entity but a heterogeneous and complex phenomenon that is context-dependent, singular notions like the integrated self may miniaturize and subjugate selfhood's possibilities (cf. Hillman, 1975) by obscuring and limiting its multidimensionality. Facets of self-experience that do not fit into preexisting images of who one really is are neglected or not assimilated. This impedes hospitality toward facets of ourselves that do not fit into the unified narrative we have constructed about ourselves. Opportunities for complicating and transforming one's sense of self are thus severely limited (cf. Sennett, 1970). The always unfinished and open nature of the self, in the view I am briefly sketching, is an achievement to be further cultivated rather than a defect to be remedied.[5] The notion of an integrated self may thus constitute what Erich Fromm (1941) might term an "escape from freedom": the ever-renewing possibility and responsibility for creating who we are.

Self-integration and self-deconstruction may both be part of what is necessary to achieve psychological health and reduce psychological suffering. I prefer a world in which we neither assume the self's sovereignty nor absolutize its provisionality. If Buddhism has correctly pinpointed the dangers of absolutizing the self, then it may now be time for Buddhists to recognize, perhaps with the help of psychoanalysis, that there is a hidden and pernicious cost to absolutizing its view of the fictionality of the self. To fail to do so also brings suffering, as the incidents in spiritual communities so vividly demonstrate.

In a world in which self-investment and empathy and care for others were seen as complementary—two interpenetrating facets of what it meant to be a human being—we might experience that liberating bifocal perspective that the poet W. H. Auden (1969) conveyed when he wrote: "cosmic trivia/we all are, but none of us are unessential" (p. 40).

Notes

1. Psychoanalysis and psychoanalysts are not without scandals and exploitation, as the Jung–Sabina Spielrein affair demonstrates. The absence of data about such incidents in psychoanalysis make it more difficult to examine. Because this aspect is not well documented, it is difficult to compare it with acting out in spiritual communities. Since this topic is tangential to the main focus of the terrain I will be exploring and will take me too far afield to explore the multiple meanings and functions of this sort of behavior, I will not discuss it here. Questions for future researchers might include such things as: Are therapeutic scandals less frequent because they are more suppressed or because they occur less often? If they occur less often, is it because of the explicit emphasis in psychoanalytic theory and training on the analysand's transference and the analyst's countertransference? And so forth.

2. It would not surprise me if this troubling doubt were dealt with by dismissing it with the ready-made conclusion that not all Buddhist teachers are enlightened, so that any disturbing incidents of egocentricity and exploitation on the part of a Buddhist teacher do not tarnish the ideal of Enlightenment. This strikes me as both a misguided and irresponsible response to incidents that should be explored more extensively. A teacher is presumably one who through discipleship (with an enlightened master?) and extensive work on him- or herself has attained significant self-understanding and self-realization. If those sanctioned to teach by indigenous practitioners who are often viewed as Buddhist "masters" do not evidence the highest possibilities for psychological and spiritual health that are theoretically posited, then one wonders who does illustrate these claims. Even if the questions I am attempting to raise were challenged on the grounds that the status and validity of Enlightenment remain unaffected by these incidents of self-blindness and are, in fact, irrelevant to them, I think it would be a shame to ignore or rationalize this conduct rather than to utilize it to explore a certain unconsciousness in the hallowed and essentially unquestioned Buddhist ideal.

3. The recent movement known as "engaged Buddhism," which utilizes Buddhist perspectives to address social issues such as ecology and the peace movement, actually illustrates rather than challenges my claim that Buddhism can lead to a restrictive detachment from the inner and outer world. For you only need to engage what was formerly disengaged. Engaged Buddhism is only necessary because Buddhism has previously fostered disengagement. Also, Buddhists can and often do engage the outer world in order to fight for social justice only to unconsciously detach from their own inner world of thoughts, feelings, and fantasies.

4. The renunciation model can also be found in Freudian analysis.

5. Adam Phillips' essay "Reflections on Buddhism and Psychoanalysis" (in this volume) spurred me to pursue this line of thinking.

References

Atwood, George, and Robert Stolorow (1984). *Structures of Subjectivity: Explorations in Psychoanalytic Phenomenology.* Hillsdale, N.J.: Lawrence Erlbaum.

Auden, W. H. (1969). *Epistles to a Godson and Other Poems.* New York: Random House.

Boucher, Sandy (1988). *Turning the Wheel: American Women Creating the New Buddhism*. San Francisco: Harper & Row.

Brown, D. and Jack Engler (1986a). "The Stages of Mindfulness Meditation: A Validation Study, Part I: Study and Results," 161–91, in *Transformation of Consciousness: Conventional and Contemplative Perspectives on Human Development*, ed. K. Wilber, Jack Engler, and D. Brown. Boston: Shambhala.

Brown, D. and Jack Engler (1986b). "The Stages of Mindfulness Meditation: A Validation Study, Part II: Discussion," 191–217, in *Transformation of Consciousness: Conventional and Contemplative Perspectives on Human Development*, ed. K. Wilber, Jack Engler, and D. Brown. Boston: Shambhala.

Engler, Jack (n.d.) *The Practice of Insight*. Unpublished manuscript.

———— (1984). "Therapeutic Aims in Psychotherapy and Meditation: Developmental Stages in the Representation of Self," 17–51, in *Transformation of Consciousness: Conventional and Contemplative Perspectives on Human Development*, ed. K. Wilber, Jack Engler, and D. Brown. Boston: Shambhala, 1986.

Goleman, Daniel (1980). "Mental Health in Classical Buddhist Psychology," 131–34, in *Beyond Ego: Transpersonal Dimensions in Psychology*, ed. R. Walsh and F. Vaughan. Los Angeles: Tarcher.

Hillman, James (1975). *Re-visioning Psychology*. New York: Harper & Row.

Kant, Immanuel (1968). *Critique of Pure Reason*. New York: St. Martin's Press.

Klein, Melanie (1960). "On Mental Health," 269–74, in *Envy and Gratitude and Other Works (1946–1963)*. New York: Delta.

Kohut, Heinz (1977). *The Restoration of the Self*. New York: International Universities Press.

Kornfield, Jack (1988, Summer). "Meditation and Psychotherapy: A Plea for Integration." *Inquiring Mind*, 10–11.

Kramer, Joel, and Diana Alstad (1993). *The Guru Papers: Masks of Authoritarian Power*. Berkeley, Calif.: North Atlantic Books.

Morrison, Toni (1993). "The Art of Fiction." *The Paris Review* 128: 83–125.

Nozick, Robert (1989). *The Examined Life: Philosophical Meditations*. New York: Simon & Schuster.

Nyanamoli, Bhikkhu, trans. (1976). *The Path of Purification*. Boulder, Colo.: Shambhala.

Rizzuto, A. M. (1994). *Sound and Sense: Words and the Paradox of the Suffering Person*. Unpublished manuscript.

Sennett, R. (1970). *The Uses of Disorder: Personal Identity and City Life*. New York: Norton.

Tworkov, Helen (1994). *Zen in America*. New York: Kodansha International.

IN PRACTICE

❑

ONE REALITY

Michael Eigen

❑

"What is your original face, before you were born?" I've always loved this koan, since first reading it forty years ago. My original face—before I was born. Just thinking this makes me breathe easier. Even now, at sixty, I feel my soul smile and my body open as I think these words.

How many things can one read at twenty and still love and learn from at sixty? Zen and Torah—I've not tired of either. I must quickly add, *my* Zen, *my* Torah, for I study neither formally, nor do I have a formal teacher. I go my way. But Buddhism and Judaism are among my umbilical connections to the universe, lifelines to the mother ship, as I swim in space.

SUZUKI AND BUBER

In 1957, I saw D. T. Suzuki speak in a big church on the seven circles of love and we had tea afterward. I was quite an idealizing youth. I worshipped

This essay appears as Chapter 10 in the author's *The Psychoanalytic Mystic* (*Esf* Publishers and Free Association Books, 1998).

wisdom and its messengers. I doubt I was able to open my mouth around Suzuki but I sucked in his presence, through my eyes, my pores. I kept looking at him and what I saw was a man being himself, not trying to make an impression, gracious perhaps, but solid as rock.

He was very old and pretty deaf and the effect of his presence may have had a lot to do with age. But an offhand remark he made stuck with me. Someone must have asked a question about activity-passivity and he responded with a delightful outburst, "Passivity, passivity. What's wrong with passivity?" He then listed Western passive pleasures he enjoyed, such as sitting in a movie, flying in planes. I instantly relaxed—the pressure to be active seemed suddenly to have lifted. It was as if I felt guilty about being passive without knowing it. I secretly liked being passive and now it was okay. So often offhand remarks have a greater impact than systematic discourse.

The same year I read Erich Fromm's *The Art of Loving*, which I liked. Fromm had just spent several months with Suzuki in Mexico that year, but when Suzuki was later asked a question about Fromm, he didn't remember him, causing some snickers among us college kids. I wonder whether there was something too activist in Fromm, something that Suzuki's remark cut through. His outburst included yet went beyond Western hyperactivity and depreciation of passivity (Aristotle's God—pure activity, the highest rationality: God forbid God should be passive, God forbid God should have a day of rest, a sabbath—the sabbath point of soul).

I saw Martin Buber speak in a big synagogue around the same time. I don't remember much about what he said (nor do I remember much about Suzuki's circles of love). But I was fascinated by the *way* Buber spoke. Too mannered, perhaps, but entrancing—the way he lowered his head into his arms after saying something, waiting for the next revelation. He took time between utterances, time to pause, to listen. For Buber, speaking was a way of listening. *Shema Yisroael*: "Hear, Israel." Buber heard, and when he heard, we heard. By speaking, Buber was teaching listening.

My memory has Buber with a flowing white beard, Suzuki clean-shaven. Both old men, Buber thick-boned with the thunder and lightning of Sinai crackling off him, Suzuki thinner and still, unafraid to let death show in his eyes. Light reflected off Buber and gathered into Suzuki. Suzuki had a lighter, ticklier touch. For Buber, listening was electrifying. There was rest, quiet, pause between, but expect to be burnt by the tongue's fire.

Buber's death between utterances was anticipatory. One emptied self in order to be ready for the next Thou surge, from moment of meeting to moment of meeting, waves of impacts. Suzuki's emptiness was not like Buber's waiting: it was emptiness itself. What a relief to be empty, not a transition to the next God surge.

Emptiness and the I-Thou moment of impact. We thrive on both. We need more than one breast, more than one eye.

IDEALIZATION OF BUDDHISM

There is hope that Buddhism will succeed where Western religions have failed. Many Westerners look to the East for what is missing in their lives. Experience teaches us that it is dangerous to think that any one system of belief will supply everything. There is always something missing, something wrong.

Healthy skepticism protects against blind faith. Healthy faith protects against nihilistic skepticism. We are made of multiple systems capable of providing some checks and balances. It is important not to expect too little or too much of a great teaching. I don't know, for example, that freedom from suffering is necessary, possible, or desirable. In the United States, for example, many think that practicing Buddhism will end suffering, rather than change one's relationship to the latter.

Bliss, ecstasy, joy, nirvana, the beatific state are real. But how does one relate to the primacy of ecstasy? How is ecstasy used? Is faith free of violence? Buddhism is supposed to be nonviolent, but is anything nonviolent in fact? Like every practice, Buddhism has casualties and involves violence to self and others in many ways. Buddhist patients have the same sins and foibles as everyone else.

OWEN

Owen is a dedicated meditator who fears he will do something destructive to those in his care. He is depressed and anxious and having trouble functioning. Yet he is filled with self-importance. As he eyes me, I can feel him placing me beneath him. I'm not worthy to be the therapist of an experienced Buddhist teacher. He does not think he should have to see a therapist after years of meditation, especially one like me. He is used to surroundings more elegant than my run-down office. He has a better self-image and sense of worth than I do. He is *someone*—and I am not even a systematic meditator.

He is taking medication cocktails, but they have failed to relieve his anxiety, depression, and fear of destruction. I wonder whether he can deepen his meditation practice, rely more on meditation than medication. But how? He complains he feels nothing, he is dead. Perhaps he is not dead enough. Perhaps he has died the wrong way—he so clings to his teacherly self.

Owen confesses that while he helps students he also has erotic liaisons with them. He is drawn to young men whose lives are in disarray. The meditation center is an erotic arena and he never knows who will attract him when. Sooner or later, though, attraction develops. He helps one in need and exacts erotic payment. He feels only a little guilty. He greatly helps the lives of those who give little in return. He uplifts, provides order and direction, for a bit of pleasure.

"Do you hear your tone?" I ask. "You seem to denigrate what they give you, as I feel denigrated by your glance."

"Yes—I do feel they owe me something. It's the least they can do. I can't help it. It comes over me. I feel it building for weeks, months, sometimes longer. I find a way to manipulate the one I want into a position where they have to give it, where it has to happen. I quietly expect it, and they seem to know what to do. They follow suit, fall into it. Then I'm enraged when they don't want to do it anymore, when they want to break free. I feel they're not grateful for all I've done for them. It plays itself out. I find another one."

"You watch with a cold eye."

"Yes. And there's nothing to do about it. I can't fight it and don't really try. I don't want to stop it. It's something that happens. It's part of my karma. It's not so bad considering the good I do. It's two people doing good for each other."

"But it doesn't solve your depression."

"It used to make me feel better than it does now. Now it's more something that happens, that runs itself out. When I was younger, it made me feel more alive."

Owen's wheels are spinning. He is caught in a progressive self-deadening process. While he is popular, sought after, in the limelight, eros deadens more than enriches him. He goes through the motions. Yet his whole life is Buddhism. He loves the Dharma—up to a point. He can give himself to transformation through the teachings only so far—no more.

The problem is not simply a matter of ego or self, but something more inclusive, more fundamental: wounds that haven't healed, have misshaped his personality, and warped the structure of his being. Owen supplied well-rehearsed versions of his personal history. Doting, controlling mother, weak, nice father. He feels his problem is not that his parents hurt him, but that they indulged him. His mother idolized him, expected him to shine.* Shine he did. He felt more catered to than injured by her domineering nature.

Yet I sense a deeply wounded, if triumphant man here. Owen can't recognize the violence done to his soul. He is, partly, a fusion of divine child and domineering/nourishing mother. I imagine myself as Owen and look through layers of personality formation. What is it like for Owen as a newborn baby, a six-month-old, an eight-month-old, and so on? What choices does the baby have, given the conditions he lives in?

I picture Owen breathing in his mother's controlling idolization, and the subsequent growth of self-idolatry. It was not that Owen feared not being idolized. It was simply all he knew. Life had never forced him to feel lowly. Owen had no idea what he missed by not feeling sufficiently wounded or violated. The wounded, broken boys he helps carry brokenness for him. He lives brokenness by proxy, vicariously. Is it possible to be out of contact with something missing, something never properly owned, perhaps something he was not allowed to have? Was a shattered baby intolerable to Owen's mother?

Owen became too strong, too fast. He became one who nourished others and was worshipped and eros was part of the brew. The self-other fusion of helper-helped seemed a piece with the idolization-nourishment Owen was born into. Apparently Owen's mother was herself nourished by Owen's submission to this idolization, and Owen remained addicted to variations of this dynamic all his life—a silent warp that made him successful, but eventually deadened him.

Owen complains about deadness, depression, anxiety, fear of destructiveness—but he does not seem wounded or shattered or broken. He does not seem torn by his panicky depression, and expects to remain its master. It is as if the bad things happening to him are foreign aberrations or don't count. They are happening to him, but are not him. He does not identify with the suffering he is enduring. Has he prematurely emptied himself of self? If so, he has done so very selectively, as can be seen from

---

* For a relevant discussion of the "idolized self," see Khan (1979), Chapter 1.

his erotic possessiveness. As a Buddhist, oughtn't he see the bad things happening to him as a result of past actions, as a challenge, as something belonging to his life task? Are there ways in which Owen isn't Buddhist enough?

As a psychologist, I would argue that Owen did not possess—he was not given—the equipment necessary to process misery, disability, limits, ordinariness, warp. Hyperdetached and critical, he was a parody of separateness. His cold eye spots flaws in me, false moves, and as a result he cannot allow much emotional flow between us. Owen lacks a full range of emotions— they are undeveloped, unlived. He became a specialist in reenacting the emotional dynamic he learned from his mother, and subtly amplified it as a meditation teacher. Unable to see his pain as intrinsic to the shape of his psyche, he'd rather get rid of or manage it. He does not have a desperate enough feel for the deformation he has undergone, and treats what haunts him now like dead skin he wishes to shed.

I picture how pleasurable meditation must have been for Owen as a young man. Inflated maternal support blossomed in the Void. He loved retreats and was generous to others. Any selfishness could easily be justified by his youth. He never really had to struggle with the warp, and if his teachers saw it, they did not press him. He kept sitting—letting life unfold. Since he was instructed not to hold on to what came up, he sidestepped wrestling with the internalized maternal idolization that, partly, fueled his meditation practice. He was a great student, and great teacher.

How did the warp slip through everyone's fingers? Owen must have been an ideal student, but did he ever work with a real spiritual master in a day in, day out way? I think of Schneur Zalman's depiction of the war between good and evil inclinations that is part of the wisdom path, and know Buddhism has equivalents. Owen somehow skipped this struggle. In Owen's case, is deadness growing where struggle might have been? Is deadness a substitute for wrestling with himself?

If only Owen would stay long enough to wrestle with me, but he no longer has to stay anywhere if he does not get his way. I suspect Owen suffers from I-Thou deprivation. He needs less emptiness. Fighting it out with an ordinary psychotherapist who has a taste for wisdom would be a start. Owen managed to incorporate the Buddhist world in clever extensions of the mother-son field, permutations of idolizing nourishment coupled with critical detachment. But he never wept through the night because of his faults.

It would be harder to bypass himself in a therapeutic relationship. If one stays in therapy, sooner or later one comes up against what is wrong with the therapy relationship. What is wrong with the therapy relationship is not something one can easily manipulate one's way out of, short of leaving, or agreeing to lie to oneself. It is something to weep over and try to change. Oddly, trying to change the unchangeable, and weeping over inability, promotes a kind of growth. The tone and texture and resonance of personality deepen.

Owen might or might not need erotic connections with young men all his life. But struggling with his warps, his limits, his personal impossible might lead to fuller, less manipulative and exploitative relationships, possibly it might even lead to more pleasure. Of course, Owen may need to be devious. He is addicted to silent slyness. But his acceptance of his style is too easy, premature. The reconciliation that comes after doing battle with oneself does not have the same offensive-defensive tone that lifelong avoidance does.

Battering his head against a wall in therapy could make Owen more appreciative of what he really takes from others. Owen denigrates the other because he does not feel the latter gives freely—a Catch-22, since Owen slyly coerces the other into giving. A basic issue in therapy is determining whether give-and-take is possible outside of coercion. It would not be surprising to learn that Owen's denigrating tongue and cold eye are manifestations of pervasive self-hatred. It is easy to imagine that the hyperidolization his mother subjected him to (deforming his growth) offset her own self-hatred as well.

Owen may well have done enough good in this life to slip into a human form again in his next incarnation. Perhaps the struggle with self will be joined a bit more in his next life. But there are opportunities in this life as well.

JESSE

Jesse sought help for what other doctors had diagnosed as chronic fatigue syndrome. He had tried a number of medical treatments but still felt listless and nauseous much of the time. Self-employed, he did very well crunching numbers for Wall Street firms.

Now in his late thirties, Jesse was a serious meditator, and had been a Buddhist for nearly fifteen years. Meditation catalyzed his creativity and heightened his already acute awareness of shifting sensations, moods, feelings. Enlivening thoughts and visions would come to him. His teachers told him to let contents of awareness freely come and go, but sometimes he was guided to slow down and direct his attention to aspects of what he was experiencing so as to better observe, control, and explore certain states. To some extent, meditation acted as a container for his sensitivity but could also be a stimulant that exploded containers, now soothing, now heightening.

As I got to know Jesse, I discerned a curious, repetitive pattern that characterized his meditation sessions. While meditating, he developed convictions about women he should see or break up with. It would dawn on him that a woman he hadn't properly considered, was really right for him. He would call her and they would get together. As time went on, he came to know, with equal conviction, that she wasn't right after all. He could do better. This sequence might involve the same woman on and off for years, or different women.

Something similar happened professionally. While meditating, he would get ideas about what sort of work would be better and how he might go about improving things for himself. He was able to make a lot of money with minimal exertion by the time I met him. He scarcely had to move three yards or put in more than a few afternoons a week (or every couple of weeks) to make more than enough for a month. However, his material success did not translate into successful relationships—unless one measures success by numbers. His insensitivity to the women in his life amazed me. He was so in touch with, so sensitive to what was right for him moment to moment that the havoc he left in his wake escaped him.

He used meditation to develop a kind of openness with women. While meditating, he would observe his feelings, so that he could be undefensive, vulnerable, and honest. Women appreciated this, but would get enraged at how controlling he was. He remained open and undefensive in the face of their rage, a high-class steamroller who managed to get his way.

I suspected that he ate himself up with his feelings and his compulsion to stay with what felt right, especially since what felt right kept shifting. He simplified work, but his emotional life was torn in two directions, toward intensity and diffusion. Perhaps his delusional openness was wearing him out. Unable to do much more than lie in bed got him out of an emotional meat grinder, at least temporarily. Illness gave his overrun psyche a reprieve.

Therapy with Jesse was not easy. He held on to the idea that therapy focuses on the past and on tracing particular patterns or problems. He expected to get a working map of his personal history and psychological life and learn how present difficulties related to past upbringing. He wanted to control what therapy should focus on and what might be achieved.

My own version of therapy tends to be more fuzzy and open. W. R. Bion (1970) suggested approaching sessions without memory, understanding, expectation, or desire. For me, psychotherapy is a psychospiritual journey. I don't have a preset idea of where it might lead. It might lead into spiritual experience, childhood trauma, inklings of future possibilities, recounting past lives. It could become, for a time, the focused cognitive-behavioral tool desired by Jesse and managed care.

Jesse wanted to keep meditation separate from psychotherapy. Therapy was to be treated as a tool to address certain problems—fatigue, nausea. It was not something he would give himself to. It did not dawn on him to think of therapy as something to discover, to wonder about, to create. Therapy was a kind of psychic engineering for him. Its business was ameliorating symptoms, not soul-making. Jesse set therapy and meditation in opposition, the former inferior to the latter. He did not experience both as outgrowths from the same psychic body.

Jesse's attitude toward therapy threw me into doubt. Isn't it reasonable to have a specific focus and to adopt a method capable of achieving success? After all, this is what insurance companies seem to feel therapy should do. Am I wrong in thinking that therapy involves one's whole being and that it is impossible and even undesirable to know where it might lead ahead of time? Am I a dinosaur for feeling that psychic life has value in its own right, and that the struggle to be open to it for its own sake is part of the "cure"?

I felt enormous pressure, as though Jesse were strangling me. How self-assured and controlling this sensitive, vulnerable man was. Or was I the controlling one? Did I try to control him by my view of therapeutic openness? His meditative openness, my therapeutic openness—how did they get into such a power struggle, a battle for control? Who was controlling whom? Was he relentlessly squeezing me more and more tightly while tightening the grip on himself as well—or was I putting the squeeze on him? How controlling ideologies of openness can be!

In fact I fed Jesse some of the things he asked for. I helped him contact early wounds and connect past trauma with present defenses. He filled in more of his story. I helped him do this, partly, to demonstrate the limits of such understanding, although the process was helpful. It gave Jesse a sense of background support that he was lacking. I supported him in his search, and the support was as important as the search. This work made him feel a little better, but the fatigue and nausea continued.

It began to dawn on me that the muted battle for control was perhaps the real work of our therapy. The struggle was a basic emotional fact, something I felt with him session to session, week to week. It was hard to pin down just where it came from. His voice was soft, even, somewhat monotonic, and his movements were slow, measured. It seemed to me that his muscles (back of neck, shoulders, lower back, sphincters, even face) were too tightly clenched. He did everything slowly, deliberately, as if he did not want to do anything faster than he could observe.

I felt overly constrained in Jesse's presence, even claustrophobic. It was as if he were trying to adapt life to his version of mindful awareness, rather than let the latter be part of life. He tried to make life conform to his vision of it and was slowly suffocating himself. Whatever feelings he experienced in my presence—anger, sadness—were quickly dampened, reported, studied, deconstructed, understood, let go. I rarely got a sense of immediate, free-flowing contact. Everything was filtered through the activity of watching. Meditation—the way Jesse used it—was making him sick.

I unsuccessfully tried to communicate my sense of being controlled by Jesse as well as the immense pressure he put on himself. I pulled back and reflected on the sense of deadlock and battle I was experiencing. My shoulders, back, and body tightened. I imagined what it was like being Jesse.

It would be easy to make something up to explain the pressure, contraction, and control, but it was more important to feel it, and continue feeling it. Weeks and months passed, and I became familiar with the tight feeling. I turned it over, tasted it, relaxed around it. We continued to talk about whatever we talked about—girlfriends, work, parents, meditation, therapy, moment-to-moment states, breakdown, never getting better, what it was like being together, this, that. I remained coiled around Jesse's tightness, in me, and eventually became less defensive-offensive about it, less uptight about the tightness. Not simply that I took it for granted, but psychosomatically I made room for it. I did not have to recoil, contract, or point at it in futile dismay.

What happened *felt* miraculous, although I'm sure there's logic to it. As the months went on, Jesse became more attractive to me. At times, I loved his expressions, the quiet twinkle in his eye, the glow of his face. I felt the tightness—his tightness in my chest and belly, the tightening skin and muscles of my face and arms and legs—but I tingled with joy sometimes just seeing him. For a few moments, the tightness melted.

When he came in, I no longer had to hold myself back somewhat fearfully, nor did I worry about his need for control. I smiled—really smiled. I liked seeing him. Nevertheless, as I sat with him, the struggle continued and pressure mounted. My inner smile would come and go. Then when I least expected it, when the self-tightening process seemed like it would last forever, Jesse's soul would tickle me, and joy would take me by surprise.

Within a year, Jesse's nauseous fatigue had lifted. I doubt that any particular thing we said or did had much to do with it. My guess is that his tightness found a place in someone else. It was not just that I let him in —I did and I didn't. Rather, the work my psyche did with the tightness kept me—and him—out. Whatever the reason, something in Jesse blocked our spontaneous contact. My attention gravitated to the barrier, to the *x* that blocked contact.

It was precisely the barrier or wall that lodged in me. Jesse's tightness obtruded, burrowed in, made room for itself. Had I resisted, *it* would have had to keep fighting for space. That I spread around it and got the feel of it opened the possibility for something more to happen.

My hunch is that Jesse's controlling tightness must have arisen in response to the traumatizing characteristics of those who cared for him. He controlled himself to better fit in and control those who threatened and nourished him. His yo-yo pattern with women suggests that his attempts to control traumatizing aspects of mother were only partly successful. And his unfortunate success in controlling his workplace (such a reduction of work life!) suggests too easy a victory over father. Jesse, too, may have had a predisposition for self-tightening as a spontaneous form of self-protectiveness and mastery.

Meditation was a way for Jesse to control his emotions. However, the more control he exercised, as he got older, the less room there was for himself. He was both master and victim of his own controlling process. To make room for himself, he assigned too great a value to moment-to-moment changes of feeling. He was compelled to follow what felt right, even though what felt right kept changing. The master of control was tossed and torn by changing emotional winds.

Jesse sat at meditation centers for years, but his need for control coupled with emotional lability and diffusion prevented him from ever really engaging another person. Meditation teachers threw him back on himself. He tried to manage himself and eventually fell ill. His meditation teachers challenged and encouraged him, but did not supply the kind of personal engagement that he so needed. Jesse needed simple, human contact, not enlightenment.

ONE REALITY

I've spoken at a number of conferences on spirituality and psychotherapy the last several years, and at each one a Buddhist has gotten up and said that practicing Buddhist meditation can shorten psychotherapy by years. They might be responding to some of my case presentations, in which psychotherapy goes on for decades. I find it fruitless to pit religion and psychotherapy against each other. I find it especially cruel for either religion or psychotherapy to advertise itself as an agent for that which it can't deliver. Hopes unfulfilled by psychotherapy are not necessarily going to be fulfilled by religion, and vice versa.

The Buddhist path requires a lifetime of practice—perhaps many lifetimes. It is no shortcut. The cases presented here serve as a warning not to idealize Buddhism, or any other path to liberation. No religion or therapeutic method holds the best cards in all games.

My use of Buddhism and Judaism is idiosyncratic and does not pass muster as being strictly true to either. I invent them as I go along and they invent me. I draw from texts and teachers and colleagues and friends—whatever hits me. If I do not draw from the Holy Spirit on a daily basis, I become a semi-collapsed version of myself. We are sustained directly by God, not only through others. We are sustained by others, not only by God.

Buddhism helps me empty myself out, Jewish prayer fills me up. There is poignant longing in Jewish prayer and song, a sweet, wailing connection to God. Tears and joy are one in it. Buddhism clears and cleans me. In meditation, chains of identities go up in smoke. What a relief to be free of self! It is like detoxifying the air we breathe.

But we learn from Owen that self re-forms. It is more than failure to be hard on himself. True, Owen does not wail repentantly about the warp that stains his efforts. He does not throw himself down, rend his garments, don sackcloth (images of soul's desire to cleanse itself). He refuses to anguish over his psychic deformations. Owen does not believe in punishing himself.

Yet over and over, gains in meditation are poisoned by the sickening feeling that tinges erotic exploitation. He has his moments of sexual exaltation, yet senses that he is acting debased. Owen is punished by success.

If one does not punish oneself for what needs punishing, sometimes punishment comes some other way. Owen and Jesse see the world as a playground filled with infinite possibilities. Life presents them with endless arrays of objects suitable for the exercise of creativity. Meditation opens space for repatterning of what is possible. But it is the very surplus of possibilities that enables Owen and Jesse to sidestep themselves. They do not have to create a boundary and say, "I'll hang in and wrestle with this."

Meditation is a way to get off the hook for them. They believe meditation will help them grow—indeed, it does. But something wrong in their relationship to meditation impedes them. Owen remains poisonously self-indulgent and can scarcely stand the taste of himself. To deaden that taste, he has become dead. Jesse could not bear the weight of his whirring whims and could scarcely get out of bed.

Individuals are both too hard on themselves and not hard enough. Often the balance needs restructuring and qualities of hardness-softness need to evolve. Missing in both Owen and Jesse is an ability to be transformed by others' responses to them. They do not—cannot—take to heart what others say to them. They can always find people who say nice things to them, and the bad things do not strike deeply enough.

Each has virtually created a world he dominates and does not have to hear or be affected by what eludes domination. Neither has linked with another in a way capable of generating the journey into self-correction. They do not grab hold of themselves and say, "This is it! The buck stops here!" They think the next moment will be different, easier. Perhaps they are waiting to grow the equipment to grapple with themselves. Meanwhile, self-deadening collapse accelerates.

Their lovers level plenty of criticisms and complaints. Owen and Jesse are good at paying lip service but, on the whole, manage to escape. They easily dismiss the lover's criticisms: the lover is reacting to rejection, is too needy, is angry because Owen or Jesse do not act as they want, the lover is not the right one, the lover is a passing moment, and so on. Owen and Jesse get off free, but pay with illness.

An inability to listen and be transformed by what one hears is characteristic of illness. What sorts of developmental deficiencies make being transformed by the other difficult or impossible? What conditions are needed to enable growth of transformational responsiveness? To what extent can psychotherapy and/or meditation and prayer enable growth of this precious capacity?

For many individuals meditation and prayer are forms of psychotherapy and psychotherapy is a form of meditation and prayer. The boundaries between them are not clear-cut. There may be a point where the branches diverge, but for most people, there is enormous overlap. Too rigid a conception of what one ought to get from which "discipline" can make it impossible to open oneself to the work of the One Reality that flows through all. We are all partners here.

References

Bion, Wilfred R. (1970). *Attention and Interpretation*. Northvale, N.J.: Jason Aronson, 1983.

Eigen, Michael (1996a). *Reshaping the Self*. Madison, Conn.: Psychosocial Press/International Universities Press.

——— (1996b). *Psychic Deadness*. Northvale, N.J.: Jason Aronson.

Khan, M. M. R. (1979). *Alienation in Perversions*. New York: International Universities Press.

Zalman, Schneur (1984). *Likutei Amarim: Tanya*. New York: Kehot Publication Society.

THE DISAVOWAL OF THE SPIRIT

INTEGRATION AND WHOLENESS

IN BUDDHISM AND PSYCHOANALYSIS

Paul C. Cooper

❑

INTRODUCTION

Common to both Freud's psychoanalysis and the Buddha's science of liberation is a distinctive emphasis on the experiential. The Buddhist critique of blind faith exemplifies the strong significance placed on personal verification of the teachings. The Zen master's directive, "Don't take my word for it, go see for yourself," parallels Freud's reluctance to provide much more than general guidelines for psychoanalytic practice.

Both Freud and the Buddha demanded of themselves and of their followers nothing less than unrelenting self-scrutiny. Persistence and hard work result in a perceptual transformation and deepening awareness of self and other. For the Buddha, self-scrutiny, facilitated primarily through the practice of meditation, results in freedom from suffering and the compassionate wish to "free all beings from the bonds of ignorance." For Freud,[1] self-awareness and knowledge, generated primarily through the process of "psychoanalytic purification," results in the ability to "love and to work well." Freud did indeed remain reticent as to the specific details of his

---

This essay is previously unpublished.

technique. However, he was quite adamant in his persistent advocacy of personal analysis as the sine qua non of personal development and of analytic training. The impact of both innovators on the human capacity for compassion and emotional healing remains undisputed. The Zen master's admonishments to "practice, practice, practice!" holds true equally for both disciplines.

Despite such commonality, one crucial question remains unexplored. How do transformative experiences, impacting as they do on the meditating analyst's psychic structure, influence the therapeutic situation? In short, solid theoretical and technical integration requires and reflects sound psychic integration. I will demonstrate below that personal integration, despite differences of meaning and/or expression, lies at the center of any discussion of the integration of religion and psychology in general, and of Buddhism and psychoanalysis in particular. Their interaction exerts a profound impact on the analyst's perception and development of both theory and technique. The following discussion examines a basic obstacle to the integrative effort and reviews the role and expression of integration from various Buddhist and psychoanalytic points of view.

DISAVOWAL OF THE SPIRIT

In his penetrating work *Transference and Countertransference*,[2] Heinrich Racker comments that "we are still children and neurotics even when we are adults and analysts," a fact that, he argues, requires our full acceptance. For the analyst this requirement depends to a large extent "on the continuity and depth of contact with himself."[3] It is this "child-self" that carries, according to Robert Lovinger,[4] our earliest contacts, and therefore our deepest internalizations, of spiritual experience. For those individuals with prior spiritual training, such internalizations can function as a lens through which they will perceive and integrate their later experiences with psychoanalysis. Similarly, personal psychoanalysis and training will influence the individual's ongoing perceptions and internalization of Buddhist practice. However, this child/spiritual self can frequently get lost in the shuffle of the demands, both real and imagined, of psychoanalytic training. Thus, the dialogue regarding the integration of Buddhism and psychoanalysis becomes an external metaphor and a necessary vehicle for an internal struggle. The analyst's regulation of personal needs in relation to the larger psychoanalytic community and maintenance of conscious contact with in-

ternalizations of earlier spiritual training and experience constitute the opposing poles of this internal conflict. The individual might, for example,
disavow both the conscious and unconscious aspects of personal spiritual
experience. Variations occur. For example, certain individuals allow the
spiritual aspects of self experience to become compartmentalized or dissolved completely. Frequently a relinquishment and resulting devaluation
of the spiritual will occur.

Developmental factors require consideration. For instance, Lovinger observes that most individuals lose contact with or complete their religious
training during early adolescence. Perhaps empty rote practices are relin-
quished. However, the more meaningful aspects of spiritual development
might remain fallow, never to be developed. Perhaps there is no longer
any interest. Those who do pursue spiritual development despite the demands of psychoanalytic training often become more committed and expressive as they resolve, through analysis, the unconscious motivations for
their initial disavowal. Still others flee from analysis and toward a deeper
commitment to a religious community or to further spiritual development.
From this camp one frequently hears the complaint that psychoanalysis is
not "deep enough" when measured by spiritual standards. My impression
is that a mutually interacting dynamic exists that reflects in the person's
experience of and relation to both areas of personal inquiry. However, both
conscious and unconscious (real and imagined) idealizations in relation to
psychoanalytic training, when not resolved, will interfere with the personal
integration of both spiritual and psychoanalytic experiences.

FREUD'S LEGACY

One aspect of the need for spiritual disavowal stems from Freud's striving
to secularize mind, an extension of Enlightenment philosophy into psychoanalytic theory. Regarding Freud's reductionist analysis of the "oceanic
feeling," Joel Kovel[5] notes that "Freud wished to see installed the Reason
that the Enlightenment, in conscious opposition to religion, had given the
world and of which he considered himself an avatar." Historically, this
issue is further complicated by Freud's incomplete knowledge of Buddhist
meditative technique. Mark Epstein[6] provides a detailed and comprehensive review of the early psychoanalytic response to meditation. He discusses
Freud's correspondence with the French writer Romain Rolland, through
which he became indirectly acquainted with the bliss-producing concen-

trative meditation techniques. However, Freud had no knowledge of the analytic forms of meditation so fundamental to the Buddhist transformational process. Therefore, he viewed Eastern meditative soteriology as a regression to the "oceanic merger state." Actually, Buddhists are also critical of those who would exclusively dwell in the bliss states available to the practitioner of concentrative techniques. For example, in addressing the importance of the thorough analysis of self and phenomena, Nagarjuna, the founder of the Buddhist "Middle Way" school, writes:

> It is not sufficient merely to withdraw the mind from conceiving a self of persons and of phenomena, or merely to stop the mind's wandering to objects, for these do not constitute realization of emptiness. If they did, then deep sleep and fainting would absurdly involve realization of emptiness.[7]

However, to return to the point, disavowal results in the analyst's loss of wholeness and in a possible hesitation to discuss spiritual issues in depth with patients and/or colleagues. The dearth of any extensive literature on the subject seems to reflect this reluctance. More significant, however, is the tragedy that results from the implicit limitations on clinical practice. The analyst, both consciously and unconsciously, comes to neglect those aspects of the patient/analyst relationship that might conflict with personal needs.

Freud's need for acceptance within the larger scientific community, writes W. W. Meissner,[8] led him to "limited conceptualization of religious experience . . . partly as a result of unresolved conflictual aspects of his own personality . . ." The disastrous historical impact of Freud's incomplete knowledge and lack of experience with Buddhist training has been compounded by a generation of followers. The result, which continues to persist, as Zdenek Chernovsky[9] notes, is the perpetuation of "a tradition of errors."

Freud's belief that religion constitutes a cultural neurosis and that personal spiritual endeavors are evidence of individual pathology continues to exert an unconscious impact on contemporary psychoanalytic thinking despite statements to the contrary. For example, in an article on the role of silence in the therapeutic situation, Mustafa Shafii[10] takes issue with Freud and views meditation "as an integrative and adaptive phenomenon, rather than as a pathological experience." However, given this consciously stated claim, Shafii nevertheless describes the process as "a controlled regression [which] helps the individual reexperience union with his earlier love object on a pre-verbal level of psycho-sexual development."[11] In this way, the meditative state is divested of any transcendent or progressive quality. This stance ultimately reduces the experience to the level of a memory or of a regression to an earlier mode of being. The ramifications of the unconscious pervasiveness of Freud's initial views in relation to the therapeutic situation will be elaborated in the case study that follows.

The above observations are neither intended to pathologize the genetic roots of religious training and spiritual experience nor are they intended to deny the existence of unresolved conflicts. Such problems require analytic attention and are manifested in an individual's spiritual orientation and associated internalizations. Rather, it is the need for disavowal that becomes an issue particularly in terms of maintaining the depth of contact with the wholeness and fullness of being so essential to our work as analysts. On this point Nina Coltart[12] comments that there "is a ludicrous falsity in any notion that for part of each day, one is sort of a practicing Buddhist and for another part, a sort of practicing analyst, and for bits in between a sort of nothing."

From this point of view, any discussion regarding the theoretical and/or technical integration of psychoanalysis and Buddhism demands unrelenting and continuous, if not ruthless, internal self-scrutiny from the synergistic vantage points available through both realms of experience. Both the Buddha and Freud demanded nothing less of themselves. Their pervasive influence on both Eastern and Western civilization and culture attests to the impact of their endeavors. We will now turn the discussion toward the expression of wholeness and integration from the various psychoanalytic and Buddhist vantage points.

WHOLENESS AND INTEGRATION

Notions of wholeness or integration find expression in all spiritual and psychological traditions. In general, as noted above, both spiritual disciplines and psychoanalysis provide systematic methods for effectively addressing the barriers and obstacles that interfere with the individual's psychic integration and the experience of wholeness. But without drawing any facile comparisons between how the two disciplines understand such experiences, I have written the following summary to draw the reader's attention to the value that wholeness carries in both psychoanalysis and Buddhist thought.

In comparing psychoanalysis and mysticism, M. L. Gottesfield[13] proposes that "the termination of therapy should leave the patient with a sense of emotional integration and harmony (union)." In 1924, in perhaps the first constructive discussion of Buddhism to appear in a psychoanalytic journal, Joe Tom Sun[14] expresses the value of integration quite clearly. He quotes the Buddha as follows: "I set up the individual mind of each one who seeks peace, bring it to quietude, unify it, gather it together." Sun continues by making the following comparison: "It would be difficult today to more clearly state the aim of an analysis, which above all is to unify the mind, to make conscious the unconscious, that is, to bring peace, an end to conflict and sorrow." This reference calls to mind Freud's famous caveat "where id was, shall ego be," which alludes to the value he placed on psychic integration.

Psychoanalyst D. W. Winnicott emphasizes that real integration, the ground of the "true self," does not imply reification. This emphasis is important for the Buddhist as well. For example, the Madyamika or "Middle Way" Buddhists tread a precarious path that avoids the reified extremes of both eternalism and nihilism. This Middle Way path is expressed in the foundational Buddhist principles of "emptiness" and "dependent arising," both of which will be explored in the case study.

In his discussion of Winnicott's work, Michael Eigen[15] observes that "in most psychological literature wholeness is associated with integration." Winnicott, however, "stresses the open-ended aspect of wholeness." As Winnicott notes: "When healthy persons come together, they each contribute a whole world, because each brings a whole person."[16] Winnicott's true self–false self concept expresses the consequences of the person's inability to obtain and/or maintain a sense of wholeness, whereby "in situations in which what is expected is a whole person, the false self has some essential lacking."[17] Following Winnicott, Harry Guntrip comments that the process of psychoanalysis "leads to a sense of integrity and wholeness."[18]

From the vantage point of self psychology Kohut and Wolf note that "the psychoanalytic situation creates conditions in which the damaged self begins to strive to achieve or to reestablish a state of cohesion, vigor and inner harmony."[19] In a later article Wolf adds that "strengthening the self takes precedence over all other possible aims."[20] Wolf also distinguishes between the experience of cohesion and solidified concepts of psychic structure. He notes the usefulness of psychological theories and concepts regarding the components of self structure. However, he considers the "metaphorical nature of the word 'self' as a label for the psychological organization that gives rise to my self experience, and . . . that reference to the self's structure, components, and cohesion is also metaphorical."[21]

Atwood and Stolorow,[22] speaking from the intersubjective perspective, address the process of "affect integration," which they view as the nexus of the healing process. However, the intersubjectivists also criticize the tendency towards reification of psychoanalytic theories and discussions of psychic structure.

Karen Horney[23] discusses the "impoverishment of the personality" and refers to the Buddhist notion of "wholeheartedness" or "sincerity of spirit," observing that "nobody divided within himself can be wholly sincere." On this point Horney quotes the Zen Buddhist scholar D. T. Suzuki, who speaks on the "spirit of sincerity" and notes that "sincerity, that is, not deceiving, means 'putting forth' one's whole being."[24]

Tibetan Buddhists refer to the quality of Buddha nature, a potential in all beings, an urge, whether conscious or unconscious, to realize the full potential of that fundamental nature. Guenther and Kawamura, in *Mind in Buddhist Psychology*, refer to "appreciative discrimination" and observe that "through 'appreciative discrimination' we would be able to discover the potential for growth and health that is in us and to develop it so that we might, and could, develop more and more into a human being."[25]

The value of wholeness and the movement toward internal integration in both psychoanalytic and Buddhist thought should be clear. Of course there are significant divergences and sources of conflict within and between the two disciplines. These differences could become sources for disavowal, particularly when they interact with the therapist's unconscious conflicts. The following case lends clarity to this point.

CASE STUDY

So how do an analyst's previous and ongoing spiritual practices influence the therapeutic situation? This case study will demonstrate one way that Buddhist study and practice can function as a filter through which the meditating analyst perceives, approaches, and integrates psychoanalytic study, training, and experience. This case also serves to illustrate the pervasiveness of the unconscious need for disavowal that, unless brought into awareness, can become a treatment obstacle.

The foundational Buddhist principles of emptiness and dependent arising, mentioned above, have influenced my orientation toward psychoanalytic concepts. This influence exerts itself in choices about training, supervision, theory, and technique. Simply stated, emptiness refers to the Buddhist belief in the impermanence or noninherent existence of self and phenomena. The realization of emptiness through both study and meditation dispels ignorance and leads to liberation. This comes about through a process of identifying and then relinquishing cherished ways in which we identify our sense of self as "concrete," "eternal," or "separate." Dependent arising, the complement to emptiness, refers to the contextual contingency of self and of phenomena. Dependent arising accounts for the experience of self both philosophically and experientially. Thus Buddhist philosophers, for the most part, accept "relative," "conventional," or "common sense" experiences of self. However, they refute absolute or inherent existence.

These contentions, combined with my experience of meditation, have led me more comfortably, for better or for worse, in the general direction of relational psychoanalytic models and toward a more "totalistic" view of transference and countertransference. This constructive position views countertransference "as the total emotional reaction of the psychoanalyst to the patient in the treatment situation [which] is useful in gaining more understanding of the patient."[26] In relation to the above Buddhist concepts, we view the therapeutic situation as an interdependently emerging transference and countertransference dynamic. This dynamic manifests in behavior, feelings, memories, and thoughts. The various ways that both the therapist and the patient identify and solidify their sense of self depends on this dynamic. Attachment to these cherished identifications can account for both resistances and counterresistances that occur during the treatment situation. As we will see, theoretical and technical stances, with certain patients, can be subsumed and more clearly understood within the context of a dependently arising transference and countertransference dynamic.

My reactions to the spiritual and creative striving of an intelligent and attractive forty-year-old woman named Ann were clearly not consistent with my conscious theoretical and personal convictions regarding both Buddhism and psychoanalysis. She entered treatment complaining of depression and anxiety that interfered with her career pursuits. Ann was the youngest sibling in a large family, and her parents' attentions were almost exclusively focused on an older sister who was a child prodigy and a highly talented and successful artist. Ann's other siblings were also accomplished artists. While Ann had enjoyed some marginal success in the creative arts, she experienced her inhibitions as a severe block to her success. Ann's inability to succeed creatively placed her at odds with her achievement-oriented family. The tone of the home environment was set primarily by the moods of Ann's mother, whom she described as an "emotionally volatile, bitter, and very angry woman." Ann's father remained "aloof." Since he was a psychologist and a professor at the local university, the family was not supposed to have any problems. As leaders in their Christian fundamentalist community they should "have all of the answers" and serve as examples to the "poor and wicked of the world." Ann became, as she put it, "the family deviant." She was expelled from high school for stealing, lying, and cheating.

Ann initially seemed serious and self-absorbed. She was controlled and controlling, and talked about herself in a flat matter-of-fact way. Ann's surface re-created the cold controlled environment in which she was raised. Her creativity revealed intense passion and underlying rage and this dichotomy found expression in her dual spiritual orientation. The free-form ecstasy produced through her movement practices contrasted with the highly disciplined rituals of her silent retreats. Ann maintained ongoing involvements with both. She obtained a residency at a Buddhist monastery and simultaneously performed with a group of whirling dervishes. In this relationship to the divine and to her creativity she experienced herself as no more than a funnel through which the spirit finds expression. Here, then, is the reification of her self-annihilation and the accompanying reification of an eternal and externalized "higher power."

This relationship contributed to my initial devaluation of Ann's spiritual and creative expressions. From my Buddhist perspective I viewed her as struggling with the conflicts created by her perceptual shifts between the extremes of nihilism and eternalism. She clearly misunderstood and misused foundational Buddhist teachings. For example, emptiness, the lack of inherent existence, for Ann meant total self-annihilation. However, I also felt my own practices were superior to hers. My biases became quite a problem during the early stages of the treatment. From a psychodynamic perspective these issues are complex and multidetermined. For example, her relation to the divine reflected her relation with an all-powerful and domineering mother. For Ann, therapy and professional success represented a separation from her mother and from her past. My devaluing attitudes related to identifications of mine with Ann's father on one level and to projections of her own overidentification with her father on another level. Actually, it was her need for a sympathetic understanding of her spiritual activities that led her to me for psychoanalytic psychotherapy. Ann's need to be taken seriously quickly became a central focus of our work together, once a week for three years.

In the United States, involvement with Buddhist practices rarely meets with family acceptance. Even with apparent approval, acceptance, or understanding, the family's covert message usually signals that the individual is not taken very seriously. But, in Ann's case, previous experiences and associated feelings, related to a lack of validation, also subjectively colored her present experiences and expectations. As a result, like many others, she understandably hesitated to discuss any involvements or interests, spiritual or otherwise. A therapist's attitude of interest and a desire to understand the patient enables the latter to negotiate feelings and concerns about risking such disclosures. Given my strong interest in spiritual inquiry, I expected a natural resonance with Ann. In fact, she expressed considerable relief when she accurately sensed my interests in her spiritual practices. However, I felt myself becoming distant as I rigidly evaluated Ann's spiritual experiences with a cold and classical skepticism. As I could not take Ann seriously, my stance conveyed a sense of infantilizing amusement. My reactions seemed much too pronounced, inconsistent with my own values, technique, and interests. I experienced a state of internal dissonance. For example, Ann would relate her experience as a passive conduit for the spirit. I would find myself silently evaluating her descriptions as a form of primitive dissociation that functioned to protect her tenuous sense of self from fragmentation. I determined that she was avoiding taking any responsibility for her artistry in case her work was criticized, rejected, or not taken seriously. To me, her passive relation to the spirit functioned as a contemporary "oceanic feeling," the return to infantile narcissism described by Freud. From this vantage point her monastic retreats appeared to be symptomatic of her pathology and an expression of her infantile needs. However, Ann became highly focused and extremely productive during these retreats, a fact that I initially ignored.

While I do not intend to deny the depth of Ann's problems, the point here relates to the emotional quality of my observations. They felt cold, critical, condescending, and disdainful, as if I were an observer looking into the cage at a freak show. Her initial diagnosis as psychotic and her occasional decompensations seemed to support my hypothesis. I did not realize at this point that we were both participating in the construction of the cage. Actually, my attitudes, to some extent, provoked her episodes of rage, withdrawal, or decompensation. I once asked: "Why can't you ever take responsibility for your creativity? You always have it coming from some higher spirit." Understandably, Ann became enraged. Furthermore, I remained silently immovable in this stance. Feeling humored in therapy recreated for Ann the actual trauma of her parents' "spider and fly" treatment. She recalled her parents' extreme swings between enthusiasm and encouragement for her creative activity and extreme criticism, rejection, and belittling. For instance, Ann took her childhood projects quite seriously. She was left feeling seduced, violated, and betrayed in almost every aspect of her relationship with both of her parents, with her siblings, with lovers, with friends, and now with me. She would express her fears that I might become abusive to her. I could not be trusted. During these episodes, Ann would lock herself up in her room for days and weeks at a time. She would come out for her sessions and quickly return home. At one point she would only talk to me by telephone. My attitudinal shifts reflected her parents' reactions described above. On the one hand I would eagerly await and enthusiastically greet her creative and spiritual expressions. However, when she would speak of spirituality, my attitude and thoughts would again suddenly shift to the devaluing outside observer. I rationalized this devaluing attitude through the double-edged sword of Freudian reason and the Buddhist refutation of the spirit. Meanwhile, the impact of the past was now spilling into the treatment and contributing to Ann's perceptions and expectations.

Ann left her family and fanatical conservative religious community after finishing high school. She journeyed North to pursue an artistic career. However, her plans were cut short when she was abducted and raped by a former acquaintance. She reported that "he held her captive" for a time but that she eventually escaped. Her parents actively encouraged and financed her return to the family nest. Despite reassurances to the contrary, they promptly proceeded to have her institutionalized and medicated against her will upon her arrival home. Ann recounts locking herself in her room in the family home for protection and for privacy. However, her father broke in, had Ann straitjacketed, medicated, and moved to a mental hospital where he was a resident psychologist.

Other details about Ann's life would certainly provide further clarification. But the point here, particularly with regard to the shift in my theoretical stance and to my own intense reactions, becomes vividly clear. Ann's father was a practicing clinical psychologist. At this point I began to view my shifting theoretical stance and its associated attitudes and feelings as part of an emerging unconscious identification with Ann's father.

She described him as removed and condescending. He was, in Ann's words, "a cold fish" who needed to insulate himself from his feelings regarding his female children. She recalls no physical or verbal affection from him after age three. As an adult she confirmed this through discussions with her older siblings. He never picked her up, touched or hugged her. This was a treatment issue since our first session. Ann wanted me to hug her. I would fantasize gratifying her wishes and would then feel guilty. I would then retreat from my discomfort into the safety of analytic distance. She recalls being used as a demonstration subject for her father's class lectures at the local university. During this stage of the treatment I too was clearly treating her as a subject, not as a person. More importantly, I was not allowing my whole self to function in the service of the treatment. I suspected that my own oedipal and boundary issues were also contributing to this reaction. I became very tough on myself. However, when considering the larger context and the idiosyncratic nature of my reaction, I still needed to ask myself: "Why would these particular feelings, thoughts, and shifts in my theoretical stance emerge at this moment with this individual?" My reactions, including the theoretical and technical stance that emerged in the context of the therapy, became the patient's "history" in the room.

Ann's mother was all-engulfing. For example, Ann felt that she was nothing but an extra set of her mother's hands. Her mother, a well-educated woman, had given up her creative aspirations for a strictly traditional family life, a decision she both regretted and resented. She lived vicariously through her children, particularly through Ann's older sister's success.

My own needs were also contending with issues of disavowal. Ann was referred to me through my training program. I was required to report on the case and to discuss my work in class and in supervision. At the time, I felt a need to be the "good adult/therapist" and follow a straight and narrow path that led to a classical formulation of the case. However, my perception of the classical stance, with the accompanying notion of the analyst as a blank screen and outside observer, was not consistent with my belief in emptiness and dependent arising. I was not allowing my totalistic orientation to inform my work. This aspect of psychoanalytic theory and technique, as noted above, connects most directly with the influence of my Buddhist practices. For me, it was time to "get serious" and be the "adult/analyst." This was the time to stop "playing around" with this "esoteric Buddhist nonsense" and with what I perceived as "unconventional" psychoanalytic principles. The "child/spiritual self" had become temporarily disavowed, as if these different aspects of my self experience could not become integrated. I could not be fully present for Ann and could not take her seriously. I was busy taking my self too seriously. Like the father, and like Ann at times, I had become aloof. This need and the accompanying perception of the institutional demands of psychoanalytic training colored my early work with Ann despite active support and encouragement by a supervisor whom I'd selected partly for her accepting attitude of my spiritual striving. Actually, the intake interviewer made the referral because of my interest in working with such individuals and partly due to Ann's request to be referred to a therapist who could relate in an accepting and sensitive way to her life as a Buddhist and as an artist. However, I had somehow disavowed this aspect of my self experience.

As I worked through these issues in my own analysis, supervision, conversations with peers, and self-reflection, the treatment began to shift. Ann became more creatively expressive. She became more flexible in her relationships and day-to-day affairs. She began to freely and openly express longing and rage for both her parents and me.

The above discussion addresses a predominant treatment theme of my unconscious identification with Ann's father, which I experienced and rationalized through my sudden theoretical shifts. However, on another level of analysis, this dynamic became, at times, an identification with Ann's own sense of self. Let me explain. You will recall that during the early phase of treatment Ann presented herself in an emotionally flat, cold, and removed way. She is very bright and prone to rationalization and intellectualization. I am vulnerable to this defensive stance myself. My defensive use of theory represents a good example. However, this identification with her father's aloofness enabled Ann to differentiate herself and to maintain a boundary in relation to her narcissistically demanding and absorbing mother and from being "swallowed up" in relationships. Her relationships rarely lasted for more than a few months. These involvements were typically sadomasochistic. Ann would "script" the relationship. She would take on a dominant role and her partners existed solely to do her bidding. For example, they would run her errands and do her shopping during her agoraphobic phases. This stance also insulated Ann from her mother's rage and intrusions. My own shifts into this distancing stance consistently occurred during times when the boundaries were slipping, such as during her creative ecstasy. These shifts also occurred at times when I could not trust my own newly developing skills as a fledgling therapist and when I felt a need to insulate myself from Ann's rage and seductiveness. However, my initial boundary was at the expense of my spiritual self and to what I considered the more creative and effective aspects of my theoretical and technical standpoint.

CONCLUSION

In retrospect, the treatment process stayed inextricably linked to my own work on myself. The more I allowed my own self into the treatment, the more I could accept Ann's creativity and spirituality. I then could work with my perceptions, her projections, and my identification with her projections, particularly with her psychologist father.

My understanding of emptiness and dependent arising in relation to the transference and to the countertransference facilitated the work. My disavowal impeded the work and caused ruptures in the treatment. Ann already disavowed what she imagined as not good enough or worthwhile in herself. She split off her own capacity for creative expression that only became accessible through her surrender to God. However, I was doing the same in an attenuated way. I surrendered to becoming an outside observer at the expense of my Buddhist experience and its influence on my technique. Like Ann, I was keeping myself at a "safe" distance. However, we remained quite connected unconsciously through the attitudes, feelings, and accompanying rationalizations that were emerging within the context of the dependently arising treatment situation, which still exerted a profound impact on our sense of self. The difficulty was ascertaining the relative nature of the emerging self experiences that during the initial stage of the treatment I experienced as solid and separate.

Whether in the vivid language of religious imagery or the highly refined language of psychoanalytic thought, both Buddhism and psychoanalysis provide comprehensive technologies that address personal integration and wholeness. Considering the highly subjective nature of both, the issue of integration involves an intensely personal process. This endeavor entails ongoing scrutiny and examination of the ways in which direct experiences with both disciplines become consciously and unconsciously internalized and integrated by the individual.

Notes

1. Sigmund Freud, "Recommendations to Physicians Practicing Psychoanalysis," in vol. 12 of *Standard Edition of the Complete Psychological Works of Sigmund Freud*, ed. and trans. James Strachey (London: Hogarth Press and Institute of Psychoanalysis, 1958), 112.

2. Heinrich Racker, *Transference and Countertransference* (Madison, Conn.: International Universities Press, 1968), 130.

3. Ibid., 131.

4. Robert J. Lovinger, *Working with Religious Issues in Therapy* (Northvale, N.J.: Jason Aronson, Inc., 1984).

5. Joel Kovel, "Beyond the Future of an Illusion: Further Reflections on Freud and Religion," *Psychoanalytic Review* 77:1 (1990): 69–87.

6. Mark Epstein, "Beyond the Oceanic Feeling: Psychoanalytic Study of Buddhist Meditation," *International Review of Psychoanalysis* 17:2 (1990): 159–66. Also, see pages 119–30 this volume.

7. Jeffrey Hopkins, *Meditation on Emptiness* (London: Wisdom Publications, 1983), 30.

8. William W. Meissner, *Psychoanalysis and Religious Experience* (New Haven: Yale University Press, 1984), 137.

9. Zdenek Chernovsky, "Psychoanalysis and Tibetan Buddhism as Techniques of Liberation," *American Journal of Psychoanalysis* 48:1 (1988): 56.

10. Mustafa Shafii, "Silence in the Service of the Ego: Psychoanalytic Study of Meditation," *International Journal of Psychoanalysis* 54 (1973): 431.

11. Ibid., 432.

12. Nina Coltart, "The Practice of Psychoanalysis and Buddhism," in *Slouching Towards Bethlehem* (New York: Guilford Press, 1992), 173.

13. M. L. Gottesfield, "Mystical Aspects of Psychotherapeutic Efficacy," *Psychoanalytic Review* 72:4 (1985): 593.

14. Joe Tom Sun, "Psychology in Primitive Buddhism," *Psychoanalytic Review* 11 (1924): 43. Also, see pages 3–11 of this volume.

15. Michael Eigen, "The Fire That Never Goes Out," *Psychoanalytic Review* 79:2 (1992): 280.

16. D. W. Winnicott, "Some Thoughts on the Meaning of the Word Democracy" (1950), in *Home Is Where We Start From: Essays by a Psychoanalyst*, ed. C. Winnicott (New York: W. W. Norton, 1986), 244.

17. D. W. Winnicott, "Ego Distortion in Terms of True and False Self," in *The Maturational Processes and the Facilitating Environment* (New York: International Universities Press, 1965), 142.

18. Harry Guntrip, *Psychoanalytic Theory, Therapy, and the Self* (New York: Basic Books, 1969), 30.

19. Heinz Kohut and E. Wolf, "The Disorders of the Self and Their Treatment: An Outline," in *The Search for the Self*, Vol. 3, ed. Paul Ornstein (New York: International Universities Press, 1991), 362.

20. Ernest Wolf, *Treating the Self: Elements of Clinical Self* (New York: Guilford Press, 1988), 95.

21. Ibid., 13.

22. George Atwood and Robert Stolorow, *Psychoanalytic Treatment: An Intersubjective Approach* (Hillsdale, N.J.: The Analytic Press, 1987).

23. Karen Horney, *Our Inner Conflicts* (New York: W. W. Norton, 1945), 163.

24. Ibid., 138.

25. H. V. Guenther and L. S. Kawamura, *Mind in Buddhist Psychology* (Emeryville, Calif.: Dharma Publishing, 1975), xxvii.

26. Otto Kernberg, *Borderline Conditions and Pathological Narcissism* (New York: Jason Aronson, Inc., 1975), 49.

from

THE PRACTICE OF UNKNOWING

Stephen Kurtz

❑

When we address ourselves to the questions of cure, we must try to discern whether the disease is primarily congenital or else rooted in a history that might have been otherwise. But in the present instance we have an additional and subtle problem. What I am calling a disease is also integral to the culture's conceptual framework. Consequently, we have the further difficulty of discerning whether any curative effort might itself be an instance of the disease.

With respect to history, Kohut (1977) suggests that disorders of the self are especially post-Freudian and the result of altered patterns in family life. In his reverence for the founder of psychoanalysis Kohut may, of course, have preferred to say that the times had changed rather than that Freud was wrong. Yet, if we read old correspondences and biographies of historical figures, we see that long before psychoanalysis, much less self psychology, people's lives reveal pervasive narcissistic damage. At the same time, his-

Excerpted from the author's *The Art of Unknowing: Dimensions of Openness in Analytic Therapy* (pages 226–44, Jason Aronson, 1989). Reprinted here with the publisher's permission.

torical frames of mind—like those of alien contemporary cultures—are arguably impossible to grasp.

To take just one example, the sense of being an individual—that almost palpable experience of oneself as a unique person living in the boundaries of one's skin—may turn out to be quite modern, linked, among other things, to the possession of a personal space. Such "rooms of one's own," as Yi-Fu Tuan (1982) notes, were unknown in medieval times and remained rare until our own. Yet, without the famous stove to which he retired in 1628, Descartes might never have arrived at a notion of existence grounded in a thinking I. What might it be like not to feel like an individual? That is something we simply cannot know.

Because of the inaccessibility of historical frames of mind, our capacity to say what is part and parcel of and what is accidental to human experience is necessarily limited. Although I shall offer some speculations, it seems to me impossible to ground them factually. What we would like to determine first is whether narcissistic damage is universal, with I-domination being merely a strategy used to counteract it. If that were the case, then I-domination could be expected to dissipate like any other by-product as the result of a self psychological cure or, on a social scale, as the result of different patterns of family interaction. If, on the other hand, I-domination is part of being human, then a self psychology cure can have no effect on it, and we must turn to other systems that treat the I itself: Zen Buddhism, perhaps, or Lacanian analysis.

I would like to sketch my own thoughts about this question without, for the present, offering very much in the way of defense. It seems to me first that the long childhood and high sensitivity of human beings make narcissistic damage inevitable. The specific sort of damage, its extent and depth, and the strategies used to deal with it must vary enormously—but, because of it, we shall not find a golden age or a people that does not suffer. No less a part of the human condition is an I that, again following Lacan (1949), tends, after some developmental turning point, to create narratives or *Gestalten*, eventually fitted to cultural templates. This I takes pleasurable control over what was primally experienced as a more aleatoric, moment-to-moment reality. Lacan calls that turning point the mirror stage, when, with a sense of triumph (sometimes heightened by the illusory power of a baby walker), the child correlates his own movements with the corresponding ones in a mirror and begins to experience his body as having the wholeness of the image he perceives there. Although Lacan would have said that the Real is ultimately ungraspable, the pre-mirror-stage experience is somehow closer to it. The task of psychoanalysis, therefore, would be to deconstruct the fictive wholes created aggressively by the I, beginning during the mirror stage, in an effort to approach the Real. To the extent that the I is an imperialistic agent colonizing the It, the analyst becomes, in this context, a kind of armchair guerrilla fighter. That this role has a certain appeal can be seen from the way Lacan was taken up by French students during the events of 1968.

The self psychologist attempts to attune himself empathically to the patient, not only to promote a certain kind of transference but also because the attunement itself is seen as curative. In accord with Winnicott (1971) and Christopher Bollas (1978), among others, many self psychologists would agree that interpretation—which is addressed primarily to the I—is often not necessary and may even obstruct the curative process. The analyst does not attune himself to the patient's I. Rather, both I's are bypassed to establish a more fundamental bond. The Lacanian analyst actively disattunes himself to the patient's I, not only to make himself "other"—the object of desire—but to establish a base camp from which to undermine the I. These very different notions of therapy are allied in their devaluing of the I and also, as one might expect, in their attitudes toward ego psychology.

It seems to me that the two views are complementary. Self psychologists may be horrified, however, by some Lacanian tactics—such as the short session—seen as crude and wounding. But the object of the analyst's attack in abruptly ending a session is not supposed to be, say, the patient's emerging grandiose-exhibitionistic self, but rather his I. It is the grandiose—imperialistic I—trying to establish its control over the It of the hour—that the analyst seeks to foil. In abruptly standing up in the middle of the patient's sentence he does what the Zen master does, when, in the midst of meditation, he suddenly raps an acolyte on the head.

If they are complementary—and it is not yet clear that they are—there is also an undeniable tension between the two. I am tempted to say that an effective assault on the I cannot be launched unless a strong, cohesive self is already present. If not, I would imagine, there is the likelihood of continuing fragmentation with a redoubling of the strategies used to counter it—not the least of which arise from the I's own gestalt-making tendencies.

At the same time, how can we discount the 2500-year experience of Buddhist spiritual practice, which suggests no prior need to repair the damage of each practitioner's childhood? Buddhist method works to cultivate an inner observer. Not an observing *ego*, for the I is itself an object of observation. Not a superego, either, for there is nothing parental, moralistic, or even containing in its stance. The observer simply observes *everything*: the body, thoughts, feelings . . . everything. Through this discipline, as I understand it, the sense of identity comes increasingly to reside in the observer until a certain critical moment when an explosion takes place. That explosion—and the altered sense of reality that follows it— are not I experiences. Consequently, ordinary language, based in the I, can neither describe nor account for them. Perhaps all that can be said— without it being clear that one is communicating anything by saying it— is that these experiences are not of fragmentation, entailing emptiness, joylessness, and loss of function. What people report is that nothing is lost—including the capacities for pleasure and accomplishment—but that everything is profoundly and permanently different.

Yet, not everyone who believes in the value of this path sets out on it, and not everyone who sets out becomes enlightened. The Buddha himself is described as a nobleman, married and the father of a son. When he left everything to become a wandering ascetic, he was motivated to do this by "*sannyāsin*"—an aversion or repugnance for the so-called good things of the world. This giving up has been described (David-Neel, 1936) as a "joyous liberation," comparable to "throwing off dirty and ragged clothing" (p. 17). It is not a sacrifice, still less the sour-grapes gesture of someone who has not been *able* to make it in conventional terms. Rather it is a step taken from the realization that the satisfactions of the I are relatively trivial and, in the end, entail more pain than they are worth. In a world where death and destructibility are inevitable, every gain—in objects, relationships, or social position—necessitates eventual loss or at least the threat of it. Seeing this, the *sannyāsin* takes himself off the path of gain and loss. He is not yet enlightened, but at least he is not an active participant in illusion.

If the Buddha is the paradigm *sannyāsin*, it is clear that he had something to give up.

People who are drawn to asceticism often reveal the bitter grandiosity of the deprived—"If I can't have everything, then I'll have nothing." "Nothing" takes on the same value as "everything." Of course, there is a certain poetic truth in this. The person who has detached himself from desire is equal, if not superior in power, to the person who can fulfill all desires at will. The difference is in motive. The *sannyāsin* is not motivated by a rageful sense of deprivation. On the contrary, having acquired a great deal, he comes to see that it does not and never will yield the happiness he'd expected. He sloughs off a dead-end existence with relief.

To my mind, a self psychology analysis can provide that grounding in fullness—that sense of having—with which the Buddha allegedly began. But can it take the patient further, toward the destructuring of an I-dominated sense of the real?

The answer, I think, depends greatly on the condition of the analyst's I. To say, as I did earlier, that the self psychologist works by attuning himself empathically puts the process perhaps too actively. To the extent that the attunement is an action—something one tries for—it will fail. The process works only when it is effortless. It works through us—one might almost say despite us. Because of this, we have all had the bittersweet experience of seeing patients go further than we ourselves have gone.

But there are limits to how much further they *can* go.

What would an enlightened psychoanalyst look like? To return to the Buddhist model, the *sannyāsin* is described (David-Neel, 1936) as "freed from social and religious laws; freed from all bonds, he walks on the path which is known to him alone, and is responsible only to himself. He is, par excellence, an 'outsider' " (p. 17). In many ways this describes the life and character of Jacques Lacan, to which I shall return. But first, a Buddhist example.

Ikkyū was a fifteenth-century Zen poet-monk—the illegitimate and unacknowledged son of an Emperor (Arntzen, 1986). He first studied with the monk Ken'ō, a man of such modesty that he had refused a seal of enlightenment (equivalent to analytic certification) and so could not pass one on. When this monk died, Ikkyū studied with another, no less austere master and attained enlightenment. He himself was then presented with a certificate, but destroyed it. At a time when the Zen monasteries were politically powerful, rich, and dissolute, Ikkyū's behavior, in this and other ways, was unheard of. Nevertheless, despite his iconoclasm, his authenticity was indisputable and he was made abbot of a subtemple in the great Daitoku-ji compound. Soon after, he sent his superior this outrageous poem:

> Ten days as abbot and my mind is churning.
> Under my feet, the red thread of passion is long.

If you come another day and ask for me,
Try a fish shop, tavern, or else a whorehouse (p. 73).

Ikkyū is the only Zen monk to have written poems about sex in a religious context—vividly erotic poems on his own amorous exploits. He
moved sex from a common but illicit activity to an integral part of spiritual
training and even an aid to enlightenment. Sonja Arntzen (1986), a com-
mentator, writes that for Ikkyū, sex was "a kind of touchstone for his
realization of the dynamic concept of non-duality that pivots upon the
essential unity of the realm of desire and the realm of enlightenment"
(p. 33). The authenticity of Ikkyū's vision was manifested in many ways,
but among them is his rejection both of conventional piety and of conventional secularism. In all of this, he meets the definition of a *sannyāsin*.

Such a concept resists cross-cultural translation. Yet there are interesting
affinities between Ikkyū and Lacan.

Lacan's character and career were equally iconoclastic and independent.
Because he had also a brilliant mind and a charismatic style, he became
the center of psychoanalysis in France. Compared to Ikkyū, however, Lacan
was less fortunate in his mentors. His analyst was Rudolph Loewenstein,
who later became a pillar of the New York society and one of the founders
of ego psychology. At that time, however, Loewenstein had come from
Germany to Paris, where the society was dominated by Marie Bonaparte.
On his rise to eminence, Loewenstein became her lover as well as the
analyst of her son. Lacan must have learned something from his work with
Loewenstein, because he managed to secure membership in the society
before completing his analysis, then broke off. Loewenstein blamed Lacan's
heterodoxy—which ultimately led to his expulsion from the International—on this failure to complete his analysis.

From the points of view of Marie Bonaparte and Anna Freud—in accord
with the Americans who then controlled the International—what was Lacan's sin? The ostensive issue was the ethics of the short session. Politically,
of course, short sessions enabled Lacan to do many more training analyses
than others and therefore to produce more disciples (Turkle, 1978). But
perhaps neither ethics nor politics was ultimately decisive. Equally crucial
was Lacan's heretical distrust of the ego—his view of it as pathological. In
"The Ego and the Id," Freud (1923) had said, "By interposing the process
of thinking, [the Ego] secures a postponement of motor discharge and controls access to motility." Stuart Schneiderman (1983) suggests that Lacan
probably understood this to mean that "the longer the postponement, the

stronger the ego." The ego, then, can only delay things and, indeed, "makes postponement something pathological" (p. 150). What can break this cycle of delay to make action possible? Only the desire of the Other. For this reason, Lacan distrusted thought that proceeded from the Ego. What makes authentic action possible are thoughts that do not come from the I, that "come to me when I do not think to think" (Schneiderman, p. 150). As with Ikkyū, the realm of desire—of which sex is emblematic—and the non-I, thought-free state of enlightenment are linked.

If we take Lacan and Ikkyū as models for the enlightened analyst, we can see in both an affinity with the Dada–surrealist sensibility—with, for example, the creativity of Duchamp. The notion of psychoanalysis as a science would be quite alien to them. Yet these men were certainly not know-nothings. Ikkyū's poetry is so steeped in allusions to classical Chinese literature that it cannot now be approached without extensive explanatory notes. Lacan similarly draws on the linguistic theory of Saussure, on a formidably extensive reading of classical and modern literature, and on a scholarly knowledge of Freud.

But they were not scientists. Their use of knowledge is unsystematic because the kind of truth they were after is outside systems. Even the sense in which they were scholars is not academic, for they were not explicators of other thinkers' quasi-sacred texts. Indeed, following the Rinzai Zen tradition,[1] an enlightened analyst might say that Freud's *Traumdeutung*, Lacan's *Ecrits*, and Kohut's *Analysis of the Self* are all so much toilet paper.

To return to my original question—whether we might take psychoanalysis to be not a science but an art—I want to say that it is an art precisely as that notion is understood in the Dada–surrealist–Zen tradition. That concept can present more difficulties in a country where the scientific/ego psychology ideals are strong and the philosophical tradition of conceptual analysis has overthrown the once-central place of aesthetics. There was an easier integration of art and psychoanalysis in France, largely because it was a group of artists and writers—Gide and his circle at the *Nouvelle Revue Française*—who first took it up in a serious way. long before the French psychiatric establishment. Although Freud himself was uncomfortable with the connection, the notion of the unconscious he introduced is central to surrealism. Through his 1907 article on Jensen's *Gradiva*, for example, that strange image of the stone woman becoming flesh became a favorite surrealist motif—the subject of paintings by Masson, Dali, and

Ernst, and even the name of Breton's gallery. René Allendy (Anaïs Nin's Paris analyst) was the chief supporter of Antonin Artaud's primal theater —arguably the most It-centered events ever staged. To bypass the I and work directly from the It is central to the surrealist ideal. That Lacan— who was close to surrealist circles—should draw on this ethos and return it to the psychoanalytic process becomes, in this light, entirely compre- hensible.

But that is history. The ongoing essence of art, understood in this way, is openness to It. Yet, because of the co-opting power of the I, one gener- ation's radical vision of It becomes the next one's I-centered orthodoxy. Kohut's heroically achieved insights are now being codified, rationalized, and glossed. In this way, they suffer the fate of Freud's, Jung's, and Lacan's visions. Explicating the texts of these visionaries quickly becomes an in- dustry. To the extent that those texts embody It, the I goes to work on them, digesting them until they too become I. Through this process, the disciple—at the same time that he expresses his idolization—castrates his mentor. Instead of assuming his own It, paralleling his master's, he achieves that power in an illusory way through the bond of discipleship and through the intellectual caging of the mentor's wild It.

The "proof" of analytic mastery is usually the final case presentation before an institute committee. Because this process is I-centered, based on the I's illusory construct of reality, passing or not passing can have very little to do with the candidate's actual condition. The proof of a Zen student's enlightenment, by contrast, is not I-centered. Ideological good behavior and political astuteness are, therefore, of no help. Since it is It- based, the evidence is as palpable to the master as a slap in the face. And, indeed, the Zen tradition is full of stories about enlightened students slap- ping their masters and the latters' pleasure in a gesture whose irreverence establishes the student's authenticity.

Lacan's *Ecole freudienne* had been perhaps the only institute to deeply question the I-centeredness of psychoanalytic training. Without arriving at a solution, it at least recognized that the process ought to be something different in kind from acquiring competence in, say, auto mechanics or law. Accession to the title took two directions. The first has been sum- marized this way: "A person is a psychoanalyst who authorizes himself to be considered as such" (Barande and Barande, 1975). Like Napoleon, one snatches the crown from the Pope's hands and places it on one's head. Of course, it is possible to be mistaken in this, but no more so than for one's judges to be. The alternative course was "the pass"—a rite so Byzantine (for example, the candidate had to convince two representatives—peers and therefore rivals—to present his case effectively for him) it is hard not to see it as a send-up of the usual process. At any rate, through these means the nature of psychoanalytic knowledge, how it can be passed on, and how the practitioner's authenticity can be recognized, were questioned by Lacan with an unparalleled seriousness. Indeed, they become the central problem of the psychoanalytic project (Turkle, 1978).

To return to the main issue of cure, then, it seems to me that I-domination is not a condition to which most psychoanalytic systems, as they now stand, can respond. They may provide a foundation for addressing it, but are too I-centered themselves to move beyond.

If analysis has largely centered itself in the I, what parts of the self have been lost to both theory and practice? Those parts of which the I cannot make sense or, alternatively, of which it can make only a specious sense.

In the Zen tradition, the correct response to a koan appears to be a non sequitur. But it is not merely a non sequitur, suggesting a kind of gim-crack idiocy. Nor is it intelligent nonsense full of will. If authentic, it is inspired—nonsense that neither cleverness nor stupidity could have produced.

In the analytic situation, a relative spontaneity is cultivated through the parallel processes of free association and evenly hovering attention. This flow of associations in both participants is monitored by the analyst's observing I, which may actively intervene when a pattern is noticed. Two difficulties immediately arise: first, how free are each person's associations? and, second, are the observed patterns present or imposed?

Since the analytic procedure is heavily aimed at character problems—the unhappy ramifications of programming by certain, in a sense, stylized interactions between parent and child—I want to say (despite the still-unresolved epistemological problems) that patterns are present that appear in the associations. Indeed, because of the programming, patterns are inevitable, and the associations are free in only the most restricted sense.

At the same time, it is no less clear that what is observed by the analyst is screened through the mesh of his theoretical outlook. To some extent, no doubt, the material will be forced to fit this mesh, so that the patterns to which he is predisposed are put there whether present or not. More benignly, the screen admits only certain shapes and thus renders others invisible. We know this retrospectively when someone formulates fresh views that spotlight seemingly new phenomena. Kohut, to my mind, did this. Those classically trained analysts who found his insights valuable (and true) now perceive their patients differently. Was what they see now always there? More importantly, I think, these changes reveal the limitations of any view and the fact that—latent or expressed—multiplicities of perspectives exist focusing on an endlessly receding reality. Is it possible to see not just one perspective (or even numbers of them) but, rather, *what is there?*

The classical controversies of knowledge theory revolve around this question. Naive realism takes the objects of perception at face value: what we see is what is there. Plato's idealism locates the real in a realm of forms, accessible perhaps only to disembodied souls. What we perceive is just a shadow of that realm. A skeptical epistemology suggests we know only phenomena; things in themselves are out of reach. In a more hopeful version, reality can be known as a theoretical construct (analogous to knowledge of atomic particles) postulated to explain the regular behavior of appearances. I realize these are caricatures of complex positions, but I think a fuller presentation would make no difference here.

Only naive realism asserts the unobstructed availability of the real. This position must capture some truth, since if large-scale stabilities did not prevail, life would not be possible. Yet we know how profoundly culture qualifies perception. Jorge Luis Borges puts this question in a historical mode through his now-classic story of "Pierre Menard" (1939). This man sets out in the twentieth century to write the novel *Don Quixote*, never having read Cervantes. He succeeds in producing the ninth and thirty-eighth chapters of the first part and a fragment of chapter twenty-two. Borges compares the following passage from the Cervantes work with a seemingly identical one by Menard: ". . . truth whose mother is history, rival of time, depository of deeds, witness of the past, exemplar and adviser to the present, and the future's counselor." For Cervantes this was just conventional rhetoric, but Menard, Borges demonstrates, has taken a serious philosophical position contra his contemporary William James. History, in Menard's view, is the origin of reality—not merely an inquiry into it. Truth in history is pragmatically based; it is what we judge to have happened. The styles are different, too—Cervantes writing with ease the Spanish of his time and Menard affecting a certain archaism. "There is no exercise of the intellect," Borges concludes, "which is not, in the final analysis, useless. A philosophical doctrine begins as a plausible description of the universe; with the passage of the years it becomes a mere chapter

—if not a paragraph or a name—in the history of philosophy" (p. 43).

Borges's surrealism delights in the audacity of all our grand illusions. It is surprising, therefore, that he did not pursue Zen with a more personal urgency.[2] Zen alone claims the possibility of seeing through illusion into reality itself. Plato's forms are not reserved for the large but still exclusive club of the unborn. Living night soil carriers may see things as they are, along with certain emperors and psychoanalysts. There is no descriptive word for what they see, but there are exclamations: *Katsu!* and *Nyoze!*

An analyst who sees his patients not from a Freudian, Jungian, or Kohutian perspective (much less an eclectic one), but rather sees them as they are, will never intervene predictably. And, in a sense, his perceptions can be neither true nor false. Such judgments apply only to checkable statements about reality, and he makes only OUTBURSTS. He does not know what to say: he exclaims.

This lack of a perspective (a perspective, after all, is just an angle on reality) begins to return to the patient the missing portions of the world —the world that is not there. As a single example, let me focus on a classic psychoanalytic concern.

Because we cannot penetrate historical minds, sex may have sometimes held meanings we can no longer fathom. But if we think of sex as an encounter with It, it seems clear that the I soon moved to hedge it round. It did this collectively through religious law and ritual, prescribing with whom and under what circumstances sex would be permissible. It did it through prostitution, making this It a commodity like any other. It did it through the use of sex for procreation or the equally purposive use of it for recreation. Vividly in pornographic works (the artistic expression of perversion), and less so in ordinary bedroom scenes, sex becomes a mise-en-scène for early childhood interactions: parent-infant, brother-sister, controller-controlled. Whether repetitions or reversals, the links with childhood, as Georges Bataille (1928) has shown, reveal these behaviors to be anything but free.

What would sex be if it were not appropriated by the I—if it were not, for instance, a language by means of which *something else* got expressed? Arntzen (1986) quotes Ikkyū:

> The rain drops of Wu-shan fall into a new song;
> Passionate fūryū, in poems and passion too.

The whole wide world and Tu-ling's tears;
At Fu-chou tonight, the moon sinks (p. 174).

I shall comment only on the second line of Ikkyū's erotic poem—one of a group entitled "Chronicle of the Dream Chamber." Introducing them, Ikkyū claims that, unlike other, more virtuous masters who dream of higher things, he dreams only of the bedchamber. It is his Way. In sex, no less than in poetry, he finds the real in a passionate burst.

The key word is *"fūryū"*—untranslatable. Fūryū has many connotations, but even when only one is intended strongly, the others are there residually. Sonja Arntzen (1986, pp. 66–67) picks out three in Ikkyū's work, noting first that the component characters of the word itself are *fū* ("wind)" and *ryū* ("to flow").

The first meaning refers to the quality of an unfragmented rustic life, which, free of artifice, flows on in attunement with the natural world.

The second meaning is erotic, sometimes specifically sexual but also including nonbody experience. One can see the connection with the first meaning: an erotic life that is not I-dominated flows mindlessly.

The third meaning—which can be linked intuitively with the others—is a kind of slang expression showing appreciation for an inspired gesture. Or it can be said of the gesture itself that it is *fūryū*. Finally, there is the implication that to appreciate a *fūryū* gesture, one must be *fūryū* oneself. Here is a classic example (from the *Blue Cliff Record*, koans 63 and 64, quoted in Arntzen, 1986):

> One day, the monks of the East and West were fighting over a cat. When Nan-ch'üan saw them he raised up the cat and said, "If someone can speak, I will not kill it." (Taking a life being forbidden.) When no one answered, Nan-ch'üan cut the cat in two. Later he recounted this incident to Chao-chou and asked what he would have done. Chao-chou took off his sandals, put them on his head, and walked away. "If you had been there," Nan-ch'üan said, "the cat would have been saved." Chao-chou's gesture was *fūryū*. (p. 81)

There are affinities between *"fūryū,"* the concept of "duende" from flamenco cante jondo, and the jazz exclamation, "far out" (mentioned, too, by Arntzen). "Far out" arose in the 1940s describing and responding to the qualities of bop and cool. In an idiom that centers on inspired improvisation, the word acclaims the musician's risk in moving through uncharted space—as well as indicating the otherness of that space. To play a far-out riff is both to confront the It and to reveal it to the listener.

"Duende" similarly belongs to an improvisational music bound, like jazz, by complex rules. It similarly values the courage to explore new depths of feeling ("cante jondo" means "deep song") that take the listener into them.

What, in psychoanalysis, would count as *fūryū*? Here is a possibility.

Once I worked with a painter as restricted in sex as she was in her work. R.'s superficially ravishing canvases—each a feminine paradise—streamed with veils of red and gold. Like them, she wore her history of victimization on the surface, almost sexily. In Richard, her husband, she found a handsome if clumsy bedmate who bruised her white skin, but always by accident. With her lover, Victor, she explored a sensual Eden of fingertip sensuality—dreamy and blind.

As our work advanced, an angel with a sword appeared. R.'s paintings became electric torture rooms—blue-black and shocking to the casual visitor. She herself wore a pendant of a cock-and-balls bound with wire. If a curious person fingered it, the thing made a hideous buzz. During these months, R. was nearly celibate.

One day R. flounced in, wearing a blond wig. The transformation announced what she would later call her "cunt period"—not those romanticized lesbian vaginas of Georgia O'Keeffe: these flowers ate flesh. They managed to be rosy-pink and inviting and at the same time stinking holes. R. called the entire show "For Dick" (she hadn't yet divorced) and titled the paintings, for example, "Too Hot Twat," "Pussy LaGore," and "Baby Lips." These names belied R.'s prudery, but the show sold out.

Not long after this success, R. showed up without the wig. Because she was beautiful, she remained so. But for the first time she seemed not to care about her looks. Abandoning painting, she turned to photography, producing abstract prints in subtle *grisailles*. Without containing a single objective referent, they seemed deeply concerned with the real.

Against this neutral-looking ground, R.'s dreams flared. At first they were complex, mythologically dense images of heroes and their goddess lovers —dressed in Venetian velvets, rubies, and pearls. Eventually all this richness resolved itself into a single frame: a phallus.

In a panic of frantic I-work, R. tried to capture this image in thought: "male power"; "penis envy"; "generativity"; "castration anxiety." It was the only truly boring phase of treatment.

As I listened to her thinking week after week, I grew increasingly exasperated—overtaken by a desperate and impotent violence. Finally, something snapped. A noise came out of me—a sound that felt, from the inside, like a deep twanging drone, growing louder and louder without losing its snarl and roll. The noise filled me until I was aware of nothing else. I felt (or perhaps I say this only retrospectively) as if the noise/I were filling the room, emanating from a glowing point source, rather than from "me."

Much later, R. revealed that while this was happening, the image of me in my chair and the phosphorescent phallus of her dreams had merged. More immediately, when the noise eventually stopped, we both stared at one another, silenced and dumbfounded. After a while a smile flickered on her face. Soon we were both grinnng, then laughing like kids with the giggles. The session ended without comment.

I shall mention only two developments that followed this event and which I take to be outcomes of it. Until then, all the men in R.'s life, and indeed R. herself, had been full of character—sparkling, sullen, brilliant . . . there was no end to the vivid adjectives that fit them. Now R. took up with B.—a quite nondescript man; she could hardly find the words to talk about him. Yet she began to love him and, from her reports, he loved her. It was certainly not an operatic love, but it was not prosaic either. To describe it, I must borrow an image from painting. Their relationship reminds me of a picture by Chardin. In an age that alternated between courtly heroics and decorative banality, Chardin chose the real. His domestic interiors and even more his still lifes capture the luminous mystery of the ordinary. R. similarly saw a god in this quite undistinguished mortal. The dream phallus, paved with sapphires and radiating light, came to rest between B.'s thighs. Not that it turned into a penis; rather, the two dimensions came to co-exist. A parallel process took place in R.'s feeling about herself, and eventually this showed up in her work. Her earlier paintings, intentionally weird, created only a momentary notoriety. Her new ones gave common, twentieth-century objects an inexplicably luminous presence. That they also made her famous was a surprising and not entirely unwelcome outcome . . .

Notes

1. Rinzai, "The Twelve Fold Teachings of the Three Vehicles Are All Old Paper for Wiping Filth," quoted in Arntzen (1986, p. 91).
2. In his lecture "Buddhism" (1980), however, Borges says, "What does it mean to reach Nirvana? Simply that our acts no longer cast shadows" (p. 75).

References

Arntzen, Sonja (1986). *Ikkyū and the Crazy Cloud Anthology: A Zen Poet of Medieval Japan*. Tokyo: University of Tokyo Press.

Barande, R., and Barande, I. (1975). *Histoire de la Psychoanalyse en France*, 11. Toulouse: Edouard Privat.

Bataille, Georges (1928). *Story of the Eye*. Trans. J. Neugroschel. New York: Berkley Publishing Group, 1982.

Bollas, Christopher (1978). "The Transformational Object." *International Journal of Psycho-Analysis* 60: 97–107.

Borges, Jorge Luis (1939). "Pierre Menard, Author of the Quixote," in *Labyrinths: Selected Stories and Other Writings*, trans. J. Irby. New York: New Directions, 1964.

David-Neel, A. (1936). *Buddhism: Its Doctrines and Its Methods*. Trans. H. Hardy and B. Miall. New York: Avon/Discus, 1979.

Freud, Sigmund (1923). *The Ego and the Id*. Standard Edition 19.

Kohut, Heinz (1977). *The Restoration of the Self*. New York: International Universities Press.

Lacan, Jacques (1949). "The Mirror Stage as Formative of the Function of the I as Revealed in Psychoanalytic Experience," 1–7, in *Écrits: A Selection*, trans. A. Sheridan. New York: W. W. Norton, 1977.

Schneiderman, Stuart (1983). *Jacques Lacan: The Death of an Intellectual Hero*. Cambridge, Mass.: Harvard University Press.

Tuan, Yi-Fu. (1982). *Segmented Worlds and Self: Group Life and Individual Consciousness*. Minneapolis: University of Minnesota Press.

Turkle, S. (1978). *Psychoanalytic Politics: Freud's French Revolution*, 106–108. New York: Basic Books.

Winnicott, D. W. (1971). *Playing and Reality*. New York: Basic Books.

THEORETICAL REFLECTIONS

❑

IS THERE AN UNCONSCIOUS IN BUDDHIST TEACHING?

A CONVERSATION BETWEEN JOYCE MCDOUGALL AND

HIS HOLINESS THE DALAI LAMA

narrated by Dr. Francisco J. Varela

❏

Joyce McDougall did not lose a moment in launching a question that was clearly burning for her, and for many of us: "I would like to ask Your Holiness if the Freudian concept of the unconscious has any corresponding ideas in Tibetan philosophy?"

He answered immediately, "First of all, within Tibetan Buddhism, you can speak of manifest versus latent states of consciousness. Beyond that, you can speak of latent propensities, or imprints (Skt. *vāsanā*; Tib. *bag chags*, pronounced *bakchak*). These are stored in the mind as a result of one's previous behavior and experience. Within the category of latent states of consciousness, there are states that can be aroused by conditions and others that are not aroused by conditions. Finally, it is said in Buddhist scriptures that during the daytime one accumulates some of these latent propensities through one's behavior and experiences, and these imprints

Excerpted from *Sleeping, Dreaming and Dying: An Exploration of Consciousness with The Dalai Lama* (Wisdom Publications, 1997), which documents the proceedings of the October 1992 Mind and Life Conference convened by His Holiness The Dalai Lama in Dharamsala, India. This excerpt (pages 77–89) is reprinted here with the permission of Dr. Varela, in conjunction with the publisher.

that are stored in the mental continuum can be aroused, or made manifest, in dreams. This provides a relationship between daytime experience and dreams. There are certain types of latent propensities that can manifest in different ways, for example by affecting one's behavior, but they cannot be consciously recalled.

"However, there are divergent views within Tibetan Buddhism, and some schools maintain that these types of latent propensities can be recalled. This issue comes up particularly in relation to the topic of mental obstructions (Skt. *āvaraṇa*; Tib. *sgrib pa*), specifically obstructions to knowledge (Skt. *jñeyāvaraṇa*: Tib. *shes bya'i sgrib pa*). There are two categories of obstructions: afflictive obstructions (Skt. *kleśāvaraṇa*; Tib. *nyon mongs pa'i sgrib pa*) and obstructions to knowledge. Afflictive obstructions include such mental afflictions (Skt. *kleśa*; Tib. *nyon mongs*) as confusion, anger, attachment, and the like. Afflicted intelligence also falls into this category, for intelligence itself is not necessarily wholesome. It may be unwholesome; it can be afflicted.

"Concerning obstructions to knowledge, one school of thought maintains that these obstructions never manifest in consciousness; they always remain as latent propensities. Even within the Prāsaṅgika Madhyamaka philosophical school there are two positions. One maintains that all the obstructions to knowledge are never manifest conscious states, but are always latent propensities. However there is a divergent view which maintains that there can be certain forms of obstructions to knowledge that are manifest conscious states.

"In one Madhyamaka text a distinction is made between recollection and certain types of activation of these propensities. A recollection is in some sense like a reenactment of the perceptual act you have performed; there is also an activation of these propensities that is not a recollection. The example given in this text takes the case of seeing an attractive woman while one is in the waking state, being attracted to her, but without taking much notice of her. Then in one's dream the woman comes to mind. This recollection is contrasted to the standard kind of recollection, because it arises purely through the stimulation of latent propensities. The propensities are stimulated and they manifest in dreams, and this process is quite unlike the process of straightforward recollection. There is another case, too, involving propensities: You engage in a certain type of action, be it wholesome or unwholesome, and through that process propensities are accumulated in the mental continuum until such time as they come to fruition. Until that happens, they are not something that can be recollected."

Joyce spoke what was in everyone's mind when she said: "It's as complicated as Freud's theory of what starts off memories and dreams. I'm very interested in what you say about these imprints that the child brings with it. The notion of an imprint passed on through centuries of man fascinated Freud; he called this our phylogenetic inheritance. The research on fetal memory observes imprints from the time the baby is in the mother's womb. Are these in any way similar to the imprints you call *bakchak*, Your Holiness?"

"It's very interesting," His Holiness answered. "At first glance, it seems that the notion of phylogenetic inheritance is quite different from Buddhism, in which these propensities are seen as coming from previous lives, carried from one life to the next by the mental continuum. However, in one of the treatises of the famous Indian Buddhist philosopher Bhāvaviveka, he mentions that calves and many other mammals instinctively know where to go to suckle milk, and that this knowledge comes as the result of propensities carried over from previous lives. The Buddhist theory of latent propensities speaks of these predominantly in terms of mental activity as opposed to the physiological constitution of the being. However, there are a lot of impulses and instincts in us which are in some sense biological and very specific to the kind of body that we have.

"For instance, Buddhism classifies sentient beings into different realms of existence, and our human existence is included in the desire realm. In this realm the bodily constitutions of living beings are such that desire and attachment are dominant impulses. So these can be seen in some sense as biological in nature. There are other propensities that are also related to one's physical constitution. For instance, it is said that the Fifth Dalai Lama came from a family lineage of many great Tantric masters who had visions and other mystical experiences. He had extraordinary experiences quite often. These may have been due, in part, to his genetic inheritance from his ancestors rather than to his own spiritual development. Very deep Tantric practice not only transforms the mind but also, on a very subtle level, transforms the body. Imagine this trait being passed down from parent to child. It seems very possible that if your parents and earlier ancestors had transformed the subtle channels, centers, and vital energies of their bodies, your own body would also be somewhat modified because of the accomplishments of your ancestors.

"Moreover, in Buddhism the *external* environment is seen in some sense as a product of collective karma. Therefore, the existence of a flower, for instance, is related to the karmic forces of the beings who live in the environment of the flower. But as to why certain types of flowers need more water, while other types need less; why some kinds of flowers grow in a particular area; and why certain types of flowers have different colors and so on—these matters cannot be accounted for on the basis of karmic theory. They must be explained mainly on the basis of natural laws and biology. Similarly, an animal's propensity to eat meat or to eat plants is related only indirectly to karma, but is directly due to physical constitution. Recall the statement by Bhāvaviveka about the calves knowing where to go for milk. Such behavior, which we consider to be instinctual, does indeed come from karma. But that may not provide a complete explanation. There may be more influences involved than karma alone."

On the Complex Inheritance of Mental Tendencies?

"This comes very close to certain psychoanalytic constructions as well as an ever-increasing interest in the individual's transgenerational inheritance," interjected Joyce. "In the course of a long analysis people discover knowledge that they have taken in unconsciously concerning their grandparents and great-grandparents—often knowledge of events that no one has ever spoken about. There has been considerable research in this area on the psychic problems of the children of survivors of the Holocaust. The survivors' children, or grandchildren, reveal through their stories, drawings, and dreams knowledge of their grandparents' traumatic experiences to which they have had no verbal access. Perhaps these psychological imprints, transmitted through the subject's genealogy, may also resemble the *bakchak* imprints from karma from generations back? Then, of course, there are purely biological genetics that make you look like your parents, but often like a previous ancestor too."

I was concerned that nonscientific concepts of time and inheritance were getting tangled up with scientific usage. "You're suggesting," I ventured, "that psychoanalysts believe the mother passes on influences to the baby unintentionally. What I hear His Holiness saying is that something comes with the mindstream of the individual that does not come through contact with the parents. Would analysts accept the idea that something comes not through the rearing of the very young, nor from genetics, but from a long-term mindstream?"

Joyce answered, "Indeed, this comes close to Carl Jung's definition of the unconscious, but it is not a classical Freudian viewpoint. However, it may be linked with what Freud called the *unknowable* in the human mind, that which we will never know but which belongs to all humanity."

"Could you give a precise definition of the unknowable?" asked the Dalai Lama, always looking to clarify terms. This is a trademark of his training, which resembles that of an analytic philosopher's in the West in its quest for terminological sharpness.

"Let me give Freud's metaphor with regard to the unknowable in the process of dreaming. When the patient is trying to understand and reconstruct, through dreams, associations, and memories, it is like unwinding a skein of wool. You can undo so much of it, but in the middle is a knot you will never be able to see into, that keeps the whole skein of wool together. This he called the unknowable and felt it was undefinable." We could not fail to notice that this was hardly a definition, and it reflected the metaphorical, almost literary, style of psychoanalytic work.

His Holiness insisted, "I've heard you say, on the one hand, there is the phylogenetic heritage, with a purely physiological basis, and I would like to clarify if there is also a mental basis. Are you saying that the child gets an inheritance also from the streams of consciousness of its two parents?" Joyce confirmed this: "From both parents, and also there are the other two aspects of lineages which are quite distinct: one purely physical, the other one mental." After pondering this rather surprising exchange, he continued, "We could make a distinction between the *grosser* level of mind and *subtle* mind. In terms of the gross mind, there could be a connection from the parents to the child if, for example, one or both of the parents has such very strong anger or attachment that physiological changes take place in their bodies as a result of these mental tendencies. In this case the mind influences the body. Thereafter they produce a child whose body is influenced by the parents' bodies. The child's body, produced by the parents' bodies, could then influence the child's state of mind so that it similarly experiences very strong anger or attachment. In this case you'd see a gross level of mind, be it anger or attachment, going from one generation to another. That's a possibility. It's not just a pure mind-to-mind relationship, but a mind-to-body and body-to-mind sequence."

"From the biologist's point of view," I insisted once again, "the only possible inheritance consists of a physiological and a morphological organism. The idea that we can inherit what our parents have learned is called a Lamarckian evolution, which standard biology sees as false. Instead, I can only inherit from my parents such things as constitution and features; anything more I learn as a young child in contact with my parents. Biologically, it's a misnomer to call that *inheritance*. The term *inheritance* is reserved for the structural parental lineage, which is only a predisposition for the imprints we acquire as early learning by being with our parents. In biology this is the difference between phylogeny (the genetic inheritance) and ontogeny, which is what I learn, once I start my life. It seems that in Buddhism the notion of mindstream is neither phylogenetic nor ontogenetic, but represents a different kind of lineage, because it comes from a transindividual mindstream. This doesn't make too much sense in current science. I just was wondering whether in psychoanalysis this third category, neither learning nor physiological inheritance, is acceptable?"

"To the extent that character traits, such as being hot-tempered and so forth, are thought to be inherited, would the biologist account for them in purely biological terms?" asked the Dalai Lama.

"This is a thorny issue, known as the nature-nurture debate. Most biologists would say that you can inherit certain tendencies for temperament, for example, but much of your actual temperament depends on the environment in which you are raised. You cannot reduce it to pure genetic factors or purely to learning, because both are involved."

His Holiness continued, "Just to round off one point here: Does biology refute the possibility that a person might have a disposition for anger which could influence their body; and then if that person has a child, the child's body would be influenced; and finally, the child's physical constitution would cause the child to have an angry disposition?"

I suggested that that would not be difficult to reformulate in biological terms. One could say, for example, that great stress or depression in a pregnant mother will physiologically affect the environment of the fetus, so much so that he or she will not be the same individual as if the mother had been normal. But biologists would call this ontogeny.

The conversation was getting sufficiently specific for others to contribute their views. Pete Engel continued with the biological track. "The whole debate over what is genetic and what is environmental has greatly changed in recent years because of studies of separated twins. There is now a belief that much more of what we consider as 'self' is inherited and much less is environmental than was previously thought in Western science. The studies have been done with identical twins who were separated at birth for various reasons, who may have grown up in different countries, with different parents, without knowing that they had a twin. When they were brought together, there were many more similarities than nonsimilarities in most cases, and many more than anybody had expected. They might, for instance, wear the same clothes or hairstyle, have the same jobs, or have married people with the same first name." His Holiness remarked that he had been aware of these studies, but that the similarities were not invariably present. Clearly, the studies had a bearing on the point, but did not prove that one could inherit traits that one's parents had learned.

The psychoanalyst rejoined the debate. "I'm not so sure," said Joyce. "We inherit, in preverbal ways, many character traits and tendencies that have marked our particular family's history and ways of reacting. Present-day psychoanalytic researchers claim that children are all born with what they call a core self, which may include characteristics that do not belong to the parents. They are not just blank screens with a genetic inheritance on which the parents are going to write the first structures of their minds. They already have minds of their own. Apart from fetal imprints, it seems to come from many generations back, though not a mindstream of knowledge that has nothing to do with either the generations or ontogeny. But certain schools of analytic thought would be ready to accept the concept of the 'third category' of innate knowledge—particularly those of Jungian inspiration."

FOUNDATION CONSCIOUSNESS AND THE UNCONSCIOUS

The discussion of inheritance seemed to have continued long enough, and I was interested in returning to parallels with the unconscious in Buddhist theory. Anyone exposed to the corpus of Buddhist theories known as Abhidharma is familiar with the notion of the *ālayavijñāna*, usually translated as the *storehouse consciousness* or the *foundation consciousness*, an existential background from which all manifestations in daily experience seem to arise, and which is accessible to direct introspection during meditation. I was curious whether the *ālaya* might be related to the unconscious.

His Holiness's response was fascinating. "The very existence of this foundation consciousness is refuted in the Prāsaṅgika system, which is generally considered by Tibetans to be the highest philosophical system in Buddhism. In brief, this foundation consciousness, or store consciousness, is believed to be the repository of all of the imprints or *bakchak*, the habits, and latent propensities that one has accumulated in this and former lives. This consciousness is said to be morally neutral, neither virtuous nor non-virtuous, and it is always the basis of latent propensities. Finally, it is nonascertaining; that is, it can have objects as contents, but it does not ascertain, or apprehend, them. Phenomena appear to it, but it does not ascertain them. But the difference between the foundation consciousness and the psychoanalytic unconscious is that the *ālayavijñāna* is manifest to consciousness. It is ever-present, and it is manifest in the sense that it is the basis or core of the identity of the person. In contrast, the psychoanalytic unconscious is something that you cannot ascertain with ordinary waking consciousness. You can have access to it only through dreams, hypnosis, and the like. The unconscious is concealed, and what becomes manifest isn't the unconscious itself, but rather the latent imprints, or propensities, that are stored in the unconscious. On the other hand, what is stored in the foundation consciousness can become conscious, and the foundation consciousness itself is always present."

"So that's the basic distinction between the Freudian unconscious and the *ālayavijñāna*: the foundation consciousness can manifest without disguise, without going through a dream?" I asked.

"Yes, it's more like consciousness itself, because it's functioning as a full-blown consciousness all the time."

"From a psychoanalytic viewpoint a baby's first external reality is the biparental unconscious. Could this include their *ālayavijñāna*? Or the baby's?" asked Joyce.

"The foundation consciousness is regarded as a continuum coming from beginningless time, a stream of consciousness that is carried through successive lifetimes. In Buddhism reincarnation is generally accepted, and according to the Yogācāra school of Buddhism, the foundation consciousness accounts for the transition from one life to another. Moreover, it's the basis on which the mental imprints are carried, in the newborn baby and in both parents separately."

The Yogācāra was an important school of Mahāyāna Buddhism that flourished in India beginning in the fourth century C.E. It was also known as the mind-only doctrine, and its proponents were idealists who held the view that no reality exists outside of consciousness, and who developed the theory of *ālayavijñāna* to account for the apparent coherence of phenomena. It was interesting to observe that in Buddhism, just as in psychology or biology, there are many conflicting interpretations. The Dalai Lama clarified his own stand: "As far as my own position is concerned, I totally refute the existence of the foundation consciousness. The reason that the Yogācāra school felt the need to posit such a category of consciousness was not because they had strong inferential grounds or experiential evidence indicating its existence. Rather they posit this out of desperation because they were philosophers who believed that phenomena must exist substantially. They wanted to believe that the self was findable under critical analysis. The self cannot be posited in terms of this continuum of the body, because the body ceases at the time of death; and this school affirms the idea of rebirth. So, in positing the self, they needed something which would carry on after death, and this has to be mental. If any other types of mental consciousness were to be posited as the self, then they could be either wholesome or unwholesome; and they could change through various stages. Moreover, there are also meditative experiences in which the individual remains in a nonconceptual state, during which all states of consciousness that are either wholesome or unwholesome cease to exist. Yet something has to carry on. For all these reasons the Yogācāra school posited the existence of an additional category of consciousness which was called the foundation consciousness. This step was taken on purely rational grounds. They were compelled to formulate this consciousness because of their rational presuppositions, rather than through empirical investigation or realization."

IMPRINTS AND THE ''MERE-I''

"How the imprints, or *bakchak*, of the mindstream fit into this picture requires an examination of other schools in Buddhism." His Holiness was referring here to the schools of thought that preceded the Prāsaṅgika Madhyamaka school, which is considered to be the most philosophically advanced in the view of the Gelugpa monastic order to which the Dalai Lama belongs. (The Gelugpa order was founded by the reformer Tsongkhapa in the fifteenth century, has grown dominant in numbers over the years, and has as its visible spiritual leaders the lineage of the Dalai Lamas.) The Prāsaṅgika school is a product of the second wave of the development of Buddhism known as Madhyamaka, led by the great scholar Nāgārjuna (c. first century). An early school of particular historical interest is the Svātantrika Madhyamaka (prominent in the fifth century), based on the writings of the Indian adept Bhāvaviveka. "The Svātantrika school says that you don't need to posit a foundation consciousness. The continuum of mental consciousness itself will act as a repository for these imprints. This is where Bhāvaviveka leaves it. However, this position is also problematic, because there's a specific state along the path to enlightenment called *the uninterrupted state on the path of seeing.* In this state one passes into an utterly nonconceptual, transcendent awareness of ultimate reality; and it's said that this state is utterly free of any tainted consciousness. That being the case, this transcendent awareness is not a suitable repository for various wholesome and unwholesome imprints. But it's not clear that Bhāvaviveka ever raised that question or responded to it.

"Now we return to the Prāsaṅgika Madhyamaka perspective, which is a critique of all the preceding views, including those of Bhāvaviveka. In response to the previously mentioned problem, the Prāsaṅgika school says you don't need to posit even the continuum of mental consciousness as the repository of latent imprints. In fact all of these problems arise because of an underlying essentialist assumption that something must be findable under analysis, something that *is* the self. People come up with different ideas: the foundation consciousness, and the continuum of mental consciousness; but they are all vainly trying to find something that is essential, something that is identifiable under analysis. And that is the fundamental error. If you get rid of that error, as the Prāsaṅgikas do, then there is nothing that can be found under analysis to be the self. You give up that task altogether, and you posit the self as something that exists purely by conventional designation.

"Then we come back to the issue of the repository for these mental imprints. The Prāsaṅgikas also assert that if you engage in a certain action, you accrue certain mental imprints which, we can say for the time being, are stored in the stream of mental consciousness. You don't need to assert an internal substantial continuum that will act as a repository for these imprints forever and ever. You don't need to assert a substantial continuum of anything that is truly, or intrinsically, the real repository for all of the imprints. You don't need it because both the mental continuum and the stored imprints exist only conventionally, not substantially. For this reason, you don't have to worry about the case of the nonconceptual state of meditation. According to the Prāsaṅgika view, the imprints are stored in the *mere-I.* Now what is the nature of this mere-I? Where is it to be found? There is nothing really to be found; it's merely something that is designated in different ways. Returning to the problematic situation of the nonconceptual state of awareness of ultimate reality: at that time, upon what are these imprints placed? Upon the mere-I, because there's still a person there, purely as a convention. So that person is the repository, but this is not a repository that can be found under analysis, as these other schools assume.

"One can speak of the 'I' being designated on the basis of the gross aggregates (psycho-physical constituents) or the subtle aggregates. Similarly, the 'I' can be designated on the basis of gross consciousness or subtle consciousness. One way of looking at this statement, that the mere-I is the repository of mental imprints, is to look at it from a conventional point of view. When a person has done an action that leaves certain imprints, he now has a certain propensity due to that experience. That's all there is to it. You don't need to posit a substantial basis that exists as the repository for that propensity. That is the Prāsaṅgika Madhyamaka view."

This subtle and elaborate explanation of how identity appears in the Buddhist tradition could not fail to arouse the questioning of our resident Western philosopher. Charles Taylor struggled to reflect his understanding of the argument thus far: "Perhaps analogies with Western philosophy might help. Hume made a famous statement about the self: 'I look within myself and I try to find a particular item which is the self'; and he failed to find one. I think you are saying in part that he was asking the wrong question by trying to find a particular element that you could single out under analysis. But you could have another view of the self as something that presents itself as a self without any continuing element. The Western analogy is that of a ship: if you change a plank on it every year, at the end of so many years you could perfectly well say this is the same ship, even though all the pieces of wood are different. You can give a causal account of why this ship is a single, continuous, causal stream. I had assumed that a similar account of continuity over lives would explain the Buddhist view of how an imprint can operate across lives in this continuing entity. It's a continuing entity because it has a continuing causal history. I thought that was going to be the answer, but instead . . ."

IN THE FACE OF THE OTHER

PSYCHIC INTERWOVENNESS IN DŌGEN AND JUNG

Gereon Kopf

❑

A comparative reading of C. G. Jung's theory of psychotherapy and the meditation theory of Zen master Dōgen Kigen[1] reveals a set of seemingly insignificant yet striking similarities concerning the relationship between self and other. Both contend that the relationship between self and other—formalized as the therapeutic relationship, in Jung's case, and the relationship between disciple and Zen master, in the case of Dōgen—plays an integral role in a person's quest for self-awareness or enlightenment. Both also acknowledge that the psychic interwovenness of patient and therapist, on the one hand, and between master and disciple, on the other, is of utmost significance for the success of the therapy and *dokusan* (that is, the instruction of the disciple by the master). Most significantly, however, a reading of Jung's theory of psychotherapy and Dōgen's meditation theory suggests that the phenomenon of psychic interwovenness necessitates a radical reevaluation of the notion of an independent self. In exploring

This essay, derived from the author's 1996 doctoral dissertation for the Religion Department of Temple University, appears here for the first time.

these theories, I will treat the relationship between therapist and patient and between disciple and master as the prototype of human relationships.

JUNG ON PSYCHIC INTERWOVENNESS

The notion that self and other actually affect each other psychically became relevant to Western psychology only when Sigmund Freud discovered a puzzling phenomenon which he called *transference*. In his analytical practice, Freud observed that some of his patients *transferred* their ambivalent feelings, which lay at the basis of their neurosis, onto the person of the therapist. As a result, the therapist found her/himself drawn into the psychic life of the patient to such a degree that it became difficult, if not impossible, to differentiate between the psychic material of the patient and that of the therapist. At the same time, however, Freud further observed instances in which, conversely, the patient was drawn into and included in the psychic life of the therapist. This reversed psychic dynamic is called countertransference.

Following Freud's observations, Jung acknowledges the deep significance of the phenomenon of transference; unlike Freud, however, he believes that this psychic phenomenon has not only pragmatic—that is, therapeutic—but also conceptual implications. To Jung, transference is most of all an instance of psychic entanglement of therapist and patient in clinical practice. He explains that during transference the therapist "literally 'takes over' the suffering of his patients";[2] he describes transferences as "demonic forces lurking in the darkness,"[3] which "twine themselves invisibly round . . . patient and doctor" like the "tentacles of an octopus."[4] Jung further likens the psychic system of a "person" to a chemical substance "which, when it affects another person, enters into reciprocal reaction with another psychic system."[5] Having described the phenomenon of transference as psychic entanglement, Jung puts forward a simple but crucial question: How is it possible that two seemingly individual psychic systems can become entangled beyond recognition of their own unique individualities? I would like to explore this dilemma by pursuing the following three questions: What is the cause of transference? How is it possible that the self "literally 'takes over' " the psychic states of an other? How does the phenomenon of transference reflect Jung's conception of selfhood?

What is the cause of transference? According to Jung, transference is caused by the existential dissociation of an overly self-conscious individual into conscious and unconscious aspects. Fundamental to this diagnosis is Jung's belief that the self-reflective self-consciousness of the "modern person" is not only a blessing, insofar as it is the key to humankind's many intellectual achievements; it is also a curse, insofar as the constitution of self-consciousness dissociates the primordial psychic unity of the human individual and, subsequently, causes an existential alienation of the self both from itself and from its environment. In order to construct itself, the self-conscious function, which Jung calls the *ego*, identifies and *represses* unwanted memories and images; it dispossesses negative emotions, memories, as well as its own unwanted and unethical thoughts and desires. This disagreeable and therefore *repressed* material, however, does not simply disappear but takes on a life of its own and emerges "against the will of the ego" in dreams, so-called Freudian slips, fantasies, and in the symptoms of mental illness. The unconscious thus conceived can be understood as an "*autonomous* intentionality," which functions independently from the will of the ego. Jung contends that it is this autonomous, unconscious intentionality which "produces" the transference process without the knowledge of the ego; on the contrary, the ego "does not make" but merely "encounters"[6] transferences.

One can deduce three ways the transference phenomenon informs the conception of self-awareness: First, the dissociation of the self is not limited to intrapsychic processes but extends to the relationship between self and other. Second, the objects of the external world lose their transcendent character (that is, their character as external objects) and become the mirror image and reflection of the self as the other changes "into the replica of one's own unknown face."[7] In other words, when the self seems to encounter a phenomenological other, it actually encounters itself. Third, and most important, the phenomenon of transference seems to blur the delineation between self and other. While psychoanalysis expanded the traditional definition of the self as "self-conscious animal" to include the unconscious dimension of human existence, it still conceived of the self as an independent and individual psychic system. In the light of transference phenomena, however, it suddenly seemed quite difficult to distinguish between "my unconscious" and "your unconscious" and, thus, ultimately, between "I" and "You," or, more generally, between self and other.

How is it possible that the self "literally 'takes over' " the psychic states of an other? In order to explain the transference of unconscious material from the self to a separate other, Jung postulates the existence of a "common ground," which he refers to as "mutual unconscious"[8] and "non-individual psyche."[9] In other words, Jung postulates a psychic dimension which transcends the boundaries and limitations of the individual. He reasoned that if self and other were two completely separate psychic systems in the sense of independent *monads*, a transference of psychic material from the one to the other would be impossible. On the contrary, the psychic entanglement between two individuals necessitates that the psyches of self and other interact with and affect each other; self and other share certain unconscious contents. Or, put differently, the human psyche transcends the boundaries of the individual self to include material which is attributed to an other. Jung did not limit this common ground to the entanglement of two individuals, though; he goes one step further and posited the universal character of this "non-individual psyche." In Jung's words, the non-individual psyche is "innate in every individual" and, at the same time, "can neither be modified nor possessed"[10] by the individual person; it is beyond "mine" and "yours." As such, it signifies a fundamental dimension of the psyche which is common to all human beings and beyond the will of the individual.

To illustrate the mechanics of the transference phenomenon, I would like to briefly mention another phenomenon of psychic interwovenness which similarly necessitates the hypothesis of the "non-individual psyche," namely *synchronicity*.[11] Jung defines synchronicity as the "simultaneous occurrence of two different psychic states" which display no causal relationship whatsoever.[12] In other words, the term "synchronicity" signifies a coincidence of two similar psychic states, which occur, seemingly independently, in separate individuals, as in the case of telepathy. Like the phenomenon of transference, synchronicity comprises instances in which one self experiences the psychic states of another person. The difference between these two psychic phenomena, however, is that, in the case of synchronicity, the self, at least theoretically, can recognize the respective psychic states as external, while, in the case of transference, the self completely lacks the capacity of discernment. At any rate, in both cases, psychic states are communicated from one self to another through the synchronization of two minds, in the sense of a "going-along"[13] with the other. In this sense, transferences occur when the psychological subject unconsciously and passively appropriates a psychic state of another person and misidentifies it "as my own." In the final analysis, transferences are characterized by a (partial) psychic correspondence between two selves or a conformity among them rather than a true encounter between two independent individuals. This correspondence is partial because it does not affect the complete psyche of the individual person.

How does the phenomenon of transference reflect Jung's conception of selfhood? As is well known, Jung developed a threefold psychological model when he identified the basic psychic aspects of human existence as consciousness, personal unconscious, and *collective unconscious*. However, since the collective unconscious coincides with the "non-individual psyche," Jung's notion of the self as "psychic totality"[14] and "total personality"[15] has to be distinguished from the everyday notions of "person" and "individual" and thus from the philosophical conception of the individual self. According to Jung, the human psyche displays a fundamental "non-individual"—that is, "collective"—dimension. In fact, Jung claims that the concepts of psychic individuality and independence are deceptive and, for the most part, illusory. Thus, it is necessary to render Jung's notion of "psychic totality" as *Self* (German: *Selbst*) in order to demarcate it from the notion of the individual "little self."

Having defined human existence as Self, however, Jung faces the difficulty of delineating individual and "non-individual" psychic elements. I believe that Jung conceives of the individual human being as an independent psychic system, characterized by a "non-individual" structure. In *Two Essays*, Jung presents his well-known analogy, by means of which he likens the "non-individual" structure of the human psyche to the universal character of a human face, which consists of two ears, two eyes, one nose, and one mouth. By the same token, the human psyche contains universal elements. However, this description does not account for the phenomenon of transference, which implies a transmission of psychic material between two seemingly independent psychic systems. By the same token, a conception of the "non-individual" psyche as collective images or material also fails to account for the phenomenon of transference, in which personal psychic states and material, and not universal imagery and symbols, are transmitted between individual psychic systems. In the contexts of transference phenomena and other occurrences of synchronicity or psychic correspondence, Jung conceives of the "non-individual" psyche as the vehicle and catalyst of these transfers rather than as the transmitted material itself; however, such a hypothesis implies a dissolution of the boundaries of the individual.

I believe that the fundamental problem inherent in these considerations lies in the basic acceptance of the one-body-one-self principle, which seems to justify the primacy of the concept of self/*Self* characteristic of most psychological theories. However, even though the assumption that every self inhabits one individual human body seems to be almost universally accepted, it is called into question by "extreme" and borderline phenomena such as Multiple Personality Disorders. One of its primary implications is the radical dissociation of the world into an inside realm (inside the body, that is) and a realm outside of body and mind. It is this underlying conceptual dualism which makes it virtually impossible to conceive of, and account for, phenomena such as transference, synchronicity, and, ultimately, other-awareness (the experience of the psychic state of an other), which imply the dissolution of the boundaries of individual psychic systems. However, the mind-body problem is a non-issue for Jung insofar as he consistently implies the unity of body and mind. He reinforces these identity assertions of body and mind when he defines the human psyche as psychic energy, which, as he suggests, mediates between body and mind. Such an energetic model would also coincide with his comparison of transference to a chemical reaction, in which both participating individual selves are transformed. Unfortunately, however, Jung does not apply this model to the hypothesis of the "non-individual" psyche and the phenomena of transference and synchronicity. I believe that an elaboration of such a model would greatly contribute to clarifying the mechanics of psychic interwovenness.

DŌGEN ON PSYCHIC INTERWOVENNESS

One of the characteristic features of Dōgen's Zen Buddhism is his frequent insistence on the importance for a disciple to study under the "right master." For example, in his "Shōbōgenzō Bendōwa," Dōgen values "practicing under a master" more highly than traditional Buddhist practices such as the *nembutsu*,[16] incense burning (*shōkō*), and silent sutra readings (*kankin*). Dōgen's own personal quest for enlightenment was shaped by his relentless search for the "right master." He spent thirteen years under a number of eminent masters such as the Tendai master Ryōkan and the Rinzai Zen masters Yōsai and Myōzen before he was ready to entrust his quest for enlightenment to the Chinese Sōtō Zen master Ju-ching.[17] I believe that his insistence of the right master illustrates Dōgen's fundamental conviction that self-awareness and, for that matter, the process of enlightenment, necessitates a self-aware other—that is, an enlightened meditation master. While it is certainly problematic if not impossible to equate Dō-gen's enlightenment (*satori*) with the notion of self-awareness (the knowl-edge the self-conscious self or even the Jungian Self has of itself), I believe that Dōgen's definition of the "Buddha-way" as the "study of the self"[18] warrants the description of enlightenment as a form of self-awareness. To demarcate the different underlying ontologies of the self, I will paraphrase and treat Dōgen's notion of "enlightenment" as selfless self-awareness. In general, I will attempt to translate the Buddhist terminology which per-meates Dōgen's writings into a conceptual language more akin to the prob-lem of psychic interwovenness.

In his fascicle "Shōbōgenzō Kattō," Dōgen explains that "the phrase 'master and student practice together' means that there is the weaving vines (*kattō*) of the Buddha-ancestors."[19] Thomas Kasulis translates the term "*kattō*"—literally "complications" or "vines"—as "intertwinings" and "(verbal) entanglements."[20] Dōgen elaborates on this psychic interwoven-ness of master and disciple when he exhorts the practitioner: "You should know that there is 'You are attaining me,' 'I am attaining you,' 'attaining me and you,' and 'attaining you and me.' "[21] Dōgen's wording clearly sug-gests that the master can experience the psychic states of the disciple from the perspective of the disciple and vice versa. As a matter of fact, the fascicle "Kattō" is full of contentions that suggest an intimate relationship between, if not the oneness of, master and disciple. In describing this in-timacy Dōgen cites the first partriarch of Zen Buddhism, Bodhidharma, who reportedly said to his disciples when he verified their attainment of enlightenment, "you attain my skin," "you attain my flesh," "you attain my bones," and "you attain my marrow." However, at the same time, Dōgen asserts the independence and individuality of disciple and master. In the sentence "you attain me," the selfhood of the disciple as well as the otherness of the master remains, in Dōgen's terminology, "unobstructed." In the case of psychic correspondence, the self "follows" the other and the borderline between the individuals blurs to such a degree that they become undifferentiatedly one (as in the experience of mystical oneness). But Dōgen maintains that in the encounter of self and other, both retain their individuality, even though "the self attains the other" and "the other at-tains the self." Even though the self experiences the psychic state of the other from the other's perspective (without abandoning itself to the psyche of the other or being absorbed by the psychic complexes of the other), self and other are not one.

These allusions to the "individuality" of self and other seem to run counter to the Buddhist doctrine of no-self. (See Masao Abe's essay in this volume.) If Zen Buddhism denies the substance and, subsequently, the individuality of self, what is the significance of the notions of "I" and "you," self and other? A Buddhist reading would interpret Dōgen's *kattō* as the Middle Path, which rejects the extremes of identity and difference: Master and disciple are identical yet different. Dōgen's notion of psychic interwovenness implies a non-individual psyche which transcends the boundaries of the individual self; the phenomenon of psychic interwovenness in which "the self attains the other" and vice versa necessitates such a non-individual dimension of human existence. At the same time, Dōgen does not substitute a universal oneness or a non-individual and collective psyche for the notion of the individual self. On the contrary, Dōgen contends that master and disciple actually encounter each other as individuals; such an encounter would not be possible in a realm of psychic oneness. He rather believes that the notions of psychic correspondence, mystical oneness, and synchronization are insufficient to describe the fundamental structure of the master-disciple relationship and, more generally, the interpersonal encounter of self and other. In the final analysis, Dōgen suggests that even though master and disciple share as "common ground" a non-individual and mutual psyche, they do not lose their individual characters. Thus, psychic interwovenness simultaneously presupposes individual and non-individual psychic elements. At this point, a note of clarification is in order: When applied to Dōgen's conceptual framework, I utilize the phrase "non-individual psyche" not in the sense of the Jungian synonyms "collective unconscious" and "archetypes" but rather to signify that which, in Jung's words, is "innate in every individual" and which "can neither be modified nor possessed" by the individual.

By claiming that an individual self can experience psychic states of the other without compromising its unique selfhood, Dōgen calls into question any dualistic, conceptual framework. If it is possible for the self "to attain the other" without dissolving its own individuality, the traditional conception of the self as a self-contained system does not apply. As I have indicated earlier, the concept of an individual self implies the conceptual delineation of self and other, inside and outside, consciousness and unconscious, and of the individual and non-individual dimensions of the human psyche. However, phenomena such as *kattō*, which allow the self to experience the psychic states of the other from the perspective of the other and yet preserve the individuality of the other, necessarily defy these conceptual dichotomies.

How does the phenomenon of *kattō* reflect Dōgen's notion of selfhood? Dōgen's descriptions of the master-disciple relationship generally indicate the existential correlativity of disciple and master, as the following quotation from the "Shōbōgenzō Sansuikyō" indicates: " 'The person sees Tokujō' means that there is Tokujō, while 'Tokujō touches the person' means that there is encountering the person."[22] However, this relatedness of master and disciple goes far beyond the truism that the definition of "master" implies the existence of disciples and discloses Dōgen's underlying notion of self. Dōgen rather defines the self in relationship to an other (*tako*) in the sense that "I recognize myself as an independent self only in relationship to an independent other." In the words of the Japanese philosopher Kitarō Nishida, "the 'I' exists as an 'I' in that it recognizes the Thou as Thou" and "without a Thou there is no 'I.' "[23] Dōgen maintains that self and other are, ultimately, interdependent. This conception of the self as *being-in-relationship* illustrates the Buddhist understanding of human existence as non-substantial. This self does not exist prior to or independent from an other, it cannot be considered an unchanging individual but should be rather conceived of as the momentary subject of an experience. To paraphrase a famous quotation by Nishida, it is not that there is a relationship because there are self and other, but there are self and other because there is a relationship.[24] Starting with the common-sense notion that self and other are interrelated, Dōgen draws its most radical conclusion—namely, the existential selflessness of self and other.

Ultimately, Dōgen suggests a radical rethinking and reversal of the Western conception of self. For the self is not an enduring individual which "has" experiences and psychic states, but constitutes an experience or, more appropriately, an awareness event. Central to Dōgen's conception of the self as an awareness event is his *logic of presencing* (*genjō*, literally "making present"). In the context of his theory of meditation, Dōgen introduces this logic in order to argue the non-dualism of enlightenment and practice. By analogy, psychic states such as emotions, thoughts, etc., can be conceived of as expressions of a non-individual psyche,[25] which contains the psychic content of self and other alike. However, defined as such, the non-individual psyche does not comprise a collective psychic structure or collective psychic imagery, but the interactivity of what Jung calls *affective complexes*, which are conventionally attributed to separate individuals such as self and other. Dōgen's underlying belief that self and other are identical yet different suggests that they are two separate, individual expressions of the same psychic content. By the same token, the self is simultaneously individual and non-individual insofar as it is an individual manifestation of non-individual content. When Dōgen identifies the "casting off of body and mind of self and other," which signifies the dissolution of the self-other dichotomy, with the "verification of myriad dharmas,"[26] he similarly implies that the self as a momentary awareness event expresses itself, the other, myriad dharmas, and, thus, the non-individual psyche. Thus defined, however, the self cannot but, in the language of psychology, "experience the psychic state of the other from the perspective of the other."

What prevents the everyday self from "attaining the other"? Dōgen's conception of the self as an expression of the non-individual psyche, which contains the psychic material of the other, poses a question: Why does everyday awareness conceive of itself as a separate and isolated self? Dōgen attributes this common conception to the self-centeredness of the self. In his "Shōbōgenzō Genjōkōan," Dōgen contends that "to practice myriad dharmas by carrying the self signifies delusion."[27] The meaning of this becomes more accessible in Tamaki's translation: "To study the surrounding world with the self as subject signifies delusion."[28] The key to understanding the incapability of the self-centered self "to attain the other" lies in Tamaki's translation of "jiko" (self) as "subject" (shūtai). There are two dimensions to the character of a subject. First, it is symptomatic of the binary experience of the world, which renders a world dissociated into pairs of opposites such as subject-object, self-other, inside-outside, etc. Second, and more important, however, it signifies a self-conscious and intentional attitude: It is the subject which experiences, knows, and acts upon the world, whereas the world is conceived of as passive, waiting to be discovered. In this case, the outside world and the external other are relegated into passivity by the self. The self-centered self misconstrues itself and the other as permanent and absolute entities and, at the same time, constructs the other in "its own image." This self-centeredness, then, prevents the self from experiencing the psychic state of the other from the perspective of the other.

In analogy, psychic entanglement has to be understood as the superimposition of the self's thoughts, desires, and expectations onto the other, which causes the self to mistakenly identify the psychic state of the other as "mine." The self-centered self does not experience the psychic state of the other from the other's own perspective but solely as a reflection of its own desires and experiences. Thus the other becomes a construct rather

than something that can be encountered by the other. These considerations echo Jung's observation that the self-centeredness of the "I" and the
concomitant psychic entanglement change the other "into the replica of
one's own unknown face."

How can the self "attain the other"? In order to "attain the other," the
self has to, in Dōgen's words, "forget the self," "cast off body and mind
of self and other," and thus "verify myriad dharmas." Contrary to everyday
awareness, which is characterized by self-centeredness, Dōgen's self-
awareness is characterized by selflessness. This selfless self-awareness transcends the dichotomies of subjectivity and objectivity, selfhood and
otherness. It even transcends the categories of body and mind and defies
the categories of "conscious" or "unconscious," "inside" or "outside." Selfless self-awareness neither constructs otherness nor superimposes its desires
and expectations onto the other; on the contrary it reveals "self" and
"other" for what they are—namely, impermanent and correlative awareness events.

This selfless self-awareness can be illustrated with the cultivation of
physical or artistic skills. A cultivated piano player, for example, does not
self-consciously move her hand in search of the right keys but, rather,
seems to play "without thinking"[29]—that is, unself-consciously.[30] The interaction between individuals cultivates what Merleau-Ponty calls a *habit-
body*. In the case of ballroom dancing as well as martial arts such as T'ai
Chi, cultivated practitioners do not perceive of each other self-consciously
as the object of each other's intentions and expectations but as separate
yet interconnected expressions of the same movement. By the same token,
groups of individuals which often work together on similar projects or in
similar situations such as in team sports are said to develop a "sense" for
each other. In either case, the self is not self-consciously aware of the other
as one is in the presence of a stranger, to use Sartre's example of the *gaze*;
on the contrary, selfless awareness of the other is pre-reflective and unself-
conscious.

Finally, Dōgen contends that this selfless, non-intentional self-awareness,
which reveals the self as a momentary awareness event, is not merely an
intellectual form of awareness but has to be cultivated through the practice
of seated meditation. It is only then that the self transforms its existential
attitude toward the world to such a degree that it ceases to superimpose
its desires and expectations onto the other. It is only then that the disciple
"attains the master."

CLOSING REFLECTIONS

Taking the psychic interwovenness of self and other as its methodological starting point, this comparison of the therapeutic relationship in Jung and Dōgen's conception of the disciple-master relationship has revealed some basic similarities as well as fundamental conceptual differences between these two thinkers. Both distinguish two forms of psychic interwovenness. First, there is the phenomenon of psychic entanglement which displays, in addition to the psychic interwovenness of self and other, the inability of the self to discern "what is mine" and "what is yours." Both thinkers contend that this phenomenon is caused by an inherent self-centered attitude of everyday awareness and an attitude which focuses on the self-conscious function of the "I." Jung and Dōgen agree not only that such an attitude is detrimental to the attainment of self-awareness but that it further tends to isolate the self from the world and, at the same time, superimposes the self's own "face" onto the other. Paradoxically, it is in my conception of myself as a separate entity that I conceive of the other as but a reflection of myself. However, while Jung maintains that the self-centered attitude of the self-conscious function "motivates" an unconscious transference of the dispossessed material of the self onto the other, Dōgen believes that the self-centered self merely mistakes the other's psychic state for its own, while de facto nothing is transferred from the one to the other.

Contrary to the phenomenon of psychic entanglement, the phenomena of *kattō* and synchronicity imply, at least theoretically, the capability of the self to identify the psychic state of the other as a psychic state external to the self. However, while Jung interprets synchronistic phenomena as well as other-awareness as instances of synchronization and, ultimately, as the oneness of two minds, Dōgen contends that it is possible for the self to experience the psychic state of the other without losing its individuality. This discrepancy, however, cannot but disclose two completely different conceptions of the self. While Jung subsumes the non-individual aspect of human existence qua collective unconscious under the notion of Self, Dōgen contends that self and other are merely manifestations of a non-individual activity and, ultimately, comprise but individual awareness events. Either position, however, demands a radical rethinking of the traditional notion of the human individual as an independent and self-contained entity and the commonly accepted one-body-one-self principle. To accommodate the notion of psychic interwovenness, any theory of the self has to consider the non-individual and the somatic dimensions of the human psyche.

Notes

1. Dōgen Kigen (1200–53), the founder of the Japanese school of Sōtō Zen Buddhism, is generally regarded as one of the most distinguished Zen Buddhist thinkers.

2. Carl Gustav Jung, *Collected Works*, Vol. 16: *The Practice of Psychotherapy*, ed. Sir Herbert Mead, Michael Fordham, Gerhard Adler, and William McGuire, trans. R. F. C. Hull, 2nd ed., Bollingen Series vol. 20 (Princeton: Princeton University Press, 1969) (hereafter abbreviated as Jung, CW 16), 172.

3. Jung, CW 16, 182.

4. Ibid., 179–80.

5. Ibid.

6. Carl Gustav Jung, *Psyche and Symbol: A Selection from the Writings of C. G. Jung*, ed. Violet S. deLaszlo, trans. R. F. C. Hull and Cary Bayes (Garden City, N.Y.: Anchor-Doubleday, 1958) (hereafter abbreviated as Jung, *Psyche and Symbol*), 8.

7. Ibid.

8. Jung, CW 16, 176.

9. Ibid., 169.

10. Ibid.

11. My interpretation coincides with that of Jungian psychologist C. A. Meier, who likens the phenomenon of transference to synchronistic phenomena. C. A. Meier, *Soul and Body* (San Francisco: The Lapis Press, 1986), 46–62.

12. Carl Gustav Jung, *Collected Works*, Vol. 8: *The Structure and Dynamics of the Psyche*, ed. Sir Herbert Mead, Michael Fordham, Gerhard Adler, and William McGuire, trans. R. F. C. Hull, 2nd ed., Bollingen Series vol. 20 (Princeton, Princeton University Press, 1969), 444.

13. Carl Gustav Jung, *The Undiscovered Self*, trans. R. F. C. Hull, 2nd ed., Bollingen Series vol. 20 (Princeton: Princeton University Press), 29.

14. Jung defines the *Self* as "psychic totality consisting of both conscious and unconscious contents." Carl Gustav Jung, *Collected Works*, Vol. 6: *Psychological Types*, ed. Sir Herbert Mead, Michael Fordham, Gerhard Adler, and William McGuire, trans. R. F. C. Hull, 2nd ed., Bollingen Series vol. 20 (Princeton: Princeton University Press, 1969), 460.

15. Jung, *Psyche and Symbol*, 4.

16. The *nembutsu*, which consists of the recitation of the phrase "I entrust myself in the name of Amida Buddha," comprises the central practice of Pure Land Buddhism.

17. The Japanese translation of "Ju-ching" is "Nyōjō."

18. Dōgen, *Shōbōgenzō*, vol. 1 (Tokyo: Daizō Shuppan Kabushiki Kaisha, 1993) (hereafter abbreviated as Dōgen, S1), 95.

19. Dōgen, *Shōbōgenzō*, vol. 4 (Tokyo: Daizō Shuppan Kabushiki Kaisha, 1993) (hereafter abbreviated as Dōgen, S4), 16.

20. Thomas P. Kasulis, "The Incomparable Philosopher," in *Dōgen Studies*, ed. Wilhelm LaFleur (Honolulu: University of Hawaii Press, 1985), 92.

21. Dōgen, S4, 15.

22. Dōgen, S1, 431.

23. Kitarō Nishida, *Nishida Kitarō Zenshū*, vol. 7: *Tetsugaku no Kompon Mondai*, 4th ed. (Tokyo: Iwanami Shoten, 1988), 85–86.

24. Nishida says that "it is not that there is experience because there is an individual but there is an individual because there is experience." Kitarō Nishida, *Nishida Kitarō Zenshu*, vol. 1: *Zen no Kenkyu*, 4th ed. (Tokyo: Iwanami Shoten, 1988), 4.

25. Dōgen identifies this non-individual dimension as "buddha-nature" (*busshō*), "enduring activity" (*gyōji*), and "total working" (*zenki*).

26. Dōgen, S1, 95.

27. Dōgen, S1, 94.

28. Koshiro Tamaki, trans., *Gendai Goyaku Shōbōgenzō*, vol. 1 (Tokyo: Daizō Shuppan Kabushiki Kaisha, 1993), 95.

29. Thomas P. Kasulis translates Dōgen's description of non-intentional awareness *"hishiryō"* as "without-thinking."

30. Shigenori Nagatomo, *Attunement Through the Body* (Albany: SUNY Press, 1992), 230.

ZEN, LACAN, AND THE ALIEN EGO

Anthony Molino

❑

Jung realized that Buddhism adapts itself to the culture that it enters. Buddhism does not represent a specific Eastern tradition: it was able to move, for example, and change, from India to China to Japan to Southeast Asia by adapting itself to the culture at-large. Thus Jung began to sense that Buddhism could become a part of depth psychology . . .
— POLLY YOUNG-EISENDRATH, *in Elaborate Selves*

❑

INTRODUCTION

Over the years, a number of psychoanalysts have expressed an interest in Zen Buddhism, undertaking comparative work aimed mostly at integrating aspects of Zen into their own theory and practice. What seems lacking throughout such research, though, is an effort to compare the theoretical underpinnings specific to Zen and Western psychotherapy as these reflect and structure different understandings of the human condition. I would like to suggest that a genuine comparison between the two systems might best be served by investigating the assumed metaphysical and metapsychological principles on which each system relies. In doing so, however, one must consider the far from unified picture offered us by present-day psychoanalysis, as well as a Zen tradition which usually eschews intellectual, conceptual or analytical explications of both its aim and worldview. To this end, I would like to focus attention on two singular figures whose

An earlier version of this essay was presented at the 1991 University of Missouri–Columbia conference entitled *History and Hysteria*. It appears here in print for the first time.

writings—while not representative of "mainstream" understandings of either Zen or psychoanalysis—nonetheless invite the kind of fertile comparison I have in mind.

Where psychoanalysis is concerned, recent writers have noted, albeit in passing, a certain similarity—at least of "style"—between Jacques Lacan and the baffling, quizzical persona of the Zen Master.[1] Yet beyond any fun but facile analogies between Lacan's short sessions and the Master's timely whack across a befuddled disciple's head, or musing on knots and Buddha-nature, little or no interdisciplinary work of a theoretical nature has explored the links between Lacan's thought and Zen.

Conversely, a notable exception to Zen Buddhism's proverbial aversion to systematized theorization is provided by the pioneering but often neglected work of Richard De Martino. Student, colleague, translator and interpreter of luminaries such as D. T. Suzuki and Shin'ichi Hisamatsu, De Martino is a fundamental figure in the postwar transplantation of Zen to American soil. If it is true—as Polly Young-Eisendrath and others have suggested—that one of the strengths of Buddhism is its flexibility in cultural adaptation, De Martino's attempt to theorize a Zen understanding of the human condition can be seen as an essential moment in the West's slow internalization of a once-alien experiential philosophy. Moreover, within the history of the dialogue between East and West, De Martino was more than an instrumental promoter whose efforts helped bring together Zen Masters and theologians, philosophers and psychoanalysts. I would suggest that while his own writings undeniably reflect an idiosyncratic understanding of Zen, they also illuminate a postwar intellectual climate in which psychoanalysis and existentialism became the privileged Western vehicles for engaging the Buddhist Other. It is this aspect of De Martino's work that I would like to acknowledge. In fact, I would suggest that his view of alienation as a *transhistorical* expression of human nature is fruitfully engaged—in a likely instance of transcultural synchronicity—by Lacan's own writings.

I

In short, we call ego that nucleus given to consciousness, but opaque to reflection, marked by all the ambiguities which . . . structure the experience of the passions in the human subject; this "I" who, in order to admit its facticity to existential criticism, opposes its irreducible inertia of pretenses and *méconnaissances* to the concrete problematic of the realization of the subject.
                                                                —JACQUES LACAN

It is thus the unswerving position of Zen Buddhism that the hub of all the ordinary man's problems or anxieties is that he lacks a firm footing in the ground of his own being as an authentic subject-I. In this view, consequently, if the ordinary man could know—or be— himself truly, then the root of all his problems and anxieties would therewith be extirpated.
                                                —RICHARD DE MARTINO

As implied by the above quotes, the question of onto-existential alienation, or "inauthenticity," is central to both Lacan and Zen. For both, the individual is split, either caught in the throes of an all-pervasive subject/object dualism (Zen) or divorced—by way of species-specific maturational processes—from the absolute subject and the Real of the unconscious. In each instance, a primordial break with an undifferentiated "natural" state is posited. What is striking, however, is to find in the work of a thinker such as De Martino a remark hinting at *a normative maturational phase* during which the onto-existential reality of the ego, and its resultant dualism, is instituted:

> . . . the norm [of] ego-consciousness . . . ordinarily first appears between the ages of two and five. . . . Forgoing, at this time, any phenomenological account of its onset and development . . .[2]

I contend that Lacan provides just such an account. It is through his conceptualization of the mirror stage, in fact, that we have at our disposal a sound basis of comparison for two of the strongest existing critiques of the Western bastion of self-identity known as the *ego*—both of which, moreover, are informed by an essential if not foundational reading of Hegel's theses on the Master-Slave relationship and the genesis of subjectivity.

II

Defined by what Richard De Martino calls "the structured function of reflective consciousness"—that is to say, by "the once actualized and thereafter reactualizable capacity of the human person to be aware or conscious of his/her own awareness or consciousness,"[3] the ego constitutes itself as a subject-knower. In becoming aware of its being aware, the ego simultaneously posits itself as the *object* of its own knowing. Thus constituted, the ego can never come to know itself as a subject. In De Martino's words:

The ego as subject is forever bound to itself and its world as object. . . . Capable of having an object solely because it is a subject, it can never be a subject except insofar as it also is or has an object. . . . Divided and dissociated in its centeredness, it is beyond its own reach, obstructed, removed and alienated from itself. Just in having itself, it does not have itself.[4]

Much in the vein of a Hegelian dialectic whereby subjectivity—or the emphasized "I" connoting self-consciousness—is generated in the encounter between two egos, De Martino's reading of Zen takes the peculiarly *human* community of Desire, in which the interplay of subject-(object)- subject unfolds, to be constitutive of the burgeoning ego of the infant. Such a reading, as I've already suggested, is remarkable in its willingness to situate the "original sin," if you will, of alienation, in a *normative* phase of developmental psychology. Essentially, this view of the child's entry into the matrix of being (and non-being) is shared by Lacan, whose own ideas concerning the alienation of the split or decentered subject also rely heavily on the philosophical foundations laid by Hegel and Kojeve. Indeed, for Lacan, a split likewise inheres in the formation and function of the *ego*, as he speaks—using language similar to De Martino's—of the "primordial Discord" from which we emerge, and of "the vital dehiscence . . . constitutive of man."[5]

III

Drawing on evidence from animal biology, whereby a mirror image of a female pigeon or migratory locust yielded the same developmental effects on the subject as those produced by a visual encounter with a live member of the species, Lacan developed his idea of the mirror stage in 1936.[6] "Occurring" at some time between the ages of six and twenty-one months (though *in actuality* the fateful event may never take place: hence the "mythical" quality of the notion), the mirror stage initially involves the subject's assumed recognition of his own bodily image, perceived as a total unity in the eyes of the mother. As I will later elaborate, this primary identification of one's "I," besides serving as the source for all later identifications, anticipates the process of bodily maturation in the apprehension of an exterior Gestalt.[7] This anticipation, in turn, on the part of a being "in Discord," precipitates the "I" in primordial form—along the lines of what Michael Guy Thompson, in his book *The Death of Desire*, calls a "mistaken identity." In fact, the perception of a "whole" self-image, in violent contrast to a surmised actual experience of internal fragmentation, leads the child to an ambivalent constitution of self-identity, where the boundaries between exterior and interior, bodily and perceptual realities are totally blurred. As Thompson explains, in a chapter called "Idolatry of the Ego" (my italics):

> Thrilled by the loving apprehension of his self-image, the infant also experiences the wish to destroy that self (formed in "bad faith") because it points to his inner chaos. . . . The paradox of this encounter is that the human infant should be initiated into his never-ending quest for the recognition of his desire through a device *that is anything but the recognition by another subject.*[8]

As one can see, what is implied is an alienation, a split or estrangement, of the burgeoning ego from the "subject," whose absolute quality of "being" forever permeates the elusive Real of the Lacanian unconscious. Again, this split occurs by virtue of the child's internalization of the unified mirror image, assumed to conflict with the actual experience of the child's (inner) fragmentation. Thus, according to Lacan, are we initiated into the tyrannical realm of the Imaginary, of freezing self images constituted and indeed structured by the desire of an alien Other, "the scene of a desperate delusional attempt to be and to remain 'what one is' by gathering to oneself ever more instances of sameness, resemblance and self-replication."[9] Such a tyranny, already prefigured by Kojeve's Hegel in the Slave's surrender of his Desire to the Master, is also astoundingly echoed by De Martino when he writes:

> The ego, however, constrained by its inner contradiction to seek its completion, is beguiled by that contradiction into just this deception. Available to itself—even as it contemplates its own subjectivity—*only in terms of some object cast of itself,* the ego naturally comes to confuse being fulfilled with "being something."

Or, to continue:

> Relying on its own projected object-image to establish itself . . . , the ego may be led to take that limited, finite impression alone to be the whole of itself, its ground, its source, and its ultimate meaning, by which it is to be sustained (and) fulfilled. . . . Virtually identifying with [its] contents, the ego focuses exclusively upon them and upon the conception of itself which they constitute.[10]

It remains perplexing that De Martino, while not a psychoanalyst or developmental psychologist, should have forgone a phenomenological account of the onset and development of ego-consciousness. Perhaps this is in part explained by the fact that his audience, at the now famous 1957 Cuernavaca conference on Zen Buddhism and Psychoanalysis (from which was derived the classic volume by the same title, which De Martino co-authored with Erich Fromm and D. T. Suzuki), was comprised primarily of psychiatrists and psychoanalysts. Also, as that was the heyday of ego psychology, at least in the United States, it is plausible to think that any such account—especially if presented by a non-specialist—might have ruffled more than a few feathers in a psychoanalytic establishment known for its theoretical conservatism. Moreover, considering the limited scope of De Martino's own familiarity with psychoanalysis at the time, it is doubtful that he could have known of Lacan's work—which was still decades away from being published in English. But whether De Martino assumed that his audience shared a monolithic understanding of the rise of ego-consciousness (that somehow corresponded with his own implied understanding) or whether the matter was not really central to his argument, the fact remains that a reading of Lacan's mirror stage fills a gap in the Zen theorization of the root causes of man's deceptive quest for being. And yet, for all of the irrefutable similarities linking Lacan with a Zen proponent like De Martino, there is in Lacan's work a major, radical revision of their common Hegelian heritage on which the French psychoanalyst's theory either rests or flounders. And it is this very revision, entailed in Lacan's reading of the mirror stage, that at the same time most seriously *challenges* the Zen understanding of ego formation and, consequently, of our human predicament.

IV

For the immediate purposes of this study, the Zen understanding of the separation of subject and object, inherent in the rise of reflective consciousness, has a singular corollary of immediate and exceptional consequence:

In dualistically distinguishing himself from that which is not himself, the ordinary man thereby "individuates" himself and is, consequently, an individual. He is uniquely and individually himself, and—in his discriminating self-consciousness—is never that which is not-himself.[11]

Illustrated here is what De Martino terms the *primary diremption* which is at the root of the ego's alienated being-in-the-world, and whose reconstitution in the attainment of *satori* (enlightenment) is at the core of Zen's philosophical idealism. From the standpoint of Zen, the rise of reflective consciousness institutes, in and of itself, *both* self and other. Both, as it were, even in their interdependence, materialize simultaneously as separate and distinct. An outgrowth of the Hegelian dialectic, whereby "to speak of the origin of Self-Consciousness is necessarily to speak of the autonomy and dependence of Self-Consciousness" (Kojeve), such a position bespeaks the necessity of the Other, even in the antagonism of its autonomous Desire. According to Zen, "twoness," if you will, is given to human consciousness; for all intents and purposes, there is no human reality that is not a social reality, no preliminary stage of development prior to the onset of reflective consciousness that marks the human being as *human*. On this score De Martino is quite emphatic: "Man is not simply born into human existence. The infant is not yet human . . ."[12]

What Lacan introduces with the mirror stage, therefore, can perhaps be conceived as an *intermediate* stage of development (between the stages of undifferentiation and reflective consciousness) which lends insight into the ego's prehistory and fixates its alienation *sub specie aeternitatis*. Situated from its inception "in a fictional direction," Lacan's inauthentic *ego* is, as suggested, the product of the infant's primordial encounter with a deceptive mirror image of itself. This encounter then serves as the prototype for a subsequent series of illusory identifications (*méconnaissances*) with other members of the human community, whereby an alien and alienating composite of external images is internalized to form a false and mangled sense of self. Thus, ever intent on grasping and fusing with the alien image, with the mirrored *Other* and its multiple object representations, we embark on our lifelong quest for oneness and unity, pawns in the play of insatiable Desire.

Consequently, while Lacan's mirror stage might initially seem to ground the Zen understanding of the ego's rise, as well as our inherent "brokenness," in a distinct phase of developmental psychology, in actuality the picture is not so simple. It might be more accurate to say that the idea of the mirror stage complements and enhances the Zen understanding. And yet De Martino, as if anticipating or indirectly addressing Lacan's position, explicitly argues against the role of the mirror in ego formation when he writes: "That which is required for the self's initial emergence is contact with another actual . . . self, *and not merely a mirror*."[13] What also follows, as I hope to show, is that Zen and Lacan differ as a result on the matter of the human propensity for aggression that stems from our inner divisiveness. For Lacan, as we've seen, it is the constitution of the ego in the mirror stage that makes a child aware of itself and of the discord that ravages its being. Aggression, then, or what Lacan calls *aggressivity*, is originally self-engendered *and* self-directed;[14] it is not, as Hegel and Zen would have it, the by-product of the alienated and objectifying encounter between *two* egos assumed to be separate and distinct. Basically, where Zen requires the presence of an extant Other, Lacan sees the Other originating in the early germs of narcissism.

In sum, from the initial "misrecognition" of one's own image in Lacan's mirror there follows a series of secondary identifications which clearly challenge De Martino's view of the ego's uniqueness and self-identity. When Lacan unequivocally states that "in the last resort, all the various formulas (*of self-identity/identification*) are to be understood in reference to the truth of 'I' as an other,"[15] there is no room for the proposed unity of self and subject that Zen envisions and indeed propounds. Effectively, then, Lacan's "truth" is the Zen position turned upside down and, in a way, emptied of itself.

V

"I have seen with my own eyes and known very well an infant in the grip of jealousy: he could not yet speak, and already he observed his foster brother, pale and with an envenomed stare." Quoting St. Augustine, Lacan suggests that the aggressivity marking the "envenomed stare" of the preverbal infant is in fact a further development of the internal discord referred to above. As he elaborates extensively on the work of Melanie Klein in his essay "Aggressivity in Psychoanalysis," Lacan discusses the phenomenon of transitivism as it applies to the concretion of the ego in the life of the infant. The latter is observed engaging in a series of identifications (primarily with its peers), which are all seen to derive from the primary identification with the mirror image. Marking this phase are behaviors of the type that have a child striking at another and saying he's been struck, or crying at the sight of another child being injured (as if he himself had been hurt). In one of his characteristically fanciful turns of phrase, Lacan describes the phenomenon as follows:

> It is by means of identification with the other that [the child] sees the whole gamut of his reactions of bearing and display, whose structural ambivalence is clearly revealed in his behavior, the slave being identified with the despot, the actor with the spectator, the seduced with the seducer.[16]

Such identifications compound and fortify the child's sense of self, leading him to look and find support for his identity in the external environment. But as Thompson argues, this intricate puzzle of *imagos* comprising the ego in no way dispels the child's self-directed aggressiveness and competitiveness: "As he strives to 'become' the Ego he thinks he is, and which finds support in the collusive confirmation of significant others *who fix the personality*, the child inhabits the spectre of an ominous and perpetual failure to be real."[17] These two "moments"—of self-directed aggression and fixing of the personality—are then understood to yield the guilt and masochism most thoroughly postulated by Klein; in addition, however, they also serve as the basis for Lacan's fourth thesis on aggressivity, expounded in the aforementioned essay, which reads:

> Aggressivity is the correlative tendency of a mode of identification that we call narcissistic, and which determines the formal structure of man's ego and of the register of entities characteristic of his world.

This thesis, in turn, sheds light on a major distinction between Zen and Lacanian reformulations of the Hegelian dialectic. Whereas De Martino speaks of the intersubjective encounter as characterized by *"a constitutive existential obligation of the 'human' being to be human or humane"*[18] (where not to be is "to debase or violate the integrity of subjectivity per se"—i.e., that of all human beings), Lacan counters with a position that is far less entrenched in the tradition of what we in the West might call classical humanism. For Lacan, the aggressiveness inherent in the ego's fundamental relationship to other people is indicative of "the intrapsychic tension we sense in the warning of the ascetic: namely, a blow at your enemy is a blow at yourself." Still, both positions do bespeak the same basic "problem": that of the ego, split at its very roots, driven to "realize" itself in what Lacan calls the *Other*, or in what Zen proclaims as the essence of enlightenment—in the "not twoness of the two," the non-dualistic duality of what, in De Martino's view of man's initial nature, is structured as an alienated and alienating subject/object relationship. As De Martino ex-claims in his groundbreaking essay "The Human Situation and Zen Bud-dhism": "Finally and fundamentally, it is not that the ego has a problem, but that the ego is the problem."[19]

But where the positions again diverge is on the possibility of such a realization of enlightenment, or *at-onement*. For Zen this possibility goes unquestioned. For Lacan, disciple and exegete of the early Freud, of the Freud of *Beyond the Pleasure Principle*, though we are compelled to seek such a realization, it is one we will never attain. Only the wish can be fulfilled, not Desire. Ever. Caught in the exhilarating, tragic, and unending dance of Desire and *jouissance*, we will forever pursue our *petits objets a*, Lacan's little-other-objects which, in a register that extends from bodily cuts and margins to punctuations of speech and experience, infill but never *fulfill* the discontinuous human landscape that ends in death. Perpetually in flight, these objects are themselves seductive, deceptive incarnations (and as such destined themselves to the mortal end that awaits all "flesh") of a universal propensity toward decay among objects of desire, even as they structure and define our *jouissance*. Or, as Ellie Ragland-Sullivan once wrote to me, commenting on Lacan's philosophy:

> . . . there is no unity, only a quest for it. And this quest fails, even when it seems to succeed. If our only unity is, as the late Lacan claimed, in our *jouissance*—which hurts us in its symptomatic fixity and rigidity—then we can never be unified, from within or without.

VI

Without addressing the more specific articulations of "separation anxiety" in general psychoanalytic theory and the "lack of object" in Klein and Lacan, psychoanalysis—starting with Freud—provides us with any number of materialist understandings of the human condition predicated on the binary opposition of presence and absence.[20] This opposition, however, extended to and contextualized within a discourse of Desire, translates the cleavage of an assumed or mythified prior unity into alternative versions of the Zen dualism of authenticity and self-alienation. For Lacan, the prime mover in our wayward attempts at reconstituting that unity is Desire itself, that which "transforms Being . . . into an 'object' revealed to a 'subject' by a subject different from the object and opposed to it" (Kojeve). Desire, that is, as postulated by a Hegelian dialectic in which the subject's ceaseless desire for recognition by the desire of another subject is what generates the "human reality" of self-consciousness. But in the Lacanian framework, where the (absolute) subject is, "a contradiction in terms, an asubjective entity"[21]—or, in Thompson's words, "*no thing* at all, except that it be grasped as a set of mutations and dialectical upheavals which point towards desire in a continuous, intentional structure of transcendence and temporality" (Thompson, p. 27)—the quest for unity is, after all, but a quest for an image: for the illusory and alienated image of the "I" mirrored in the eye of the Other. Unlike Zen, in Lacan there is no "true self" to be regained, no pristine relation of self and world that can return us to Eden and the realization of Desire. Or, as another Frenchman, Albert Camus, knew well, there can be no final resolution to "the deep, mysterious ancestral need [for unity] which alone abolishes the all too real dualities and antinomies with which we struggle."[22]

Finally, we all sense what Anthony Wilden means when, in his commentary on Lacan's Rome Discourse, he writes: "The subject's profoundest desire is to be 'One' again." Freud understood something similar when he struggled with Romain Rolland's ephemeral "oceanic feeling," cited at the beginning of *Civilization and Its Discontents*. In any case, human discontent is such that our "ego" is alienated whether it's lying on the analyst's couch in Paris or New York or prostrated before the Master in a Kyoto temple. But for all their similarities, the two worldviews of psychoanalysis and Zen Buddhism remain fundamentally at odds. On the one hand, as expressed by Lacan, psychoanalysis would likely view Zen as a jeweled and marvelous essay on the discourse of Desire—except that it ultimately bears the hallmark of delusion. On the other hand, seen from the vantage point of Zen Buddhism, Lacan probably articulates one of the more cogent critiques of a shared notion of "reality" which itself is inherently delusional—only to remain stuck in the quagmire of *samsara*, the damning cycle of birth-and-death. Ultimately, East and West diverge, with little or no room for compromise. (Something Jung had already intuited, in his foreword to Suzuki's *Introduction to Zen Buddhism*.) For Lacan, though the lack of object looms as the condition and result of desire, two egos, existing in reflective consciousness and constituting one another as objects, are doomed to embark on a pathological quest for an identity that is sadly illusory.[23] For Zen, far from being at the root of neurosis and psychosis, to discover or *actualize* the transcendent "I" is a moral imperative; we are, in a way, compelled to enter our "true" or "authentic" nature, which remains inaccessible so long as we, as *egos*, inhabit the logic of duality in which reflective consciousness reveals itself. For subject/object, mind/body, self/other, being/non-being, time/space and the ultimate, all-encompassing duality of life/death, all reflect, in De Martino's words, "the cleavage both within and without itself, [in which] the ordinary ego is unable to effect a genuine reconciliation of the many contrasting elements which go to make its existence."[24]

Of course, it is not the purpose of this paper to take sides in a philosophical debate of dimensions that far exceed this author's expertise. However, in outlining some of the basic tenets of Zen and Lacanian theory as I understand them, this paper will hopefully contribute to the dialogue and cross-fertilization of ideas begun by Jung, Fromm and D. T. Suzuki, and most recently invigorated by the likes of Jeffrey Rubin, Polly Young-Eisendrath, John Suler and numerous others. The implications of such a dialogue are far-reaching, even as the very comparison between Zen and Lacan is far from exhausted. In this study, for example, I've done little more than outline parallels in De Martino's and Lacan's respective conceptualizations of Desire, especially as it relates to the genesis of subjectivity. Similarly, the respective cultural contexts of these two authors and their particular relationships to Existentialism (De Martino knew Tillich well; Lacan knew Sartre and most of the French scene) could serve as the basis for a more detailed account of common historical and philosophical influences. A closer reading of both Lacan and Zen, moreover, could help evidence and illustrate philosophies of knowledge which, derived from their respective notions of the ego, are likely to converge on some points and diverge on others. Further research might also be conducted on what Lacan and De Martino both identify as the *structural* aspects of the division of the subject. And the assumed analogies between Lacan's short sessions and the Zen koan also warrant more focused attention, especially as they reflect encoded experiences and definitions of "reality." The Lacanian canon itself is interspersed with references to Buddhism that warrant closer study. The following, from Lacan's "Function and Field of Speech and Language," is but one such example:

> But this mystery [of the transference] becomes clarified if it is viewed within the phenomenology of the subject, insofar as the subject constitutes himself in the search for truth. One only has to go back to the traditional givens—*which the Buddhists could provide us with . . .*—to recognize in this form of transference the normal error of existence, under the three headings of love, hate and ignorance.[25]

Finally, the implications of ego-formation in both instances—through a parallel study of the irremediable "gaps" postulated by Lacan and what De Martino terms "the abyss and despair of the yawning inner hiatus"[26]—can help shed light on Lacan's—and subsequent—diagnoses of the "social hell" of contemporary man. But such investigations, at least for the time being, will have to wait. Hopefully, they will find room in a comparative project of greater scope for which this paper serves as a preliminary exercise.

Notes

The author would like to express his gratitude to Jeffrey Rubin for his critical attention to earlier versions of this essay.

1. See especially Schneiderman, 81. Similar echoes are found in Borch-Jacobsen's *The Absolute Master* and, in this volume, the essay by Stephen Kurtz.
2. De Martino, "The Human Situation and Zen Buddhism," in *Zen Buddhism and Psychoanalysis*, 142–43.
3. De Martino, from a 1983 classroom communication during his course "Zen and Western Psychotherapy" at Temple University in Philadelphia.
4. De Martino, "The Human Situation and Zen Buddhism," 144.
5. See Lacan, "The Mirror Stage as Formative of the Function of the I as Revealed in Psychoanalytic Experience," 4, and "Aggressivity in Psychoanalysis," 21, in *Écrits*. The similarity in language is noteworthy: where Lacan talks of *dehiscence*, De Martino in his writings uses the word *diremption*.
6. Lacan's paper on the mirror stage, while published in 1949, was prefigured in 1936, in an address to the 14th Congress of the International Psychoanalytic Association in Marienbad. Whereas the French *stade*, or stadium, emphasizes the notion of the spectacle, as well as a combat arena (here reprising the Hegelian theme of the "fight to the death" between Master and Slave), the English translation—with its theatrical allusion—elaborates nevertheless on the alienation and "deceptions" the stage promotes.
7. Lacan cites the organic insufficiency ("specific prematurity," or partial fetalization) of the human infant at this stage of development.
8. Thompson, *Death of Desire*, 21.
9. Bowie, *Lacan*, 92.
10. De Martino, "The Human Situation and Zen Buddhism," 146–47. (My italics.)
11. De Martino, "The Zen Understanding of the Fundamental Problem of the Ordinary Man," 29. By "ordinary man" is meant the human person characterized by reflective consciousness, and to that extent unenlightened or "unactualized."
12. De Martino, "The Human Situation and Zen Buddhism," 142.
13. My italics. See footnote 55 to De Martino's "The Zen Understanding of the Initial Nature of Man."
14. Lacan, "Aggressivity in Psychoanalysis."
15. Lacan, in Thompson, 27.

16. Lacan, "Aggressivity in Psychoanalysis," 19.

17. Thompson, 23. Psychoanalytic findings confirming the two moments of self-directed aggressiveness and fixing of the personality are given by Lacan in both cited articles. He refers primarily to dreams of *le corps morcelé*, in which the dreamer's body appears fragmented or dismembered (images "codified," so to speak, in the paintings of H. Bosch) and to dreams which have a stadium or arena as their scenario (symbolizing both the enclosure and fortification of the ego and the battleground on which bodily discord with the image ravages the infant).

18. De Martino, "The Zen Understanding of the Initial Nature of Man," 48.

19. As a way of underscoring the idiosyncratic quality of De Martino's reading of Zen (as well as of my use of it as a basis for comparison with Lacan), Jeffrey Rubin has commented in a personal communication: "The assumption here—undemonstrated—is that duality is always conflictual. Secretly privileged is the paradigm of oneness—which has its own blind spots. Assuming that duality is always conflictual is an inherently alienated and alienating view of human life." See Rubin's own contribution to this volume, "The Emperor of Enlightenment May Have No Clothes," excerpted from his *Psychotherapy and Buddhism: Towards an Integration* (Plenum, 1996), in which the author elaborates extensively on this view. See also Joel Kramer and Diana Alstad's *The Guru Papers: Masks of Authoritarian Power* (North Atlantic Books, 1993).

20. For a detailed discussion of separation anxiety in the lives of Zen students and masters, see Krynicki. For an analysis of Lacan's "lack of object," developed from his reading of Freud's *Fort/Da* anecdote in *Beyond the Pleasure Principle*, see Wilden, 188–92.

21. Wilden, *The Language of the Self*, 190.

22. The remark is taken from the introduction by Paul Viallaneix to Camus's *Youthful Writings*.

23. On this score, I offer the reflections of Christopher Bollas, excerpted from my earlier *Elaborate Selves*: "I don't think we can be engaged by the human other in such a way that they can cease to be an object for us. In our psyche we will always be unconsciously or consciously objectifying them. But the 'other,' the human other, in particular, does have a profound subjective effect upon us; in the sense that our subjectivity is restructured by their processional effect."

24. De Martino, "The Zen Understanding of the Initial Nature of Man," 35.

25. "Function and Field of Speech and Language," in *Écrits*, 94 (my italics). As an aside, also consider Lacan's reference—in the concluding paragraph of his essay on the mirror stage—to another Eastern tradition, that of the Vedanta, when he writes of "the ecstatic limit of the 'Thou art that.' "

26. De Martino, "The Human Situation and Zen Buddhism," 150.

Bibliography

Bowie, Malcolm. *Lacan*, Cambridge, Mass.: Harvard University Press, 1991.

Camus, Albert. *Youthful Writings* (P. Viallaneix, ed.), New York: Vintage Books, 1977.

De Martino, Richard. "The Zen Understanding of the Initial Nature of Man." Unpublished article derived from chapter 1 of the author's Ph.D. dissertation, *The Zen Understanding of Man*, Philadelphia: Temple University, 1969.

————. "The Zen Understanding of the Fundamental Problem of the Ordinary Man," chapter 2 of above dissertation.

————. "The Human Situation and Zen Buddhism," in *Zen Buddhism and Psychoanalysis*, New York: Harper & Row, 1960.

Jung, Carl G. *Psychology and the East*, Princeton: Princeton University Press, 1978.

Kojeve, Alexandre. *Introduction to the Reading of Hegel*, Ithaca: Cornell University Press, 1969.

Krynicki, Victor. "The Double Orientation of the Ego in the Practice of Zen," *American Journal of Psychoanalysis* 40(3), 1980.

Lacan, Jacques. *Écrits: A Selection* (trans. by Alan Sheridan), New York: W. W. Norton, 1977.

Molino, Anthony, ed. *Elaborate Selves: Reflections and Reveries of Christopher Bollas, Polly Young-Eisendrath, Michael Eigen, Samuel and Evelyn Laeuchli, and Marie Coleman Nelson*, Binghamton, N.Y.: Haworth Press, 1997.

Scheiderman, Stuart. *Jacques Lacan: The Death of an Intellectual Hero*, Cambridge, Mass.: Harvard University Press, 1983.

Thompson, Michael Guy. *The Death of Desire*, New York: New York University Press, 1985.

Wilden, Anthony. *The Language of the Self*, Baltimore: Johns Hopkins University Press, 1968.

THE COUCH AND THE TREE

❏

THE FERTILE MIND

Joseph Bobrow

❏

So . . . there was nothing left for me but to remember the wise saying that there are more things in heaven and earth than are dreamed of in our philosophy. Anyone who could succeed in eliminating his pre-existing convictions even more thoroughly could no doubt discover even more such things.   —FREUD, 1918

> To study the Way is to study the self.
> To study the self is to forget the self.
> To forget the self is to be enlightened by all
>   things of the universe.
>   —DOGEN, in Aitken, 1992

❏

The nature, knowledge, use, and enjoyment of the mind are areas of growing importance in psychoanalysis. Melanie Klein writes of the epistemophilic instinct, the desire to know, reflected in the wish to enter the mother's body and apprehend its contents and treasures from the inside out. The mother's body—nipple, breast, skin, arms; vagina, womb, organs, blood vessels, the blood itself—is one metaphor. The mother's mind, however, is another. We want to know our own mind *and* the other's mind, to keep the other "in mind," and to be kept "in mind" by him or her. A "meeting of minds," however transient, can have particular depth and poignancy.

In this essay, I suggest that the desire for knowledge of the mind of self and other may be broadened to include the desire for direct knowledge of the essential nature of our own life and death, our existence itself, and that of all beings. In Buddhism this is called *bodhicitta,* or aspiration for awakening. In Zen, getting to the heart of the matter, realizing our mind, the body of knowledge, is fundamentally not a matter of inside or outside.

An earlier version of this essay appeared in *Soul on the Couch*, Charles Spezzano and Gerald Gargiulo, eds. (The Analytic Press, 1997). It is reprinted here with the permission of the author, in conjunction with the editors and publisher.

Curiosity about origins is at work here. The question "Where did I come from?" refers, or course, to the intercourse of one's parents, to the womb of the mother, the penis of the father, and the minds of both. The koan* "Show me your original face before your parents were born," speaks to another dimension of human curiosity. Children's questions—"Where do I (or baby brother or sister) come from?" or "I know I came from Mommy and Daddy but where did you, Mommy and Daddy, come from?"—although in part deflective, contain more than a kernel of real inquiry. Our response as parents, "From each of our mommies and daddies," leads us back to the mysteries of the beginnings of time and creation, which are animate in the present.

The notion of mind is evolving dramatically within psychoanalysis. Freud's early formulations, based on the thermodynamic model of the times, wherein there were determinate and determinable causes and quantifiable relations between discrete elements that could be measured in quantifiable terms, have given way to several revisions. The impact of ego psychology, object relations, self-psychological theory, and infant developmental research has led to new models of the mind. Intersubjective models do not view the mind as residing solely in the brain or the psyche of the patient or, for that matter, the analyst. The analyst does not simply stand outside the situation, objectively observe the productions of the subject, and make uncontaminated clinical interventions that result in a change in the subject's mental condition. New developments in how the mind and the analytic situation are construed reflect a fundamental paradigm shift in fields as diverse as biology, cognition, physics, and cosmology. The Zen view of mind, ancient as it is, overlaps with and may help bring into focus, some of these changes in the psychoanalytic view.

The word *sesshin*, a Zen meditation retreat, literally means "to touch the mind." How do we do this? This mind, like the self, is empty. Although this emptiness, also called *shunyata* or the shining void, may sound barren, it is neither anomie nor vacuum, but rather the absence of self as absolute and continuous in time and space. Charged with potential, boundless and without measure, it is the fundamental ground of Zen. In psychoanalysis we can see its action in generative, nondefensive silence, sometimes called

---

* Koans are meditative, metaphorical themes usually drawn from spontaneous, everyday encounters between students and teachers, the folk stories of Zen. A koan is literally a "matter to be made clear." Koans are windows, facilitating discovery of the sacred in the particulars of one's daily experience.

the fertile void, a deep, cooperative mutuality into which pieces can gather, and out of which surprises, discoveries, and new movement emerge. Some think this is the goal of psychoanalysis, some think it underlies its method, free association. Perhaps it is both.

The mind contains nothing absolute, proprietary, or permanent; it is essentially insubstantial. We might say "I am walking, I am loving, I am eating, I am imagining." But is there really a mind *separate from* the activities? Enclosed by the skin? Perhaps pulling the strings: a core motivational nexus driving the machine? Wise teachers are everywhere, would we but recognize them. In *The Gateless Barrier* Robert Aitken Roshi (1990) relates a surprising encounter.

> Te-shan was a well-established scholar who lectured frequently on the Diamond Sutra, an important Mahayana Buddhist text, in Western Szechuan province. He apparently felt threatened by the Zen teaching of realization that is not established on words and was wary of transmission outside tradition. So he traveled several hundred miles south to Hunan province with the avowed purpose of stamping out such heresy.
>
> On the road to Li-chou with its many Zen monasteries, he stopped at a wayside refreshment stand. Here he met a great teacher of Zen who, like others of her sex, the Chinese recorders sadly fail to identify by name. Te-shan didn't pay any particular attention to her, but she discerned the potential of her new customer as he asked for *tien-hsin*. This Buddhist term means "refreshment," but the old woman played with its etymology: "punctuate the mind."
>
> "Your reverence," this wise old woman politely asked, "what sort of literature do you have there in your cart?" . . . "Notes and commentaries on the Diamond Sutra," he replied shortly. The old woman [said] . . . "I hear the Diamond Sutra says, 'Past mind cannot be grasped, present mind cannot be grasped, future mind cannot be grasped.' Which mind does Your Reverence intend to . . . refresh?"
>
> Duh! For all his wisdom, Te-shan was confounded by the old woman. He recognized in a moment that he had been mistaken—not only in overlooking the virtue of the tea seller, but also in his "knowledge" of the sutra. (p. 180)

It is surprising and mysterious that although empty of permanent identity, this mind laughs, weeps, takes the children to school, goes to the bathroom, cooks dinner, makes love, gets lost, and finds its way.

The very insubstantiality of the mind implies and makes possible its complementary feature: interdependence. The image is the Jewel Net of Indra (Cook, 1977; Cleary, 1983). Each of us is a point in a net in which there are mirrors at each knot of a vast web, and each point reflects and contains every other point of the web. This is not unlike the hologram. It is precisely *because* the self and the mind have no absolute substance that we literally make up each other, we are composed by one another. We are all intimately connected, multicentered selves. Thich Nhat Hanh, a Vietnamese Zen teacher, says we "interare," with all beings. This is in the same spirit as Winnicott: we cannot say infant without saying mother, we cannot say mother-baby unit without saying father (because father is part of mother's unconscious). We cannot say "paper" without saying tree, leaves, rain, sun, earth, lumberjack, storekeeper. They are all inherent in the piece of paper. *This* is because *that* is. Buddhists call this *paticca samuppada*, mutual causality, or dependent co-arising.

To come alive is to realize this interpenetration. Neville Symington (1994) uses the felicitous phrase "fertile mutuality" to describe this, and unpacks the ways in which, through our unconscious response to trauma, in our deepest emotional response to ourselves and others, we either self-centeredly repudiate this fertility and encapsulate ourselves, or we embrace it, giving rise to what he calls "the lifegiver."

The Buddha sat in meditation under the bodhi tree until he saw into the nature of human suffering (and of course, his own). Legend has it that at dawn one day he looked up and glimpsed the morning star. Everything fell away and he exclaimed, "I and all beings have at this moment attained the way" (Cleary, 1990). Enlightenment in Zen is simultaneously the enlightenment of bushes and grasses, tadpoles and quasars, ancestors and infants. In realizing our own essential nature, we realize the nature of all things.

A story Stephen Mitchell (1993) tells about taking a walk with his daughter illustrates this point.

When my daughter was about two or so, I remember my excitement at the prospect of taking walks with her, given her new ambulatory skills and her intense interest in being outdoors. However I soon found these walks agonizingly slow. My idea of a walk entailed brisk movement along a road or path. Her idea was quite different. The implications of this difference hit me one day when we encountered a fallen tree on the side of the road, about twenty yards from our house. The rest of the "walk" was spent exploring the fungal and insect life on, under, and around the tree. I remember my sudden realization that these walks would be no fun for me, merely a parental duty, if I held on to my idea of walks. As I was able to give that up and surrender to my daughter's rhythm and focus, a different type of experience opened up to me. I was able to find in that another way for me to be that took on great personal meaning for me. (p. 147)

Not only was Mitchell brought to life in a new way, so was his daughter, delighted I'm sure by the shift, and so were the many creatures in the fallen tree, including the fungi and insects.

Charles Spezzano (1995) quotes Adam Phillips, who referred to the psychological dimension of unconscious affective communication as a "hidden black market," the obscured exchange and mutual composition of our emotional lives. I think the modern technological innovation called the "worldwide web" is *already* palpably and dynamically active, but we are unaware of its activity. In a lecture, Robert Stoller once related a story Ralph Greenson told him about how Greenson "knew" a relative had been in an accident, although the two of them were thousands of miles apart. "The subject was quickly dropped," Stoller said. How do patients know when our silence is retributive, or when our attention has wandered and we are no longer with them in the same receptive way? We know that they know, even if they do not let themselves perceive it. Each of us also knows, each of us communicates affectively in such a way, yet we don't know that we are doing it, nor do we know how. It is *as if* there *were* an actual web: touch here and the message gets across there, instantaneously. Though we often can't decode it, we experience its effects.

In *Emotion and Spirit*, Neville Symington writes of the "unseen emotional action" within and between people. Awareness and transformation in this field *is* the spiritual work of psychoanalysis. While such unconscious activity may not be apparent, it is there, active, and we can and must become aware of it. It is not secret; in fact it takes shape and operates in our daily interactions. What is meant, after all, by the oft heard statement about parenting, "It's not what you say but who you are"? If we are unaware of its activity, as we commonly are, no matter how "enlightened," mature, helpful, and insightful we may be, we remain out of touch and fundamentally encapsulated. We may value our freedom of thought, but unless we become privy to this "web," our freedom itself can function as a prison.

This intimately interdependent field, the fundamental ground of Hua-Yen Buddhism, is described in lyrical detail in the *Avatamsaka Sutra* written about two thousand years ago (Cleary, 1983). It bears an uncanny resemblance to the "intersubjective field" of contemporary psychoanalysis. Neither tradition, of course, holds a patent on it. Whitman was familiar with this web: "I am vast, I contain multitudes," he writes in "Song of Myself." So, in her own way, is a seriously troubled patient of a colleague who said to her analyst: "If I don't have the experience of people in me, and me in them, my life and my death have no meaning. My life is counting on being in you and you in me."

Autonomy and separateness were terrifying and unintegrated for this woman. While we are insubstantial and interconnected creatures, there is still something mysteriously unique and distinctive about our actions, about each point in the net, the mark we leave in our wake, the way distinctive tendencies coalesce as our person. This absolute uniqueness, represented in infinitely rich variety (the *Nirmanakaya*), is, in Buddhist philosophy, one of the three "Bodies of the Buddha," or aspects of awakening, that are embodied in our moment-to-moment, daily life experience. The other two are clarity-emptiness (the *Dharmakaya*) and interdependence-oneness (the *Sambogakaya*). For purposes of discussion, these aspects are distinguished; in deepest experience, they do not oppose each other at all.

BLIND SPOTS

It is a common misconception of meditative practitioners that spiritual practice and insight bring, ipso facto, an exemption from life's emotional vicissitudes and imperfections—ultimate salvation. However, the fruits of either path—psychoanalytic or contemplative—can be hijacked at any point along the way, exploited for motives outside our awareness, and turned into something else. We must ask "In the service of what?" Even insights themselves can obstruct our true emotional activity. Our understanding can become like a frozen and stale intellectual object. Zen practice, while emancipatory in purpose, can itself be used to obscure awareness of what is happening internally and interpersonally, just as analyst and analysand too can collude, ignoring or unconsciously encouraging an obfuscating or deadening process.

A seasoned Buddhist teacher with deep insight into essential nature and a well-developed psychological sensibility makes the point at a seminar that there is fundamentally "nothing to know." As he says so, however, he conveys precisely the opposite: that he *does* know and the others do not. He is not aware this is happening, but others are. A therapist has insight into corruption being a key element in the dynamics of perversion, yet she is totally unaware that her own activities set in motion conditions which undermine the integrity of a clinic where she is a key staff member. A parent complains that his child eats too many sweets; within minutes, completely unaware of any connection to what he just said, the parent fills

up on the candies himself. A group of experienced psychotherapy profes-
sionals meet for a week, with expert facilitation, to iron out interpersonal
tensions. The meeting ends with unanimous agreement as to its efficacy.
Within days, things explode and schisms are rampant.

Symington describes how this process develops in the analytic situation.
For him, understanding—spiritual or psychological—is not an abstract
event, detached from the emotional field between two people. Rather, the
analyst's experience in the analytic field and his interpretive activity become vehicles for bringing into consciousness such split-off psychic activity, much of which he sees as destructive in nature, and for liberating
integrity. Enlightenment and truth here begin with the awareness of this
unconscious emotional activity. Insight, conscience, freedom, and compassion develop in concert.

None of us is exempt. Each new self-representational structure is a discovery and may also become the next blind spot, an obstacle to further
learning. Language helps us to symbolize effectively and creatively as we
live through a mode where "things in themselves" can be concrete and
frightening. This developmental achievement itself, however, can serve to
avoid a deeper encounter with ourselves and our fellows as we actually are,
and with sacred yet surprisingly ordinary "things in themselves."

DEATH, KNOWING, AND ILLUSION

For many, fear of death seems related not only to physical deterioration,
the loss of capacities we've taken for granted, and their psychological impact. It also presents us with the sheer unpredictability and the seeming
randomness of life—the limits of our ability to know. Waiting for the
results of medical tests can evoke this kind of feeling. Helplessness indeed:
magical thinking can return in the most "mature" among us; belief in a
powerful, protective, or at least a *knowing*, deity can appear in the most
hardened of atheists. Buddhism is known as the "Middle Way," originally
a path distinct from both asceticism and blind sensual indulgence. Here
the Middle Way might be the cultivation of a way to be with oneself (and
others) that mitigates the rush either to all-knowing authority worship on
the one hand or to mind-numbing hopelessness and its consequences on
the other.

But death is not simply the passing of this body; we know the body
wears out. Death is there in each lived moment, a gateway. In notes that

were to become an autobiography, Winnicott (1978) wrote: "Oh God! May I be alive when I die." Perhaps accepting and even learning to rest in the not-knowing, in the mystery, is a springboard to wisdom and to the "peace which passeth understanding." I'm reminded of how Bion responded to Grotstein when the latter, in analysis with Bion, said that he thought he understood an interpretation Bion had made. "I was afraid of that," Bion replied (Grotstein, 1995).

It is not simply that spiritual experience (and particularly its cultivation or avoidance, as it were, in much organized religion) is intrinsically obsessive, as Freud thought, though it may be put by an individual or group at the service of obsessional defenses. Rather, obsessiveness and other "defenses," manic and otherwise, can arise in the wake of burgeoning awareness of the immediacy, the vividness, the empty, spacious playground of existence. A colleague was describing the experience of absorbed delight in the presence of the work of Manet. She worried that there might be some omnipotence attached to it. Omnipotence, however, couldn't be further from the experience itself; omnipotence would be the attempt to reproduce at will such an experience, to bring it under one's control.

The nature of the mind and the self in psychoanalysis is explored in the debate about discontinuous versus continuous experience. Mitchell (1993) explores this issue cogently in an essay entitled "On the Illusion of the Experience of a Separate Self," a revised version of which is now called "Multiple Selves, Singular Self." The original title captured a useful tension in the contrasting meanings of "illusion." Illusion, in the Winnicottian sense, is at the heart of play and freedom of mind. Yet the word is also used to describe self-deception. One must have a discrete sense of self to function effectively and to live a fulfilling life, just as one must have, for example, a relatively differentiated body image and developed ego structure. To have a sense of self with threads of continuity to organizing story lines, a sense of historicity is critical. However, upon examination (psychoanalytic or meditative), the structures of the mind, the constellations of me-you patterns through which we construct our experience of the world and ourselves, are far more fluid than we thought; in fact one might say they are illusory.

Charles Fisher (1992) examines the experience of the troubled adolescent and young adult. He suggests: "A sense of identity, defined as inner sameness and continuity, is like a snapshot of a system which is in constant motion. It captures features which are characteristic and familiar, but creates the illusion that we are organized in a more static way than we really are" (p. 454).

It is this very perception, and the experience that comes from it, that can be the springboard for change. And yet, says Mitchell, too much discontinuity may result in dread of fragmentation—"the discontinuities are too discontinuous"—while too much continuity leads to paralysis and stagnation. The fundamental purpose of Zen practice lies not in the balancing of this dialectic tension but in facilitating direct experience of a realm where the distinctions themselves fall away and no longer constrain perception. During the course of Zen practice, as in daily life itself, one can get caught up in, can collapse into, either the world of emptiness or the world of form.

ILLUMINATION AND THE ORDINARY

Self-knowledge or "touching the mind" is, in Zen, the *experience* that dualistic notions such as continuity and discontinuity, self and other, form and emptiness, are not fundamentally separate: not two, not even "one." In the *Heart Sutra* (trans. in Aitken, 1993) we come to the heart of the matter: emptiness *is* form, form *is* emptiness.

The particular is itself the universal. The sacred—the fertile void itself —is reflected in the particular, in each being, as it comes forth anew in each moment. Deep realization of this in the moments of one's daily life brings a change of heart. Hakuin Zenji in the *Song of Zazen* (sitting meditation, Aitken, 1993) writes: "All beings by nature are Buddha as ice by nature is water. Apart from water, there is no ice, apart from beings, no Buddha" (p. 179).

However, like unseen emotional action, this knowledge is obscured from ordinary consciousness. (Bandying around the concepts without integration through practice can lead to self-justificatory mischief: "It's all one, we're all empty, I am Buddha," and so on, can be used to rationalize all manner of narcissistic, ignorant, and cruel behavior.) Our most cherished views of self and other, of our very existence, must give way, must literally fall away. This relinquishment—for Symington the result of an act of freedom, an unconscious choice at the deepest strata of our being in the context of a fertilizing analytic relationship; in Zen the natural fruit of sustained practice, of nonjudgmental, nondualistic attentiveness and deep meditative inquiry—is the core action at the heart of transformational or transcendent experience: both much used but perhaps somewhat trivialized notions these days.

The apparent paradox is that only by "forgetting the self" can we truly come to ourselves, can we come to *experience* the stuff of the self as sacred. Self and object fall away. Yamada Roshi (old teacher), at the time a middle-aged businessman and Zen student, was returning from work in Tokyo one day. While reading a book on the train, he came upon the line "Mind is none other than the mountains and rivers and the great wide earth, the sun, the moon and the stars" (Dogen, in Kim, 1980, p. 148). He had read the words many times before, but they had not come alive for him. Now everything fell away and there was only great laughter. What was so funny? Through an experience of empty infinity we can know *directly* (in contrast to *knowing about*) the personal and the sacred as identical. While habitual and narrow views, including the dualism of deluded and enlightened beings, did fall away for Yamada Roshi, it was less the kind of falling apart which we associate with fragmentation and dread than it was a *falling into fertility*. Meister Ekhart said: "The eye with which I see God is the very same eye with which he sees me." Soen Sa Nim, a Korean Zen teacher, used to say: "God is always calling but the phone is busy." I might add that she doesn't give a name when she calls. You can try to pick up the message later, but it is like reheating cold coffee.

Our personal experience is not extinguished, but rather is enriched in the realm of time and space, meaning, purpose, intention, choice, responsibility. We reinhabit the world of coming and going, shopping, getting to work, and feeding the baby. And we are the same, but not the same. "Singing and dancing are the voice of the *Tao*" (the awakened Way), writes Hakuin. And not only singing and dancing, but weeping and feeling angry. Suffering does not disappear forever. It is rather that *our relation to suffering is subverted*. No cessation of suffering or unending *Nirvana* takes its place, as some think the Buddha's teaching in the Four Noble Truths on suffering and the ending of suffering implies. Rather, just as I see, just as I hear, just as I feel, that's it! The fog has cleared, the internal mediatory dialogue has sloughed off, and the vividness can shine through, born of neither subject nor object, yet right in the midst of, and *as*, the very "obstruction" itself. Obstructions do not permanently vanish; it is simply that when they arise, they no longer obstruct. Thought, imagery, affective and sensory experience, memory, personal history, and meaning do not disappear forever. As Hakuin writes: "This very place is the Lotus land, this very body, the Buddha." Rather than being buffeted around, we are "coming and going, never astray."

With understanding of the emptiness, oneness, and uniqueness of the mind comes a sense of freedom and, simultaneously, compassion for all beings. Things have been turned on their axis, and each moment, each being—including the one right here, with this particular birthdate, birthplace, these particular parents, this particular gender, skin color, height, weight—each one just as it is, in its very ordinariness, its good, bad, and ugliness, is infinitely precious. The other is none other than myself and yet, simultaneously is completely other: distinct, unique, sacred. All beings, animate and inanimate, are none other than the multicentered mind itself. We can see how this contrasts with the collapsed, concrete, "things in themselves" of Melanie Klein's paranoid-schizoid position.

LIBERATION ON TWO TRACKS

I became interested in the interplay between and possible integration of psychoanalysis and Zen practice as I realized, over the years, that these two paths of inquiry, understanding, and healing spoke to discrete yet cross-fertilizing capacities and activities of the mind. My sense, however, is that we can't really "get it together"; it *is* together. Articulating how this is so, and not altogether so, is the enjoyable and perhaps impossible challenge.

Early on, a dream helped. I was preparing to return to Hawaii (where I had studied Zen and founded a nursery school) after some years on the East Coast, where I was finishing my graduate studies. I awoke one morning with a dream: "East, West, Center." My associations were first to the East-West Center, a facility at the University of Hawaii which my Zen teacher had helped direct earlier in his career. Then there was a temporal association: I had first been in the Far West, then in the East, and now I was going to stop off in San Francisco for my orals. Next, there was a spatial one: East (Cambridge and New York), West (Hawaii), Center (San Francisco). Then it occurred to me that I'd just finished my studies in Western psychology and was returning to complete studies in Eastern meditative practice. These associations were interesting but incomplete. My attention drifted, and after a minute or so, it hit me: East, West (two streams) and center! But in this moment, the "center," such as it was, was no longer a theoretical integration of a dialectic but an experience curiously unidentified with, yet not strictly separate from, myself. Further, the "East" and the "West" (as separate entities) seemed to have long since gone! Recently, nearly twenty years after this dream, I realized something I had not been aware of. During a class on dreams, it dawned on me all of a sudden, yet as if I had always known it, that the dream also represented my reworking of conception, birth, and differentiation from parents who had spent time separately on opposite coasts of the country. This may illustrate what I referred to earlier as the multidirectional continuum of curiosity about origins, in both its personal-historical and its more broadly existential aspects.

The clarifying and ongoing integration of the sacred with the personal, the ineffable with the affectively human, is a lifelong task, as is, in its own way, the integration of insight and new experience into the human character in an analysis, and in our (often unaddressed but inevitable) postanalysis lives. "The challenge of course," writes Mitchell, "is to find a way to integrate the depths of self experience discovered in the 'unreal' analytic situation into the 'realities' of ordinary life" (p. 148). The parallel in Zen training is: How is insight into life and death, *gnosis*, the fruit of meditative practice on and off the cushion, lived in the hurly-burly of everyday life? Life ensures there is no shortage of opportunities.

Although the key unconscious decision may involve, as Bion wrote, whether or not to evade frustration, and although this inner work is painful, unpredictable, and never how we imagined, neither is it just grim. Suffering is not enough. Both paths can be joyful, as implied in Freud's notion of the "playground," Vamik Volkan's "pleasure of knowing" (1995), and Hakuin's "singing and dancing." When afflictions are no other than enlightenment, psychic suffering, though not eliminated, is like the ebb and flow of the tides, illusion and reality like the play of shadows on the ocean, and the waves themselves present the "incredible lightness of being" alive and awake.

The ability to experience ourselves in novel ways is at the heart of successful negotiation, not only of adolescence and young adulthood, as Fisher writes, but of psychoanalysis and life itself, at every point along the developmental spectrum. In Zen, suffering is said to be caused by attachment, *not* attachment to each other, or the attachment of a baby to its parents. Zen scholar and teacher Katsuki Sekida once said: "Nonattachment, all I hear is non-attachment! If you weren't attached you'd be dead!" (Aitken, 1992).

Rather it is our unconscious predilection for protective, sometimes destructive, and always narrow, limiting, and fundamentally illusory views of self and other that lies at the source of our anguish. Becoming aware of how such views permeate our mind, our bodies, our affective and relational experience, our very lives—how they literally constitute and constrain our "identity"—is the beginning of Zen practice.

Jack Engler describes the apparent conflict inherent in the fact that what in psychoanalysis is a developmental achievement—that is, differentiating a separate self (or, we might say, mind)—is in Buddhism the very source of suffering. As Yasutani Roshi, one of the first Zen teachers to come and teach in America, said: "The core delusion is that I am here and you are there." But this, despite being axiomatic in most contemplative traditions, is not quite accurate. I don't think it is the *separate* self (or the autonomous mind), illusory as it is, that is the problem—to the contrary—but rather the habitual, automatic, and tenacious attachment to constricting versions of such a self and its relations to others that informs and shapes our experience and behavior.

Engler concludes with the notion that "one must have a self before one loses it," a notion that has gained much popular currency. That is to say, from an expanded developmental perspective, both are achievements, but having a self precedes letting go of the self. I suggest, however, that the two are not mutually exclusive; nor are they simply sequentially related. Rather, we must *both* have (create) *and* not have (lose, destroy, see into) a self. Further, we must struggle with, ultimately accept, and hopefully come to enjoy their differentiation, their interpenetration, their necessary though incomplete integration, and their falling away in each moment of fresh, lived experience.

Rather than having to construct a self *before* we can discover no self, as Engler suggests, I think it *takes* a (distinctive, personal) self to fully embody our essential (no-self) nature. And as one unravels, experiences, and realizes the empty, multicentered nature of all beings and of consciousness itself, the (particular, personal) self and its unique qualities are potentiated, brought to life and fruition. This seems closer to the experience of contemporary psychoanalysis, to the edge of current meditative practice, and to life itself.

References

Aitken, Robert (1990). *The Gateless Barrier (Wu-men Kuan)*. Translated and with commentary by Robert Aitken. New York: North Point Press.

———. (1992). *Zen Talks, Essays and Prefaces*. Honolulu: Honolulu Diamond Sangha.

———. (1993). *Encouraging Words*. New York: Pantheon.

Cleary, Thomas (1990). *Transmission of Light (Denkoroku)*. Translated and with an Introduction by T. Cleary. San Francisco: North Point Press.

———. (1983). *Entry into the Inconceivable*. Honolulu: University of Hawaii Press.

Cook, Francis (1977). *Hua-yen Buddhism*. Philadelphia: University of Pennsylvania Press.

Engler, Jack (1986). "Therapeutic Aims in Psychotherapy and Meditation: Developmental Stages in the Representation of the Self," in K. Wilber, Jack Engler, and D. Brown (eds.). *Transformations in Consciousness*. Boston: Shambhala.

Fisher, Charles (1992). "Beyond Identity: Invention, Absorption and Transcendence." *Adolescent Psychiatry* 18: 448–60.

Freud, Sigmund (1918). "From the History of an Infantile Neurosis." *Standard Edition*, 17:12. London: Hogarth Press, 1955.

Grotstein, James (1995). From a seminar on psychoanalytic technique, April 1995. Psychoanalytic Institute of Northern California.

Kim, Hee-Jin (1980). *Dogen Kigen—Mystical Realist*. Tucson: University of Arizona Press.

Mitchell, Stephen (1993). *Hope and Dread in Psychoanalysis*. New York: Basic Books.

Spezzano, Charles (1995). "How Psychoanalysts Learn." Paper delivered at a symposium at the Psychoanalytic Institute of Northern California entitled "What Is Contemporary about Contemporary Psychoanalysis?"

Symington, Neville (1994). *Emotion and Spirit*. New York: St. Martin's Press.

Volkan, Vamik (1995). From a seminar on the psychoanalytic treatment of narcissism. Psychoanalytic Institute of Northern California, January 15, 1996.

PARADOX

John R. Suler

❏

THE MEANINGS OF PARADOX

A paradox is a statement or behavior that is seemingly inconsistent, absurd, or self-contradictory, yet in fact true. As a derivative of the Greek *para* (contrary) and *dokein* (think), it signifies a countering of reason. It thrusts one, literally, into "nonsense" by challenging common sense and violating one's basic assumptions about reality. Many paradoxes embody the self-contradiction that arises when a statement implicitly turns back and reflects on itself, asking whether or not it is to be taken as an example of the idea it proposes. The classic example is, "Everything I say is a lie." If the statement is an example of the idea it asserts, it negates itself as it affirms itself. Paradoxical injunctions such as, "Disobey me!" turn disobeying into obeying and obeying into disobeying when the command turns back and enlists itself as an example of its own directive.

This self-contradiction arising from the action of the self attempting to

This essay is taken, in its entirety, from the author's *Contemporary Psychoanalysis and Eastern Thought* (State University of New York Press, 1993). It is reprinted here with the permission of the publisher.

grasp or reflect on itself may take the form of a paradoxical conflict between different levels of self-examination. Hofstadter (Hofstadter & Dennett, 1981) gives the example of the statement "This sentence contains one error." On a manifest level, it is incorrect because there are no errors— but on a deeper level it is correct because it is incorrect in the estimation of its error, which in turn shows that it is in error, and so on. It is simultaneously both correct and incorrect. The paradoxical self-contradiction is rooted in the interpenetrating opposition of self-representations. The existence of the paradox itself points to the existence of these different and disparate layers of self-representation.

Hofstadter suggests that paradoxes are the consequence of a long-recognized dilemma: An object bears a special and unique relationship to itself. It is restricted in its ability to act on itself in the way it acts upon all other objects. A pencil cannot write on itself; a fly swatter cannot swat itself; people cannot directly see their own faces. Hofstadter (Hofstadter & Dennett, 1981) concluded:

> We can come close to seeing and understanding ourselves objectively, but each of us is trapped inside a powerful system with a unique point of view—and that power is also a guarantor of limitedness. And this vulnerability—this self-hook—may also be the source of the ineradicable sense of "I" (p. 278).

In Zen Buddhist training, paradoxes known as koans are presented to students to stimulate their progress toward satori, the state of enlightenment. The student must produce a solution to the puzzle even though there seems to be no logical answer. Some koans are one-liner questions: What is the sound of one hand clapping? When the many are reduced to the one, to what is the one reduced? Without using your mouth, body, or mind, express yourself. Show me your face before your parents were born.

Other koans are presented as a paradoxical situation that challenges the student to determine its solution or meaning:

- A monk asks the master if a dog has a self. The master replies, "Mu!" (which translates as "not" or "none," or perhaps more accurately as the prefix "un" or "non").
- A man dangles over a deep precipice, hanging only by his teeth that clench the root of a tree. A Zen master appears and asks, "What is your true self?"
- A master holds a staff above the head of his student. "If you say this is a staff I will strike you. If you say it isn't a staff I will strike you. If you say nothing I will strike you."

- A man grew a goose in a bottle until it became too big to stay inside. If the bottle is smashed it will kill the goose. If nothing is done, the goose will smother.

Psychotherapists in the West, particularly adherents of the strategic or paradoxical schools (e.g., Haley, 1963; Seltzer, 1986; Weeks, 1985), often cite Zen koans as an example of how immersing a person into paradox can culminate in therapeutic insight and relief from symptoms. Yet few studies have focused specifically on the application of the koan and the underlying Zen psychology of paradox as a model for understanding psychotherapy. Such a focus can reveal the various elements of paradoxical self-contradictions that underlie psychological transformations—including the shift in one's perspective of reality, the conflict of internal representations and levels of self, the interweaving of self-affirmation and negation, and the puzzling dynamics of the self that turns back to capture, understand, or reflect on itself.

ENTERING THE PARADOX

For no apparent reason, a bright student miserably fails an entrance exam into graduate school. A patient who frequently cancels sessions claims that her psychotherapy is not going deep enough, so she wants to come every other week. Like a character from a Woody Allen film, a lonely man states that he would never join any organization that would have him as a member. By pointing out these self-contradictory behaviors, the therapist presents to the patient a paradox that seems to violate logic and common sense. These patients are disputing themselves by presenting an idea and then countering that idea, all in one breath—as if they have taken both sides in an argument in which the distinction between the subject and object is unclear. Although it may disturb the person to realize he or she is knotted into a self-contradiction, this personal paradox, similar to the koan, entices curiosity, for the person realizes there is more going on below the surface than meets the eye. By stepping back into the observing self to see him- or herself entangled in paradox, the patient gets his or her first alluring scent of a dispute between different layers of selfhood. As Kapleau (1980) stated, the koan is like candy to coax a reluctant child, to stimulate the thirst for realization. Observing the dilemma from an objective viewpoint allows the patient to feel its outer shape and texture, yet quickly realize that this approach is insufficient. To untangle the knot of self-contradiction, the patient must enter right into it.

The patient's initial advance on the paradox typically involves the attempt to unravel it intellectually. But the paradox ultimately frustrates and cracks open any rational attempt to resolve it, for the solution is not logical. The koan has no answer; the answer is to be something different. The solution is an experience. As sophisticated as the person's intellectualizations may be, they are an illusion, a defense. Rational explanations meet only silence or another question from the therapist and a nonsensical retort or flat-out rejection from the Zen master, as in the response "Mu!" At first this situation amplifies the person's attempts to grip it logically, cognitively. The struggle for a solution becomes an ordeal of "figuring out," a crisis of thinking that lasts as long as the person persists in cogitating an answer. The teacher has led the student down a blind tunnel, to the edge of a precipice, where the realization that intellect will not suffice forces the student to make a quantum leap out of it. Consistent with the principle of both psychoanalysis and Eastern philosophy that "intellect is a good servant but a bad master" (Watts, 1958), the koan sets a trap that breaks the back of rationality. And, as Kopp (1976) stated, one cannot get out of a trap until one first gets into it.

The crisis generated by the paradox quickly spreads into realms of one's personality other than the intellect. During the Zen student's meditation on a koan and the therapy patient's contemplation of a personal paradox, a variety of conflicting affects, ideas, and memories surface. The paradox is a digging, churning tool that penetrates directly into the roots of who we are. Multiple components of one's self structure are jostled, loosened, forced to the surface. During meditation, conflicting layers of self-representation often take the form of vivid, almost hallucinatory images known in Zen as *makyo*. The paradox becomes all-consuming; one's whole being enters it. The self is at war with itself as the conscious and unconscious realms clash. Even the koan, which started off as a benign brain teaser that seemed external to oneself, now becomes the center of a desperate struggle around personal issues. The sane and irrational reasons that led the student to Zen are uncovered and questioned. The problems of one's life are uncovered and questioned. The koan is a struggle for one's very existence. One becomes the self in contradiction with itself. "He feels like a man seeking something he has forgotten, something he has to remember at any cost, because his life depends on it" (Herrigel, 1960, p. 43).

The student has entered the stage of the Great Doubt, which corresponds to the dark nights of psychotherapy when despair, hopelessness, and exhaustion prevail. Kapleau (1980) uses the analogy of taking away a blind man's staff and spinning him around. The person is confused by and doubts everything—her- or himself, the teacher, the validity of the learning process. As stated in Zen: "Rivers are no longer rivers; mountains no longer mountains."

One has reached an internal deadlock. The koan, according to Zen lore, becomes a "red-hot iron ball stuck in one's throat." Like repeating the same word over and over again until it loses its meaning, this stage marks a satiation effect, where the prolonged focus on self-contradiction brings one to the brink of cognitive and perceptual freezing, disintegration, and reorganization (Kubose & Umemoto, 1980). Gestalt therapists called it the *impasse* (Perls, 1976), whereas psychoanalytic theorists described it as a form of nonbeing, a stage of hesitation, where patients block and there is nothing to be said or done (Bion, 1963; Winnicott, 1971). It is the condition of catastrophe and oblivion, the surfacing of the no-self that grounds existence. It is the intrapsychic tangle of doubt, confusion, and crisis that precedes the religious conversion experience. Watts (1975a) told the story of a psychiatrist who asked a Zen master how he deals with neurotic people. "I trap them," he said. "And how do you do that?" the psychiatrist replied. "I get them where they can't ask any more questions." Haidar Ansari spoke similarly of a voice in the night that whispered to him, "There is no such thing as a voice whispering in the night!"

From this deadlock of the Great Doubt springs a sudden insight that expands one's perspective of reality. The old assumptions and perceptions of oneself and the world—one's "old hometown" (Mountain, 1983) —are recognized as illusions and are discarded. For the Zen student, it is a clearer, broader view of the ontology of self and other. So, too, it is for the psychotherapy patient, although the insight specifically reveals the unconscious transferential and parataxic distortions that warp one's day-to-day perceptions of self and other. The bright college student realizes he sabotaged his exam because he fears his success will enrage and destroy his father. The patient who wants more from therapy and cancels her sessions realizes she dreads where the therapy is leading her and how her therapist will react to what they discover. The man who rejects any organization that would have him as a member discovers that he really hates himself.

The self-contradiction that led to insight loses its grip. The double bind forces the person outside the previous frame of reference, expands the individual's model of the world, "decontextualizes" the seemingly paradoxical symptom (Osmer, 1981; Seltzer, 1986). The koan and the patient's personal paradox now can be left behind, like discarding a brick that was used to knock open a jammed door or a tissue that was used to blow one's nose and clear the head (Suzuki, 1956; van de Wetering, 1978). The paradox was a finger pointing to the moon. It indicated a direction; it motioned toward another, deeper level of the self, something unverbalizable. It pointed to the unconscious.

The cracking open of the double-binding self-contradiction and the insightful reframing of one's crisis can only occur if, in the words of Zen, one "lets go of the hold" which corresponds to the Taoist principle of *wu wei*. One must let things happen of their own accord. Theories about paradoxical therapy (Frankl, 1967; Haley, 1963; Seltzer, 1986; Weeks, 1985) have documented how a person's desperate attempts to control or eliminate a problematic behavior only perpetuate and exaggerate the symptom. The insomniac who tries to force himself to sleep never will; the phobic who worries about avoiding an anxiety attack inadvertently triggers it. The paradoxical intervention amplifies the problem until the person, reaching the limits of exhaustion and despair, finally lets go of it, allowing change to be spontaneous. Old concepts, rationalizations, and perspectives are swept away, creating space for a transformation.

So, too, the psychotherapy patient and the koan student are caught in a paradoxical dilemma: The harder they try for spontaneity, insight, or enlightenment, the less likely they will achieve it. Like the student who is confronted by the Zen master's staff, they are caught in *samsara*, the action of the grasping self that tries to get "one up" (Watts, 1975a) on something that cannot be consciously grasped. When a martial arts student asked his *sensei* how long it would take for him to become a master, the *sensei* replied, "Ten years." The student seemed disturbed. "I can't wait that long. What if I work twice as hard, come to every class, and practice every day—how long then?" "Twenty years," the *sensei* replied.

Even the attempt not to grasp is just another form of grasping that blocks spontaneity and fulfillment. Compulsive people who force themselves to play never have fun. Meditators who try hard not to focus their attention on anything in particular are focusing their attention on not-focusing, resulting in poor meditation. Conscious attempts to let go and let things happen miss the mark of the spontaneous, willing self. As noted by James (1960) in his studies of religious conversion and by Kris (1952) in his work on the creative process, the final trigger for an experiential breakthrough is an unself-conscious self-surrender, a relinquishing of control to the unconscious, to something beyond the conscious self. The tendency to cling to one's illusions and symptoms because they are familiar, out of a fear of the unknown, must be bypassed. Desperately hanging on the edge of the precipice, one must simply let go. Paradoxically, losing oneself is finding oneself.

PARADOXES WITHIN AND BETWEEN

Similar to exploring the koan in Zen training, psychotherapy probes the paradoxes of human nature, although the insights usually center specifically on the paradoxical aspects of emotional disturbances and psychological change, rather than on the deeper ontological aspects of selfhood. As noted by the strategic therapists (Seltzer, 1986; Weeks, 1985) and by Freud in his concept of the neurotic paradox, attempts to cope with one's problems often perpetuate them through anticipatory anxiety and other cyclical, self-fulfilling mechanisms. A woman with an avoidant personality so desperately wants to be loved that she cannot tolerate the possibility of being rejected, so she avoids other people, which makes her even more lonely and desperate for love. Because a paranoid man thinks other people are out to hurt him, he acts critical and hostile, which makes others want to hurt him. Psychoanalytic theory also has clarified how symptoms are compromise formations that are both adaptive and maladaptive, that simultaneously reveal and conceal the unconscious, resulting in a paradoxical meshing of seemingly contradictory ideas and affects. Obsessive-compulsives are controlled by their desire not to be controlled, masochists use helplessness to be powerful. Haley (1963) suggested that determining who is responsible for these symptoms becomes a metaparadox atop the paradox of the symptom itself. Your parents may be blamed, but they couldn't help themselves; you, too, are not to blame because you also are driven by your unconscious—but in therapy you are expected to take control of it. A patient once complained that he was not responsible for his problems because it was his unconscious that caused them. Capturing the paradoxical essence of human nature, the therapist responded, "Whose unconscious is it, anyway?" Finally, consistent with Eastern philosophy, psychoanalysis reveals how even reality and fantasy are paradoxically intertwined, how a simple memory is both truth and self-deception.

Although these self-contradictions are relevant mostly to the psychotherapy context and may only be peripheral issues to the Zen student, they do tap the more fundamental paradox that is the essence of the koan and the underlying Taoist philosophy of yin and yang: that human nature, in fact all of nature, embodies the balance, inseparability, and interpenetration of opposites. This principle became a key feature of Jung's theory of personality and was also implied by Freud—as in, for instance, his concept of ambivalence, that contradictory emotions are two aspects of the same attachment to a significant other and therefore exist side by side in the unconscious. The personal paradox in psychotherapy is the self-contradiction resulting from only one side of the ambivalence being conscious, whereas the other remains unconscious, with the two disparate levels of self in conflict with each other. Within the intrapsychic world, A and not-A do not mutually exclude each other. Psychological dynamics violate Aristotelian logic, which is why the koan is designed to break intellectualization. Instead, human nature follows a form of "paradoxical logic" (Fromm, Suzuki, & DeMartino, 1960) or "dialectics" (Seltzer, 1986; Weeks, 1985) in which all ideas, affects, and behaviors generate their opposites and demand a resolution. The concept of the unconscious itself embodies paradox: Its very essence is the negation of consciousness ("unconscious"), and yet, according to classical theory, the unconscious itself does not negate contradictions and does not even know of "no."

The self is a complex, changing constellation of forces, properties, and relationships. Paradoxes within it abound. The variety of interpretations and interventions that constitute psychotherapy—which often are forgotten by the patient, even though they were entirely effective—probe these various paradoxes within the realm of the individual's unique personality dynamics. Koans, which also are set aside once they have fulfilled their usefulness, reveal the underlying, more universal paradoxes within the ontological realm of self and other. But these realms of the personal and universal, following the course of the yin and yang, are intertwined. The individual personality is rooted in the deeper ontology of self, and the ontology of self achieves expression through the individual personality. Realization of paradox on one level invariably affects the other. Drawing on the works of Jung, Federn, Winnicott, and Bion, Eigen (1986) masterfully uncovered these paradoxes or "reversals," as he called them, which fuel the conflicts of the individual and sink to the deeper self/other ontology—paradoxes of hate and love, unity and chaos, boundaries and fusion. These are the paradoxes that spring from the "psychotic core" within everyone, the core touched by Zen training and intensive psychoanalysis.

The paradoxes within the individual dovetail into the paradoxes between self and other. People use symptoms to place others into self-contradictory double binds; they attempt to control or get "one up" on others without openly acknowledging the fact that they are attempting to control (Haley, 1963). These double binds often take the form of implicit or explicit demands for spontaneity and genuineness, such as, "You ought to love me," "Don't be so obedient," or "You should enjoy this" (Jichaku, Fujita, & Shapiro, 1984). In psychotherapy the person plays out these paradoxical strategies to control the therapeutic relationship, often placing the therapist in a damned-if-you-do/damned-if-you-don't, goose-in-the-bottle dilemma. For example, if the therapist agrees to the patient's request to come less often, she may feel rejected and quit therapy; if the therapist suggests that the patient come every week, she may feel pressured and quit therapy. Like the koan, interpreting this predicament points the patient to the unconscious, where deeper, conflicted aspects of self contradict the conscious mind and gave birth to the paradox.

In their relationship with patients, therapists amplify the paradoxes of control, spontaneity, and genuineness to the point where the patient relinquishes attempts to be one up and discovers genuine spontaneity (Haley, 1963; Seltzer, 1986; Watts, 1975a). The therapeutic context creats a variety of such double binds. The clinician stands for autonomy, maturity, and independence, but encourages dependency and regression. Therapy is supposedly voluntary, but missed appointments are interpreted as resistance. The therapist directs the patient to control the therapy session, but makes it appear that he or she is not being directive at all and that everything is the patient's initiative. In fact, the therapist's attempts not to influence the person become a profound form of influence that invariably directs the patient into the unconscious. Most of these interpersonal double binds seem to apply specifically to psychoanalysis, although Seltzer suggests that elements of paradox exist in all therapies. Clinicians are both detached and intimate; they want to help patients change and accept them as they are; the path to cure requires the patient to express and sometimes exaggerate the symptom (the regression, in psychoanalysis, that is essential for progression). In their most intense form, the simultaneously frustrating and gratifying contradictions of the therapy context, which often occur on different levels of communication, cause a disruption of reality testing and create the feeling that one is losing one's mind, being destroyed, or being engulfed by the other (Searles, 1965).

The relationship between Zen student and master also captures these paradoxes about control, authority, and spontaneity. The student believes that the master is implicitly demanding, "Be enlightened!"—which is as paradoxical as the therapist apparently demanding, "Be genuine and spontaneous!" Like the therapist, the master refuses to give any answers and throws back the student's question with a terse "Mu!"—which frustrates the student to the point of crisis and self-disintegration. And yet the master is also a reassuring presence, the authority whose very existence proves that an answer exists, who acts as a container and holding environment for the student's psychological and spiritual storm. The master is the teacher, but "Zen has nothing to teach." If the student says the staff is or is not a staff, or says nothing, the master will strike the student. What can the student do? The staff, the Zen symbol of control and authority, is elusive, unnameable. Who is responsible for one's situation in life, for one's psychological and spiritual problems? Who is responsible for having an insight? At the peak of this interpersonal paradox, if the student can let go of his illusions about self and other, about who controls whom and who gives insight to whom, then the source of spontaneity and genuineness is revealed.

The koan and the personal paradox in therapy are always a question. The student and patient look to the master and therapist for an answer. But the request is turned back. Asking the question implies that the person already has the answer. Turning back the question reveals its source: The source of the question is within the questioning—within the illusive, willing self. When the insight occurs, the person knows it with certainty; acknowledgment from the authority figure is superfluous. The issue of control and authority is largely superfluous. The Zen student could seize the staff from the master, affirming that he ultimately is the authority on himself and responsible for himself, his spontaneity, his insights. Although this is indeed true, the path of the koan runs even deeper than this.

BEYOND WITHIN AND BETWEEN

Zen training points to a state of mind that transcends paradox, that is beyond the notions of "within" and "between" individuals. This state transcends the paradoxical futility of the self that attempts to step back and objectively grasp or gain insight into itself. It moves beyond the consciousness of a distinction between self and other. It is the conscious mind that has no object as the target of its awareness.

The koan moves one in this direction through the act of negation or renunciation. As a paradox, it both affirms and negates the affirmation. When asked if a dog has a self, the master's reply, "Mu!" undoes and negates the concepts of dog, true nature, and "having," as well as undoes or un-asks the question itself. It negates the questioner, just as the master turns away from the questions, ideas, feelings, and other bits of self that the student offers as a solution to the koan. The crisis through which the koan leads the person entails the stripping away, piece by piece, of the layers to the personality until one experiences a "dropping out of the bottom of the self" (Sato, 1968). The act of negating is the act of letting go of one's old ideas and attainments, a letting go of one's own identity.

Paradox is the fuel that drives the deautomatizing and retraversing of the self-as-structure through the activation of the observing self. In Zen training and psychotherapy, attaining insight is becoming aware of the various self-contradictory qualities of one's behavior, personality, defenses, thought patterns. In Zen one even becomes aware of the self-contradictory situation of knowing you are thinking, attending, and remembering without being able to know or grasp the "you" who is thinking, attending, and remembering. Stripping away each psychological and ontological layer, a string of paradoxes drives one deeper and deeper into the source of the self. One comes to recognize that all the features of the object self—including self and object representations, thoughts, attention, memory—are not the core self. Transcending these features of the self-as-structure is the observing self that is conscious of these features but which cannot be observed itself—the self that is featureless, without boundaries or content. Frankl (1967) described this phenomenon as the self that detaches from symptoms through the technique of paradoxical intention, that leaves the psychological plane and enters the "noological" space where new meanings and attitudes about one's symptoms can be chosen freely. To instruct the phobic patient to deliberately pump up an anxiety attack will pop him out of the anticipatory anxiety that created the symptom—will make him fail at the task and even laugh at himself as he steps back and, with a sigh of relief, observes his paradoxical dilemma. In psychoanalysis, the excitement and even elation that patients experience when they gain insight into their conflicts spring from the sense of freedom associated with the activation of the observing self. Paradox forces one to step back to a position of wider scope, like stepping out of a mud field to see where you are headed. Self-contradictory behaviors are seen in a new light, are reframed. From this new perspective, there no longer is the feeling that one is trapped within the paradox, but rather the sense that one has encompassed the paradox. Fresh, informed actions—free will—now seem possible. Centered within this illusive observing and willing self, one feels stabilized, unfettered. One experiences that distinctive yet ungraspable sense of "I-ness."

While clearing one's head through koans in Zen training and personal paradoxes in therapy, one encounters the same questions. Who is it that has this conflict, that symptom? Who is it that experiences this anxiety, this crisis, this paradox? Paradoxes point to deeper layers of the personality and highlight the opposing polarities of the self, but they also point to a place where one can be free from these aspects of the object self and live within the observing self that stands beyond the paradox. The observing self is the origin of the possibility for having a new perspective, of being able to see past the illusions and distortions of the object self. Zen compares this self to a mirror that reflects but is not altered by the act of reflecting. It is your face before your parents were born, your expression of who you are without using your mouth, body, or mind.

The final paradox in Zen, which points to the observing self in its purest form, is the state of mind in which the observing self observes itself, which cannot be observed. This is the consciousness of consciousness that has no content, the awakening in the unconscious, a consciousness of nothing, as occurs when two mirrors face each other and when the eye sees itself. It is the true self in its most pristine state—the no-self and no-mind, a state of emptiness, void, enlightenment that holds absolute freedom and is replete with possibility and potential. Total negation paradoxically leads to complete affirmation, for the chipping away of the self by the koan allows the koan to sink to the level of being and willing in the purest form. This true self that is no-self is a state of completeness, the sound of one hand clapping, the place to which the one returns that transcends all polarities, contradictions, and paradoxes of the self: good/bad, unity/disunity, assertion/denial, being/nonbeing. The goose is out of the bottle, and the bottle is unbroken.

This no-self also transcends the distinction between self and other that is the illusion of the rationalizing, discriminating mind. The koan reveals that the world is an interdependent whole, that the self is that whole, and that the self/other duality is an illusion. Separation is experienced within union and union within separation. This insight helps one transcend the crippling, paradoxical message imposed by society: You are independent, but you must not be so independent that you realize you are not independent (Watts, 1975a). The very act of resolving the koan forces the person to abandon the subject/object dichotomy. "The inability of the koan to be resolved as an object by the ego as subject is, in fact, precisely the inability of the ego as ego in its subject-object bifurcation to resolve the existential contradiction which is that bifurcation" (Fromm, Suzuki, & DeMartino, 1960). Only when the self becomes its innermost contradiction does it become subjectless and objectless. In a more down-to-earth style, Watts (1975b) framed the subject/object paradox in terms of the dilemma frequently experienced in science. As we study the world, we continually uncover more questions than we discover solutions—as if the world is running away from us. But what is it that always retreats when you try to pursue it? Yourself.

Expressed in classic Buddhist terms, this most basic paradox is the paradoxical inseparability of relative and absolute truths. Relative truth—the protocol of logic, distinctions, cause and effect—guides our everyday, conventional experience of ourselves and the world. Relative truth is the life of the individual and the dynamics of the individual mind. Absolute truth is the vision of unity—of the emptiness—that binds the collection of relative truths. It is the universal mind that transcends cause and effect, conditions, and categories. However, even though the absolute transcends and contains the relative, the relative and absolute are identical; hence the paradox that arises when a class of things is equated with a thing that is a member of that class (Jichaku, Fujita, & Shapiro, 1984). The life of the individual is the life of the universal, as illustrated by Jung in his concept of the collective unconscious, or in the idea that ontological development recapitulates phylogenic development. The individual mind is the universal mind, the particular is the general. If not, how could psychoanalysis derive any "laws" of intrapsychic dynamics, or physics derive any laws of nature?

By emphasizing the no-self and the mystical union of self and other, Zen seems to depart from Western psychotherapy. Many writers have stated that psychotherapy is not designed to produce enlightenment. However, as I have discussed previously elsewhere, there are many indications that in-depth psychotherapy taps and utilizes the pregnant emptiness and self/other dissolution that is the state of no-self. Although they use a variety of technical and not so technical terms—such as unconscious, undifferentiated ego matrix; symbiotic oneness; fertile void; blanking out; or simply "holes"—many therapists describe how their patients often contact an inner emptiness, oblivion, or boundlessness. Dangling over the abyss, frightened by it, they may at first attempt to fill the void with talking, acting out, materialism, or more symptoms; but eventually they discover that the dive into this emptiness reveals it as the source of insight, possibility, and spontaneity. When asked to show your true self, giving the answer means letting go and falling into this emptiness.

As a state of mind in which the self/other barrier dissolves, boundlessness becomes the source of empathy and the transformational merging of patient and therapist. This is revealed in the story of the Zen master whose first insight was his recognition that everyone he met had his own face. So too the psychotherapy patient, during the moment of empathic merging with the therapist, realizes the I in the you and the you in the I. The therapist also, in making an empathic interpretation that is truly rooted in his own experience, transcends the paradox of simultaneously forgetting and being aware of himself, of being both the patient and therapist.

The resolution of the personal paradox, like that of the koan, springs from this condition of merging. One must enter that transitional space where separation is a form of union, where the subjective and objective are interpenetrated—an intermediate zone of me-and-not-me that encompasses both external reality and one's own internal capacity to create. Winnicott (1971) thought of this transitional phenomenon as a stepping-stone to separation and individuation. The koan and the personal paradox in therapy are types of transitional objects that serve as stepping-stones in the opposite direction of separation and individuation. They lead to the no-self that counterpoises and highlights one's separation and individuation.

Like the koan, all forms of intensive psychotherapy deal directly or indirectly with the fear of the loss of self, whether it takes the form of anxiety about personal loss or injury, separation, or, ultimately, death. After all, the most basic paradox is that we are all born to die and that death gives life meaning. In his analysis of the existential therapies, Yalom (1980) discussed how death anxiety is a primary source of psychopathology and how "boundary" experiences, which involve the temporary loss of self, produce powerful psychological transformations. Paradoxically, psychological well-being and the integrity of self are generated from the oscillation and interpenetration of self and no-self. Through the act of negation, the crisis of self, and letting go, the paradox immerses the individual into this existential awareness. A Chinese allegory tells of a monk who embarks on a long pilgrimage to find the Buddha. After many years, he crosses a wide river to the land where the Buddha lives. There is a corpse floating on the water. It comes closer. The monk loses all control and wails, for he recognizes the corpse—it is his own. That moment is his liberation.

Here we return to themes from my earlier work, for the most funda-

mental, knowable manifestations of the self express themselves in paradox—the paradoxical dualities of self and no-self, self and other. Neither
self nor no-self, self nor other, alone accounts for who we are. Zen is quick
to point out that we are and aren't at the same time; that when we die
we both die and don't die; that we are both two and one simultaneously.
When we speak of the most basic, graspable expressions of the self, we
must contradict ourselves. The mathematician Gödel once demonstrated
that any sufficiently powerful logical system will eventually lead to a conclusion that cannot be proven true or false within that system, that will
even violate the basic assumptions of the system (see Hofstadter, 1980).
Self-contradiction is intrinsic to any and all entities, including intrapsychic
systems and all facets of selfhood. The primary function of the paradox is
to point to something that lies beyond that entity—something deeper,
more fundamental, a wider frame of reference that includes and surpasses
that entity—something that cannot be named. The paradoxical dualities
of self/no-self and self/other are these pointing fingers that motion toward
the "true" self that can be signified, but not comprehended directly. As
Eigen (1986) stated: "I am but am not my I."

THE PARADOX OF THE WILLING SELF

As an undergraduate student, I attended a university in which the psychology program, a strong bastion of behaviorism, offered little in the way
of psychodynamic or humanistic theory. To expand my education, I felt
compelled to take courses in philosophy, sociology, and religious studies
One of these was an introductory religion course with Thomas Altizer, a
scholar recognized in academia for his philosophy of Christian Atheism,
and known by his students as eccentric and charismatic. With wild, fiery
eyes and graying hair that always appeared windswept—as if he had just
stepped in from a metaphysical storm—he gave me the impression that he
had one foot in this world and the other in a reality that only he understood.

One afternoon I visited him during office hours to discuss my term paper.
The discussion turned to Nietzsche, who, along with Kierkegaard, was his
favorite philosopher. He talked of Nietzsche's vision of the "will to power"
with a conviction and fervor that could inspire even the most stolid of
skeptics. Nevertheless, I decided to raise a doubt. Drawing on my background as a psychology major, I mentioned the established fact that

Nietzsche, toward the end of his life, became schizophrenic (the final outcome of general paresis, a prolonged, untreated syphilitic condition). How, I asked, could we reconcile Nietzsche's philosophy with this fact? How do we take into consideration his being completely mad?

Altizer looked me stright in the eye and replied, "Maybe he willed it."

What exactly did that mean? Isn't that like willing the fact that you have brown eyes, or that there's a tornado in the next county, or that you were born? It didn't make sense. Then again, somewhere in my head, maybe it did—because most things that don't make sense quickly slip away from memory, but this idea stuck with me.

Several years later, in graduate school and during my clinical internship, I learned how to do psychotherapy. My early psychoanalytic training impressed one fact upon me: My patients will do anything to prevent themselves from getting better. They benefit in some paradoxical way from their psychopathology—the phenomenon known as "secondary gain." When I told one supervisor about my difficulty in following what one of my patients talked about, he described how some people unconsciously break connections between their thoughts, causing their ideas to be disjointed, with no overall rhyme or reason to their story. How amazing, I thought at that time, are our patients' strategies to prevent us from understanding and helping them! Of course, such insights are basic tenets of traditional psychoanalysis. In fact, some analysts believe that the essence of treatment is the analysis of the resistance to therapeutic progress.

This philosophy is firmly rooted in Freud's classical model of intrapsychic determinism. All emotions, behaviors, and thoughts are vectors arising from the complex interaction of unconscious drives. They are locked into place. Psychological symptoms, the compromise formations of these dynamics, are also locked in. The person is locked into conflict. There is no free will, no agency in this intricate knot of intrapsychic forces. Only the analyst can untangle the binds and launch the patient toward a new, healthier equilibrium.

But psychoanalytic theory has changed since Freud's time. In object relations theory and especially self psychology, we no longer find this explicit assumption that people are passive victims of jammed, counterbalanced, and redirected intrapsychic energies. Theories that emphasize the self rather than drives as the cornerstone of psychological functioning have reopened the psychoanalytic world's eyes to the vicissitudes of inner agency and volition. Kohut (1977, 1984) described the self as a joyfully experienced, independent center of initiative, a developing, coordinating agent that is the superordinate dynamic of personality structure and functioning. He spoke of a tension arc between one's ambition and ideals—a teleological rather than biological energy that is the core of the self's propulsion through development. Predating Kohut, Rank (1945) labeled even more specifically this "cosmic primal force" that launches the person toward the actualization of autonomy, psychological well-being, and creativity. He called it "will."

The concept of will has a long history in the theories of personality and psychotherapy. Most notable are the works of Leslie Farber (1966), Otto Rank (1945), Rollo May (1969), Viktor Frankl (1969), Silvano Arieti (1972), and Allen Wheelis (1956). In his widely acclaimed book on existential psychotherapy, Yalom (1980) claims that the most basic goal of therapy is to liberate will, which brings choice and responsibility. It is the will to heal and develop, the will to find the meaning and purpose of one's existence. At the most basic level, it is the will to create one's identity: the willing of the self.

The psychoanalytic literature on object relations and self psychology are filled with descriptions of these vicissitudes of will. From his comprehensive research on infant development, Stern (1985) concluded that acquiring a sense of "agency" constitutes a fundamental step in building the core sense of self. In their pioneering work on infants, Mahler, Pine, and Bergman (1975) claimed that the child holds the "lion's share" of responsibility for moving through development. Although the parents' skills, or lack thereof, surely affect the child's evolving sense of self, some children are much stronger, more determined, or willful than others in seeking what they need, even from pathological caretakers. Kohut (1977) similarly noted how children, if thwarted or hurt by one parent in their attempt to develop a cohesive self, will bypass that person to connect to the other parent—and if that person fails, to aunts, uncles, neighbors, or any potentially significant other. Even much later in life, people will reopen old developmental lines and resume building neglected sectors of their self via relationships with new "father" or "mother" figures—a boss, teacher, father- or mother-in-law.

All these theories, implicitly or explicitly, share two basic assumptions about the nature of will. The willing self strives for the creation of a cohesive, harmonious, stable, and unified self structure. It also drives toward connectedness to what is not the self, to the other. Object relations theory and self psychology both maintain that the self's path toward cohesion and integration is achieved through this connectedness, through such processes as mirroring, idealizing, twinning, and internalization. In Plato's *Symposium*, Socrates, too, spoke of the life force, Eros, as the drive toward connectedness to the other—an always open-ended, searching energy that pushes toward higher and higher forms of connectedness, that is, the source of creativity and life.

Yet the path of the willing self is paradoxical. The willing of the self begins and ends at paradox. The intrinsic drive to develop the self, to find its origin, seems to originate from an ungraspable source, from the no-self. Ultimately, this drive leads to the transcendence of self, to the no-self. This movement from and to no-self also follows the paradoxical path of affirming the self via the process of negating it. By activating the observing self through the deautomatization of psychic structure and function, by canceling conscious overthought to actualize internal unity and spontaneity, the negation of self gives birth to its willful affirmation. The movement toward integration and connectedness necessarily entwines with the dimensions of no-self and not-self. At their frontiers contemporary psychoanalytic theory and self psychology have begun to probe this insight. These frontiers mark a transition between psychoanalysis and Eastern thought. The fulfilling of the self entails the opening to the interpenetrating action of no-self. To will the self is to will the negation and transcendence of self. The willing of connectedness culminates in the recognition that, from the start, there never was any disconnectedness.

To immerse oneself into no-self, one must relinquish conscious control of the self. Rooting into the no-self, attaining connectedness and unity with the other, require letting go. Willing the self is spontaneous, unselfconscious abdication. Willing embraces surrender. When you hang over a precipice, holding on only by a tree root clenched between your teeth, the will to speak of your true self is the will to let go of it. Farber (1966) spoke of the conscious experience of will in which we decide and act in the situation at hand, and contrasted this with the deeper, more fundamental realm of will that is unconscious, that we realize only after the act, that provides propulsion but eludes immediate, direct scrutiny. Paradoxically, this primary realm of will is a willing without conscious willing: One must surrender to its action.

> I can will knowledge, but not wisdom; going to bed, but not sleeping; eating, but not hunger; meekness, but not humility; scrupulosity, but not virtue; self-assertion or bravado, but not courage; lust, but not love; commiseration, but not sympathy; congrat-

ulations, but not admiration; religiosity, but not faith; reading, but not understanding (Farber, 1966, p. 15).

Nietzsche's vision of the will to power also is a vision of paradox—the paradox of the self willing its own creation. To return to the source of self, to create the self from chaos and void, to will the self's continuing evolution, one simultaneously becomes both the creator and the created. The subject and object become one. This is the paradox embodied by the immersion into the not-self and no-self. To realize the interpenetration of self and no-self is to will the becoming and unbecoming of the self, and to be willed by that becoming and unbecoming. Ancient rituals embodied this paradox by allowing the participants to reenact the role of the gods who created humankind and world: simultaneously, the participants were both god and mortal, creator and created, self and world (Eliade, 1959, 1976). Zen meditators participate in this quintessential form of creativity each time they complete their meditation session, when they rediscover and re-create themselves by emerging from the no-self of *zazen* (Suzuki, 1970); during that moment of returning to their everyday self, they both create and are created. At this primary, paradoxical level of the will, the distinction between voluntary and involuntary collapses into the recognition that the two are really one. Willing seems to come from nowhere in particular, but its effects are witnessed everywhere. According to Watts (1975b), this realization is the essence of enlightenment:

> . . . the difference between what you do and what happens to you, the voluntary and the involuntary, seems to disappear. This feeling may be interpreted as the sense that everything is voluntary—that the whole universe is your own action and will. But this can easily flip into the sense that everything is involuntary. The individual and the will are nothing, and everything that might be called "I" is as much beyond control as the spinning of the earth in its orbit. But from the Taoist standpoint these two views fall short. They are polar ways of seeing the same truth: That there is no ruler and nothing ruled. What goes on simply happens of itself without either push or pull, since every push is also a pull and every pull a push. . . . This is, again, the principle of "mutual arising" (p. 53).

This paradoxical vision of a willful creating that arises from nowhere, that fuses the creator and created, may seem far removed from our everyday experience. But, intuitively, we all recognize the manifestations of this paradox everywhere around us. We easily note the extraordinary examples, such as Viktor Frankl (1963), who, from his encounter with nihilism, torture, and death in a Nazi concentration camp, uncovered a joyful purpose in life—his "will to meaning." For those of us who are psychotherapists, we see people using their own bootstraps to climb out of symptoms and create a new sense of self. All of us see children willing their own becoming.

A few months ago I reread Kurt Vonnegut's *Breakfast of Champions* (1975). It's a story about the ordinary people of a small city who seem trapped by their own lives, filled with despair by a fate over which they have no control. A renowned artist who sells a painting to the city arrives for the dedication ceremonies. The painting, entitled *The Temptation of Saint Anthony*, consists of a single vertical stripe of Day-Glo orange reflecting tape on a background of avocado green. At first the people are outraged. That isn't art, they protest, a child could do it. The artist leaps to his own defense:

> I now give you my word of honor that the picture your city owns shows everything about life which truly matters, with nothing left out. It is a picture of the awareness of every animal—the "I am" to which all messages are sent. It is all that is alive in any of us . . . It is unwavering and pure, no matter what preposterous adventure may befall us. A sacred picture of Saint Anthony alone is one vertical, unwavering band of light . . . (p. 221).

He is a rip-off artist, but his point is well made. He points to awareness, consciousness—the immutable, ungraspable self that is the universal connectedness and union of all selves. No matter what befalls us, it is all that is alive; it is the source of becoming and will. Most important, the people immediately understand his point. The willing of the self is intuitively known to all.

Here Vonnegut draws us into the paradox of the willing self that is both the creator and the created. Can the characters of a novel truly understand the nature of their own will? After all, they are just created people in a created story. Vonnegut answers this question by placing himself into the story line as himself, the writer, as well as another character in his own story. As the master of the novel, he informs the protagonist that he created him, momentarily transports him to the surface of the sun as convincing evidence of this fact, and then, paradoxically, sets the protagonist "free." But as a character in his own novel, Vonnegut surprises himself when the plot takes "unpredicted" turns. A dog jumps out at him and scares him half to death. But didn't he create the dog and that scene? Why should it surprise and scare him? He is the novelist and the character, the creator and the created all at once.

Not unlike Nietzsche, who was mad, he wills the very predicament that befalls him. It is this willing ourselves into predicaments—and out of them—that is a primary concern of psychoanalysis and Zen.

The mystical qualities of paradox and the Zen koan may strike Westerners as bizarre, alien, irrelevant to their own lives. But once again we see that the final outcome of Zen is simple and familiar. Mountains are once again mountains, and rivers are once again rivers. Zen is one's everyday mind: You eat when you are hungry and sleep when tired. In a way similar to the outcome of psychotherapy, one lives in the spontaneity of the willing self and accepts one's predicaments and life rather than blaming oneself or others. The solution to the paradoxical problems that trouble our personal lives, as well as to the universal paradoxes of being human, is to see that they are not to be felt as problems. This simple realization is not unlike Freud's idea that psychoanalysis turns an extraordinary misery into an everyday suffering. As Watts (1975a) noted, the Zen master, too, has shortcomings, but has learned to accept them as perfectly and simply human, unlike people who are at odds with their humanity and are attempting to be angels or demons. The difficulty, according to Watts, is that self-acceptance can never be a deliberate act; it is as paradoxical as kissing one's own lips. The liberating realization is that one's self can only be genuine, spontaneous, and unfettered in its willfulness if one lets go of the struggles to own it as property. Like the solution to the koan, once grasped as ungraspable, the self becomes free to move on its own accord.

References

Arieti, Silvano (1972). *The Will to Be Human*. New York: Quadrangle Books.

Bion, Wilfred R. (1963). *Elements of Psychoanalysis*. New York: Aronson.

Eigen, Michael (1986). *The Psychotic Core*. Northvale, N.J.: Jason Aronson.

Eliade, Mircea (1959). *The Sacred and the Profane; The Nature of Religion*. New York: Harcourt, Brace & World.

——— (1976). *Myths, Rites, Symbols*. New York: HarperColophon Books.

Farber, Leslie (1966). *The Ways of Will*. New York: Basic Books.

Frankl, Viktor E. (1963). *Man's Search for Meaning*. Boston: Beacon.

——— (1969). *The Will to Meaning*. New York: World.

Fromm, Erich, D. T. Suzuki, and R. DeMartino. (1960). *Zen Buddhism and Psychoanalysis*. New York: Harper and Row.

Haley, Jay (1963). *Strategies of Psychotherapy*. New York: Grune and Stratton.

Herrigel, Eugen (1960). *The Method of Zen*. New York: Vintage Books.

Hofstadter, Douglas R. (1980). *Gödel, Escher, Bach: An Eternal Golden Braid*. New York: Random.

Hofstadter, Douglas R., and C. Dennett. (1981). *The Mind's I: Fantasies and Reflections on Self and Soul*. New York: Bantam.

James, William. (1960). *Varieties of Religious Experience*. New York: Longmans, Green (originally published 1902).

Jichaku, P., G. Y. Fujita, and S. I. Shapiro. (1984). "Double Bind and the Zen Koan." *Journal of Mind and Behavior* 5: 211–21.

Kapleau, P. (1980). *The Three Pillars of Zen: Teaching, Practice and Enlightenment*. New York: Anchor Books.

Kohut, H. (1977). *The Restoration of the Self*. New York: International Universities Press.

———— (1984). *How Does Analysis Cure?* Chicago: University of Chicago Press.

Kopp, Sheldon B. (1976). *If You Meet the Buddha on the Road, Kill Him! The Pilgrimage of Psychotherapy Patients*. Toronto: Bantam.

Kris, Ernst (1952). *Psychoanalytic Explorations in Art*. New York: International Universities Press.

Kubose, S. K., and T. Umemoto. (1980). "Creativity and the Zen Koan." *Psychologia: An International Journal of Psychology in the Orient* 23: 1–9.

Mahler, Margaret, F. Pine, and A. Bergman. (1975). *The Psychological Birth of the Human Infant*. New York: Basic Books.

May, Rollo (1969). *Love and Will*. New York: W. W. Norton.

Mountain, Marian (1983). *The Zen Environment: The Impact of Zen Meditation*. New York: Bantam.

Osmer, H. (1981). "Paradoxical Treatments: A Unified Concept." *Psychotherapy: Theory, Research, Practice* 18: 320–24.

Perls, Frederick S. (1976). *Gestalt Therapy Verbatim*. New York: Bantam.

Rank, Otto (1945). *Will Therapy and Truth and Reality*. Trans. J. Taft. New York: Knopf.

Sato, K. (1968). "Zen from a Personological Viewpoint." *Psychologia: An International Journal of Psychology in the Orient*, 11: 3–24.

Searles, Harold F. (1965). *Collected Papers on Schizophrenia and Related Topics*. New York: International Universities Press.

Seltzer, L. F. (1986). *Paradoxical Strategies in Psychotherapy: A Comprehensive Overview and Guidebook*. New York: Wiley.

Stern, Daniel N. (1985). *The Interpersonal World of the Infant: A View from Psychoanalysis and Developmental Psychology*. New York: Basic Books.

Suzuki, Daisetz T. (1956). *Zen Buddhism*. Ed. W. Barrett. New York: Doubleday.

Suzuki, Shunryu (1970). *Zen Mind, Beginner's Mind*. New York: Weatherhill.

van de Wetering, Janwillem (1978). *A Glimpse of Nothingness: Experiences in an American Zen Community*. New York: Pocket Books.

Vonnegut, Kurt (1975). *Breakfast of Champions*. New York: Dell.

Watts, Alan (1958). *The Spirit of Zen*. New York: Grove Press.

———— (1975a). *Psychotherapy East and West*. New York: Vintage Books (originally published 1961).

——— (1975b). *Tao: The Watercourse Way*. New York: Pantheon.

Weeks, Gerald R. (1985). *Promoting Change Through Paradoxical Therapy*. Homewood, Ill.: Dow Jones-Irwin.

Wheelis, Allen (1956). "Will and Psychoanalysis." *Journal of the American Psychoanalytic Association*, 4: 285–303.

Winnicott, D. W. (1971). *Playing and Reality*. London: Tavistock.

Yalom, Irvin D. (1980). *Existential Psychotherapy*. New York: Basic Books.

WHAT SUFFERING TEACHES

Polly Young-Eisendrath

❑

Zen Master Dogen has pointed out that anxiety, when accepted, is the driving force to enlightenment in that it lays bare the human dilemma at the same time that it ignites our desire to break out of it. —PHILIP KAPLEAU, 1969

❑

There is a dearth of methods and theories about how suffering can be useful in the contemporary world. The elite ranks of medicine, psychiatry, biology, and sometimes even psychology show an almost uniform lack of interest in the value of suffering. The focus instead is on avoiding or eliminating it. This contemporary strategy tends to increase our worst fears—that pain and suffering are intolerable and wasteful of our energy. As a practicing Buddhist and psychoanalyst, I see it differently. Hardships are the major catalysts for change and development in our lives; they wake us to how we create suffering through our own attitudes and intentions, our actions and relationships.

I'm writing, though, against a strong current that includes a widespread assortment of psychiatric and New Age formulas for how to stay happy and in control, as well as the hard-core scientific ideologies of genetics and brain chemistry that promise us cures for all major diseases and problematic moods—even the possibility of conquering death. Trying to find a gene

Adapted from Polly Young-Eisendrath, *The Gifts of Suffering*, © 1996 by Polly Young-Eisendrath. Adapted by permission of Addison Wesley Longman, Inc.

for criminality, a physical basis for happiness, and ever better drugs for our negative moods, we have directed our gaze to Nature to locate the origin of our suffering. This is a grave error from the perspectives of Buddhism and psychoanalysis.

SEEING YOURSELF OR BLAMING NATURE

Much of our suffering originates with our own discontent, emanating from the evaluations and attitudes that arise in protecting ourselves and separating ourselves out from the context of our own engagement. As a Jungian psychoanalyst, I look upon much of this discontent as arising from the psychological complexes that derive from our emotional adaptations of childhood. These complexes, archetypal at core, drive us to create images of grandiosity and devaluation and dominance and submission both within ourselves and between ourselves and others. The ego complex, with its core of an archetypal self (the universal predisposition to create an identity of coherent individual subjectivity), forms as the central complex of personal identity. Defenses of the ego can lead to suffering through shame, envy, fear, pride, or guilt as we feel ourselves separated off or isolated from others. Tendencies to identify with and/or project complexes of Terrible Parent and Victim Child are universal emotional difficulties of adulthood that are sometimes rigidified as aspects of personality, and sometimes felt as neurotic inner conflicts. If we can map the psychic terrain of our subjective lives, we can begin to find a path to freedom—that middle path between repression and enactment.

As we attempt to explain more and more of our personal difficulties through biology and genes, society and culture encourage us to avoid such a path. We are invited to put down the mirror of self-recognition and to stop our search for a self-awareness that could set us free. Naturally this leads to endless confusions about how and why anyone should fund a long-term psychotherapy or psychoanalysis.

From the perspective of Buddhist teachings, dropping the mirror of self-recognition can result in falling into the lowest realms of hell where we are continuously driven by greed, ignorance, fears, and cravings into terrible states of misery and restlessness. I fear that I see these hellish states in every shopping mall, every subway, every parking garage and supermarket that I enter. People have lost their ability to know how to be human.

They often appear to be drifting around in the confusions of greed, igno-rance, and fear—perhaps searching for something to relieve their misery.

NEUROSIS AND AUTHENTIC PAIN

Without the capacity to see how we create a lot of our own difficulties, we are morally and spiritually adrift on all levels of existence. In our so-ciety, we are deeply perplexed about the increase in violence and suicide and destruction among young people, especially in our cities. But it is obvious that there is no widespread understanding or teaching of the "ethic of suffering": that one is the creator of oneself and that whatever one does, one becomes heir to those intentions and actions.

To put this basic Buddhist teaching of *karma* into psychoanalytic lan-guage, I borrow some words from Roy Schafer (1978), who describes the process of development in an effective psychotherapy or analysis:

> . . . the analysand progressively recognizes, accepts, revises, refines, and lives in terms of the idea of the self as agent. This is to say that, in one way or another and more and more, the analysand sees himself or herself as being the person who essentially has been doing the things from which he or she was apparently suffering upon entering analysis, and from many other problems as well that will have been defined only during the analysis itself (p. 180).

Through the ethic of suffering we come to recognize a boundary between our own subjectivity and what lies beyond our control. Our thoughts, feel-ings, intentions, and actions become ours, and we recognize the powers of being conscious, of making meaning. Knowing our own subjective freedom, we are able to surrender more fully to the effects of loss, aging, illness, and death which are the inevitable natural processes of life.

Jung talks about the difference between neurosis and authentic pain. Neurosis arises from the ways in which, conscious or unconscious, we are dissatisfied, thrown off-center, full of childish wishes and complaints. This neurotic suffering distracts us from the authentic and inevitable miseries of life, according to Jung. Without a true understanding of the constraints and limitations of human existence, we have no knowledge about what it means to be *human* (not animal, not divine). We have no answers to life's major questions: Who are they? (the mystery of our parents in childhood), Who am I? (the perennial question of adolescence), and Who are we? (the exquisite question of adulthood). When we get caught in the unending repetitions of our neuroses, we lack the inner freedom even to ask these human questions, much less seek their answers.

Within the contemporary ideology of biological psychiatry, genetic engineering, and psychopharmaceutical remakes, there is no felt personal connection between our actions and their consequences, no belief that anxiety may be the springboard for development, that illness and loss are the impetus to wake up to discoveries of self-knowledge. Our cultural messages have themselves become neurotic: stay young forever, try to escape the boredom that arises from sealing off your inner life, and protect yourself from too much insight.

A famous story about the Buddha Shakyamuni tells of his encounter with a teenage mother whose infant has died. She is frantic with grief and outrage and has traveled from village to village, carrying her child on her hip, looking for a miracle that will bring the child back to life. Someone tells her that only the Buddha, who is preaching in a nearby town, would be capable of such a miracle. When she arrives at the town and finds the crowds around the Buddha, she pushes her way through and stands before him.

"If you would perform a miracle and bring my child back to life, I would do anything in return," she says with touching sincerity. The Buddha sees the depth of her grief and responds, "If you bring me a mustard seed from a home in which there has been no death, then I will perform the miracle." This sounds like a small task and she readily agrees, setting off with the deepest gratitude in her heart.

She travels from this village to that, carrying her dead child and asking at each house if there has ever been a death. She hears about many difficult deaths and much disease and her heart is opened to other people's pain. Eventually, she realizes that all families have been touched by death and she returns to the Buddha.

"I know now what you were trying to teach me," she says. "I am not alone in my misery. All people must endure death, not only their own but that of others around them." The Buddha gently offers to perform a funeral for her child and then to teach her how suffering can be alleviated. Thus she becomes one of his most dedicated followers and eventually a powerful teacher in her own right.

THE MEANING OF LIMITATION

Keeping our attention on the limits and constraints of human life arouses spiritual yearning. In both psychoanalysis and Buddhism, practitioners discover the meaning of limits—of time, wishes, desires, control, responsibility, omnipotence, ideals, power, and even love. These limits teach us. From the facts of our discontent, dependence, vulnerability, and lack of omnipotence and omniscience, we learn what it means to be truly human. These "negative" experiences open our hearts and allow us to connect to others through gratitude and compassion. Moreover, they insist that we ask those fundamental questions: Who are they? Who am I? Who are we?

The only real freedom from suffering and death is to accept them, to be interested, and to begin to see how they connect us to ourselves through meaning and to others through compassion. Although we may discover many cures for illnesses and some relief for pain, we cannot transform our own discontent without recognizing how we create it.

This is at the heart of the Four Noble Truths of Buddhism, the first teachings of the Buddha Shakyamuni after his supreme enlightenment. Although the core teachings of the Noble Truths are often translated into English as teachings about "suffering," it would probably be more accurate to call them teachings about discontent. The Sanskrit word translated as "suffering" is *dukkha*, which literally refers to off-centeredness, like a wheel riding off its axle or a bone out of its socket. So I refer to the Noble Truths as teachings about discontent.

Taken as a whole, the Noble Truths state that discontent has an identifiable cause, and if this cause can be eliminated, then so can its effect. In other words, the goal of Buddhist practice and theory is to achieve lasting contentment. This is understood as possible only when the actual causes of discontent have been eliminated. Most forms of Buddhism teach that the ultimate root of discontent is the concept of a permanent, lasting individual self. Many practices and theories of Buddhism demonstrate that nothing in reality corresponds to the notion of our having a permanent, lasting self or soul.

In fact, nothing is permanent and lasting in human life—not our most up-to-date knowledge, not ourselves, not any of the world as we know it. It is all subject to change. When we can experience this impermanence as the fact of our existence and live within its reality—that is, within the ongoing death and rebirth from moment to moment of existence—then we are attuned to the nature of being human. What grounds us and keeps us centered in this existence is the recognition of our actual interdependence or interbeing—our connection to all that exists. When we have a proper sense of ourselves as impermanent, with the freedom to eliminate discontent, our hearts are opened by compassion to everything that lives and suffers from limitation. There is an almost natural sense of purpose that arises from such compassion, some inspiration about how one might help others with the knowledge that has come from one's own suffering.

NEGATIVITY AND DEPRESSION

This sense of purpose brings greater order, creativity, and transcendent coherence to our lives, allowing us to move more smoothly through inevitable miseries and losses, appreciating the riches they provide in the context of the demands they make on us. With all of our contemporary concerns about depression, we would do well to note that negativity turned inward as depression, or outward as conduct disorder, could be greatly alleviated by recognizing its sources. Whatever the biological counterparts to mood change may be—and there is no doubt that our biochemistry is intimately related to our consciousness—no medication will do more than relieve symptoms. Our lack of modesty in making claims about "cures" for depression will only set us up for more suffering. We have not demonstrated that depression is a biological disorder any more than we have demonstrated that human life is a by-product of certain carbon compounds. Depression simply has a bigger story, a larger drama, than that of neuro-transmitters and brain chemistry.

Depression is a transitory mood, one that we all experience from time to time, and its symptoms may be relieved in part through medication. All depression contains some fundamental discontent, some serious disappointments and failed expectations. All depression, in one way or another, arises out of and is continued by shame or resentment or disappointment or despair at the limitations of one's own life or life in general. Depression is surely a story about discontent more than it is about biochemistry.

No one really knows how or why the antidepressant medications work, how long they will work or whether they will eventually have harmful side effects if taken over years. We do not know, with any clarity, "the" biochemical cause of depression, nor do we have an overall biological understanding of the condition. And yet some psychiatrists still claim that we have defeated it through medication.

I am not in any way opposed to the appropriate use of antidepressants. By relieving some symptoms, they can help people concentrate and begin to explore the roots of discontent. But we need to be alert to harmful ideologies that focus our gaze on Nature as the root of our suffering, rather than on our own attitudes and intentions.

In my experience with symptomatic depression in analysis and psychotherapy, I have found that patients—both medicated and not—gradually recognize the roots of their discontent by coming to see and know their own psychological complexes. They become resilient as they discover how cycles of mood changes are connected with attitude and intention, with internal images and disclaimed thoughts or memories. Their resilience, an ability to thrive even in the face of depression, comes from a knowledge of both the causes and the impermanence of their moods. Then these patients can reduce their despair, resentment, fear, false pride, envy, and self-pity, sometimes even eliminate them. These emotions are the ultimate ongoing culprits of intransigent depression in all of the cases I have treated.

SOCIAL ETHIC OF SUFFERING

As a society we need far more opportunities to hear stories of suffering and resilience, to explore our own experiences of discontent, and to be mentored or guided through fundamental transitions from suffering to compassion and self-knowledge. This would allow us to engage with the ethic of suffering—the knowledge that we create the conditions of our own lives through our intentions, attitudes, actions. Such knowledge might enable us to cope more effectively with our cultural symptoms of idealization.

In Western societies we have a long history of idealizing ourselves through visions of heroic control and dominance—over ourselves, our environment, others. Our contemporary platform of a "free market economy" is one in which environmental resources are used without knowledge of future effects, often without any thought of the consequences of our actions. We separate ourselves out as individuals, from other species, even from other humans, and bring Nature under our dominion.

This kind of idealized control has often led to a tendency to feel exempt from the natural limitations of life, limitations that may now have put our own species at greater risk of extinction. Many aspects of Western culture—from our stories of heroes and geniuses to our theories of bringing Nature under our control—arise from beliefs in the rights of an individual self to promote itself in isolation. From the perspective of Buddhism, this way of thinking causes ultimate harm to all.

The human ability to think abstractly, manipulate symbolic concepts apart from concrete situations, and theorize about ourselves is perhaps the greatest resource of our species. It derives from an experience of a separate self, the very condition that can run amok in a need to control and dominate.

In fact, some theorists argue that humans are characterized, as a species, by a sort of "instinct" of competence. This instinct emerges in our predisposition to separate ourselves out from our experience and then to evaluate our experience negatively. As psychologist and researcher Mihaly Csikszentmihalyi (1933) says of this universal human characteristic:

> The . . . reason that the freely roaming mind usually attends to negative thoughts is that such a pessimistic bias might be adaptive—if by "adaptation" we mean an increased likelihood of survival. The mind turns to negative possibilities as a compass needle turns to the magnetic pole, because this is the best way, on the average, to anticipate dangerous situations. (p. 35)

This instinct of competence seems to me to be unchecked in our society. We don't question the limits of its usefulness. Both Buddhism and psychoanalysis, as I said above, insist that we face the limits of our control and, in facing those limits, allow ourselves to awaken to the knowledge of our dependence, a mature dependence when it is grounded in both giving and taking. The knowledge of mature dependence—of our interconnection with and responsibility to other living beings—is not readily available at this time in America.

Our economic system has achieved world dominance, but it is grounded in competition and individualism. Although we have the potential, through the valuable methods of democracy, for complex responsiveness to a range of needs and points of view, we seem more and more to be immersed only in competence and control—my pocketbook and my safety—with the results of greater and greater self-protection and isolation. Rather than being able to foster an image of shared goals and interdependence, many Western societies end up protecting only those forms of life that are essential to their own economic stability. In large part, this is the result of a fundamental belief in individual rights to happiness, even when these put other beings at risk for greater and greater adversity.

THE LESSON

Unless we can begin to see the problems of our inherent discontent and grandiosity, we may put our species at risk of suffering catastrophes that result from unchecked competence. Although negative thinking might have benefited us earlier in the evolutionary process, compelling us to greater and greater manipulation of the environment to fulfill our needs, it may now put us out of business if we cannot respond wisely to the demands for cooperation, collaboration, and limitation that seem to characterize our future on this planet.

What suffering teaches us today is the necessity of developing personal responsibility for our own subjective lives, in order to awaken thoughtful compassion about the critical limitations that face our own and other species here on earth. This is what I have learned from practicing Buddhism and doing psychoanalysis for thousands and thousands of hours. My patients in therapy have taught me the path of resilience—from suffering to self-awareness, then on to compassion, self-knowledge (of what it means to be human), and a sense of purpose in life. What is so striking about the capacity to thrive in adversity, known now as resilience, is how resilient people have a meaningful story that places them in a context of helping others for some larger purpose. This might seem like a sort of sleight-of-mind trick if it did not come from the authentic struggles to develop personal responsibility in the face of misery. Instead, it seems to me to be a fundamental witnessing of why human life is so interesting. From psychoanalysis and Buddhism, I have learned how a mature spirituality can develop from a confrontation with one's own neurosis, one's individual suffering.

Our meanings and intentions are vitally important in shaping our lives. When we shift the paradigm for our own perceptions—the grounds of meaning and expectation—then the perceived also changes. Subject and object are joined in the ground of our perceptions. The account of a world resting on consciousness may still seem far-fetched in terms of most Western psychology and philosophy, but it is not unfamiliar from the perspective of some theories of contemporary physics, and it seems immediately apparent when we dissolve our belief in a strongly bounded, separate, individual self. When we conceive of the self as wholly interdependent and impermanent, as a function rather than a thing, then we appreciate more deeply our true freedom in this world. It is the freedom of making new meanings, of opening ourselves especially to the conditions of our own limitations and exploring these into the roots of our suffering.

When we cross the bridge from self-protection and isolation to gratitude and compassion, then we have changed the world. Without the ordinary occasion of human suffering—our own discontent—there would be no bridge.

References

Csikszentmihalyi, Mihalyi (1993). *The Evolving Self: A Psychology for the Third Millennium*. New York: HarperCollins.

Kapleau, Philip K. (1969). *Zen Bow*. Rochester, N.Y.: Rochester Zen Center Publication.

Schafer, Roy (1978). *Language and Insight*. New Haven: Yale University Press.

THE CONTRIBUTORS

MASAO ABE has been, since the death of D. T. Suzuki, the leading exponent of Zen Buddhism in the West. A student of Shin'ichi Hisamatsu and a member of the Kyoto School of Philosophy, he was for many years professor of philosophy at Japan's Nara University. Over the past two decades, Dr. Abe has been on the faculty of Columbia University, the University of Chicago, the University of Hawaii, and Claremont Graduate School. The author of numerous scholarly articles on the relationship between Buddhism and Western thought, he is best known in English for the volume *Zen and Western Thought*, a collection of his most important essays.

FRANZ ALEXANDER, M.D. (1891–1964), was among an early group of prominent psychoanalysts to emigrate from Hungary to Berlin in the 1920s. A precursor of ego psychology and an early contributor to the development of a psychoanalytic criminology (see his 1929 *The Criminal, the Judge and the Public*, written with Hugo Staub), he was one of the first psychoanalysts to investigate, in his 1931 article "Buddhist Training as an Artificial Catatonia," the relationship between psychoanalysis and Buddhism.

JOSEPH BOBROW, PH.D., began his Zen practice with Robert Aitken Roshi in 1972. An independent Zen master in the Diamond Sangha tradition, he founded the Harbor Sangha of San Francisco in 1988. A clinical psychologist with long-standing interests in psychoanalysis and Buddhism, Dr. Bobrow is the author of "Coming to Life: The Creative Intercourse of Psychoanalysis and Zen Buddhism," which appeared in *The Soul on the Couch* (Spezzano and Gargiulo, eds., The Analytic Press, 1997).

NINA COLTART (1927–97) studied modern languages at Oxford before training in medicine and working in the British National Health Service as a psychiatrist. She was for many years a member of the British Psychoanalytic Society, as well as a leading representative of the society's Independent Group. The author of three books—*Slouching Towards Bethlehem, How to Survive as a Psychotherapist*, and the final essays collected in *The Baby and the Bathwater*—Dr. Coltart passed away as this book neared completion.

PAUL C. COOPER, M.S., N.C.Psy.A., is a supervising and training analyst with the National Psychological Association for Psychoanalysis. He maintains a private practice in New York City.

HIS HOLINESS THE DALAI LAMA (Tenzin Gyatso) is the Fourteenth Dalai Lama. Spiritual and political leader of the people of Tibet, in 1959 he was forced into exile in India as a result of the Chinese invasion of his country. Since 1987 he has convened the Mind and Life Dialogues, seeking to bridge traditional Buddhist thought and Western science. (His conversation with Joyce McDougall, here excerpted, is from Mind and Life IV, held in Dharamsala in 1992.) In 1989 he was awarded the Nobel Peace Prize. Among the Dalai Lama's many publications are: *Tibetan Buddhism, The Key to the Middle Way, Freedom from Exile, The Science of Mind, Ocean of Wisdom*, and *The Way of Tibetan Buddhism*.

RAM DASS discusses his transformation from Dr. Richard Alpert into Baba Ram Dass in his 1971 book *Be Here Now*. Formerly a professor of psychology at Harvard, he began experimenting with hallucinogens there in the 1960s, together with Timothy Leary, before moving to India, where he apprenticed with a spiritual guru for a number of years. A prominent figure of the counterculture of the 1960s, he has since returned to the West from India and was known to be working recently with AIDS patients.

TAKEO DOI, M.D., was originally at Tokyo University before training at the Menninger Foundation in the 1950s and later at the San Francisco Psychoanalytic Institute. A former director of the National Institute for Mental Health, he is highly regarded as a cross-cultural theorist whose work has greatly influenced social scientists and Japan specialists. He is best known for his books *The Anatomy of Dependence*, an essential study of *amae* psychology (the psychology of emotional dependency frequently evidenced in Japanese relationships), and *The Anatomy of the Self: The Individual versus Society*.

MICHAEL EIGEN, PH.D., is a senior faculty member and control/training analyst for the National Psychological Association for Psychoanalysis in New York City. A supervisor and clinical associate professor of psychology at New York University's Postdoctoral Program in Psychotherapy and Psychoanalysis, he is the author of *The Psychotic Core; Coming Through the Whirlwind; The Electrified Tightrope; Reshaping the Self; Psychic Deadness*; and *The Psychoanalytic Mystic*.

GEORGE R. ELDER holds an M.Div. in church history from Union Theological Seminary and a Ph.D. in Buddhist studies from Columbia University. For many years a professor in comparative religions at Hunter College (CUNY), he currently resides with his family in

Florida, where he practices as a Jungian therapist and writes. Author of several scholarly essays, his most recent and major work is *The Body: An Encyclopedia of Archetypal Symbolism*.

JACK ENGLER, PH.D., is a supervising and training psychologist at Harvard Medical School and the Cambridge Hospital Department of Psychiatry. After training at the Menninger Foundation, McLean Hospital and the Yale Psychiatric Institute, he spent several years in India and Burma studying Buddhist Vipassana meditation as a Fulbright Research Fellow. The co-author of three books, including *Transformations of Consciousness* (with Ken Wilbur and Dan Brown) and *Worlds in Harmony* (with His Holiness the Dalai Lama), Dr. Engler is affiliated with both the Insight Meditation Society and the Barre Center for Buddhist Studies in Barre, Massachusetts.

MARK EPSTEIN, M.D., has a private practice in New York City and has been an instructor at New York Hospital–Cornell Medical Center. A graduate of Harvard College and the Harvard Medical School, he is consulting editor to *Tricycle: The Buddhist Review*, and the author of *Thoughts without a Thinker: Psychotherapy from a Buddhist Perpsective*. His most recent book is *Going to Pieces without Falling Apart: A Buddhist Perspective on Wholeness*.

MARK FINN, PH.D., is Chief In-patient Psychologist at New York's North Central Bronx Hospital, Albert Einstein College of Medicine. He is the editor of the volume *Object Relations Theory and Religion*.

ERICH FROMM (1900–80) was a leading member of the Frankfurt School and a pioneering figure in the neo-Freudian movement that sought to root and apply psychoanalysis in the social sphere. Trained in Berlin, and one of the first psychoanalysts to leave Germany for fear of Nazi persecution, Fromm taught extensively and wrote prolifically, ever intent on the construction of bridges and syntheses between psychoanalysis, ethics, and the world's major intellectual and spiritual traditions. Included in his researches were seminal studies on Marxism, Judaism, ethology, and, of course, Zen Buddhism. In addition to Zen Buddhism and Psychoanalysis, his titles include: *Escape from Freedom*, *To Have or to Be?*, and *The Anatomy of Human Destructiveness*.

SHIN'ICHI HISAMATSU (1889–1980) was a member of the Kyoto School and disciple of Kitaro Nishida, Japan's greatest modern philosopher. Arguably this century's leading philosopher of Zen, Dr. Hisamatsu was professor of religion and Buddhism at Kyoto University from 1932 to 1946, and founder of the FAS Zen Society. He is well known in the West for his conversations with figures such as C. G. Jung and Paul Tillich. Among his many significant publications are the eight volumes of his collected works (*Hisamatsu Shin'ichi Chosaku Shu*) and the volume *Zen and the Fine Arts*.

KAREN HORNEY (1885–1952), an orthodox psychoanalyst for the first fifteen years of her career, helped pioneer the application of Zen Buddhism to psychoanalysis. A "neo-Freudian," as well as a protofeminist in the world of psychoanalysis, along with Erich Fromm, Harry Stack Sullivan, and others she initiated a move away from the discipline's biologically inspired tenets to highlight cultural factors in the understanding of neurosis.

Her works include *The Neurotic Personality of Our Time*, *New Ways in Psychoanalysis*, *Our Inner Conflicts*, *Neurosis and Human Growth*, and the posthumous *Final Lectures*.

CARL GUSTAV JUNG (1875–1961) was Freud's chosen successor before major conflicts of temperament and theory precipitated their break in 1927. The founder of analytical psychology, Jung placed at the center of his theory and worldview the notion of a collective unconscious: an ancestral psychic substrate common to all humankind that inspires and evidences the species' essential spiritual sensibilities. Arguably the foremost interpreter and scholar of those sensibilities of his day and beyond, Jung had concerned himself with Eastern philosophy and culture from the early stages of his researches. One of the great facilitators in the dialogue between East and West, his writings on the subject—which intersperse the twenty volumes of his *Collected Works*—are collected in the volume *Psychology and the East*.

HAROLD KELMAN, M.D., D.MD.SC. (1906–77), was a Fellow of the American Psychiatric Association and charter member of the Academy of Psychoanalysis. He was also editor of the *American Journal of Psychoanalysis*, as well as dean of the American Institute for Psychoanalysis. A close associate of Karen Horney's, Dr. Kelman was a pioneer in bridging East and West via numerous scholarly articles published in the 1950s. His major work, *Helping People*, was an exposition of Horney's approach enriched with his own experience.

AKIHISA KONDO, M.D., is a key figure in the transplantation of Zen Buddhism to Western soil. Born in 1911, this Japanese psychiatrist trained in the late 1940s and early 1950s at the Karen Horney Institute in New York, where he was instrumental in introducing a number of psychoanalysts—most notably Erich Fromm and Horney herself—to D. T. Suzuki. Deeply committed to fostering a clinical approach that could integrate in practice the insights of East and West, Dr. Kondo combined in his work not only psychoanalysis and Zen, but the specific tenets of Morita therapy as well.

GEREON KOPF, PH.D., studied at Eberhard-Karls-Universität Tübingen and Temple University, where he received his Ph.D. in religious studies. A Japan Foundation Fellow at Obirin University in Machida City, Japan, he has focused his research on the relationship of Zen Buddhist philosophy to Western psychology—with a particular emphasis on Jung's analytical psychology. Author of several papers on the notions of "person" and "self" in Japanese Zen Buddhism, he is assistant professor of the history of religion at Luther College.

JACK KORNFIELD, PH.D., was trained as a Buddhist monk in Thailand, Burma, and India and has taught meditation worldwide since 1974. One of the key teachers to introduce Theravada Buddhist practice to the West, he has focused for many years on integrating and bringing alive the great Eastern spiritual teachings in an accessible way for Western students and society. He is a husband, father, psychotherapist, and founding teacher of the Insight Meditation Society and the Spirit Rock Center in California. His books include *Seeking the Heart of Wisdom*, *A Still Forest Pool*, *Stories of the Spirit*, *Stories of the Heart*, and *A Path with Heart*.

STEPHEN A. KURTZ, M.S.W., received his training at Oxford University, Columbia University, and Hunter College School of Social Work. His work has appeared in several of the major psychoanalytic journals (*Journal of the American Psychoanalytic Association, The Psychoanalytic Review, Free Associations*), and he has also published extensively on art and cultural criticism. He is the author of *The Art of Unknowing: Dimensions of Openness in Analytic Therapy*.

JOYCE MCDOUGALL, ED.D., is a training and supervising analyst with the Paris Psychoanalytic Institute and Society. She lectures frequently in Europe, the United States, and South America, and is the author of several acclaimed books, including *Theatres of the Mind, Theatres of the Body, Plea for a Measure of Abnormality*, and *The Many Faces of Eros*.

JAN MIDDELDORF is an instructor and training and supervising analyst at the Colorado Center for Modern Psychoanalytic Studies. He also maintains a private practice in Albuquerque, New Mexico. Among his interests are the study of narcissism and the formulation of an integrative psychoanalytic viewpoint.

MOKUSEN MIYUKI, PH.D., is professor of religious studies at California State University–Northridge. Formally educated in both Japan and the United States, he is a graduate of the C. G. Jung Institute in Zurich, Switzerland. A Buddhist priest and practicing Jungian analyst, he is the author, with J. Marvin Spiegelman, of *Buddhism and Jungian Psychology*.

ANTHONY MOLINO, PH.D., is a psychoanalyst, translator, and anthropologist. He has received numerous awards for his translations of modern Italian poetry and theatre and has edited two books of interviews: *Elaborate Selves* and *Freely Associated: Encounters in Psychoanalysis with Christopher Bollas, Nina Coltart, Michael Eigen, Joyce McDougall and Adam Phillips*. His forthcoming works include *Where Id Was: From Normalization to a New Ethics in Psychoanalysis* (edited with Christine Ware), and a volume on the present-day relation between psychoanalysis and ethnography.

SHOJI MURAMOTO, PH.D., studied psychology and philosophy at the universities of Kyoto, Zurich, and Osaka. He is presently professor of psychology at Hanazono University in Japan, where he also counsels students. Editor-in-chief of *The Japanese Journal for Humanistic Psychology*, as well as author of many papers on Zen and psychology, he is the author of *Jung and Goethe* and *Jung and Faust*.

V. WALTER ODAJNYK, PH.D., is a student of Zen meditation as well as a Jungian analyst. Trained in Zurich, he is in private practice in New York City. Dr. Odajnyk is the author of *Jung and Politics* and *Gathering the Light: A Psychology of Meditation*.

ADAM PHILLIPS was formerly Principal Child Psychotherapist at Charing Cross Hospital in London. He is the author of several volumes, including *Winnicott; On Kissing, Tickling, and Being Bored; On Flirtation; Terrors and Experts; Monogamy* and the recent *The Beast in the Nursery*.

JEFFREY B. RUBIN, PH.D., has practiced both psychoanalysis and Buddhist meditation for over twenty years. He has taught psychoanalysis and Buddhist theory and practice at Yeshiva University and Goddard College, and has been a faculty member of the Object Relations Institute, the Postgraduate Center for Mental Health and the C. G. Jung Foundation in New York City, where he works in private practice. He is the author of several volumes, including *Psychotherapy and Buddhism: Toward an Integration; A Psychoanalysis for Our Time: Exploring the Blindness of the Seeing I;* and of the forthcoming *Close Encounters of a New Kind: Essays on Psychotherapy and Buddhism.*

JOHN R. SULER, PH.D., is professor of psychology at Rider College. In private practice in the Philadelphia area, he is the author of *Contemporary Psychoanalysis and Eastern Thought,* as well as many published papers on the relationship between psychoanalysis, Taoism, and Zen Buddhism.

JOE TOM SUN. Pseudonym of psychoanalyst Joseph Thompson. His "Psychology in Primitive Buddhism" is the earliest known published investigation of the parallels and convergences between psychoanalysis and Buddhism.

DAISETZ TERITARO SUZUKI (1869–1966) was, until his death, the world's foremost authority on Zen Buddhism and the most instrumental in transplanting Zen to the West. For many years professor of Buddhist philosophy at Kyoto's Otani University, Suzuki advanced Western knowledge of the East immeasurably with his groundbreaking English-language publication of 1927, *Essays in Zen Buddhism* (Vol. 1). The author of countless seminal works in both Japanese and English, he also collaborated with Erich Fromm and Richard De Martino on the 1960 classic *Zen Buddhism and Psychoanalysis.*

WILSON MILES VAN DUSEN served extensively in the U.S. Merchant Marine during World War II before training as a clinical psychologist and going on to become an expert on the world's mystic traditions. A mystic himself, currently affiliated with the Philemon Foundation of California, he is the author of *The Natural Depth in Man* and *The Presence of Other Worlds: Psychological and Spiritual Findings of Emanuel Swedenborg.*

FRANCISCO J. VARELA, PH.D., after graduating from Harvard University as a biologist, worked with a number of universities, as well as with the Max Planck Institute for Brain Research in Germany, before assuming his current position as Director of Research at the National Council for Scientific Research in Paris. The author of ten books and over 150 articles on neuroscience and cognitive science, he is the editor of *Sleeping, Dreaming, and Dying: An Exploration of Consciousness with The Dalai Lama,* derived from the 1992 Mind and Life Conference.

ALAN W. WATTS (1915–73) was best known as an interpreter of Zen Buddhism in particular and of Indian and Chinese philosophy in general. The author of over twenty books on the philosophy and psychology of religion, Watts was —together with Thomas Merton, Aldous Huxley, and Eugen Herrigel, and alongside the Beat Generation—one of the foremost Western exponents of a 1960s sensibility that resonated deeply with Eastern psychology and thought. Among his titles: *The Way of Zen, The Spirit of Zen, Psychotherapy East and West,* and *Tao: The Watercourse Way.*

POLLY YOUNG-EISENDRATH, PH.D., is a psychologist and Jungian psychoanalyst practicing in Burlington, Vermont. Clinical associate professor of psychiatry at the University of Vermont Medical College, she has published and lectured widely on topics of resilience, women's development, couple relationship, and the interface of psychoanalysis and spirituality. The most recent of her eight books include *The Gifts of Suffering, The Cambridge Companion to Jung* (edited with Terence Dawson), and *Gender and Desire.*